PLANNING

AUSTRALIA
LBC Information Services
Sydney

CANADA AND THE USA
Carswell
Toronto

NEW ZEALAND
Brooker's
Auckland

PLANNING

By

Neil A. Collar, LL.B, LL.M., DIP.L.P.,
Solicitor and Legal Associate of the R.T.P.I.
Brodies, W.S.
and
Part-Time Tutor, University of Edinburgh

EDINBURGH
W. GREEN/Sweet & Maxwell
1999

First published 1994

Second edition published 1999

Published in 1999 by W. Green & Son Limited
21 Alva Street
Edinburgh EH2 4PS

Typeset by LBJ Typesetting Ltd
Kingsclere

Printed in Great Britain by
Redwood Books Ltd, Kennet Way, Trowbridge, Wiltshire

No natural forests were destroyed to make this product
only farmed timber was used and replanted

A CIP catalogue record of this book is available from the British Library

ISBN 0 414 01292 5

PREFACE TO SECOND EDITION

The need for a second edition of this book largely arose from the consolidation of the planning legislation into four new Acts of Parliament. This has forced planning practitioners to learn a new set of section numbers, and refer to section 75 agreements instead of section 50 agreements. In the five years since the first edition of this book was published, there have been several other significant legislative changes, including local government reorganisation, and changes to the Use Classes Order and the Planning Inquiries Procedure Rules. The courts have also clarified and developed various legal issues. In particular, a Scottish appeal to the House of Lords has resulted in an explanation of the role of the development plan in determining planning applications. Many new policy documents have also been issued by the Scottish Office.

With the approach of the Millenium, this second edition also reviews the future of planning law, particularly with the arrival of the Scottish Parliament, which has land-use planning among its legislative powers, and the incorporation of the European Convention on Human Rights.

The law is stated as at February 28, 1999. Where possible, subsequent changes have been referred to, such as the establishment of the Scottish Parliament. Mention is also made of various consultation papers, which are likely to result in changes to the law in the next few years.

My thanks go to all those at Brodies and Greens who assisted with the production of the second edition.

This second edition is dedicated to my wife Paula, for her support and understanding.

NEIL COLLAR
Edinburgh
June 1999

PREFACE TO FIRST EDITION

"Does the Englishman still fondly believe that his home is his castle when the Executive has the following powers over it?
(1) To knock it down.
(2) To take possession of it, without notice to the owner, but with 14 days notice to the occupier, and without previous payment of the price.
(3) To close the King's highway which gives access to his house.
(4) To direct the colour with which his doors and fences may be painted.
(5) To confiscate his property illegally if he, for example is fighting in Asia for his country and so unable to appeal to the Courts within 28 days from any illegal act.
(6) To seize it and pay as compensation less than its value."

(Mekie & Williams: *Town and Country Planning Law*)

The outrage at the growing power of the Executive felt by the authors of this statement is clear. Yet the basic premise of this statement which was written in 1946 remains valid today: the State has considerable powers over land under private ownership.

Town and country planning, to give its full title, is one of the powers exercised by the State to control building and other work on land which is in private ownership. Since 1947 any landowner wishing to develop his/her land must seek permission from the State before carrying out that development. If this permission is refused, the landowner is unable to carry out the development but has no right to claim compensation from the State as a result. In such circumstances, how can "the Englishman still fondly believe that his home is his castle"? It is therefore surprising, but perhaps a tribute to the results which it has achieved, that the planning system enjoys almost universal support.

This book is written as an introduction to Scots planning law, a subject which has grown in importance over recent years. It is intended for use by any person coming into contact with the planning system, whether in their professional or private life. In particular, Chapter 10 provides a guide to members of the public on the opportunities for participating in the system. Inevitably some readers will use this book as a general reference text. With this in mind, it is recommended that any reader unfamiliar with the operation of the planning system should first read Chapter 2, which describes the "nuts and bolts", before selectively reading other chapters.

For many years Young and Rowan-Robinson's *Scottish Planning Law and Procedure* has been the bible for those involved in the Scottish planning system. This book is not a replacement for their comprehensive work but is intended as an introduction for those who are unfamiliar with the subject. It should also be of use where a more up-to-date text is required, as many areas of planning law have changed since *Scottish Planning Law and Procedure* was published in 1985.

With one exception, the law is stated as at January 31, 1994. It has been possible to address the introduction of the plan-led system on March 7th, 1994, although this change in the law came too late in the publishing process for a detailed discussion on its implications to be included. The existence of other provisions of the Planning and Compensation Act 1991 which have yet to come into force, is also noted.

The starting point for this book was my LL.M. thesis, "The Effects of Judicial Intervention on Planning Conditions," for which I owe a continuing debt to my supervisor Sue Nott and the University of Liverpool for the award of a research studentship. I also thank Paul Watchman for guiding my first steps as a practising planning lawyer. Many people have assisted with the production of this book. Particular thanks must go to my parents for their constant encouragement. I am also grateful to the partners of Brodies, W.S. and my colleagues for their support. As a novice to legal publishing, I greatly appreciated the help offered by everyone at Greens. And to all my friends, thank you.

NEIL A. COLLAR,
Edinburgh,
February 1994.

CONTENTS

TABLE OF CASES

TABLE OF STATUTES

TABLE OF STATUTORY INSTRUMENTS

TABLE OF SCOTTISH OFFICE GUIDANCE AND DIRECTIONS

TABLE OF ABBREVIATIONS

A.C.	Appeal Cases (Law Reports)
All E.R.	All England Law Reports
B.P.P.	British Parliamentary Papers
Ch.D./Ch.	Chancery (Law Reports)
CLEUD	Certificate of Lawfulness of Existing Use or Development
CLOPUD	Certificate of Lawfulness of Proposed Use or Development
DPO	Development Procedure Order
E.A.	Environmental Assessment
E.G.	Estates Gazette
E.G.C.S.	Estates Gazette Case Summaries
E.G.L.R.	Estates Gazette Law Reports
E.I.P.	Examination in Public
E.P.A.	Environmental Protection Act 1990
ESA	Environmentally Sensitive Areas
E.Z.	Enterprise Zone
F.	Session Cases 1898–1906 (8 Volumes), edited by Fraser
GDO	General Development Order
GDPO	General Development Procedure Order
GPDO	General Permitted Development Order
G.W.D.	Greens Weekly Digest
I.P.C.	Integrated Pollution Control
J.L.S.S.	Journal of the Law Society of Scotland
J.P.L.	Journal of Planning Law
K.B.	King's Bench (Law Reports)
L.G.R.	Local Government Reports
L.J.(K.B.)	Law Journal Reports (King's Bench)
M.L.R.	Modern Law Review
NHA	Natural Heritage Area
N.H.S.A.	Natural Heritage (Scotland) Act 1991
N.I.D.	Notice of Intention to Develop
NNR	National Nature Reserve
NPPG	National Planning Policy Guideline
NSA	National Scenic Area
O.J.L.S.	Oxford Journal of Legal Studies
P. & C.R.	Property and Compensation Reports
PAN	Planning Advice Note
P.C.A.	Planning and Compensation Act 1991
PDO	Permitted Development Order
P.L.	Public Law
P.L.I.	Public Local Inquiry

P.L.R.	Planning Law Reports
R.T.P.I.	Royal Town Planning Institute
Q.B.	Queen's Bench (Law Reports)
S.C.	Session Cases
S.C.L.R.	Scottish Civil Law Reports
SDD	Scottish Development Department
SEnvD	Scottish Environment Department
S.I.	Statutory Instrument
S.L.T.	Scots Law Times
S.L.T. (Lands Tr.)	Scots Law Times Lands Tribunal Reports
S.L.T. (Sh.Ct.)	Scots Law Times Sheriff Court Reports
SOIR	Scottish Office Inquiry Reporters
SPA	Special Protection Areas
SPEL	Scottish Planning and Environmental Law
S.P.L.P.	Scottish Planning Law and Practice
SPZ	Simplified Planning Zone
SSSI	Site of Special Scientific Interest
TCPSA	Town and Country Planning (Scotland) Act 1972
TPO	Tree Preservation Order
T.P.Rev.	Town Planning Review
U.L. & P.	Urban Law and Policy
UCO	Use Classes Order
W.L.R.	Weekly Law Reports

ILLUSTRATIONS

CHAPTER 1

EVOLUTION OF PLANNING LAW

Planning law is the creation of statute, unlike many other areas of law. 1.01
The development of the statutory provisions applicable to town and
country planning is traced in the first part of this chapter and provides an
historical perspective for the current planning system, which is examined
in subsequent chapters.

The activity of planning initially evolved in tandem with the planning
system, with statute setting out the objectives of planning. However,
under the present system, statute provides the framework rather than the
objectives for the activity of planning. The evolving planning profession
and academic thought has led to many theories of planning. The second
part of this chapter examines some of these theories, and considers
whether there can ever be an answer to the question: "What is
planning?"

PRE-1909—ORIGINS OF PLANNING LAW

Prior to the advent of state control of land use under the planning system, 1.02
the feudal nature of Scottish land ownership provided an important facility
for the private planning of land use. Feudal land tenure allows the feudal
superior to impose restrictions on what the landowner may do on his own
land. For example, the carrying on of trades and businesses likely to have
an injurious effect on neighbouring landowners may be prohibited. One of
the greatest feats of town planning—the creation of Edinburgh's New
Town—was achieved almost a century before the introduction of statutory
planning powers.[1] The uniformity of development was secured through
title conditions requiring the consent of the feudal superior to be obtained
before development could proceed. However, title restrictions can vary
considerably and not all feudal superiors in Scotland could be relied upon
to impose such high standards. Events were to show that some form of
state control was necessary.

The origins of planning law lie in the dramatic changes in nineteenth-
century British society caused by the Industrial Revolution, with an
influx of people from the countryside into the towns, attracted by
employment in the expanding factories. Houses were hurriedly constructed to meet the demand, often close to the factories. There was no
control over standards of construction, resulting in houses in close and

---

[1] Youngson, *The Making of Classical Edinburgh* (1966).

1

unregulated proximity with little or no regard to the requirements of proper ventilation and sanitation. People were living in slum conditions.

Model industrial villages, such as New Lanark and Port Sunlight (close to Glasgow and Liverpool, respectively), provided a powerful precedent of how workers could be housed in pleasant and healthy surroundings, underlining the need for action to combat the existing slum conditions of many towns and cities. Organisations such as the Garden City Association, formed in 1899, promoted development of well laid out towns, with extensive open spaces and houses with gardens. Well designed and laid out towns were seen as the way to assure human happiness and eradicate social problems.

1.03   Insanitary housing conditions were struck at by the introduction of the Public Health Acts. Local authorities were given powers to secure proper standards of drainage and sewage, and also to make bye-laws regulating the size of rooms, space between houses and width of streets.[2] Local authorities also had powers to remove insanitary dwellings and supply new houses for the working classes.[3] However, there was still a need for local authority powers to deal with more general land-use problems, such as the separation of incompatible uses.

By the beginning of the twentieth century, there was an increasing awareness of the ill-effects caused by the physical environment of the industrial towns and cities. With the political trend towards democracy and social equality, marked by the beginnings of the welfare state in the budget of 1909, action was required to improve living conditions. A healthy workforce was required to build the *Dreadnoughts*, the mighty battleships constructed in great numbers by Britain and Germany during the power struggle in the years leading to the First World War. It was recognised that urban conditions were inimical to health, and that degeneration of the population had led to reduced labour efficiency.[4] There was an increasing realisation that Britain had lagged behind other countries, including Germany, in the guidance of the growth of towns. As war became more likely, memories revived of the ill-health of British men enlisting to fight in the Boer War,[5] such ill-health caused by the squalid dwellings in British cities.

Two explanations therefore underlie the general acceptance of the principle of town planning in 1909.[6] First, it was a logical extension of earlier legislation concerned with housing and public health. Secondly, it was clear that the effect of rapid urban and industrial change required a more comprehensive approach than the public health bye-laws.

[2] Public Health (Scotland) Act 1897 (60 & 61 Vict., c. 38), s. 181.
[3] Artisans Dwellings (Scotland) Act 1875 (38 & 39 Vict., c. 49), replaced and repealed by Housing of the Working Classes Act 1890 (53 & 54 Vict., c. 70).
[4] Cd. 2175 (B.P.P., 1904, xxxiii).
[5] Cherry, *The Politics of Town Planning* (1982), Chap. 2.
[6] Ashworth, *Genesis of Modern British Town Planning* (1954), Chap. 7.

1909–1939—Town Planning

Town planning was born in the Housing, Town Planning, Etc. Act 1909,   1.04
which conferred a power upon local authorities to prepare town planning
schemes for their area[7]:

> "with the general object of securing proper sanitary conditions,
> amenity, and convenience in connection with the laying-out and use
> of the land, and of any neighbouring lands."

The scope of town planning was therefore wider than that of the old
sanitary and housing legislation, covering the additional objects of
amenity and convenience.

The power conferred on local authorities by the 1909 Act was
discretionary, and the cumbersome procedure for the preparation of
town planning schemes provided little incentive for exercise of their
powers.[8] Moreover, schemes could only be prepared for land about to be
developed or likely to be developed, and the Act did not provide for
control of building development in the countryside or redevelopment of
built-up areas. Statutory town planning was confined to the physical
layout of land and buildings, ensuring standards of amenity and convenience. However, local authorities had the power to take a comprehensive approach to development: where previously new buildings had to
satisfy public health bye-laws, the impact of those buildings on the
amenity and convenience of the surrounding neighbourhood now had to
be considered. Town planning was born.

Town planning schemes were the principal instrument of town plan-   1.05
ning until 1947. The provisions of the operative scheme controlled
development and the authority ceased to have planning control over
individual development, unless zoning provisions required its consent for
certain uses. The scheme was essentially a zoning plan, dedicating
certain areas or zones to specified uses such as industrial use, open space
and residential development. It left no doubts about what forms of
development were permitted, but this certainty meant that the scheme
was inflexible. To give more flexibility zones were often dedicated to a
predominant use which was allowed without consent, while other
specified uses were prohibited or required the consent of the local
authority.[9] Schemes also provided limits on the number of buildings, the
space around them, and their appearance. Planning schemes were
entirely regulatory in nature, and did not secure that development would
take place, merely providing that if it did take place in any particular
part of the area covered by the scheme, it would be controlled in certain
ways.

After the First World War, there was a desperate shortage of housing
and calls for "homes fit for heroes". Social pacification through

---

[7] 9 Edw. 7, c. 44, s. 54—applicable to Scotland by virtue of s. 53.

[8] Fewer than 10,000 acres of land in England and Wales had been brought under
planning control by 1919—Griffiths, "The Law of Property (Land)" in *Law and Opinion in
England in the Twentieth Century* (Ginsberg ed., 1959), p. 127.

[9] For detailed discussion, see Abercrombie, *Town and Country Planning* (1st ed., 1933);
Mekie and Williams, *Town and Country Planning Law* (1946).

improved housing provision was a clear antidote to fears of bolshevism and industrial unrest following the Russian Revolution.[10] This was combined with increased planning powers in the Housing, Town Planning, Etc. (Scotland) Act 1919.[11] During the war there had been a considerable extension of government powers, and it was felt safe to increase local authority planning powers in that light. The 1919 Act introduced compulsory town planning for the council of every burgh with a population of 20,000 or more. These councils were required to produce town planning schemes by January 1, 1926. Although some of the procedural obstacles to the preparation of schemes were removed, there was no attention paid to the most fundamental criticisms and, in particular, there was still no question of planning a town as a whole.

One innovation of the 1919 Act was the introduction of interim development control[12] for the period between the passing of a resolution to prepare a scheme until the scheme became effective, which could be several years. There was no obligation on developers to apply for permission, but a grant of planning permission under interim development control preserved the right to compensation if the development conflicted with the scheme eventually approved. Thus interim development control was purely negative in character, neither obliging nor assisting anybody to do anything. To avoid any liability to pay compensation, the authority would rely on the projected provisions of the planning scheme when granting planning permission.

1.06   The first statute to deal exclusively with town planning was the Town Planning (Scotland) Act 1925, which consolidated existing planning law.[13] This was followed by the Town and Country Planning (Scotland) Act 1932,[14] which extended the planning powers of local authorities by providing that town planning schemes could be made over any land, urban or rural, containing buildings or not. The objects of town planning schemes now included[15]:

> "preserving existing buildings or other objects of architectural, historic or artistic interest and places of natural interest or beauty, and generally of protecting amenities whether in urban or rural portions of the area."

However, the 1932 Act also removed any requirement upon authorities to prepare town planning schemes, leaving planning as a voluntary activity. It also reintroduced the cumbersome procedures for preparing or modifying a scheme. The growing complexity of planning law was reflected in the size of the 1932 Act: 55 sections and five Schedules, compared to the 22 sections and four Schedules of the 1925 Act.

---

[10] Committee on Building Construction in Connection with the Provision of Dwellings for the Working Classes, Cd. 9191 (B.P.P., 1918, vii).

[11] 9 & 10 Geo. 5, c. 60.

[12] s. 37. See Mekie and Williams *ibid.*, Chap. V, "Interim Development".

[13] 15 & 16 Geo. 5, c. 17. The Housing Etc. Act 1923 (13 & 14 Geo. 5, c. 49) had extended planning powers to areas of aesthetic or historic interest, whether developed or not.

[14] 22 & 23 Geo. 5, c. 49. See *Encyclopaedia of the Laws of Scotland* (1933), Vol. 14, "Town and Country Planning".

[15] 1932 Act, s. 1.

Post-1939—The War Years

During the Second World War public opinion swung behind the need 1.07
for effective town and country planning. As a relief from the struggle for
survival, hopes had centred on the drive for reconstruction and it was
increasingly expected that bold and imaginative planning would create a
better Britain. After all, if the war could be planned, why not peace?
State direction was seen as the way forward. At last, public opinion was
prepared to subordinate private interests in land to the public interest in
a planned environment.

The Blitz saw the heart of many British cities and towns destroyed by
bombing. Since extensive rebuilding was inescapable, there was an
opportunity to improve cities as a whole. It was realised that unless
proper planning was implemented, the end result would be a total lack
of improvement. There was a need to treat the city as an entity, and not
to concentrate on the devastated areas in isolation. Planning could deal
with the enormous demand for housing and redevelop congested and
inadequate areas of towns and cities.

The Government saw the possibilities of using the planning system as
a political tool to achieve reconstruction of society after the war.[16] As a
result it commissioned three reports to examine the future role of
planning. The Barlow Report[17] recommended decentralisation of industry to allow redevelopment of congested urban areas, and a reasonable
balance of industrial development throughout the country. This led to
the establishment of the new towns. The Uthwatt Report[18] tackled the
problem of compensation. Since planning powers were first conferred,
the possible liability to pay compensation to landowners had left many
authorities unwilling to control development. The report recommended
that rights to development in all land outside built-up areas should be
vested in the State on payment of fair compensation. This would allow
local authorities in the future to divert land to uses not chosen by the
owner, without automatic liability to pay compensation. It also recommended that control over development should be secured by speedy
legislation bringing all land within interim development control, to
prevent development prejudicial to post-war reconstruction plans. The
Scott Report[19] called for local planning to become compulsory rather
than permissive, and for the approval of the local authority to be
required for any development during the period of interim development
control.

Following the recommendation of the Uthwatt Report, the Town and 1.08
Country Planning (Interim Development) (Scotland) Act 1943[20]
extended interim control of development throughout the country,

---

[16] See generally Cullingworth, *Peacetime History of Environmental Planning 1939–69*
(1975), Vol. 1, "Reconstruction and Land-use Planning 1939–1947".

[17] Royal Commission on the Distribution of the Industrial Population, Cmd. 6153 (1940)
(B.P.P., 1939–40, iv, 263).

[18] Reports of the Expert Committee on Compensation and Betterment, Interim Cmd.
6291 (1941) (B.P.P., 1940–41, iv, 205); Final Cmd. 6386 (1942) (B.P.P., 1941–42, iv, 15).

[19] Report of the Committee on Land Utilisation in Rural Areas, Cmd. 6328 (1942)
(B.P.P., 1941–42, iv, 421).

[20] 6 & 7 Geo. 6, c. 43.

through the statutory fiction that all authorities were in the process of preparing a town planning scheme. Local authorities were also given the power to enforce interim development control. Previously, enforcement action could only be taken once a town planning scheme was operative and a development did not conform with its provisions. The 1943 Act enabled the authorities to take enforcement action against development which threatened their planning proposals or was not in accordance with the terms of the grant of permission, before any scheme was approved. However, there was still no requirement for planning permission to be sought from the local authority before development could proceed.

The Town and Country Planning (Scotland) Act 1945,[21] known as the "blitz and blight" Act, empowered local authorities to undertake the actual development of their own areas. For the first time, local authorities could buy land simply and expeditiously for planning purposes, particularly for redeveloping as a whole war-damaged or obsolete and badly laid out areas.

Thus by 1945, local authorities had extensive planning powers unheard of before the war. The 1943 Act extended existing powers, while the 1945 Act introduced major new powers. However, a complete overhaul of the planning system was still necessary to allow reconstruction after the war.

1947 ACT AND BEYOND

1.09   In dealing with the principal recommendations of the Uthwatt and Scott Reports, the Town and Country Planning (Scotland) Act 1947[22] heralded a new era of planned society. For the first time, local authorities were given comprehensive planning powers, and the whole country was subjected to planning control. The Act had five main purposes[23]:

(a) to provide a framework, or pattern, for land use against which day-to-day development could be considered (the development plan);

(b) to bring all development under control, making it subject to the permission of local authorities or central government;

(c) to deal with specific problems of amenity, including the preservation of trees and woodlands, and of buildings of special architectural and historic interest, and control of outdoor advertisements;

(d) to solve the compensation and betterment problem[24]; and

(e) to extend the powers of authorities to acquire and develop land for planning purposes, and the scale and scope of grants from central funds to local authorities carrying out the acquisition and clearing of land.

---

[21] 8 & 9 Geo. 6, c. 33.

[22] 10 & 11 Geo. 6, c. 53.

[23] *Ministry of Town and Country Planning Report 1943–51*, Cmd. 8204 (B.P.P., 50–51, xx, 133).

[24] For a brief explanation of this problem, see Moore, *A Practical Approach to Planning Law* (1987), pp. 2–3. Also, Grant, *Urban Planning Law* (1982), pp. 18–20.

Perhaps the most important measure in the 1947 Act was the introduction of a universal requirement to obtain consent from the local authority for any development. This control was created by nationalising all development rights in land, leaving owners with the existing (1947) use rights in their land. As all development rights were vested in the state, its permission had to be obtained for any proposed development. Unlike the non-obligatory nature of interim development control, consent was required before development could commence. This was a considerable extension of the proposals of the Uthwatt Report, which had restricted control to undeveloped land outside town areas. The effect of these provisions cannot be exaggerated. Owners were left with no absolute rights to develop their land, build upon it, or even change its use. This was a radical encroachment on rights of private property.

With the universal requirement for planning permission, the town planning scheme became meaningless, as there was no need to impose specific restrictions on the use of particular land. However, the advantage of the town planning scheme had been that the developer knew with considerable precision what development could be undertaken, and this advantage was retained with the introduction of development plans. Under the 1947 Act development plans had to be prepared for every area in the country, to outline the way in which each area was to be developed or preserved.

The development plan was conceived essentially as a statement of development proposals and the intentions of the local authority with regard to the development of their area, and was intended to show only broad land-use allocations. Unlike the town planning scheme, the development plan carried no guarantee that planning permission would be granted even if development proposals were in harmony with the plan. However, in considering an application for planning permission, the authority had to consider the provisions of the plan and "any other material considerations". In addition, the plan was not intended to be a final statement, even of the broad intentions of the authority. It was to be reviewed every five years, and amendments could be made at any time. It was hoped that the new system of flexible development plans would cure the rigid and static nature of town planning schemes.

The importance of the 1947 Act cannot be overstated. It made planning a compulsory function of all local authorities. Pre-war Britain had been largely free from any operative planning control, but following the 1947 Act every piece of land in Britain was under development control, with a universal requirement to obtain consent before development could commence. The Act imposed unheard of limitations on the rights of landowners, and conferred unprecedented and largely unfettered discretionary power on local authorities. This was the true birth of planning.

1947–1997—50 YEARS OF PLANNING LAW

Although the 1947 Act introduced the most sweeping planning powers yet conferred upon local authorities, disillusionment soon set in. The system rapidly became bogged down with details and cumbersome procedures. Development plans were too detailed and quickly became   1.10

out of date. Changes to the system of development plans were proposed, to distinguish policy and strategic issues from detailed tactical issues.[25] This proposal was implemented through the introduction of the new two-part development plan in the Town and Country Planning (Scotland) Act 1969. Structure plans, which would require the approval of the Secretary of State, would set out and justify broad land-use policies for the area, policies for the management of traffic, and measures for the improvement of the physical environment. Structure plans would not contain detailed land allocations, which were left for the local plans to cover. Local plans were to set out the detailed plans for the area within the framework of the structure plans. The 1969 Act also provided for increased public consultation in the planning process.

The introduction of structure plans was seen as the opportunity for achieving more broadly based types of planning, stressing economic and social ends (theories of social and economic planning are discussed below). However, central government adopted a restrictive approach to social and economic policies in structure plans.[26] Social policies were rarely permitted to be incorporated as specific policies or proposals, and non-land-use criteria were excluded. Although the structure plan offered an opportunity to lay out broad policies and strategy, that policy and strategy related to land use. A similar approach is taken today.

The non-financial provisions of the 1947 Act, and the system of structure and local plans, still survive largely intact, consolidated in the Town and Country Planning (Scotland) Act 1997.[27] The Planning and Compensation Act 1991 improved the enforcement regime (Chapter 7), but its principal change was the introduction of the plan-led system, whereby planning decisions must be made in accordance with the provisions of the structure and local plans unless material considerations indicate otherwise (Chapter 3).[28]

Local government reorganisation in 1996 removed the two-tier system of local government by abolishing the regional councils. The new unitary councils are therefore not subject to the checks and balances exercised by the regional councils on the district councils, which included the power of the regional council to call in for determination an application which had been submitted to the district council for their determination. The new structure plan areas designated by the Secretary of State (Chapter 3) require many of the new unitary authorities to work together in preparing structure plans.

---

[25] Planning Advisory Group (PAG) Report, *The Future of Development Plans* (1965).

[26] Jowell and Noble, "Structure Plans as Instruments of Social and Economic Policy" [1981] J.P.L. 466.

[27] c. 8. Other provisions are in the Planning (Listed Buildings and Conservation Areas) (Scotland) Act 1997 (c. 9), Planning (Hazardous Substances) (Scotland) Act 1997 (c. 10), and Planning (Consequential Provisions) (Scotland) Act 1997 (c. 11).

[28] TCPSA, ss. 25 and 37(2). The force of this provision has been blunted by the decision of the House of Lords in *City of Edinburgh Council v. Secretary of State for Scotland*, 1998 S.L.T. 120 that the assessment of the material considerations is a matter for the decision-maker (Chapter 3).

Towards the Millenium

With the approach of the Millenium, it seems appropriate to review the 1.11
future of planning law, particularly with the arrival of the Scottish
Parliament, which has land-use planning among its legislative powers
(Chapter 2).

The current system has bedded-down since the introduction of the
universal requirement for planning permission in 1947. Although there
have been many changes, particularly the division of the development
plan into structure and local plans, and the introduction of the plan-led
system, the structure of the planning system is largely the same, centered
around the activities of development planning and the control of
development through the requirement for planning permission.

The introduction of the plan-led system emphasises the importance of
development plan policies in the operation of the planning system. The
content of these policies is guided by the policies issued by the Scottish
Office, principally in the National Planning Policy Guidelines (NPPGs).
It is within this national policy that most of the recent innovations in the
planning system can be found, such as the introduction of the sequential
approach for retail development. Significantly, the concept of sustainable
development does not appear in any of the planning statutes, and its role
in the planning system is entirely driven by national planning policy.
Ironically, the making and role of such policy is not regulated by the
1997 Acts, unlike the preparation and adoption/ approval of structure
and local plans. National planning policy is no more than a material
consideration (Chapter 5), albeit that there are checks and balances
enabling the Scottish Office to ensure compliance.

Among the issues suggested for consideration by the Scottish Parliament are whether planning legislation should refer to sustainable
development and NPPGs, whether there is a continuing need for
structure plans and whether sub-national planning guidance should be
prepared as an alternative, and whether planning controls should
be extended to cover agriculture, forestry and the marine environment.[29]
There has also been a suggestion that the Lands Tribunal should be
given jurisdiction for variation and discharge of section 75 agreements.[30]
Although there does not appear to be a demand for radical change in
the planning system, the proposed land reforms, including access to land
and the creation of national parks, will have implications for planning.
The external influence of planning is also reflected in the new concept of
community planning.[31] It also remains to be seen whether the incorporation of the European Convention on Human Rights will have a
significant impact on the planning system (Chapter 8).

The delays in the planning system remain a concern. The Scottish
Office Planning Audit Unit has been addressing decision-making by
planning authorities. Changes have been made to the Inquiry Procedure

---

[29] Consultation Paper "Land Use Planning under a Scottish Parliament" (Scottish
Office, January 1999).
[30] Scottish Law Commission Discussion Paper No. 106, "Real Burdens" (October 1998).
[31] McFadden *Report of the Community Planning Working Group*, SPEL 70:119.

Rules to reduce the length of planning inquiries (Chapter 8). There is concern that the preparation of development plans is taking too long and that there is insufficient monitoring and review of these plans, and recommendations have been made to improve the management of the process.[32]

OBJECTIVES OF PLANNING

1.12   Since the 1932 Act no indication has been given in the Planning Acts of the objects for which planning powers are conferred. The Town and Country Planning (Scotland) Act 1997 (TCPSA) does provide guidance on the contents of structure and local plans (Chapter 3). When determining applications for planning permission, the planning authority are directed to have regard to the provisions of the development plan and to any other "material considerations", and must determine the application in accordance with the provisions of the plan unless the material considerations indicate otherwise.[33] As the power to determine such applications is conferred by the TCPSA, legal theory states that such considerations must be planning considerations. But what is "planning"?

Throughout the years, writers have suggested a variety of objectives, which have altered as the planning system has developed.[34] Every person involved in the planning process has a different conception of the objective of planning—a personal planning theory. Thus one of the problems of planning is that it promises to be all things to all men and therefore satisfies no one objective. However, the flexibility of the planning system has the advantage of being able to adjust to new philosophies and ideas as they arise, such as the concept of sustainable development, whereby planners may be seen as trustees of the environment for future generations.

In general terms, planning seeks to preserve the environment while improving it by careful control of development, moving towards the ultimate goal of a healthy and civilised life. However, a more detailed analysis is required to explain the purpose of the planning system.

Town and country planning is predominantly about land use. However, writers have argued that interpreting "planning" as being concerned solely with land use is unduly confining, and that social and economic factors should be on a level par with land-use considerations.[35] In the sense that town planning is an activity carried out in the public

---

[32] "Review of Development Planning in Scotland" (Scottish Office, March 1998).

[33] TSCPA, ss. 25 and 37(2).

[34] *e.g.* Abercrombie, quoted in Hall, *The Containment of Urban England* (1973), Vol. 2, Chap. 1; Hall himself, *ibid.*; Foley, "British Town Planning: One Ideology or Three?" (1960) 11 British Journal of Sociology 211 and in Faludi, *A Reader in Planning Theory* (1973); Bruton (ed.), *The Spirit and Purpose of Planning* (1974); Simmonds, "The Conflicting Aims of Planning", in *Contemporary Issues in Town Planning* (Willis ed., 1986).

[35] Faludi, *supra*, p. 291. The systems analysis approach of the 1960s viewed towns as complex systems where physical, economic and social environments were interrelated: see Ravetz, *The Government of Space—Town Planning in Modern Society* (1986).

interest, there must be a social element within it. The "public interest" must be an amalgam of the social values and interests of the population. Furthermore, the social origins of town planning lay in concerns for public health. Man's environment was conceived as the determinant of his happiness and behaviour, and early town planners believed that social problems could be eradicated by engineering the environment. Modern theories are less interventionist, providing a framework not to fashion behaviour, but rather to present the widest range of opportunities to enable individuals to fulfil their social objectives.[36]

There is also an economic dimension to planning, as it represents government intervention in the land market to correct deficiencies.[37] For example, the factory owner has no incentive to minimise pollution from the smoking factory chimney. The planning system therefore intervenes to balance the social costs of this pollution against the social benefits of the factory development, thereby providing for socially optimal use of land. The planning system also has the ability to change land values. Proposals for major developments such as roads can cause planning blight, with property values in the vicinity of the development plummeting. The reverse is also true: a grant of planning permission for a plot of land invariably increases its value. The Thatcher Government of the 1980s emphasised this economic dimension, believing that the planning system could be used to encourage economic prosperity.[38]   1.13

Various influences act as a brake on the pursuit of wider social and economic objectives,[39] and limit the extent of planning powers. Planning is a professional activity and must be influenced by the opinions and theories of the planning profession.[40] More importantly, planning functions within a political and legal structure, and this structure acts as a limiting factor. Planning is a political function, both in the sense that it is a power vested in government, central and local, and also because it is a process of choice and must therefore have an inherently political nature.[41] Planning powers are vested in local government, subject to the guidance of central government, which initiates all planning legislation. At every stage of the planning process, politicians take the final decisions, enabling the planners to claim political neutrality, although this claim is undermined by the reliance often placed on their advice by

---

[36] Cherry, *Town Planning in Its Social Context* (1970); Loughlin's social-needs model—"Planning Gain: Law, Policy and Practice" (1980) 1 O.J.L.S. 61 at pp. 74–75; Broady, *Planning for People: Essays on the Social Context of Planning* (1968).

[37] See generally, Broadbent, *Planning and Profit in the Urban Economy* (1977).

[38] Michael Heseltine, quoted in Cherry, *The Politics of Town Planning* (1982), Chap. 4; Address by Mrs. Roe M.P., Parliamentary Under Secretary of State, D.O.E. [1988] J.P.L. 517.

[39] See generally, M.L. Harrison, "Development Control—Influence of Political, Legal and Ideological Factors" (1972) 48 T.P. Rev. 254; Regan, "Pathology of British Land-use Planning" (April 1978), *Local Government Studies*.

[40] For example, Healey, McDougall and Thomas (eds), *Planning Theory—Prospects for the 1980s* (1982).

[41] See generally, Blowers, *The Limits of Power: The Politics of Local Planning Policy* (1980); Cherry, *The Politics of Town Planning* (1982); Goldsmith, *Politics, Planning and the City* (1980); Hayward and Watson (eds), *Planning Politics and Public Policy* (1975); Keating, *The City that Refused to Die—Glasgow: The Politics of Urban Regeneration* (1988).

the politicians.[42] While the planner may argue that his advice is apolitical, it must be influenced by his own values and those of the planning profession.

The political influence on planning is demonstrated by the changes made to the planning system by the Thatcher Government. The political impetus was to promote economic growth by simplifying the planning system, and concepts such as the Urban Development Area, Enterprise Zones and Simplified Planning Zones represent political manipulation of the planning system to encourage industrial development.[43]

1.14   In general, the political will does not favour a truly comprehensive and broadly based planning system, as this is too reminiscent of communist-planned economies. This philosophy is manifested in the government approach to the contents of structure plans, which confines policies to land-use factors. Writers may argue for planning to be given an explicit social and economic role, but this is resisted by the politicians. The political context of planning has limited it to a passive and negative character, responding to pressures for development rather than initiating development.[44] Local authorities have few positive planning powers enabling them to take active steps to achieve the policies promoted in development plans. Instead the development control function is emphasised and planning appears negative in character. Treating planning on this application-by-application basis provides no possibility for applying broad theories of social and economic planning. Thus the political framework within which planning operates has placed considerable limitations on what it may achieve.

Planning is also a legal activity, with its powers derived from statute and subject to judicial control, which is a further limiting factor on the extent of planning powers,[45] as will be demonstrated in later chapters. One writer concluded that the judiciary appear sympathetic towards individual property rights at the expense of the public control of land use represented by planning powers.[46] This serves as a reminder that the law and its institutions are not wholly neutral, and that the personal planning theories or values of the judiciary must influence its decisions on the breadth of planning powers.

As a result of these diverse influences, only general comments can be made about the extent of planning powers. The objectives attributed to planning powers reflect the prevailing political, legal, social and economic influences. Planning is predominantly concerned with the use of land, but social and economic considerations have a varying influence.

---

[42] See Elkin, *Politics and Land-use Planning: The London Experience* (1974), Chap. 5; McAuslan, *Land, Law and Planning* (1974), p. 360 "The Role of Planning Officials", and p. 401 "The Actual Determination by the Committee".

[43] Redman, "Simplifying the System?" [1989] J.P.L. 563.

[44] Blowers, *supra*.

[45] See generally, McAuslan, *Land, Law and Planning* (1974), "Planning Law's Contribution to Problems of an Urban Society" (1974) 37 M.L.R. 134, "The Plan, the Planners and the Lawyers" 1971 P.L. 247; McEwan, *Planning Law and Ideological Disorder* (1982).

[46] McAuslan, *The Ideologies of Planning Law* (1980), and article of same name (1979) 2 U.L. & P. 1. See also, Griffiths, *The Politics of the Judiciary* (3rd ed., 1985), Chap. 9, in particular, p. 202.

Planning powers are exercised to preserve and enhance the environment, but only to the extent permitted by such influences as the political framework within which planning operates. The question "What is planning?" cannot be answered fully, because the activity of planning is not static and it changes or develops to reflect prevailing influences. This can be seen from the significant role of planning in promoting sustainable development (Chapter 5), despite the absence of any mention of sustainable development in the Town and Country Planning (Scotland) Act 1997.

CONCLUSION

The evolution of planning law has not been a linear process, but a pattern of successive actions and reactions, with great leaps and small steps. Despite this fitful evolution, two trends have consistently influenced legislation. The preparation of town planning schemes and development plans has always been slow. Successive Acts have attempted to speed up the preparation process, as well as searching for a way of ensuring flexibility and comprehensiveness. The solution has yet to be found. The problems identified with the present system have changed little since the beginnings of statutory planning: the consequence of the length and complexity of procedures for preparation of development plans is that policies are frequently out of date before the plan is adopted; and plans are excessively long, too detailed and contain policies irrelevant to planning.[47] The other problem has been the delays in the development control process, a consistent problem since 1947.

A criticism frequently made of statutory planning is that it has consistently promised far more than it could hope to deliver. However, this is a result of inflated claims of what planning can achieve, made when the powers available have been insufficient to attain the desired aims. Immediately after major town planning legislation has been passed there have been periods of optimism and enthusiasm in planning, for example, in 1909, 1947 and 1969. However, this has given way to disillusionment once it is realised that what could be achieved was much less than was expected. Since 1947, planners have sought an increased scope for town planning, but central government has consistently taken the view that planning and the development plan is solely concerned with land use and the quality of the physical environment.

After 90 years of statutory town planning, and more than 50 years of the universal requirement to obtain planning permission, it is interesting to trace the evolution of development control. The first planning powers were permissive and geographically limited (1909 Act). After some compulsory planning (1919 Act), planning became voluntary once again, although planning control could be exercised over more areas of land. After the Second World War, planning became both compulsory and comprehensive, covering all land. Since 1947 this has remained the

1.15

---

[47] One example of an irrelevant policy is the frequent statement in structure plans that the local authority has declared the area a nuclear-free zone.

situation, although in the late '80s some control was removed from local authorities. The universal requirement to obtain planning consent for development has been a feature of development control since the 1947 Act. This process is modelled on the voluntary process of interim development control which existed, in some form, since the 1919 Act. The tools of development control have been in existence since 1919, and only their function and importance have changed.

THE PLANNING SYSTEM

Subsequent chapters examine in detail the important elements of the   2.01
planning system. However, to appreciate its full magnificence and
complexity, one must understand the basic "nuts and bolts" of the
system, including the personnel who operate the system, and the tools
which they use.

TERRITORIAL LIMITS

Planning control extends only to the mean low water mark around the   2.02
coast.[1] From this point to the 12-mile limit of British territorial waters,
there is no control over activities other than that exercised by the Crown
Estate Commissioners in their capacity as landlords of the seabed. This
creates an inherent weakness in statutory designations such as National
Scenic Areas (Chapter 9), which cannot extend to the seabed and
inshore waters beyond low water mark, and arguably prevents effective
coastal management. An extension of the jurisdiction of planning
authorities to the 12-mile limit has been recommended.[2] It is intended
that the siting of marine fish farms will be brought within planning
control.[3]

PERSONNEL

(a) Parliament

Much of the basic structure of the planning system comes from   2.03
legislation passed by Parliament in the form of Acts of Parliament and
statutory instruments (below).

Planning is within the legislative competence of the Scottish Parliament. However, the power of the Scottish Parliament to legislate is
limited by the requirement that its legislation be compatible with
European Community law and certain rights created by the European
Convention on Human Rights. In addition, its jurisdiction does not
extend to matters reserved to the Westminster Parliament, which include

---

[1] *Argyll and Bute D.C. v. Secretary of State for Scotland*, 1976 S.C. 248; 1977 S.L.T. 33.
[2] Report from the Select Committee on the Environment (1992, H.C.).
[3] "Marine Fish Farm—Review of Planning Arrangements" (The Scottish Office,
December 1997).

aspects of electricity, oil and gas, coal, nuclear energy, energy conservation, road transport, rail transport, marine transport and air transport.[4]

(b)   European Community

2.04   It is an objective of European Community (now European Union)
policy to preserve, protect and improve the quality of the environment.
The competence of the Community to adopt measures concerning
planning has been recognised,[5] subject to the principle of subsidiarity
whereby it can only act if Member States cannot achieve the objectives
of the proposed action. European Community law has already introduced environmental assessment (Chapter 5) and several statutory
designations protecting areas of land (Chapter 9), and further initiatives
from Europe can be anticipated. Work is proceeding on the European
Spatial Development Perspective, which is not an additional European
layer of statutory planning and aims to provide a perspective rather than
being prescriptive.[6]

(c)   Secretary of State for Scotland/Scottish Executive

2.05   Until the formation of the Scottish Parliament in July 1999, the
Secretary of State for Scotland has executive responsibility for
the planning system in Scotland, and is the Scottish equivalent of the
Secretary of State for the Environment. After the Scottish Parliament
has been formed, the First Minister will be appointed, and he/ she will
appoint the Scottish Ministers. The First Minister and the Scottish
Ministers will form the Scottish Executive and have the executive
responsibility for the Scottish planning system. The Secretary of State for
Scotland will remain associated with the Westminster Parliament. For
ease of reference, the remainder of this book continues to follow the
approach of the Town and Country Planning (Scotland) Act 1997 in
referring to the Secretary of State rather than the Scottish Executive.
        The executive responsibility for the planning system includes:

  (i)   initiating new legislation governing the planning system and
         piloting it through Parliament;
  (ii)   taking ministerial responsibility for the activities of the Scot-
         tish Office Development Department (SDD) and the Scottish
         Office Inquiry Reporters (SOIR) (below);
  (iii) drawing up national planning policies and issuing guidance on
         policy matters in the form of National Planning Policy
         Guidelines (NPPGs), Planning Advice Notes (PANs) and
         circulars (see below);
  (iv)   giving strategic or regional guidance to be taken into account
         by authorities drawing up development plans (Chapter 3);
  (v)   approving structure plans and considering, and if necessary
         calling-in for decision, proposed local plans (Chapter 3);

---

[4] Scotland Act 1998 (c.46).
[5] Maastricht Treaty, Art. 130s.
[6] Mackinnon, "European Spatial Development Perspective", SPEL 71:8.

(vi) determining appeals against a range of planning decisions (Chapter 8), normally by delegating the decision to a reporter;

(vii) calling-in applications for planning permission for decision (Chapter 5);

(viii) listing buildings of historical and architectural interest (Chapter 9).

Of course, many of these functions are not carried out by the Secretary of State personally, but on his behalf by the SDD, the SOIR and Historic Scotland.

In determining appeals and called-in applications, the Secretary of State considers the planning merits of the matter and generally has the same powers, and is subject to the same legal restrictions, as the planning authority.

(d) Scottish Office Inquiry Reporters

The SOIR are responsible for administering planning appeals and the public inquiries system (both for planning and other statutory regimes). Where the Planning Acts require an appeal against a planning decision to be submitted to the Secretary of State, the notice of appeal should be forwarded to SOIR who will advise on further procedure and organise the administrative aspects of the appeal (Chapter 8). 2.06

SOIR maintain a list of reporters to hear appeals, either by written submissions or at a hearing or public inquiry, and to chair hearings and public inquiries. There is a small core of full-time reporters supplemented by part-time reporters. All reporters are professionally qualified, and have experience in planning or a related discipline. SOIR appoint a reporter to each appeal or inquiry, and the parties have no say in this process.

A wide range of planning appeals has been delegated by the Secretary of State to reporters for decision, to the extent that over 90 per cent of appeals are now decided by reporters. The Secretary of State retains the right to "claw-back" for his decision any appeal within these delegated classes. In a delegated appeal, the reporter hears the evidence at the hearing or inquiry, or considers the written submissions, and issues his decision letter. Where the decision is to be made by the Secretary of State, the reporter hears the case and reports to the Secretary of State, usually with a recommendation on its disposal. The decision on the appeal is made by the Secretary of State who can reject any recommendation made in the report.

The reporter is the master of procedure at a hearing or public local inquiry. He is entitled to adopt an interventionist role and to ask witnesses questions, rather than merely note the evidence brought out during examination by the parties. In reaching conclusions, the reporter is entitled to make use of his planning experience and expertise.[7] In common with the planning authority, the reporter is obliged to take account of all material considerations and not merely those raised by the

---

[7] *Narden Services v. Secretary of State for Scotland*, 1993 S.L.T. 871.

parties at the inquiry or in their written submissions.[8] Where the reporter identifies a planning issue which he considers may be material to the decision, but which has not been addressed by either party, the reporter is not entitled to reach a conclusion on that issue and found upon it as a factor material to his decision without giving the parties an opportunity of commenting upon it.[9]

(e)   Planning Authorities

2.07   It is left to the planning authorities to operate the grass-roots level of the planning system. They are responsible for implementing the policies of the Secretary of State, preparing development plans, determining applications for planning permission, and enforcing planning controls. Following the creation of unitary authorities in the local government reorganisation in 1996, each of the local authorities now has responsibility for development control and preparation of the local plan for their area. Some authorities have responsibility for preparing structure plans for their area, and others have shared responsibility with other authorities. The Secretary of State has designated 17 structure plan areas, six of which extend to the districts of more than one planning authority (Chapter 3).

(f)   Councillors

2.08   The planning powers vested in the local authorities are exercised by the elected councillors, either in a full meeting of the council or a planning sub-committee. Although more minor decisions may be delegated to planning officers for decision, the councillors will typically take decisions involving adoption of planning policies and development plans (see below and Chapter 3), determination of applications for planning permission (Chapter 5), and decisions on enforcement action (Chapter 7).

In making decisions on the exercise of these powers, the councillors are advised by the Director of Planning (or the holder of the equivalent position) and the officers in his department. However, they are not bound to follow the recommendation of the professional planners.

There is (and will always be) a continuing debate about the wisdom of conferring the final say on planning decisions to councillors. Some argue that the decisions are best left to the professional planning officers, rather than councillors who may have little or no knowledge of the planning system. However, others would respond that these officers are too hidebound by their professional theories and that the councillors can be relied upon to bring common sense into decision-making, if necessary acting contrary to the advice given by the planning officers. Furthermore, our democratic ideals of government frown upon vesting power in unelected officials. However, the democratic pressures upon councillors, particularly from concerned local residents, may not always result in the

---

[8] But see *Anwar v. Secretary of State for Scotland*, 1992 S.C.L.R. 875.
[9] *Anduff Holdings v. Secretary of State for Scotland*, 1992 S.L.T. 696; *cf. Ladbroke Racing Ltd v. Secretary of State for Scotland*, 1990 S.C.L.R. 705.

best decision from a planning viewpoint. All that can be said with any confidence is that each side of the debate can be supported by examples of planning decisions proving the strength of their argument. Most of those involved in the planning system are comfortable with the present decision-making process, if perhaps not entirely happy. The Nolan Committee upheld the current system of permitting councillors to make decisions contrary to officers' recommendations, but recommended good practice guidelines, training for councillors and effective external scrutiny where necessary.[10]

Where planning powers are conferred by statute upon the planning authority, the power must be exercised by the authority and no other person or body. However, the authority can competently delegate its powers to sub-committees (of councillors) or planning officers.[11] Where a discretionary power is conferred, the authority can (or is sometimes obliged to) take into account the views of other bodies and persons on how that power should be exercised, but cannot allow those views necessarily to dictate its decision.[12]

The procedures for determining applications for planning permission vary between authorities. Some have delegated extensive decision-making powers to planning officers. Others operate a form of list system whereby the councillors sitting on the planning committee receive lists of applications and the officers' recommendations thereon. Unless a councillor indicates that an application should be discussed at the committee meeting, the application is deemed to be determined in accordance with the recommendations and the decision is issued under delegated powers. This form of system reduces the number of applications debated by the councillors. Many authorities still conform to the traditional approach of requiring all applications other than those of a minor and non-controversial nature to be decided at the committee meeting.

(g) Planning Officers

Councillors are rarely professional planners and may have limited knowledge of the planning system. Their council duties are not paid as a full-time job and they cannot be expected to attend to the administrative work required before decisions can be made. As a result, councillors require the advice and administrative assistance of the planning department (following local government reorganisation, departmental names have changed, and in some councils planning may form part of the responsibility of departments such as environment, regulatory services, community services or enforcement services).

Members of the planning department are responsible for administration of all planning functions up to the point at which a decision must be taken by the councillors, or appropriate delegates. In making the decision, the councillors must take into account the professional recom-

2.09

---

[10] McFadden, "The Nolan Committee on Planning", SPEL 63:96; and "Nolan on Planning: The Government's Preliminary Response", SPEL 68:65.

[11] Local Government (Scotland) Act 1973, s. 56, as amended.

[12] *Ynys Mon B.C. v. Secretary of State for Wales* [1993] J.P.L. 225.

mendation of the planning department, but may choose to reach a contrary decision. It is therefore vital to appreciate that any views or advice offered by a planning officer cannot dictate the eventual decision by the councillors and will not bind them.[13] However, officers normally have enough experience of the decisions reached by their councillors to be able to predict their decisions with a reasonable degree of accuracy, and their advice should be seriously considered. Planning officers and clerical members of the planning department have responsibility for:

(i)   maintenance of the statutory registers which must be available for public inspection (below);

(ii)   drafting development plan proposals and organising publicity and consultation in relation to those proposals;

(iii) pre-application discussions with potential developers, which may include advising on relevant policies and possible alterations to proposals;

(iv)   responding to communications or queries from members of the public (most authorities maintain a scheme whereby a duty planning officer is always available to speak to members of the public);

(v)   preparing reports on applications for planning permission and, where appropriate, deciding these applications in terms of delegated powers (below);

(vi)   preparing cases for appeals and giving evidence on behalf of the authority at inquiries (the Royal Town Planning Institute (RTPI) advise their members not to give evidence where a decision has been made contrary to their recommendation and their professional opinion will not allow them to support that decision, not least because their true opinion is likely to be exposed during cross-examination and used to support the opposing side);

(vii) checking compliance with planning consents or the need for planning permission to be obtained for works, and recommending to the councillors when enforcement action should be taken (Chapter 9).

The extent of the duties of planning officers can be seen in the procedure leading up to determinations of applications for planning permission (Chapter 5). An application is submitted to the department. Compliance with the statutory requirements is checked, and the application registered. Responsibility for handling the application is given to a planning officer, who is a qualified planner. The officer will consult the appropriate bodies in connection with the application. He will prepare a report to the councillors, taking account of the development plan, consultation responses, representations received from the public and any other material considerations. This report will recommend to the councillors how they should determine the application. If the Director of

---

[13] *Western Fish Products Ltd v. Penwith D.C.* [1981] 2 All E.R. 204; *cf. Camden LBC v. Secretary of State for the Environment* [1993] J.P.L. 1049.

Planning (the chief planning officer) does not have delegated powers to decide the application, the report is presented to the councillors who will make their decision.

Most councils have formally delegated the exercise of various planning powers in minor or uncontroversial circumstances to the Director of Planning. For example, the Director may be authorised to decide all applications for planning unless the application is either recommended for approval contrary to the provisions of the development plan, it raises controversial or major planning issues, a councillor requests that the application be decided by the committee, or objections to the proposed development are received.

Membership of the RTPI is usually a prerequisite for employment as a planning officer. The RTPI has laid down professional standards of conduct to be met by its members and will investigate complaints concerning failure to comply with these standards.

(h) Developers

Developers are the life-blood of the planning system. For all the views 2.10 of the planning authority expressed in the development plan, there are few opportunities to put these views into practice unless and until developers seek permission for proposed developments. Although the requirement to obtain planning permission (Chapter 4) is an onerous burden placed upon landowners, the planning system protects them from over-restrictive control by providing rights to challenge planning decisions (Chapter 8) and imposing a policy in favour of development whereby planning authorities must justify refusals of permission (Chapter 5). The inability to obtain permission in some circumstances undoubtedly leads to dissatisfaction. However, the development control system also provides landowner/developers with some guarantee that their amenity will not be adversely affected by development on surrounding land.

Although accepting the need for the planning system, developers complain that the process for obtaining permission is too slow, that planning officers and authorities have no sense of commercial reality, and that there is too much interference with matters of detail, such as design, which are not planning issues.

(i) Official Bodies

Depending upon the nature of a development, various official bodies 2.11 must be consulted and asked for their views, such as Scottish Natural Heritage, the Scottish Environment Protection Agency and community councils. These bodies also have a role to play in the formulation of development-plan policies and proposals. However, their views cannot dictate the decision reached by the planning authority.[14]

---

[14] *Ynys Mon B.C. v. Secretary of State for Wales, supra.*

(j)   Public Interest

2.12   The planning system is broadly intended to control development in the public interest. Without interest and input from members of the public, the system cannot maintain the public confidence which it requires to function efficiently.

Chapter 10 examines public participation in the planning system in more detail. Both the development-plan and development-control parts of the system contain many requirements for matters to be publicised to alert members of the public to their opportunity to lodge representations and have their views taken into account as part of the decision-making process.

The weakness in the planning system perceived by members of the public is their lack of any right of appeal against a decision to grant planning permission. This omission confines them to use of the judicial review procedure (described in Chapter 8), which only allows the legality and not the merits of the decision to be challenged, and is therefore of limited value. As Chapter 10 explains, this omission can be linked to the presumption in favour of development. Put simply, to require a land-owner to obtain permission before developing his land is restrictive enough, but to allow a member of the public to challenge any grant of permission would be going too far. However, this leaves the unsatisfactory position that members of the public have no means of reversing a decision which they consider to be wrong on planning merits, but which was made legally. The Nolan Committee rejected the introduction of third party appeals.[15]

(k)   New Towns

2.13   The new town development corporations have been wound up. The corporations had no planning powers as such, but in terms of Special Development Orders made for each new town, other than Glenrothes, they were entitled to authorise development within land which they owned or had previously owned which conformed with the proposals approved by the Secretary of State in those orders. This authorisation is equivalent to a grant of planning permission.

(l)   Courts

2.14   According to British constitutional theory, Parliament makes laws and the courts apply those laws. The courts have been responsible for fleshing out many of the statutory planning provisions, through the process of statutory interpretation. For example, the seemingly wide discretionary power vested in planning authorities to impose "such conditions as they think fit" is now subject to a series of legal restrictions declared by the courts (Chapter 6). In addition, through the use of common law concepts such as natural justice and fairness, the courts seek to secure procedural fairness within the planning system. The introduction of the European Convention on Human Rights into the

---

[15] McFadden, *supra*.

United Kingdom is likely to increase the role of the courts (Chapter 8). In addition, issues regarding the competence of legislation passed by the Scottish Parliament will be raised in the courts.

The role of the courts must be contrasted with that of the Secretary of State/reporter deciding an appeal. The jurisdiction of the courts is limited to reviewing the decision to ensure that all legal requirements have been met, and the judges are not entitled to intervene where they consider that the decision is wrong on its merits. Even where a decision is declared to be illegal, the court cannot change that decision but must quash it and return the matter to the decision-maker for a fresh decision to be made in a legal manner. In contrast, the Secretary of State/reporter determines the matter as if application had been made to him in the first instance, and is entitled to reach a decision on the merits of the matter.

The powers of the courts are examined in Chapter 8.

(m) Ombudsman

Complaints relating to both decisions and actions of planning author-   2.15
ities can now be made direct to the Commissioner for Local Administration in Scotland—the Ombudsman (Chapter 8).

LAW AND POLICY

The planning system is a mixture of law and policy.[16] Planning author-   2.16
ities and other participants must act according to the law, and compliance mechanisms, such as judicial review and prosecution, exist to
enforce the law. The skeletal legal framework is fleshed out by policy,
which is necessary to ensure that the wide discretionary planning powers
are exercised consistently, both within districts and throughout the
country.

One of the keys to understanding the planning system is appreciating the difference between law, which must be observed at all times, and policies, which are not binding, with departures from policy being competent in individual cases.

Law

The Act and Treaty of Union (1707) guaranteed the preservation of   2.17
Scots law and a separate Scots legal system. The distinct nature of Scots
law is carried into planning law, with different Acts of Parliament and
statutory instruments applying to Scotland (some apply to the whole of
Britain). However, despite separate legal provisions, the law in Scotland
is very similar to that applicable to England and Wales, with many of the
differences relating to the separate Scottish local government and court
structure. Where appropriate, subsequent chapters highlight the dif-

---

[16] Extracts of planning law and policy are contained in Henderson (ed.), *Scottish Planning Sourcebook* (1989); *Scottish Planning Encyclopedia* (Greens) and *Scottish Planning—Legislation and Guidance* (the Stationery Office). Information may also be obtainable from appropriate websites (below).

ferences, to avoid any confusion. In consequence of the similarities between the two sets of planning law, reference is made to court decisions from England and Wales in the absence of any decision of the Scottish courts.

(a) Acts of Parliament

2.18   The basic framework of the planning system in Scotland is laid down by the Town and Country Planning (Scotland) Act 1997 (referred to in subsequent chapters as the TCPSA), and the Planning (Listed Buildings and Conservation Areas) (Scotland) Act 1997 (PLBCASA), the Planning (Hazardous Substances) (Scotland) Act 1997 and the Planning (Consequential Provisions) (Scotland) Act 1997. There are several other statutes which affect the planning system, such as the Local Government (Scotland) Act 1973 and the Wildlife and Countryside Act 1981.[17]

Acts of Parliament are frequently amended by subsequent legislation. When referring to Acts, either in an official form or in a commercial publication, it is therefore necessary to check whether or not any subsequent amendments have been incorporated into the text.

(b) Statutory Instruments

2.19   The TCPSA and other statutes confer power upon the Secretary of State to prepare regulations (also variously known as statutory instruments or delegated legislation). These are placed before Parliament and published by the Stationery Office.[18] In many cases these regulations prescribe detailed procedural codes for various parts of the planning system. The principal statutory instruments affecting the planning system in Scotland are the Use Classes Order, the General Permitted Development Order and the General Development Procedure Order (the latter two orders were previously contained in the single General Development Order). Reference to these and other statutory instruments are made in subsequent chapters. As with Acts, care must be taken to ensure that account is taken of subsequent amendments. For example, the General Permitted Development Order has been amended by 11 subsequent statutory instruments since its publication in 1992.

(c) European Community Directives

2.20   As noted above, the influence of the European Community (now the European Union) on planning is increasing. Directives, such as that on Environmental Assessment, oblige Member States to incorporate provisions into their national law within a specified period. If the provision has not been incorporated by the end of this period, an individual may be able to rely on the provisions of the directive when bringing an action in the Scottish courts (Chapter 8). This is known as the direct effect of European Community law.[19]

---

[17] Text of some Acts is available on the internet: www.hmso.gov.uk. Information on forthcoming legislation can also be obtained: www.Parliament.uk.

[18] Text of some statutory instruments is available on the internet: www.hmso.gov.uk.

[19] For example, *Kincardine and Deeside D.C. v. Forestry Commissioners*, 1992 S.L.T. 1180. Information on European Union legislation is available on the website: europa.eu.int

(d) Case Law

Under our unwritten constitution, Parliament is responsible for mak- 2.21
ing laws, and the courts are responsible for interpreting those laws and
declaring how they should apply in particular circumstances. Court
decisions can therefore be used as authoritative statements on the
meaning of legal provisions and their application in practice. Within
the legal system, court decisions form precedents which often bind
judges hearing future cases to decide those cases in a particular way.
Previous decisions can therefore be used as an indication of how a future
case might be decided. The weight to be given to a court decision
depends upon various factors such as the position of the court in the
hierarchy, the planning expertise of the judge(s), and the extent to which
the decision is applicable only to the facts and circumstances of
the particular case. Subsequent chapters refer to court decisions where
these decisions explain or illustrate how a legal provision may be
applied.[20]

Despite Scotland having a different legal system from the rest of
Britain, there are few differences between the planning laws and
widespread use is made in Scotland of case law from the English courts.
While a decision of an English court (other than the House of Lords) is
not binding on a Scottish judge, it will be very persuasive. With the
introduction of the European Convention on Human Rights (Chapter
8), the case law of the European Court on Human Rights will become
relevant.

(e) Comment

It is of concern that the planning system, which is supposedly open to 2.22
public participation, is regulated by such a myriad of legal sources. For
example, the landowner who wishes to know whether planning permission is required for a proposed development must consult the TCPSA,
the General Permitted Development Order and the Use Classes Order.
Assuming the landowner can obtain copies, he then has to interpret
these provisions. It is a common criticism that the drafting of Acts of
Parliament renders them impossible to read and difficult to understand,
and planning law is one of the prime examples of this criticism. It is little
wonder that our landowner gives up in disgust, only to be threatened by
the planning authority with enforcement action for failing to obtain
planning permission. When one of the underlying principles of Scots law
is that ignorance of the law is no excuse, it seems unacceptable that an
activity such as planning, which touches on the activities of so many
members of the public, is regulated by laws which are often inaccessible
to those persons, even after their best efforts.

---

[20] The following case law is available on the internet—Court of Session judgments:
www.scotcourts.gov.uk; House of Lords judgments: www.parliament.the-stationery-
office.co.uk/pa/ldjudgment/ldjudgmt.htm; English court decisions (a fee may be payable):
www.smithbernal.com.

Policy

2.23   Contrary to popular belief, the law supports the use of policy, within certain confines. Policies promote consistent decision-making which, in turn, ensures that every person is treated equally and in the same manner. Policies also provide a degree of certainty. What the law seeks to discourage is the blind, unthinking application of policy, which can lead to injustice in some cases. In every case, the decision-maker should consider whether the circumstances of that case justify making an exception to the policy. As has already been observed, one of the keys to understanding the planning system is appreciating the difference between law, which must be observed at all times, and policies, which are not binding, with departures from policy being competent in individual cases.

Consistency does not mean immutability of policies or their interpretation. The decision-maker need not adhere slavishly to a policy or a previous interpretation of it, but must clearly explain the reasons for not doing so in a particular case. Fairness may require notice of the change to be given to affected parties (Chapter 8 discusses the concept of legitimate expectations). For example, an appeal decision was quashed on the ground of unfairness where, by reason of the decision-maker's inconsistency in the interpretation and application of his policy, a person dealing with him had been taken by surprise and had had no adequate opportunity to meet the new approach before the relevant decision was made.[21]

(a)   Development Plans

2.24   The development plan, consisting of the structure and local plan for the area, contains the policies and proposals of the planning authority with regard to use of the land in that area (Chapter 3).[22] When exercising planning powers, the authority is generally required to have regard to the provisions of the development plan, so far as material, and to any other material considerations, and to act in accordance with the provisions of the plan unless material considerations indicate otherwise (commonly referred to as "the plan-led system").[23] This does not amount to a requirement to always follow the policies and proposals contained in the plan, as is recognised by provision of a procedure for granting permission contrary to the terms of the plan (Chapter 5). The House of Lords have indicated that the assessment of the facts and the weighing of the considerations is for the decision-maker, and the courts will only intervene where the assessment of the considerations is irrational or perverse.[24]

Draft development plans are a material consideration in the planning process, but do not carry the full weight of a development plan until approved/adopted (Chapters 3 and 5).

---

[21] *Barnet Meeting Room Trust v. Secretary of State for the Environment* [1993] J.P.L. 739.
[22] There is only limited development plan information available on the internet: Hollywood, "Planning, Environment and the Web", SPEL 68:75.
[23] TCPSA, ss. 25 and 37(2).
[24] *City of Edinburgh Council v. Secretary of State for Scotland*, 1998 S.L.T. 120.

Views are being sought as to whether structure plans should be replaced by sub-national planning guidance.[25]

(b)   Scottish Office

The SDD periodically issues statements of national planning policies   2.25
to planning authorities.[26] These form one of the material considerations to which the planning authority must have regard in exercising its planning powers, but the authority is not bound to comply with the policy. As the policy will be applied by the Secretary of State/reporter in determining any appeal against the exercise of power by the authority, the sanction underlying such statements of policy is that by failing to comply with the policy the authority risks losing such an appeal and having to pay the costs incurred by the appellant (Chapter 8).

The TCPSA does not empower the Secretary of State to issue national planning policy. Indeed, the Act does not refer to national planning policy, which therefore has no statutory role, other than its role as a material consideration. Among the issues suggested for consideration by the Scottish Parliament are whether planning legislation should refer to NPPGs, and whether structure plans should be replaced by sub-national planning guidance.[27]

Previously circulars contained advice and guidance on both policy and procedural matters, but now are used primarily to explain the operation of new legislation and other administrative procedures. National Planning Guidelines are being replaced by NPPGs, which provide statements of planning policy on land use and related matters. The effectiveness of NPPGs is being reviewed.[28] Planning Advice Notes (PANs) are intended to identify and disseminate good practice and to provide advice.

In the absence of any SDD policy, reference can be made to the policy of the Department of the Environment (DETR) which, though it applies to England and Wales, often represents the policy which would be laid down by SDD (Chapter 5).

(c)   Non-Statutory Policies

While it is clearly preferable for all relevant policies of the planning   2.26
authority to be contained in the development plan, there are instances where this is not possible. An urgent policy response may be required to an issue which has come to prominence since adoption of the plan. Alternatively, a policy may require to be stated in such detail as is not

[25] Consultation Paper "Land Use Planning Under a Scottish Parliament" (Scottish Office, January 1999).
[26] These statements are not published, but are available on request from Scottish Office Development Department. Many of the statements are reproduced in the publications noted above (n. 16) and can be found on the Scottish Office website: www.scotland.gov.uk. Other relevant websites are: Government information service: www.open.gov.uk; Department of the Environment: www.detr.gov.uk; Scottish Environment Protection Agency: www.sepa.org.uk; and Scottish Natural Heritage: www.snh.org.uk.
[27] Consultation Paper "Land Use Planning Under a Scottish Parliament" (Scottish Office, January 1999).
[28] "Review of National Planning Policy Guidelines", SPEL 68:66.

suitable for inclusion in the plan, such as development briefs for particular sites or design guides for certain types of development. As a result, policies other than those contained in the development plan may be applicable to an exercise of planning powers by the authority (such policies are commonly referred to as non-statutory policies). These policies form one of the material considerations to be taken into account by the authority.

(d) Directions by Secretary of State

2.27   The Secretary of State has power to issue directions to planning authorities restricting the grant of planning permission for a particular development or type of development.[29] A variety of directions have been issued authorising authorities to grant permission for certain types of development only after specified procedures have been followed. These often include notification of the proposed decision to the Secretary of State to allow exercise of his call-in powers (Chapter 5). The directions are attached to circulars issued by SDD.

DEVELOPMENT PLANS AND DEVELOPMENT CONTROL

2.28   The planning system can be divided into two parts: development plans and development control.

The development plan and its significance for the planning system is discussed in the next chapter. The development plan is an expression of the views of the planning authority with regard to the future use of land within its district. In this sense it operates as authoritative guidance to developers on the views of the authority. However, the plan does not relieve developers of the need to obtain planning permission, even in circumstances where the proposed development is entirely in accordance with the provisions of the plan. The development control process provides the authority with the opportunity to prevent development which is not in accordance with its views as expressed in the plan.

What authorities lack are positive powers to achieve the objectives outlined in the plan other than compulsory purchase powers. At present the function of the development plan is to encourage developers by showing which developments are likely to be given permission. However, if these developments are not attractive to developers, no application for planning permission will be forthcoming. The complete vision of the planning authority will be replaced by piecemeal development.

Unlike the passive development planning, development control is a negative process. If work amounts to "development" and does not enjoy permitted development rights, planning permission must be obtained before that work can commence. The development control process determines when permission is required (Chapter 4), the procedure for obtaining that permission (Chapter 5), the restrictions which may be

---

[29] Town and Country Planning (General Development Procedure) (Scotland) Order 1992, art. 17.

placed on any permission granted (Chapter 6), and the enforcement action which may be taken if work commences without permission or in breach of the terms and conditions of a permission (Chapter 7). Where an application for planning permission is lodged, the development control process involves determination of that application according to the law, policy and planning merits of the proposed development.

EFFECT OF PLANNING PERMISSION

The consequences flowing from a grant of planning permission are 2.29 examined in Chapter 5. Every grant of planning permission carries a time limit for the commencement of development. If no start is made within that time limit, the permission expires. Once a start has been made, the permission exists in perpetuity and there is no time limit for completing the development, unless there is an express condition attached to the permission specifying such a time limit or the planning authority serve a completion notice. As a result, it is only possible to take enforcement action where a negative condition, such as a restriction on use, is breached or where there is a failure to comply with a positive obligation which is subject to an express time limit.

PLANNING INFORMATION

For the planning system to operate efficiently and maintain the confi- 2.30 dence of all involved in or affected by it, information must be freely available. Planning authorities are required to keep registers detailing such matters as the progress and decision of applications for planning permission, enforcement action, and the progress with alteration or repeal and replacement of development plans.[30] These registers must be kept up-to-date and available for public inspection, along with copies of the development plan. Copies of the agenda for the planning committee meeting and any reports to committee must be available to the public at least three days prior to any meeting.[31]

In contrast to the availability of information from planning authorities, the various items of law and policy which are relevant to the planning systems are not easily obtainable and in many cases are difficult to understand even if an up-to-date copy can be obtained.

---

[30] For example, TCPSA, s. 36, and art. 10 of the Development Procedure Order 1992, as amended. Illsley, Lloyd and Lynch, "Public Access to Planning Information in Scotland", SPEL 64:123. There is a limited amount of local authority information available on the internet: Hollywood "Planning, Environment and the Web", SPEL 68:75.

[31] Local Government (Scotland) Act 1973, s. 50B.

CHAPTER 3

DEVELOPMENT PLANS

3.01   Since 1947 the development plan has been a central feature of the planning system. This role has heightened following the introduction of the plan-led system (below). The plan is an expression of the views of the planning authority (possibly as modified by the Secretary of State) with regard to use of the land within its district, formulated after consultation with official bodies and the general public. It also provides the framework within which the authority exercises its day-to-day control of development. Rather than being a prescriptive rule book, the development plan provides authoritative guidance to those wishing to develop land.

The deficiency associated with development plans lies in the lack of any positive power conferred upon the planning authority to implement its views as expressed in the plan. Unless the authority has a legal interest in the land concerned, it cannot implement the proposals identified in the plan. These proposals therefore amount to no more than encouragement for developers to submit applications for planning permission for those proposed land uses. In this sense planning authorities have few positive planning powers and are restricted to the negative role of approving or rejecting proposals made by developers, which inevitably leads to piecemeal implementation of the development plan proposals. With the onset of the recession in the early 1990s, many authorities took a more active role in attracting potential developers to undertake development projects. This active role extended to assembling sites, often through use of compulsory purchase powers, and obtaining planning permission for the development.

Structure plans require the approval of the Secretary of State, who may impose modifications, but local plans are approved by the initiating authority, although the Secretary of State has powers to call-in local plans for decision.

The Review of Development Planning in Scotland undertaken for the Scottish Office in 1997 found that the legislative framework for development planning remains broadly sufficient to enable the expeditious preparation and review of development plans, with safeguards for public involvement before plans are completed. However, it also found that there is scope for more effective management of the plan-making and review process, and for consolidated national policy guidance and more best practice advice. For development plans to be more effective, the contribution of key implementation agencies, such as local enterprise companies, Scottish Natural Heritage, Scottish Homes, Scottish Environmental Protection Agency, the water and sewerage authorities and others, needs to be made more effective. The Review made recommendations for improving these aspects of the system.

The Consultation Paper "Land Use Planning under a Scottish Parliament" issued in 1999 sought views on matters such as the continuing need for structure plans, or, as an alternative, sub-national planning guidance, and other possible changes to development planning procedures.

PLAN-LED SYSTEM: INTERACTION BETWEEN DEVELOPMENT PLAN AND DEVELOPMENT CONTROL

Although the development plan expresses the views of the planning   3.02
authority with regard to the use of the land within its district, it does not remove the need to seek planning permission for development (Chapter 4). Indeed, even a development which conforms to the provisions of the plan is not guaranteed to obtain planning permission. The development plan system can therefore be distinguished from the rigidity of the zoning systems used by many other countries, whereby proposals in accordance with the zoning either cannot be refused consent or enjoy deemed consent without the necessity for an application (as in the British system of enterprise zones and simplified planning zones, Chapter 9).

When determining an application for planning permission, the planning authority is directed to have regard to the provisions of the development plan, so far as material to the application, and to any other material considerations.[1] The authority must also determine the application in accordance with the provisions of the development plan unless material considerations indicate otherwise.[2]

Although these provisions impose a presumption in favour of the development plan, this does not amount to a requirement that the authority decide all applications according to the terms of the plan. The authority has to decide in light of the whole plan whether the proposal accords with it, and then if there are material considerations of such weight as to indicate that the plan should not be accorded priority. The House of Lords have stated that the assessment of the facts and the weighing of considerations remains in the hands of the decision-maker. The assessment of the considerations can only be challenged on the ground that it is irrational or perverse.[3] The law does not require a material consideration to have any special weight to overcome the presumption in favour of the development plan.[4] These provisions are discussed further in Chapter 5.

The House of Lords' decision indicates the following approach[5]:   3.03

- The decision-maker must consider the development plan, identify any provisions in it which are relevant to the question before him and make a proper interpretation of them. His

---

[1] TCPSA, s. 37(2).
[2] s. 25.
[3] *City of Edinburgh Council v. Secretary of State for Scotland*, 1998 S.L.T. 120.
[4] *St. Albans D.C. v. Secretary of State for the Environment* [1993] J.P.L. 370.
[5] *City of Edinburgh Council, supra*, Lord Clyde at p.127G–L.

decision will be open to challenge if he fails to have regard to a policy in the development plan which is relevant to the application or fails properly to interpret it.

- He will also have to consider whether the development proposed in the application before him does or does not accord with the development plan. There may be some points in the plan which support the proposal but there may be some considerations pointing in the opposite direction. He will require to assess all of these and then decide whether in light of the whole plan the proposal does or does not accord with it.

- He will also have to identify all the other material considerations which are relevant to the application and to which he should have regard. He will then have to note which of them support the application and which of them do not, and he will have to assess the weight to be given to all of these considerations. He will have to decide whether there are considerations of such weight as to indicate that the development plan should not be accorded the priority which the statute has given to it.

- Having weighed these considerations and determined these matters he will require to form his opinion on the disposal of the application.

- If he fails to take account of some material consideration or takes account of some consideration which is irrelevant to the application, his decision will be open to challenge. But the assessment of the considerations can only be challenged on the ground that it is irrational or perverse.

- It is undesirable to devise any universal prescription for the method to be adopted by the decision-maker. Different cases will invite different methods. It should be left to the good sense of the decision-maker, acting within his powers, to decide how to go about the task before him in the particular circumstances of each case.

Some importance thus now attaches to the decision whether the proposed development accords with the development plan. In some instances, this decision will rely on the interpretation of the policy. It appears that interpretation of a provision of the development plan is accepted as a ground for legal challenge,[6] although the courts are likely to follow the tenor of the approach taken by the House of Lords and only intervene if the interpretation is perverse and irrational. The Court of Appeal in England has indicated that if the wording of the development plan is capable of more than one meaning, the courts will only intervene if the decision-maker adopts and applies a meaning which is perverse or otherwise bad in law.[7] A judge has observed that it is easy to conceive of situations where it would be perverse for a decision-maker to reject factual evidence. When the question is one of value judgment

---

[6] Lord Clyde, supra; *e.g. Rafferty v. Secretary of State for Scotland*, 1998 G.W.D. 16–818, *Greater Glasgow Health Board v. Secretary of State for Scotland*, 1996 S.C.L.R. 808.
[7] *R. v. Derbyshire C.C., ex p. Woods* [1998] Env. L.R. 277.

such as "Will this spoil the view?", it is much easier for a decision-maker to reject even unanimous opinion evidence on this basis of agreed facts without that rejection being castigated as unlawful by the courts.[8]

Until the plan has been approved by the Secretary of State (structure plans) or adopted by the authority (local plans), the policies and proposals in the plan are no more than a material consideration.[9]

The importance of the development plan is further emphasised by the special procedures which must be followed by the planning authority when it proposes to grant permission for a development which is contrary to the provisions of the development plan (Chapter 5).

SURVEY AND MONITORING

Planning authorities have a duty to keep under review the matters which may be expected to affect the development of the district or the planning of its development, including: 3.04

(a) the principal physical and economic characteristics of the district, including the principal purposes for which land is used, and of any neighbouring districts which might be expected to affect the district (the authority should consult with the authority responsible for that district about those matters);

(b) the size, composition and distribution of the population of the district (whether resident or otherwise);

(c) the communications, transport system and traffic of the district (and of any neighbouring district so far as they may be expected to affect the district);

(d) any other relevant considerations; and

(e) any changes already projected in any of these matters and the effect which those changes are likely to have on the development of the district or the planning of such development.

The planning authority can institute a survey of the whole or part of their district, examining these matters.[10]

Following the adoption of the development plan, the planning authority can anticipate the need to alter or replace the development plan by keeping these matters under review and monitoring changes in the environment, development pressures and political priorities, and the inter-relationships of these changes. As part of this monitoring process, some authorities prepare an annual or biennial monitoring statement indicating the extent to which the plan strategy and its component policies are still relevant and whether any alterations are required.

---

[8] *R. v. Leominster D.C., ex p. Pothecary* [1998] J.P.L. 335.

[9] *City of Glasgow D.C. v. Secretary of State for Scotland and William Hill (Scotland) Ltd,* 1992 S.C.L.R. 453; S.P.L.P. 36:56.

[10] s. 4. See also s. 11(2).

DEVELOPMENT PLAN

3.05   Although the TCPSA refers to "the development plan", there are
actually two separate plans[11]:

> (a)   the structure plan, and any alterations to it, together with the
> notice(s) of approval by the Secretary of State; and
> (b)   the local plan, and any alterations to it, together with a copy of
> the resolution(s) of adoption by the planning authority or the
> notice(s) of approval by the Secretary of State.

There are operative structure plans covering the whole of Scotland, and
all have been updated at least once. Following local government
reorganisation in 1996, the new structure plan authorities are preparing
structure plans for their districts. National coverage of local plans is
nearing achievement. However, a high proportion of plans are more
than five years old, and many have no immediate prospect of review or
replacement.[12]

There is a trend towards authorities undertaking environmental
appraisal of their development plans. This involves testing the likely
environmental impacts of the aims, policies and proposals contained in
the plan.

STRUCTURE PLAN

3.06   The structure plan is intended to deal with strategic matters and
statements of broad policy, the details of which will be fleshed out by the
local plan. All structure plans require to be submitted to the Secretary of
State for approval before the plan can take effect, and the Secretary of
State can impose modifications contrary to the wishes of the authority.

Structure plans contain the land-use planning policies and proposals
which co-ordinate the requirements for development land with the
protection of the environment at the strategic level. The purpose and
function of structure plans are to provide:

> (a)   a framework for the promotion of development and regenera-
> tion through private and public sector investment;
> (b)   a strategic approach to conserving and enhancing the quality
> of the natural and built environment;
> (c)   the basis for decisions on planning applications and appeals
> which individually or cumulatively raise issues of more than
> local significance; and
> (d)   the context for local plans.

Structure plans are intended to be built around a vision of an area
extending beyond currently programmed developments and provide a

---

[11] s. 24.
[12] "Review of Development Planning in Scotland" (Scottish Office Central Research
Unit, 1998), p. 10. Information on structure and local plan progress is contained in the
Planning Bulletin published by the Scottish Office Development Department, Planning
Services.

long-term perspective on the balance to be struck between development and conservation. This long-term view will normally require a time horizon extending at least 10 years beyond the expected date of approval of the plan.[13]

The provisions relating to the preparation of regional reports, and the identification of action areas and comprehensive development areas, have been repealed.

Content

Structure plans should contain at least five main elements[14]:   3.07

    (a)   indication of how international and national obligations or policies affect an area;

    (b)   an overall long-term development strategy;

    (c)   a complementary strategic approach to conserving and enhancing environmental quality;

    (d)   policies and proposals that provide a sound basis for development control; and

    (e)   priorities for implementation.

Issues covered in the structure plan normally include urban and rural strategies; new housing; major industrial, business, retail and other employment-generating developments; regional transportation and infrastructure; urban and rural environments; mineral working and protection of mineral resources; waste disposal, land reclamation and re-uses; tourism, leisure and recreation; and indicative forestry strategies.

The structure plan is a written statement, accompanied by diagrams, drawings and other descriptive matter to explain or illustrate the proposals in the plan. These form part of the plan,[15] but in the event of any inconsistency the provisions of the written statement prevail.[16] The written statement is accompanied by a key diagram (not on a map base) which shows at a glance the policies and general proposals applicable to areas within the district, allowing reference to be made to these policies and proposals within the written statement without reading the entire plan.[17]

The written statement contains[18]:   3.08

    (a)   The authority's policies and general proposals in respect of the development and other use of land in the district, including measures for the conservation of the natural beauty and amenity of the land, the improvement of the physical environment, the management of traffic, and suitable waste disposal

---

[13] PAN 37, "Structure Planning" (revised 1996), paras 3 and 15.
[14] *ibid.*, para 8.
[15] s. 7.
[16] Town and Country Planning (Structure and Local Plans) (Scotland) Regulations 1983 (S.I. 1983 No. 1590), reg. 10.
[17] reg. 9.
[18] s. 7(1); reg. 7.

sites or installations.[19] Measures for the conservation of natural beauty and amenity include policies encouraging the management of features of the landscape which are of major importance for the migration, dispersal and genetic exchange of wild species of flora and fauna by virtue of their linear and continuous structure (such as rivers with their banks or the traditional systems of marking field boundaries) or their function as stepping stones (such as ponds or small woods).[20]

(b) The relationship of the proposals to general proposals for the development and other use of land in neighbouring districts which might be expected to affect the district covered by the structure plan.

(c) The existing social, economic and physical structure of the district to which the plan relates and the needs and opportunities for change.

(d) The resources likely to be available for the carrying out of the policies and general proposals formulated in the plan.

(e) The broad criteria to be applied as respects the control of development in the region, including guidance on the application of these criteria, where appropriate, in local plans.

(f) Such other matters as the planning authority considers relevant.

The written statement should be laid out so that the policies and proposals are clearly distinguishable from the other contents. A reasoned justification of the policies and proposals by reference to the results of the survey and any other information should also be included.[21]

In formulating its policies and general proposals, the planning authority must secure that the policies and proposals are justified by the results of the initial survey and any fresh survey and by any other information obtained. It must also have regard to current policies with respect to the economic planning and development of the region as a whole and the resources likely to be available for the carrying out of the structure plan proposals.[22]

The determination of the generality or otherwise of proposals contained in a structure plan is a question of degree. It is generally accepted that structure plans should not contain site-specific proposals. However, it is competent for the structure plan to refer to a general locality within which the boundaries should be determined by the local plan.[23]

Structure Plan Areas

3.09 Responsibility for the preparation of structure plans formerly rested with the regional and islands councils. Following local government reorganisation in 1996, this responsibility has been transferred to the new

---

[19] Waste Management Licensing Regulations 1994, Sched. 4, para. 7.
[20] The Conservation (Natural Habitats, Etc) Regulations 1994, reg. 37.
[21] reg. 6.
[22] s. 7(2).
[23] *Falkirk District Council v. Secretary of State for Scotland*, 1994 G.W.D. 5–309, SPEL 43:41.

unitary authorities. The Secretary of State has designated 17 structure plan areas in respect of which structure plans are to be prepared (fig. 3.1). For the six structure plan areas which extend to the districts of more than one planning authority, the authorities concerned are to jointly carry out the structure plan functions in accordance with the arrangements which they agree for the purpose.[24]

Existing structure plans continue in force. Where the new structure plan area is different from the area in respect of which a structure plan is in force, the planning authority must prepare and submit to the Secretary of State for his approval a structure plan for the area. The Secretary of State may direct a planning authority to undertake this exercise within a specified period.[25]

The structure plan must be submitted with a copy of the report of any survey which has been carried out. This copy report must include an estimate of the changes, during such period as the authority consider appropriate, likely to occur in the matters which the authority are obliged to keep under review (see survey and monitoring, above). A report must also be submitted of the results of their review of these matters, together with any other information on which the proposals are based.[26]

Before the structure plan is submitted to the Secretary of State, the planning authority must consult any other planning authority who are likely to be affected by the plan.[27]

Fig. 3.1   Structure Plan Areas (and relevant planning authorities)

Shetland Islands
Orkney Islands
Western Isles
Highland
Moray
Aberdeen and Aberdeenshire (two unitary authorities)
Dundee and Angus (two unitary authorities)
Perthshire and Kinross
Stirling and Clackmannan (two unitary authorities)
Falkirk
Fife
Edinburgh and Lothians (West Lothian, City of Edinburgh, Midlothian and East Lothian Councils)
Borders
Dumfries and Galloway
Ayrshire (South Ayrshire and East Ayrshire Councils)
Glasgow and Clyde Valley (West Dunbartonshire, East Dunbartonshire, North Lanarkshire, South Lanarkshire, City of Glasgow, East Renfrewshire, Renfrewshire, Inverclyde)
Argyll and Bute

[24] s. 5 and Designation of Structure Plan Areas (Scotland) Order 1995.
[25] s. 6(1)–(3).
[26] s. 6(2), (6), (7).
[27] s. 6(8).

Where the structure plan area includes the district of more than one planning authority, and the authorities are unable to agree on a joint structure plan, each authority may include in the plan submitted to the Secretary of State alternative proposals, accompanied by a statement of the reasoning behind the proposals.[28]

Procedure for Preparation or Alteration of Structure Plan

3.10   The TCPSA prescribes the procedure for the preparation and approval of the first structure plan for an area. As structure plans now exist for all areas in Scotland, these procedures no longer apply. However, these procedures are described below because they are commonly used for proposals for alteration, or repeal and replacement of existing structure plans, as the statutory requirements for such proposals are very general in nature (see below). Specific provisions apply to the preparation of structure plans where the new structure plan area is different from the area in respect of which a structure plan is in force (see above).

The planning authority may at any time submit to the Secretary of State proposals for alterations to or repeal and replacement of the structure plan for the district. Such proposals may relate to the whole or part of their district.[29] The authority are required to consult every other planning authority who are likely to be affected by the proposals, give such publicity (if any), and undertake such consultations (if any), as they think fit.[30] The discretionary nature of this requirement makes it difficult to challenge in court the procedure adopted by the authority.[31]

An expedited procedure is often used for alterations to an existing plan. This may be appropriate where the alteration involves a small change of planning policy with minor effects in the area and the public interest will not be prejudiced because of reduced publicity and consultation. The publicity given to the alteration may be limited to notice of the right to lodge representations with the Secretary of State following adoption of the alteration by the authority and its submission to the Secretary of State for approval. If the authority opts for an expedited procedure, a statement explaining the absence (or limitation) of the publicity and/or consultation must be submitted along with the proposals, and the Secretary of State may return the proposals with a direction to publicise the application or consult relevant persons or bodies.[32]

For these reasons, although the following description of the procedures refers to preparation of plans, the same procedures can be used for the alteration, or repeal and replacement of existing structure plans.

At various points in the procedure described below and in fig. 3.2 the planning authority or the Secretary of State is required to give notice by advertisement. This requirement is satisfied by publication of a notice in

---

[28] s. 6(4) and (5).
[29] s. 9(1) and (2).
[30] s. 9(4); reg 21.
[31] *Glasgow for People v. Secretary of State for Scotland*, 1991 S.C.L.R. 775; 1992 S.P.L.P. 35:16.
[32] s. 9(5)–(9).

the *Edinburgh Gazette* and, in each of two successive weeks, in at least one local newspaper circulating in the region.

Fig. 3.2 Preparation/Alteration of Structure Plan

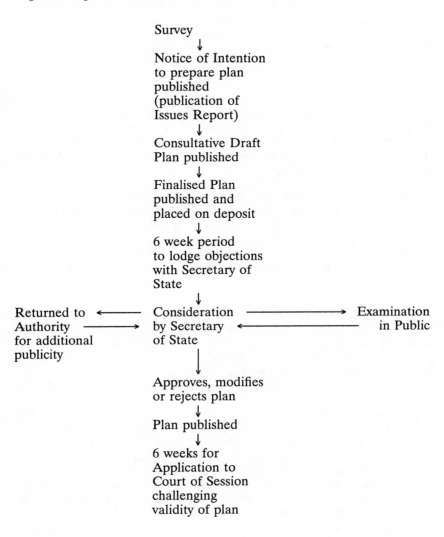

(a) Survey

Although there is no longer a statutory requirement to institute a fresh survey of the area, the procedure for preparing a structure plan may still commence with the authority undertaking some form of survey of the area and publishing the report of the results of the survey. The information in the report forms the basis on which the policies and proposals to be contained in the structure plan are prepared. 3.11

(b)   Advertisement of Intention to Prepare/the Issues Report

3.12   Notice is given by newspaper advertisement of the intention of the
planning authority to prepare a structure plan.[33] Adequate publicity must
also be given to the matters which are proposed to be included in the
plan. The planning authority can comply with these requirements by
publication of an Issues Report, seeking views on potential issues to be
tackled by the plan. The Issues Report performs the dual function of
stimulating interest and providing a structure for responses from the
public.

(c)   Consultative Draft Plan

3.13   The consultative draft plan is published by the authority after considering responses to the survey report and/or Issues Report. It is presented
in substantially the same form that the written statement in the adopted
structure plan will take, and contains the matters which the authority
propose to include in that plan.

Notice of publication of the consultative draft plan will be given by
advertisement, stating that representations in relation to the plan should
be lodged with the authority within a specified period of not less than
four weeks.[34] Copies of the plan are sent by the authority to all other
planning authorities which are likely to be affected by the proposals
(including local authorities within the district to which the plan relates),
and other appropriate bodies such as Scottish Natural Heritage and
Historic Scotland.[35]

(d)   Finalised Plan

3.14   All representations and responses from the consulted bodies are
considered by the authority, together with all statements of government
policy, and the finalised plan produced. If there are substantial changes
to the draft plan, the authority may advertise the opportunity to lodge
representations in connection with these changes and reconsult the
various bodies for their views.

Following the adoption of the plan by resolution of the authority, the
finalised draft plan and report of the survey are placed on deposit. Two
certified copies of the plan are submitted to the Secretary of State for
approval, accompanied by a report of the survey and a statement of the
steps taken to publicise the report and the right to make representations
thereon, the opportunity offered to make such representations and the
consultations with other authorities and bodies.[36] The publicity and
consultation statement should also clearly indicate which parts of the
draft plan were amended to take account of representations received.

Notice is given by newspaper advertisement of the placing of the plan
on deposit and its submission to the Secretary of State, and of the right

---

[33] reg. 11.
[34] s. 8(1); reg. 3.
[35] reg. 4.
[36] TCPSA, s. 8(6); reg. 12.

to submit objections to the plan to the Secretary of State within a six-week period.[37] Copies of the plan must be made available for public inspection, and be accompanied by a statement of this time limit for lodging objections to the Secretary of State.[38] An entry is made in all the planning registers in the district.

(e) Approval by Secretary of State

At the end of the six-week deposit period the plan is considered by the   3.15
Secretary of State. If he considers that the publicity procedures have not been carried out properly, the plan is returned to the authority with a statement of the reasons for its return and a direction to take remedial action and resubmit the plan within a given period (with modifications if appropriate). Any person who lodged an objection to the plan with the Secretary of State is informed that the plan has been returned to the authority. The authority publishes notice by advertisement of the return of the plan. After the required steps have been taken, the plan is resubmitted to the Secretary of State in the same manner as before, and notice of resubmission advertised and given to any party which lodged an objection with the Secretary of State to the original plan.[39]

If the plan is not returned in this way, the Secretary of State proceeds to consider its provisions, taking into account any objections which were properly lodged, and any matters thought relevant, whether or not these matters were taken into account in preparing the plan. The Secretary of State may also consult with any planning authority or other person or body, and consider their views on the plan.

An examination in public (EIP) may be held by the Secretary of State into any matter affecting his consideration of the plan,[40] although recent practice suggests that the EIP option has fallen into disuse. At least four weeks notice of the holding of the EIP must be given by advertisement.[41] Unlike a public local inquiry (Chapter 8), no person or body, including the planning authority, has an absolute entitlement to take part. It is for the Secretary of State to decide which bodies or persons should be invited to take part in the EIP, although the rules of natural justice might require that a party be heard (Chapter 8). The reporter conducting the EIP on behalf of the Secretary of State has the power to invite additional bodies or persons to take part, if this appears desirable to him.

Following consideration of the plan and any EIP, the Secretary of State issues his decision letter either approving the plan (in whole or in part and with or without modifications and reservations) or rejecting it, giving a statement of his reasons for the decision.[42] If any intended modification of the plan would materially affect its content, notice of the

---

[37] reg. 13.
[38] s. 8(4) and (5).
[39] s. 8(7)–(11); regs 14 and 15.
[40] s. 10(4)(b); SDD Circular 6/1985, "Code of Practice for the Examination in Public of Structure Plans".
[41] reg. 17.
[42] s. 10(1)–(10).

modification must be given by advertisement and to the planning authority, and to such other persons as the Secretary of State thinks fit, and an opportunity offered for representations to be made. The Secretary of State will consider any objections made to the proposed modifications, before making a final decision on the plan.[43] Notification of the decision of the Secretary of State on the plan is given to the authority, and such persons as he thinks fit, and notice given by advertisement.[44]

In making his decision on the structure plan, the Secretary of State must consider the relevant policy guidance issued by the Scottish Office. If he decides not to follow that guidance, sufficient reasons must be provided.[45]

(f)   Publication of Approved Plan

3.16   Following approval of the plan by the Secretary of State, the authority must arrange for the plan to be reproduced, incorporating the Secretary of State's decision letter and any modifications. Copies must be made available for public inspection and purchase. Each copy must contain the statement that the validity of the plan may be challenged by making an application to the Court of Session within six weeks (see below).[46]

LOCAL PLANS

3.17   Local plans are intended to apply the strategic guidance of the structure plan by showing the detailed land-use policies within a much smaller area. Unlike structure plans, local plans do not require approval by the Secretary of State. As a general principle, the Secretary of State will only intervene in the local planning process in exceptional circumstances.[47]

The functions of the local plan have been described as[48]:

(a)   stimulating and encouraging development where appropriate;
(b)   indicating land where there are opportunities for change;
(c)   applying national and regional policies;
(d)   giving a clear locational reference to policies for the development, change of use or conservation of land, and to proposals for development;
(e)   showing how those who have an interest in the area, for example, the authority, private owners, residents, commerce, industry, developers and investors, could contribute to implementation of the plan;
(f)   providing an adequate basis for development control; and

---

[43] reg. 18.
[44] reg. 19.
[45] *Scottish House Builders Association v. Secretary of State for Scotland*, 1995 S.C.L.R. 1039, SPEL 52:109
[46] regs 43 and 44.
[47] PAN 49, "Local Planning", para. 5.
[48] PAN 30, "Local Planning", para. 1, now replaced by PAN 49.

(g) indicating the intended future pattern of land use and development in the area by showing how existing development and the policies and proposals of the plan fit together.

Every planning authority must prepare local plans for all parts of their district. Two or more authorities may prepare a joint local plan extending to parts of each of their districts. Different plans may be prepared for different purposes for the same part of any district. Where there is a contradiction between the provisions of any two or more local plans relating to the same area of the district, the provisions of the plan most recently adopted or approved shall prevail.[49] The trend is towards preparation of district-wide plans to avoid such inconsistencies or contradictions. Subject plans may be prepared to deal with a self-contained subject.[50]

Local plans should have a minimum five year timespan, although many elements, such as those dealing with conservation, can continue indefinitely subject to regular review, refinement or adjustment.[51]

Content

The local plan consists of a written statement and a key diagram based   3.18
on the Ordnance Survey map, and known as the proposals map. This shows at a glance the policies and proposals applicable to individual areas of land within the district, allowing reference to be made to these policies and proposals within the written statement without reading the whole plan.[52] The plan may also include diagrams, illustrations and other descriptive matter, but in the event of any inconsistency, the provisions of the written statement will prevail.[53] Although not a statutory requirement, the written statement should also include a summary of the survey findings.

The written statement formulates the planning authority's detailed proposals for the development and other use of land within its district or for any description of development or other use of such land. It includes measures for the conservation of the natural beauty and amenity of the land, the improvement of the physical environment and the management of traffic. Measures for the conservation of natural beauty and amenity include policies encouraging the management of features of the landscape which are of major importance for the migration, dispersal and genetic exchange of wild species of flora and fauna by virtue of their linear and continuous structure (such as rivers with their banks or the traditional systems of marking field boundaries) or their function as stepping stones (such as ponds or small woods).[54]

The statement specifies[55]:

---

[49] TCPSA, s. 11(1) and (4); reg. 27(2).
[50] *e.g.* Forth and Clyde Canal, or mineral extraction.
[51] PAN 49 "Local Planning", para. 62.
[52] reg. 26.
[53] reg. 27(1).
[54] The Conservation (Natural Habitats, Etc.) Regulations 1994, reg. 37.
[55] s. 11(3); reg. 25.

(a) the character, pattern and function of the existing develop-
     ment and other use of land within the district or part of the
     district to which the plan relates, and the needs and oppor-
     tunities for change;
(b) the implications of current policies and general proposals
     contained in the relevant structure plan for the district, or any
     part of the district to which the local plan relates;
(c) the resources likely to be available for the carrying out of the
     policies and proposals formulated in the plan;
(d) the criteria to be applied as respects the control of develop-
     ment within the district, or any part of the district to which the
     plan relates; and
(e) such other matters as the planning authority considers
     relevant.

The policies and proposals formulated in the local plan should be set out
so as to be readily distinguishable from the other contents, and be
accompanied by a reasoned justification.[56] The absence of a reasoned
justification may form the grounds for a legal challenge (see below), but
it may be difficult to show that substantial prejudice results.[57] The
planning authority has a duty to ensure that the proposals contained in
the local plan conform generally to the structure plan as it stands,
whether or not it has been approved by the Secretary of State.[58]

Procedure for Preparation or Alteration of Local Plan

3.19   At various stages in the procedure described below, there is a
requirement to give notice by advertisement. In most cases, this amounts
to a requirement to publish an advertisement in each of two successive
weeks in at least one local newspaper. However, in relation to publication of the finalised plan and of adoption of the local plan, advertisement in the *Edinburgh Gazette* is also required.

(a) Survey

3.20 Planning authorities have a duty to institute a survey of their district for
the purpose of preparing a local plan, in so far as not already done,
taking into account any matters necessary for the formulation of their
proposals. This duty extends to keeping those matters under review
during and after the preparation of the local plan.[59]

It is open to the Secretary of State to direct a planning authority to
prepare as soon as is practicable a local plan for (part of) its district, or
proposals for the alteration, repeal or replacement of, a local plan. Such
a direction can only be given before approval of the structure plan for
the district by the Secretary of State. The authority must be consulted
prior to issuing the direction.[60]

---

[56] reg. 24.
[57] *Mackenzie's Trs v. Highland R.C.*, 1994 S.C.L.R. 1042, SPEL 46:93.
[58] s. 11(5).
[59] s. 11(2).
[60] s. 14.

Fig. 3.3 Preparation/Alteration of Local Plan

Survey
↓
Notice of Intention
to prepare Plan
published
(publication of
Issues Report)
↓
Consultative Draft
Plan published
↓
Finalised Plan
published and
placed on deposit
↓
Local Plan Inquiry
into outstanding
objections
↓
Notice of Proposed
Modifications published
and 6 weeks allowed
for representations
↓
Notice of Intention
to Adopt published
↓
Secretary of State
has 28 days to call-in
plan for decision
↓
Adoption of plan
by resolution and
publication of
adopted plan

(b) Advertisement of Intention to Prepare a Local Plan

The procedure for preparation of a local plan begins with the planning   3.21
authority giving notice by newspaper advertisement of its intention to
prepare a local plan.[61] This may be combined with publication of an
Issues Report, identifying the key issues to be addressed in the plan, to
stimulate public discussion. The Report also serves as a framework for
responses from the public, which are considered as part of the preparation of the draft plan.

In preparing the draft plan, the authority must consult any other
authorities whose areas form part of the district to which the plan

---

[61] reg. 28.

relates, and other appropriate bodies, and take their views into consideration.[62]

(c) Consultative Draft Plan

3.22   The consultative draft plan is published by the authority in substantially the same form as the final written statement will appear. It serves to ensure that adequate publicity is given in the district to matters arising out of the survey and to those matters proposed to be included in the plan, and to give interested parties an opportunity of making representations in respect of those matters.[63] Notice of publication of the draft plan is given by advertisement and a period of not less than four weeks specified for representations to be submitted to the authority.[64] Representations received during that period are considered by the authority and may result in alterations to the provisions of the draft plan.

(d) Finalised Plan

3.23   The finalised plan is produced by the authority after considering the responses to the consultative draft plan. It represents their final view on the policies and proposals which should be contained in the local plan once adopted, and is therefore in the form of the plan which they propose to adopt. However, the finalised plan is subject to a period of public consultation, and the representations received may result in amendment of the policies and proposals. Included in or with the finalised plan is a statement of the steps taken by the authority to publicise the preparation of the plan, the opportunities given for representations to be submitted, the consultation process, and the authority's consideration of the views received.[65]

Notice is given by advertisement in both a local newspaper and the *Edinburgh Gazette* that the finalised plan has been placed on deposit and copies are available for public inspection and that representations may be submitted to the authority within six weeks from the first date of advertisement.[66] Forms for making objections should be made available at the places where copies of the plan are available for inspection. Objections should be made in writing, stating the name and address of the person making the objection, the matters to which the objection relates and the grounds on which it is made.

Copies of the finalised plan are sent to the Secretary of State and other local authorities whose areas are wholly or partly within the district covered by the plan or whose interests appear likely to be affected.[67] Entries relating to the finalised plan are made in the register kept by the planning authority for public inspection and in the registers of other authorities to whose area the plan relates.

---

[62] reg. 4(2).
[63] TCPSA, s. 12.
[64] reg. 3.
[65] s. 12(5); reg. 30(2).
[66] s. 12(3) and (4); reg. 30(1).
[67] regs. 29 and 30.

(e) Local Plan Inquiry

Where an objection to the finalised plan has not been withdrawn by an   3.24
objector after resolution of the matter by the authority, that person or
body can require a local plan inquiry to be held to hear that objection.[68]
However, this right does not necessarily prevent the planning authority
granting a planning permission which effectively prejudges the objection
before it has been considered at the local plan inquiry provided the
objections were taken into account in the determination of the planning
application.[69]

The inquiry is chaired by a reporter appointed by the planning
authority from a list prepared by the Secretary of State, and therefore
represents an opportunity for the objector to attempt to convince a
planning expert independent of the plan preparation process of the
soundness of the objection. The objector can either present his case at
the inquiry, or in writing or request that the reporter considers the terms
of the objection originally submitted. The authority has an opportunity
to respond.

The procedure for local plan inquiries is similar to the broad outlines
of the public local inquiry procedure (Chapter 8), but with some
differences.[70] Responsibility for organising the inquiry lies with the
planning authority rather than the Scottish Office Inquiry Reporters
(SOIR).[71] The authority must give notice of the inquiry by advertisement
at least four weeks before the date of the inquiry and serve notice upon
each objector (unless their objection has been withdrawn) and on such
other persons as it thinks fit.[72] At the same time as publishing the
advertisement, the authority must make available for public inspection at
its office copies of the objections which are to be considered at the
inquiry.

The reporter may hold a pre-inquiry meeting with the authority and
objectors. Notice of this meeting will be served upon the authority and
objectors, and given by newspaper advertisement. The purposes of the
meeting are to agree a timetable for the inquiry, and identify the issues
and the areas of agreement and disagreement between the parties.
Objections can be divided into general policy issues and more site-
specific matters, and an attempt made to group them together at the
inquiry accordingly. A copy of the agreed timetable will be circulated to
all parties.

Unlike public local inquiries, the advance circulation requirements
applicable to local plan inquiries are minimal. The parties already have
prior notice of the case to be presented by each other: the authority will
rely on the provisions of the finalised plan, and the objector's case is
contained in the objection. If the objection gives insufficient information
to allow proper preparation for the inquiry, the reporter can request

---

[68] s. 15(2).
[69] *Watson v. Renfrew District Council*, 1995 S.C.L.R. 82; SPEL 50:68.
[70] SDD Circular 32/1996, "Code of Practice for Local Plan Inquiries". No procedural
rules have been prescribed.
[71] Circular 1/1996 outlines the planning authority's responsibilities.
[72] reg. 34.

amplification. Where the parties propose to rely on other written material (known as documents, previously referred to as productions) at the inquiry, agreement will normally be reached at the pre-inquiry meeting on the exchange of copies of this material. In the absence of such agreement, parties may adhere to the usual public local inquiry procedure of exchanging documents four weeks before the inquiry. Copies of all documents should also be sent to the reporter.

3.25   Where an objector proposes to refer at the inquiry to alternative sites for proposed development or suggest that a policy should apply to an area different from that shown on the plan, notification of this intention should be sent to the authority and the reporter as early as possible in advance of the inquiry.

The procedure at the inquiry is a matter for the discretion of the reporter, but is intended to be informal. For each objection or group of objections, the objector presents his case first, the planning authority responds, and the objector has the right of reply. The evidence presented by the authority will take the form of testimony of witnesses, including planning officers. Objectors may present evidence through their own testimony, or lead witnesses, who may be concerned individuals or expert witnesses. Unless the testimony to be given by a witness is short, it is normal practice for a written statement of that testimony to be prepared (known as a precognition), and circulated to the reporter and other parties present at the inquiry. Most reporters follow the procedure for planning appeal inquiries and require circulation of precognitions two or more weeks before the inquiry commences. The use of precognitions in this manner aids the reporter's note-taking. Following his initial testimony, each witness may be cross-examined by the other parties, re-examined, and questioned by the reporter, in the same way as at public local inquiries. After all the evidence has been presented in relation to the objection or group of objections, the parties make their closing submissions in reverse order, and the inquiry then moves to consider the next objection.

While the evidence presented at the inquiry should involve general policy issues, in practice these are often overshadowed by site-specific arguments in which developers seek to protect development proposals. This results in the case presented at the inquiry being more in the form of an appeal against a refusal of planning permission, leading to more detailed cases and longer inquiries. Landowners who are uncertain of their long-term development proposals will seek the widest possible allocation for their land in the plan to avoid restricting the available development options. These are inevitable consequences of the introduction of the plan-led system, whereby it is important for development proposals to be in accordance with the provisions of the development plan.

At some point during or after the inquiry, the reporter will make a site inspection which the parties are entitled to attend (the reporter will probably have made an unaccompanied inspection in advance of the inquiry). The purpose of the inspection is to confirm the physical characteristics of the site, and the reporter may ask the parties to confirm points raised at the inquiry in this regard. The reporter will not allow the parties to use the site inspection as an opportunity to reopen arguments on the merits of the objection, plan policy or proposal.

The cost of organising the inquiry and employing the reporter is paid 3.26 by the authority.[73] The objectors must bear their own costs, and there is no provision for an award of expenses (in contrast to public local inquiries).

Where an objector also has an outstanding appeal to the Secretary of State concerning a matter similar to the content of the objection, the SOIR may suggest to the objector and the authority that the appeal inquiry could usefully be conjoined with the relevant part of the local plan inquiry. Both parties must consent to conjoining the inquiries. As the same issues may underlie both the objection and the appeal (indeed, the objection is often submitted in support of the proposed development which is the subject of the appeal), the time and expense of two separate inquiries can be avoided.

Conjoining inquiries is not without its potential difficulties, although these do not tend to arise in practice. For the local plan inquiry, the reporter is paid by and reports to the authority, but in the appeal inquiry the reporter is employed by the Scottish Office and reports to the Secretary of State. In the conjoined inquiry, the reporter would therefore be paid, at least in part, by the authority which initially refused or delayed in determining the application for planning permission which is the subject of the appeal. This raises an appearance of bias possibly rendering the decision illegal (Chapter 8). It is arguable that this potential illegality cannot be cured by the consent of the objector/appellant to the conjoining. One solution may be to hold both inquiries back-to-back, closing one before opening the other, and taking as read at the later inquiry the evidence presented to the earlier inquiry. Difficulties may be encountered with this solution if members of the public who were not present at the earlier inquiry, and therefore did not hear, or have an opportunity to challenge, evidence given at that inquiry, wish to participate in the later inquiry. A better solution may be for two reporters to chair the conjoined inquiry, one to report on the local plan objection and the other on the appeal. However, this solution negates much of the benefit offered to the SOIR by conjoining and is unlikely to be attractive to them.

Another problem is that confusion often reigns during a conjoined 3.27 inquiry, with the participants finding it difficult to distinguish local plan from appeal issues.

Where the inquiry is conjoined, the authority must comply with the local plan inquiry requirements and SOIR is bound by the appeal inquiry procedural requirements, resulting in two sets of advertisements. At the inquiry itself, the appeal procedure takes precedence, and the objector/appellant presents his case first.

Following the local plan inquiry, the reporter prepares a report which is sent to the authority for consideration. The report will show the following matters for each objection or group of related objections: a summary of the arguments advanced by the objectors and by the authority, a summary of any other arguments or facts advanced at

[73] s. 16

the inquiry which are relevant to consideration of these objections, the reporter's findings of fact, and his recommendation, if any, as to how the authority should deal with the objection.

On receipt of the report of the inquiry, the authority must consider whether to accept the recommendations made by the reporter. It is open to the authority to ignore the report completely, provided that reasons for this approach can be given. The authority may decide to adopt the plan without change, propose modifications, or abandon the plan. A reasoned statement of its decision whether or not to take action in light of the report is prepared and made available for public inspection along with copies of the report.[74] Each objector is notified by the authority of the decision in relation to his objection and sent a copy of the statement and report, or informed of the opportunity to inspect them. Before rejecting the reporter's recommendations, the planning authority must have regard to all material considerations and give adequate reasons for their decision. In one case, although the court found no substance in the contention that the authority had failed to take account of relevant considerations, an absence of reasoned justification was found for the authority's decision to take no account of the possibility of the implementation of a planning permission which would have a material effect on the future development of the area, but the appeal was dismissed because the appellant failed to show how they would suffer prejudice.[75] Reasons which recapitulate arguments advanced at the local plan inquiry are not necessarily inadequate, especially if the authority differ from the reporter on a question of planning judgment.[76]

(f) Modifications to Finalised Plan

3.28   Where modifications to the finalised plan (other than drafting or technical matters of a minor nature) are proposed by the authority following consideration of objections or an inquiry report, a list of the modifications and the reasons for proposing them is prepared by the authority and made available for public inspection. Notice of the proposed modifications is given by newspaper advertisement and served on all objectors who have not withdrawn their objections. A six-week period must be allowed for representations to be submitted with regard to the proposed modifications.

Any objections made to the proposed modifications are considered by the authority and a further inquiry must be held to hear unwithdrawn objections which do not relate to matters considered at the previous inquiry. A further inquiry may also be held to hear other objections.[77] Even if no further inquiry is held, the authority is obliged to consider all representations received in relation to the proposed modifications.

---

[74] reg. 35.
[75] *Mackenzie's Trs v. Highland R.C., supra.*
[76] *Peel Investments v. Bury MBC* [1999] J.P.L. 74, distinguishing *Stirk v. Bridgenorth D.C.* (1997) 73 P. & C.R. 439; *Miller v. Wycombe D.C.* [1997] J.P.L. 951.
[77] reg. 37; *Warren v. Uttlesford D.C.* [1996] J.P.L. B127.

(g) Adoption by Planning Authority

Prior to final adoption of the plan by the authority, notice of its 3.29
intention to adopt the plan is given by newspaper advertisement and
served on objectors whose objection has not been withdrawn. Copies of
the plan in the form which the planning authority proposes to adopt are
made available for inspection and sent to the Secretary of State. The
authority must certify by recorded delivery to the Secretary of State that
this notice has been given. The plan can only be adopted 28 days after
sending this certification. Within the 28-day period the Secretary of State
may direct that the plan cannot be adopted until the authority receives
notification that the plan is not to be called in for decision by the
Secretary of State.[78] The procedure following call-in by the Secretary of
State is considered below.

If no such direction is received, on the expiry of the 28 days the
authority may adopt the plan by resolution.[79] Adoption of the plan is
advertised (both in a local newspaper and in the *Edinburgh Gazette*), and
notice served on those who have requested notification and on such
other persons as the authority thinks fit, indicating where the plan can be
inspected. Two certified copies of the adopted plan must be sent to the
Secretary of State not later than the date on which such notice is given.[80]

Following adoption, copies of the plan must be available for inspection and purchase at the authority's offices and at the office of every
other local authority to whose area the plan relates. Each copy must
contain a statement detailing the right to question the validity of the
plan by making an application to the Court of Session (see below).[81]

(h) Powers of Secretary of State

At any time between receipt of the finalised local plan and its 3.30
adoption, the Secretary of State has a general power to call in the plan
for decision whereby it will have no effect until approved by him.[82]

Following the call-in, if the Secretary of State decides not to reject the
plan, he must take into account any objections to the plan made in
accordance with the regulations. Objectors have no right to demand an
inquiry unless no inquiry has been held by the authority. If an inquiry is
to be held, an opportunity to participate must also be offered to the
planning authority and such other persons as the Secretary of State
thinks fit. At least four weeks' notice of the inquiry must be given by
newspaper advertisement and notice served on the objectors and such
other persons as the Secretary of State considers appropriate.[83] In
considering the plan, the Secretary of State may consult with other
planning authorities or persons, and take into account any relevant
matters irrespective of whether such matters were considered in the
plan.

---

[78] ss. 17(4) and (5), 18(1) and (2); reg. 38.
[79] s. 17(1) and (2).
[80] reg. 39.
[81] regs 42, 43 and 44.
[82] s. 18.
[83] reg. 40(1).

After considering the plan, the Secretary of State may either approve it in whole or in part and with or without modifications, or reject it. The planning authority must be notified of any proposal to modify the plan, unless the Secretary of State is satisfied that the modifications will not materially affect any policy or proposal in the plan. On receipt of notification of proposed modifications, the authority must give notice of the modifications by advertisement (unless such advertisement was carried out previously) and serve notice on such persons as it thinks fit. Any objections to the modifications are considered by the Secretary of State who decides whether or not to hold an inquiry.[84]

The Secretary of State notifies his decision in writing to the planning authority which gives notice of the decision by advertisement and serves notice on persons who have requested notification and such other persons as the Secretary of State may direct.[85] Copies of the local plan as approved by the Secretary of State are made available for public inspection and purchase at the offices of the planning authority.

In addition to the power to call in the plan for decision, the Secretary of State may direct the authority at any time prior to the adoption of the plan to consider modifying it in specified respects. After such a direction, the authority cannot adopt the plan unless it either satisfies the Secretary of State that the necessary modifications have been made, or the direction is withdrawn.[86]

(i) Procedure for Alteration or Replacement of Plan

3.31   Similar procedures apply to the alteration, or repeal and replacement of a local plan.[87] If the planning authority regard the alteration as too minor to justify full publicity and consultation, when submitting the plan to the Secretary of State it should include a statement giving a brief account of the publicity and consultation undertaken or its reasons for not undertaking any publicity or consultation. The Secretary of State may call in the alterations if the publicity and consultation carried out is unsatisfactory. The expedited procedure normally involves no publicity until the finalised alteration is placed on deposit. A change to a policy contained in a validly adopted local plan cannot be made by the planning authority merely issuing a different document without giving the public notice of the changes or an opportunity to lodge representations.[88]

On average, replacement local plans take four years to prepare and adopt.[89]

Relationship between Structure and Local Plan

3.32   The planning authority has a duty to secure that the proposals contained in the local plan conform generally to the structure plan as it stands (whether or not it has been approved by the Secretary of State),

---

[84] s. 19; reg. 40(2) and (3).
[85] reg. 40(4).
[86] s. 17(4) and (5); *e.g. H.J. Banks v. Midlothian Council*, 1996 G.W.D. 22–1304, SPEL 56:75.
[87] s. 13.
[88] *Falkirk D.C. v. Secretary of State for Scotland*, 1991 S.L.T. 553.
[89] "Review of Development Planning in Scotland" (see n. 12), p. 11, para. 4.

and cannot adopt a local plan which does not conform to an approved structure plan.[90]

APPLICATION TO COURT OF SESSION CHALLENGING VALIDITY OF PLAN

An action may be raised in the Court of Session challenging the validity 3.33
of a structure or local plan within six weeks from the date of publication
of the first notice of the approval or adoption of the plan or its
alteration, repeal or replacement.[91] No challenge will be possible outside
this time limit (Chapter 8).

The action may be raised by any "person aggrieved" by the structure
or local plan or any alteration, repeal or replacement of the plan. This
includes a neighbouring planning authority[92], but not the planning
authority responsible for preparing the plan where it seeks to challenge
modifications made by the Secretary of State.[93] The Court has rejected
the argument that "person aggrieved" has a different meaning for the
purposes of challenging the validity of a development plan from other
legal challenges (see Chapter 8). A landowner who had a legitimate
interest in the policies and proposals in the plan and the way in which
the council dealt with their objections to those policies and proposals
was a "person aggrieved".[94] A member of the public whose property was
not directly affected by the policies and proposals in the plan and took
no objection to them during the plan process was not a "person
aggrieved".[95] It has been suggested that the term will include objectors,
persons selected to appear at an examination in public (structure plan)
or who participated at a local plan inquiry, bodies which have to be
consulted in the making of a plan, and any person whose property is
affected by a plan.[96] It would also seem to include bodies consulted
during the plan process.[97]

The grounds of challenge are that the plan is not within the powers
conferred by the TCPSA in relation to development plans, or that any of
the regulations made under the TCPSA have not been complied with in
relation to the approval or adoption of the plan, alteration, repeal or
replacement. These grounds of challenge are discussed in detail in
Chapter 8. A failure to comply with the Regulations only invalidates the
plan if substantial prejudice results, and this may be difficult to show.[98]

The Court of Session has the power to suspend in the interim the
plan, its alteration, repeal or replacement, either generally or only in so
far as it affects the applicant's property. When considering an application
for an interim order, the nature and degree of harm likely to be suffered

---

[90] ss. 11(5) and 17(3).
[91] s. 238.
[92] *Central R.C. v. Secretary of State for Scotland*, 1991 S.L.T. 702; S.P.L.P. 33:49.
[93] *Strathclyde R.C. v. Secretary of State for Scotland*, 1989 S.L.T. 821.
[94] *Mackenzie's Trs v. Highland R.C.*, 1994 S.C.L.R. 1042, SPEL 46:93.
[95] *Lardner v. Renfrewshire Council*, 1997 S.L.T. 1027, SPEL 62:81.
[96] Young and Rowan Robinson, *Scottish Planning Law and Procedure* (1985), p. 530.
[97] *Glasgow for People v. Secretary of State for Scotland* (n. 31, *supra*).
[98] *Mackenzie's Trs, supra*.

by the parties to the appeal by the grant or refusal of the order is not the only issue. The public interest lies in the plan taking effect. The question whether the operation of the plan should be suspended is therefore dealt with by an assessment of the strength of the competing arguments, albeit on a prima facie basis.[99]

Following a successful challenge, the court has the discretion to quash wholly or partly the plan, alteration, repeal or replacement, either generally or in so far as it affects the applicant's property. The approval by the Secretary of State of the Strathclyde Structure Plan Update 1992 was quashed because of his failure to adjudicate in the dispute on the criteria to be used in calculating housing land supply.[1]

READING DEVELOPMENT PLANS

3.34 Planning authorities are obliged to make copies of the development plan available at their offices for public inspection free of charge. Copies can also be purchased for a small fee (typically between £10–£20, although copies of draft plans may be more expensive due to the cost of the limited print run). They are also obliged to maintain a register containing information on the development plan and any proposals to alter, repeal or replace it, together with an index map showing the plan boundaries.[2]

When consulting the provisions of the structure or local plan, reference should be made initially to the key map or diagram which shows the policies and proposals applicable to particular sites. This will allow the appropriate provisions to be found in the written statement without reading the entire text.

Attention should be paid to the term used to describe any particular provision, and to any glossary explaining the interpretation of that term. The weight to be given to the provision may depend upon which "label" is used. For example, "proposal" is used to denote action which the authority intends to take within the short term, whereas "policy" denotes a longer-term intention. A "recommendation" is made where the authority wishes to indicate its views to another body which has control over the result sought. Most of the written statement is not expressed in the form of proposals, policies or recommendations, and can be used for little more than background information. A proposed development is only contrary to the plan if it does not conform with a proposal, policy or recommendation. The general aims expressed in the plan cannot derogate from its specific policies.[3]

---

[99] *Mackenzie's Trs, supra.*
[1] *Scottish House Builders Association v. Secretary of State for Scotland*, (n. 45.).
[2] Town and Country Planning (Structure and Local Plans) (Scotland) Regulations 1983 (S.I. 1983 No. 1590), regs. 42–45.
[3] *Bearsden and Milngavie D.C. v. Secretary of State for Scotland*, 1992 S.L.T. 917; S.P.L.P. 36:55, *per* Lord Justice-Clerk Ross.

OBJECTING TO DRAFT PLANS

With the enhanced status of development plans resulting from the plan- 3.35
led system, it is important for all persons, whether developers, landowners or members of the public, to monitor changes to development
plans. Such monitoring has several different objectives:

(a) landowners/developers should ensure that any proposals for
     development of their land, even if uncertain or long-term, will
     be consistent with the plan;

(b) landowners/occupiers will also be anxious to preserve land
     value and amenity by ensuring that the plan does not contain
     proposals which may have a negative effect on land value, such
     as allocating neighbouring land for a sewage works;

(c) members of the public should ensure that the plan makes
     provision for the proper planning of their neighbourhood,
     town or area, or any items or issues of special interest or
     concern to them.

It is important to note that publicity requirements attached to the plan
process do not include notification to individual landowners of proposals
to change policies applicable to their land. It is therefore conceivable
that land previously allocated for housing could be reallocated for
agricultural use without the knowledge of the landowner and to his
financial loss. Although this would not necessarily prevent a successful
application for planning permission for housing, under the plan-led
system the agricultural zoning would give the authority an easy reason
for refusing permission.

Monitoring draft plans in this way will inevitably lead to submission of
objections. This can be done by completing the form obtainable from the
authority, or submitting an objection in writing. The objection itself
should specify the provision(s) of the plan to which the objection relates,
and explain the reasons for the objection. For local plans, the form also
seeks a (preliminary) indication of whether the objector wishes to appear
at a local plan inquiry.

There are no limits to the content of the objection. It may relate to a
provision contained in the plan, or point to something omitted from the
plan. It may concern a minor error or a complex policy issue. No
particular expertise is required, and a strong argument can often be
made on the basis of general local knowledge. The only essential
element is that the objection identify the provision in the plan and the
result sought by the objector in relation to that provision (*i.e.* removal,
modification, etc.).

In pursuing the objection, one should be aware of the constraints on
the authority. For instance, if the provision in the plan relates to a
development which has already been granted planning permission, the
authority cannot change that provision as it has no power to stop the
development from proceeding, short of revoking the permission and
exposing itself to a claim for compensation. Landowners or developers
should also be realistic, and accept that authorities can rarely allocate
sites for what amounts to any possible development idea which might
arise during the next decade.

Campaigning against planning issues is examined in more detail in
Chapter 10.

CHAPTER 4

DEVELOPMENT CONTROL I—THE NEED FOR PLANNING PERMISSION

The keystone of the planning system is the requirement to obtain 4.01
planning permission for any development of land. It provides a means
for planning authorities to control unsuitable development either by
refusing permission or granting permission subject to conditions (Chapters 5 and 6), and the other elements within the system flow from the
requirement for planning permission. Development plans have little
practical effect until their policies are applied in the determination of
applications for planning permission. Unless there is a breach of
planning control caused by the failure to obtain planning permission or
to observe the terms and conditions attached to a grant of planning
permission, planning authorities have few enforcement powers over land
short of compulsory purchase.

To determine whether planning permission is required, the following
questions must be asked of the proposed activity (see fig. 4.1):

(a) Does it fall within the statutory definition of "development"?
(b) Is it an activity which is declared not to amount to "develop-
     ment", for example, in terms of the Use Classes Order
     (UCO)?
(c) Is planning permission deemed to be granted for the proposed
     activity, for example, in terms of the Permitted Development
     Order (PDO)?

Depending upon the answer to any of these questions, an application for
planning permission must be submitted before the proposed activity can
be commenced. In practice, these questions are asked in reverse,
principally because of the ease of reference of the UCO and PDO as the
main sources of exemptions. The thorny question of "development" is
only considered if the UCO and PDO fail to exempt the proposed
activity from the need for planning permission.

This may be expressed diagrammatically, thus:

Fig. 4.1   The need for Planning Permission

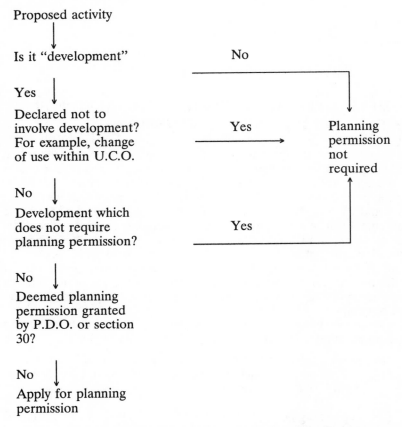

Proposed activity

Is it "development"   No

Yes

Declared not to
involve development?   Yes   Planning
For example, change   ⟶   permission
of use within U.C.O.   not
                                             required

No

Development which
does not require   Yes
planning permission?

No

Deemed planning
permission granted
by P.D.O. or section
30?

No

Apply for planning
permission

It is a question of the facts and circumstances of each individual case
whether the proposal falls within the requirement for permission. There
is a procedure for obtaining a formal answer from the planning authority
on the need for planning permission, with a right of appeal to the
Secretary of State.

REQUIREMENT FOR PLANNING PERMISSION

4.02   Planning permission is required for the carrying out of any development
of land or buildings,[1] which is defined as the carrying out of[2]:

(a)   building operations,
(b)   engineering operations,
(c)   mining operations, or

---

[1] TCPSA, s. 28.
[2] s. 26.

(d)   other operations in, on, over or under land, or
(e)   the making of any material change in the use of any building or other land.

Building, engineering, mining or other operations are generally described as operational development. This description highlights the difference in character between these forms of development and material changes of use. It is possible for an activity to involve both operational development and change of use.

The question of whether what is proposed amounts to "development" and, therefore, requires planning permission is one of fact and circumstances for the planning authority, or the Secretary of State on appeal, to decide. As a result, the courts will be reluctant to interfere unless the decision is unreasonable.

The imprecise definition of terms such as "building operations", combined with the residual term "other operations", gives ample scope for disputes with planning authorities on this question. For example, prior to statutory intervention (see below), the courts decided that demolition could be a building operation[3] or an engineering operation,[4] thereby requiring planning permission, or an operation for which planning permission was not required.[5] In an appeal decision the reporter held that provision of a limited number of unmarked and unfenced private graves did not constitute a material change of use from grazing land, and digging those graves by hand was not an engineering operation. Planning permission was therefore not required.[6]

Operational Development

(a)   Building Operations

Planning permission is required for building operations, which include   4.03
demolition of buildings (discussed further below), rebuilding, structural alterations of or additions to buildings, and other operations normally undertaken by a person carrying on business as a builder.[7]

A "building" is defined as including any structure or erection, and any part of a building.[8] Size, permanence and degree of attachment of the structure are factors to be considered.[9]

As a result of the confusion caused by conflicting court decisions (see above), the Planning and Compensation Act 1991 added demolition to the list of building operations, thereby requiring planning permission for demolition of a building. However, the Secretary of State also issued a

---

[3] *Cambridge City Council v. Secretary of State for the Environment* [1991] J.P.L. 428 (reversed on appeal); *Glasgow District Council v. Secretary of State for Scotland*, 1982 S.L.T. 28, *per* Lord Justice-Clerk Wheatley at p. 32.
[4] *Coleshill v. M.H.L.G.* [1969] 1 W.L.R. 746.
[5] *Cambridge City Council v. Secretary of State for the Environment* [1992] J.P.L. 644 (CA).
[6] *The Scotsman*, December 3, 1992.
[7] TCPSA, s. 26(4).
[8] s. 277.
[9] *Barvis Ltd v. Secretary of State for the Environment* (1971) 22 P. & C.R. 710. The concept of fixtures in property law may provide a useful parallel see, for example, Gordon, *Scottish Land Law*, Chap. 5.

Direction that the demolition of certain types of building do not require planning permission.[10] In addition, an amendment was made to the PDO requiring approval for demolition to be sought from the planning authority in certain circumstances.[11] These provisions are examined below.

In consequence of these provisions, it may be important to determine whether works are demolition or another form of building operation. This is a question of fact in each case.[12]

The effect of the provisions is that many forms of demolition outwith residential areas do not require any sanction from the planning authority (although a demolition warrant might be required under the Building (Scotland) Act 1959); most other demolition has to be notified to the authority, who can then exercise control over the method of demolition and any site restoration proposals; and only the demolition of part of a building is likely to require an application for planning permission.

4.04	The effect of the Direction is that demolition of specified types of buildings is not development and therefore does not require planning permission. The Direction only applies to demolition of a building, and not to demolition of part of a building. The buildings specified in the Direction are:

(i)	All buildings other than dwellinghouses, buildings containing one or more flatted dwellinghouses, or buildings having a mutual wall with, or having a main wall adjoining the main wall of, a dwellinghouse or a building containing flat(s). For this purpose, a building is not to be regarded as a dwellinghouse or containing a flat if its use as a dwellinghouse is ancillary to any non-residential use of that building or other buildings on the same site. In addition, each house in a pair of semi-detached houses is to be regarded as a building, as is every house in a row of terrace houses, whether or not, in either case, the house is in residential use.

(ii)	Any listed building (as listed building consent will be required—Chapter 9).

(iii)	A building in a conservation area (conservation area consent will be required—Chapter 9).

(iv)	A building which is a scheduled monument under the Ancient Monuments and Archaeological Areas Act 1979 (scheduled monument consent will be required).

(v)	Any building with a cubic content not exceeding 50 cubic metres measured externally.

(vi)	The whole or any part of any gate, fence, wall or other means of enclosure.

For buildings outwith these categories, the PDO Class 70 grants deemed planning permission for demolition, unless the building has been ren-

[10] Town and Country Planning (Demolition which is not Development) (Scotland) Direction 1995, attached to Circular 15/1995.
[11] Class 70 inserted by S.I. 1994 No. 3294.
[12] *Shimizu Ltd v. Westminster City Council* [1997] 1 All E.R. 481.

dered unsafe or uninhabitable by the action or inaction of any person
having an interest in the land on which the building stands, and it is
practicable to secure safety or health by repair works or works for
affording temporary support. The PDO also does not apply to demolition of part of a building.

The PDO imposes a prior notification procedure for demolition. This
procedure does not apply to the types of demolition declared by the
Direction not to be development (see above) or to demolition of part of
a building. It also does not apply to excluded demolition, which is
demolition necessary to implement a planning permission for redevelopment of the site, or required or permitted to be carried out by statute or
by any provision of a section 75 agreement.

The prior notification procedure involves the submission of an application to the planning authority for a determination as to whether their
prior approval will be required for the method of the proposed
demolition and any proposed restoration of the site. The application
must contain a written description of the proposed development. Neighbours must be notified of the submission of the application using the
procedure for planning applications (see Chapter 5), and the application
must include a certificate stating that the neighbour notification procedure has been carried out.

If, after 28 days from the date of receipt by the planning authority of 4.05
the application, the authority have not made any determination as to
whether the approval is required or notified the applicant of their
determination, development can commence. Development can also start
if the applicant receives written notice of their determination that their
prior approval is not required. If the authority notify the applicant within
the 28-day period that their prior approval is required, the development
cannot start until that approval is given.

Where the prior approval of the authority is required for demolition,
the development must be carried out in accordance with the details
approved. If no prior approval is required, it must be carried out in
accordance with the details submitted with the application. The development must be carried out within five years from the date of the approval,
or, where no approval was required, from the date of receipt of the
application.

Internal maintenance or improvement works or other alteration of a
building (other than structural alterations) do not require planning
permission unless the works materially affect the external appearance of
the building.[13] The distinction between alteration, which does not require
planning permission, and rebuilding works, which do need permission,
may be difficult to draw.

In considering whether the works materially affect the external 4.06
appearance of the building, what must be taken into account is the
external appearance of the building, and not its exterior. The alteration
must be one which affects the way in which the exterior of the building is
or can be seen by an observer outside the building. The degree to which

---

[13] s. 26(2)(a). Listed building consent is required for internal works which affect the
character of a listed building (Chapter 9).

the alteration is capable of being seen by observers is also relevant, from any vantage point on the grounds or in or on any neighbouring building. Whether the external appearance is materially affected depends on part of the degree of visibility, and must take into account the nature of the particular building which it is proposed to alter, including whether it is listed (Chapter 9). The effect on the external appearance must be judged for its materiality in relation to the building as a whole, and not by reference to a part of the building taken in isolation.[14]

The statutory wording suggests that when assessing the effect of the proposed works on the external appearance of the building, no account should be taken of the appearance of the surrounding area. Canopies, grilles, roller shutters, stone cladding, and replacement windows are all works which may materially affect the external appearance of a building.

Planning permission is also required for works to provide additional space below ground, such as lowering the floor level or creating a basement.

The PDO grants deemed planning permission for many forms of building operations, including those within the curtilage of a dwelling-house and agricultural buildings (see below). For example, planning permission is deemed to be granted for painting a building. This deemed permission does not extend to listed buildings and buildings situated in conservation areas. However, planning permission is only required if the painting of such a building amounts to development because it will materially affect the external appearance of the building.

(b) Engineering Operations

4.07   Engineering operations are defined as operations usually undertaken by or under the supervision of an engineer or which would require engineering skills, irrespective of whether an engineer is actually involved,[15] including the placing or assembly of a tank in inland waters for the purpose of fish farming[16] and the formation or laying out of means of access to roads.[17]

Planning permission is not required for the following works, which might be considered to be engineering operations: works carried out on land within the boundaries of a road by the local roads authority for the maintenance or improvement of that road; and works carried out by the local authority or statutory undertakers for inspecting, repairing or renewing any sewers, mains, pipes, cables or other apparatus, including the breaking open of any road or other land for that purpose.[18]

(c) Mining Operations

4.08   Mining operations include the removal of material of any description from a mineral-working deposit, from a deposit of pulverised fuel ash or other furnace ash or clinker, or from a deposit of iron, steel or other

---

[14] *Burroughs Day v. Bristol City Council* [1996] 1 P.L.R. 78.
[15] *Fayrewood Fish Farms v. Secretary of State for the Environment* [1984] J.P.L. 267.
[16] s. 26(6).
[17] s. 277.
[18] s. 26(2)(b) and (c).

metallic slags, and the extraction of minerals from a disused railway embankment.[19] For the purposes of the PDO, mining operations are defined as the winning and working of minerals in, on or under land, whether by surface or underground working.

Unlike building and engineering operations, mining is a continuous operation lasting for many years. Special controls apply to mining operations (Chapter 9). The removal of each shovelful constitutes a separate mining operation and it will therefore be rare for unauthorised mining operations to become lawful.[20]

(d)   Other Operations

There is no definition of what amounts to "other operations". It has   4.09
been suggested that these are operations of a positive, constructive and identifiable character[21] which result in some physical alteration to land.[22] Arguably the definition of development is not intended to comprehend every operation on land. Clearly there are some operations on land which should not require planning permission, for example, mowing a lawn. The phrase "other operations", therefore, does not refer to all other operations.[23] Indeed, it has been suggested that this residual category may be restricted to operations similar to building, engineering or mining operations.[24]

For practical purposes, "other operations" will include any form of operational development which does not fall within the other categories, but which the planning authority or the Secretary of State may reasonably consider requires planning permission—for example, any excavation and levelling works which cannot be considered engineering or mining operations.[25]

Material Change of Use

Following nationalisation of development rights in 1947, owners were   4.10
left with their existing (1947) use rights and required to obtain planning permission from the State for any material change of use of land or buildings.

Certain changes of use are declared to be material and therefore require planning permission[26]:

(a)   Sub-division of a single dwellinghouse resulting in its use as two or more separate dwellinghouses. In contrast to the PDO, this provision extends to sub-division of flats.

(b)   Deposit of refuse or waste materials on land, notwithstanding that the land is already used for that purpose, if either the superficial area of the deposit is thereby extended or

---

[19] s. 26(5).
[20] *Thomas David (Porthcawl) Ltd. v. Penybont RDC* [1972] 1 W.L.R. 1526.
[21] *Coleshill, supra. per* Lord Wilberforce at p. 765.
[22] *Parkes v. Secretary of State for the Environment* [1978] 1 W.L.R. 1308, *per* Lord Denning at 1311 E.
[23] *Cambridge City Council v. Secretary of State for the Environment, supra.*
[24] *cf. Coleshill, supra, per* Lords Wilberforce and Guest.
[25] Young and Rowan-Robinson, *Scottish Planning Law and Procedure* (1985), p. 123.
[26] s. 26(3) and (7).

the height of the deposit is extended to exceed the level of the land adjoining the site.

(c) Use of any external part of a building for the display of advertisements, if it is not normally used for that purpose. However, if the advertisement is displayed in accordance with the Control of Advertisement Regulations (Chapter 9), planning permission is deemed to have been granted.[27] Flags and lighting used by businesses may require advertisement consent.[28]

These changes of use should be distinguished from the changes of use which are declared not to involve development and, therefore, do not require planning permission[29]:

(a) The use of any buildings or other land within the curtilage of a dwellinghouse (see below), as for any purpose incidental to the enjoyment of the dwellinghouse does not amount to a material change of use and, therefore, requires no planning permission. Where a granny flat was not intended to be used as a separate dwelling, its use was incidental to the main dwelling and no planning permission was required.[30] Keeping up to 44 dogs as a hobby was not an incidental use of the dwellinghouse.[31] Subject to the provisions of the PDO planning permission may be required for erection of the buildings.

(b) The change of use to agricultural or forestry use (including afforestation) of land and any building occupied together with the land does not require planning permission (Chapter 9).

(c) A change of use within any class specified in the UCO (see below).

Whether any other change of use is "material" and therefore requires planning permission is a question of fact and degree for the planning authority, or the Secretary of State on appeal, to decide and the courts will only interfere with an unreasonable decision. There is no general guidance on when a change of use will be considered "material". Some assistance is provided by case law, but much of this area of planning law remains conceptual in nature.[32]

The first step in assessing whether a material change of use has occurred is the identification of the area of land or the building to be used as the reference point against which the change can be judged. This area of land or building is known as the "planning unit".

4.11   The correct identification of the planning unit may be of crucial importance to the planning authority or the owner. In general, the larger the planning unit, the less likely that a change of use will be material.

---

[27] s. 184.
[28] *Taylor v. Secretary of State for Scotland*, 1997 S.L.T. 535, *Great Yarmouth B.C. v. Secretary of State for the Environment* [1997] J.P.L. 650.
[29] s. 26(2)(d), (e) and (f).
[30] *City of Glasgow District Council v. Sec. of State for Scotland* 1997 S.C.L.R. 711.
[31] *Wallington v. Secretary of State for the Environment* [1990] J.P.L. 112.
[32] See Young and Rowan-Robinson, *op. cit.*, p. 125 *et seq.*

For example, a lean-to building in a car-breakers yard had been used as the yard office and for retail sales of car parts salvaged from vehicles broken up on the site. New owners used the lean-to for the sale of new vehicle parts and camping equipment. They appealed against an enforcement notice on the ground that the planning unit was the whole yard and that looking at the site as a whole, the intensification of the retail sale use was insufficient to amount to a material change of use. The Secretary of State held that the planning unit was the lean-to and there had been a material change of use. The court tended to agree with the Secretary of State, but found that he had applied the wrong test and returned the matter to him for re-decision.[33]

A court also found that the wrong test had been applied in reaching the conclusion that outbuildings were used as one unit for the purposes of holiday accommodation comprising 10 apartments rather than as 10 single dwellinghouses.[34] Identification of the planning unit is a question of the facts and circumstances of each case, but some broad criteria have been suggested.[35] If there is a single main use, perhaps with secondary activities which are incidental or ancillary to that use, the area of land occupied as a single holding (the unit of occupation) is the planning unit. Where the occupier carries on a variety of activities, the unit of occupation may still be the planning unit. However, if these activities occupy separate and distinct areas, each area which can be identified as being used for a different main purpose forms a separate planning unit (the unit of activity replaces the unit of occupation).

In general, the unit of occupation is the planning unit unless and until some smaller unit can be recognised as the site of activities which amount to a separate use both physically and functionally. Physical separation of plots of land within the same occupation may cause the individual plots to form separate planning units.

The planning unit may be larger than the unit of occupation, but only in exceptional circumstances.[36] This avoids the possibility of enforcement action directed against an occupier sharing a planning unit with others (except for joint occupiers) in respect of activities carried on by the other occupiers over which he has no control. Thus the Secretary of State on appeal rejected the argument that a whole group of lock-up garages previously used for a taxi business, but gradually let singly or in groups to different persons, formed a single planning unit. The appropriate planning unit was the unit of occupation and each garage individually occupied became a separate planning unit. Enforcement notices alleging a material change of use were validly directed against garages in separate occupation where vehicle repairing was being carried out.[37] Similarly, the individual units within the Metro Centre shopping centre are occupied in their own right, and each is therefore a separate planning unit.[38]

---

[33] *Burdle v. Secretary of State for the Environment* [1972] 1 W.L.R. 1207.
[34] *Moore v. Secretary of State for the Environment, The Times*, Feb. 18, 1998.
[35] *Burdle, supra, per* Bridge J.
[36] *Rawlins v. Secretary of State for the Environment* [1989] J.P.L. 439; *Kwik Save v. Secretary of State for Wales* (1978) 37 P. & C.R. 170.
[37] *Johnston v. Secretary of State for the Environment* (1974) 28 P. & C.R. 424.
[38] *Church Commissioners v. Secretary of State for the Environment* [1995] 2 P.L.R. 99.

4.12   After the planning unit has been identified, it is possible to consider whether there has been a material change of use within it. Once again, this is a matter of fact and degree to be determined by the planning authority or the Secretary of State on appeal. Relevant factors in assessing the materiality of a change of use are the character and intensity of the various uses, the degree to which the uses are dependent on each other, the proportion of the planning unit devoted to each activity, and any planning effects on the locality.

Determining whether a change of use is involved can raise difficult questions. For example, helicopters landing on or taking off from a vessel floating but not moored on the River Thames could constitute a change of use of the river bed.[39]

If the general character of the use remains the same, but there is a change from one particular purpose to another particular purpose, there may not be a material change of use. Where land was used as a railway storage depot, there was no material change of use when it came to be used for storage of motor vehicles mainly destined for rail transport instead of coal for transport by rail. What should be considered is the character of the use of the land, not the particular purpose of a particular occupier.[40] However, a change from one leisure activity to another is capable of constituting a material change of use if the particular nature of the type of leisure activity has changed.[41] The change of use of a caravan site from holiday purposes to permanent residential purposes can be a material change of use.[42] The courts have also held that a dwellinghouse does not cease to be used as such because it is managed for the commercial purposes of holiday or other temporary lets.[43]

4.13   The character of the use is determined by the primary or main use. Changes in ancillary or incidental uses do not involve a material change of use, provided the subordinate and dependent character of the ancillary use is preserved. Once an ancillary use is no longer subordinate and linked to the main use, or has become a main use in its own right, a material change of use may have occurred. Thus, in terms of a planning permission for a quarry operation, backfilling the quarry with waste material from the quarrying operation was ancillary to the main activity. When the quarry came to be used for dumping refuse from outside, the ancillary dumping use had become a main use. The character of the use had altered and a material change of use had occurred.[44] Similarly, keeping up to 44 dogs in a dwellinghouse as a hobby amounted to a material change of use because it was not incidental to the enjoyment of the dwellinghouse.[45]

The size of the area devoted to a use is not conclusive. The use of cubicles for viewing films in a sex shop was held not to be ancillary to the

---

[39] *Thames Heliport plc v. Tower Hamlets LBC* [1997] J.P.L. 448.
[40] *East Barnet UDC v. British Transport Commission* [1962] 2 Q.B. 484.
[41] *Shepherd and Love v. Secretary of State for the Environment* [1992] J.P.L. 827.
[42] *Forest of Dean D.C. v. Secretary of State for the Environment* [1994] E.G.C.S. 138.
[43] *Moore, supra.*
[44] *Alexandra Transport v. Secretary of State for Scotland*, 1974 S.L.T. 81.
[45] *Wallington, supra.*

main retail use.[46] Although residential use of a caretaker's flat in an office building may be ancillary to the principal office use, it is often considered that these are two physically separate and distinct primary uses, and the flat and the office therefore form separate planning units.

It may also be relevant to consider whether the change of use will have material or relevant planning considerations, such as adverse effects on the locality. The limited environmental health effects of the sale of heated food from a shop was a factor in the decision that there had been no material change of use.[47]

Creation of a new planning unit is not conclusive evidence of a material change of use. As the general rule is that the planning unit is the unit of occupation, a new planning unit is therefore formed when part of a site is sold or leased to another person. However, the primary use may remain as before,[48] in which case there is no material change of use (with the exception of a sub-division of a dwellinghouse into two or more dwelling-houses which is always a material change of use). In contrast, a material change of use caused by an ancillary use becoming a main use in its own right will not necessarily result in the creation of a new planning unit unless it occupies a separately identifiable part of the site.

If existing use rights are lost, the planning unit has a nil use and planning permission will be required for any new use or resumption of the previous use. Confusingly, this is often referred to as the creation of a new planning unit, when what is meant is that there has been a fresh start or new chapter in the planning history.

Demolition of a building results in the right to continue its use being extinguished. Resumption of that use thereafter requires planning permission.[49] Rebuilding operations would probably require planning permission in any case, but there may be circumstances in which permission would not be forthcoming for a resumption of the use, for example, a disco in a residential area.

Loss of existing use rights may also occur when a planning permission 4.14 is implemented. Where planning permission was granted for construction of retail units, but a unit was used as an air terminal in terms of a separate permission, resumption of the retail use required fresh planning permission.[50] If the existing use is supplanted or superseded by another use, the right to resume the existing use is lost and planning permission will be required for its resumption, even if the change to the supplanting use did not require planning permission.[51] The erection of a building will not of itself result in the loss of existing use rights.[52]

A temporary discontinuance of use does not lead to loss of existing use rights.[53] As a result, no planning permission is required to resume

---

[46] *Lydcare v. Secretary of State for the Environment* [1984] J.P.L. 809.
[47] *City of Glasgow District Council v. Secretary of State for Scotland*, 1985 S.L.T. 19.
[48] *R. v. Kensington and Chelsea RLBC, ex p. Europa Foods Ltd* [1996] E.G.C.S. 5.
[49] *Iddenden v. Secretary of State for the Environment* [1972] 1 W.L.R. 1433, Buckley L.J., p. 1440; see also App./6/90/p.4225/1 [1992] J.P.L. 579.
[50] *Regent Lion Properties v. Westminster C.C.* [1991] J.P.L. 569.
[51] *J.L. Engineering v. Secretary of State for the Environment* [1993] E.G.C.S. 24.
[52] *Jennings Motors v. Secretary of State for the Environment* [1982] 1 Q.B. 541.
[53] *Paul v. Ayrshire County Council*, 1964 S.C. 116; 1964 S.L.T. 207.

the discontinued use, unless the land has been used for some different purpose in the meantime. In contrast, where a use has been abandoned, the land has a nil use and planning permission will be required for any use, including resumption of the former use.[54] In distinguishing between a temporary cessation of use and abandonment, at least four factors should be considered: the physical condition of the land or building; the length of the period of non-use; whether there has been any other use; and evidence of the owner's intentions.[55] Any action inconsistent with retention of the right to resume the use, such as removal of petrol tanks and pumps at a filling station, will also be relevant. Cessation of a car sales use for four years was sufficient grounds to find that the use had been abandoned.[56]

It is important to determine when a change of use occurs. Although land is converted to allow a new use, there is no change until the land is actually put to the new use.[57] If the change of use has occurred gradually over a period, it will be necessary to identify the point at which the change became material. At that point any failure to obtain planning permission results in a breach of planning control which may be the subject of enforcement action (Chapter 7).

Operations and Uses Declared Not to Involve Development

4.15   The following operations and uses are declared not to involve development and therefore will not require planning permission[58]:

(a)   internal maintenance or improvement works or other alteration of a building (other than structural alterations), unless the works materially affect the external appearance of the building (see Building Operations, above):

(b)   works required for the maintenance or improvement of a road which are carried out by a local roads authority on land within the boundaries of the road;

(c)   works carried out by a local authority or statutory undertaker for the purpose of inspecting, repairing or renewing any sewers, mains, pipes, cables or other apparatus, including the breaking open of any road or other land for that purpose;

(d)   use of any buildings or other land within the curtilage of a dwellinghouse for a purpose incidental to the enjoyment of the dwellinghouse as such (see Material Change of Use, above);

(e)   use of any land for the purposes of agriculture or forestry (including afforestation) and the use for any of those purposes of any building occupied together with land so used (Chapter 9);

---

[54] Planning permission for operational development can never be abandoned, but may be incapable of implementation (see Chap. 5).

[55] *Trustees of Castel-y-Mynach Estate v. Secretary of State for Wales* [1985] J.P.L. 40.

[56] *Hartley v. MHLG* [1970] 1 Q.B. 413.

[57] *Caledonian Terminal Investments v. Edinburgh Corporation*, 1970 S.C. 271; 1970 S.L.T. 362.

[58] s. 26(2).

(f)   a change of use within the terms of the UCO (see below);
(g)   demolition of any description of building specified in a direction given by the Secretary of State to planning authorities generally or to a particular planning authority (see Building Operations, above).

DEVELOPMENT WHICH DOES NOT REQUIRE PLANNING PERMISSION

Notwithstanding the definition of "development", planning permission is   4.16
not required in certain restricted circumstances.[59] In consequence of the
substitution of the 10-year immunity period for changes of use without
planning permission, for the previous rule that only changes prior to
1965 were immune (Chapter 7), the only important categories are:

(a)   if on July 1, 1948 land was used on occasions for a purpose other than its normal use, whether or not at regular intervals, permission will not be required for use of the land for that other purpose on similar occasions on or after December 8, 1969 if the land has been used for that other purpose on at least one similar occasion between July 1, 1948 and before the beginning of 1969;
(b)   planning permission is not required for resumption of the normal use of the land on the expiry of a temporary planning permission (Chapter 5), provided that use was not in breach of planning control (Chapter 7);
(c)   where planning permission has been granted by a development order, such as the PDO (see below), planning permission is not required for resumption of the normal use of the land, provided that use was not in breach of planning control; and
(d)   where an enforcement notice has been served in respect of any development of land, planning permission is not required to change the use of the land to any use which would have been lawful if that development had not been carried out. Uses which are immune from enforcement action are deemed to be lawful (Chapter 7).

In addition, planning permission is not required for development on
Crown land or any other land which is undertaken by the Crown
(Chapter 9).

DEEMED PLANNING PERMISSION (PERMITTED DEVELOPMENT RIGHTS)

In certain circumstances planning permission is deemed to have been   4.17
granted and no application for permission is therefore necessary. The
main source of deemed planning permission (sometimes referred to as
permitted development rights) is the Permitted Development Order (see
below).

---

[59] s. 28 and Sched. 2.

Deemed planning permission for the display of an advertisement in accordance with the Control of Advertisement Regulations,[60] development in Enterprise Zones and Simplified Planning Zones and development by a planning authority is discussed in Chapter 9.

PERMITTED DEVELOPMENT ORDER

4.18   From March 13, 1992 the Permitted Development Order (PDO) has replaced the General Development Order (GDO) as the main source of deemed planning permission/permitted development rights.[61] The layout of the PDO is different, but the majority of the permitted development rights remain the same, although exercise of these rights in conservation areas and within the curtilage of listed buildings is more restricted than before, and there is a reduction in the scope of the deemed permission for agricultural development.[62]

Planning permission is deemed to be granted for developments within the descriptions printed in **bold** type in Schedule 1 of the PDO. The sub-paragraphs below each description specify the circumstances in which there is no deemed planning permission granted (although planning permission will only be required if the proposed work falls within the definition of development). Important terms are defined in article 2(1) or the appropriate part of Schedule 1.

For example, class 9 is in the following form:

(1) The stone cleaning or painting of the exterior of any building or works.

(2) Development is not permitted by this class—

(a)   for the purposes of advertisement, announcement or direction;
(b)   where the building or works are in a conservation area;
(c)   where the building is a listed building.

The effect of class 9 is that planning permission is deemed to be granted for stone cleaning or painting of the exterior of a building. If the circumstances fall within one of the exceptions, an application for planning permission will be required only if the stone cleaning or painting falls within the definition of development. For example, there is no deemed planning permission for stone cleaning a building in a

---

[60] s. 184. See Chap. 9.

[61] s. 30; Town and Country Planning (General Permitted Development) (Scotland) Order 1992 (S.I. 1992 No. 223), as amended by S.I. 1992 Nos 1078 and 2084, 1993 No. 1036, 1994 Nos 1442, 2586 and 3294, 1996 Nos 1266 and 3023, 1997 Nos 1871 and 3060, 1998 No. 1226. "Research on the General Permitted Development Order & Related Mechanisms" (Scottish Office, 1998) recommends changes to the PDO to simplify its operation.

[62] Compensation claims had to be submitted by March 13, 1993 for loss suffered as a result of this removal of permitted development rights and a subsequent refusal of an application for planning permission: TCPSA s. 77, as amended.

conservation area, but planning permission will only be required if the cleaning will materially affect the exterior of the building (see Building Operations, above).

The 1992 PDO introduced a prior notification and approval procedure for certain categories of permitted development, including agricultural and forestry buildings and operations (chapter 9), demolition (see above), and some public utility developments. It is a condition of permitted development for these classes that prior notification is made to the planning authority, which then has the opportunity to control aspects of the development in the interests of amenity.

The prior notification procedure involves submission of an application to the planning authority to determine whether their prior approval is required. Work cannot proceed until notification is received from the planning authority that its prior approval is not required, or its approval is received, or 28 days have elapsed since the application was lodged and the authority has reached no decision. The prior approval requirement is restricted to the siting, design and external appearance of the building.

There is a right of appeal to the Secretary of State against the refusal of prior approval, the grant of approval subject to conditions, or, having decided that the prior approval is required, the failure of the planning authority to determine the prior notification application within two months of its receipt.[63] Any appeal must be lodged within six months of the decision or within six months of the expiry of the two-month period.

The work must be carried out in accordance with the approved details, or, if no approval is required, in line with the details submitted with the application. It must also be carried out within five years of the date on which approval was given, or if no approval was given, the date of the application.

The PDO cannot permit development[64]:   4.19

    (a)   in breach of any condition attached to a grant of planning permission or deemed permission granted in terms of another order;

    (b)   in connection with a building, if the building operations involved in the constructions of that building are unlawful (Chapter 7);

    (c)   in connection with an existing use, if that use is unlawful;

    (d)   involving the formation, laying out or material widening of a means of access to a trunk or classified road, or which creates an obstruction to the view of persons using any road used by vehicular traffic, so as to be likely to cause danger to such persons (with some exceptions);

    (e)   entailing the laying or construction of a notifiable pipeline other than by a public gas supplier;

    (f)   any development which requires or involves the demolition of a building (but not part of a building), other than as permitted by class 70; and

---

[63] s. 47 and Development Procedure Order, arts 14 and 23.
[64] art. 3 as amended.

(g)   any development which, if it were the subject of an application
      for planning permission, would require environmental assess-
      ment, other than the categories of developments specified in
      article 3(10)—the effect of this provision is to remove permit-
      ted development rights for any development which, but for
      those permitted development rights, would require environ-
      mental assessment.

Any deemed planning permission granted by the PDO for development
which is likely to have a significant effect on a European site in Great
Britain (either alone or in combination with other plans or projects), and
is not directly connected with or necessary to the management of the
site, is subject to a requirement to obtain the approval of the planning
authority before commencing development.[65] European sites are important nature conservation sites protected by the Habitats Directive,
including special areas of conservation (see Chapter 9). This requirement applies to any development which has not yet started. In addition,
any development begun and not completed should not be continued
until approval from the planning authority has been obtained. The
authority can only approve a development after having ascertained that
it will not adversely affect the integrity of the site.

Permitted development rights conferred by the PDO may be removed
for any particular development or class of development within a
specified geographical area (frequently a conservation area), by an
article 4 direction.[66] If an article 4 direction removes permitted development rights for work and a subsequent application for planning permission for that work made within 12 months of the direction is refused, a
claim for compensation may arise.[67] It is also competent to restrict future
exercise of permitted development rights by imposing a condition upon a
grant of planning permission (Chapter 6).

The PDO specifies 71 classes of permitted development listed in
Schedule 1, Parts 1–25, ranging from development within the curtilage of
a dwellinghouse to development at amusement parks. As many of the
classes are of specialised interest only, the following discussion concentrates on the provisions which are likely to have a wider effect.

Part 1   Development Within the Curtilage of a Dwellinghouse

4.20   It is important to note that the definition of "dwellinghouse" for the
          purposes of the PDO does not include a building containing one or more
          flats, or a flat contained within such a building. The permitted develop-
          ment rights specified in Part 1 therefore do not extend to a flat, which is
          defined as a separate and self-contained set of premises, whether or not
          on the same floor, forming part of a building from some other part of
          which it is divided horizontally.

          Neither the PDO nor the TCPSA define "curtilage". Broadly, the
          curtilage of a building includes any land or building used for its

---

[65] art. 3(1) as amended; Conservation (Natural Habitats, Etc.) Regulations 1994, regs
60–63
[66] art. 4.
[67] TCPSA, s. 77.

comfortable enjoyment or serving the purpose of the building in some necessary or reasonably useful way, although not marked off or enclosed in any way.[68] The curtilage of a typical dwellinghouse is its garden.

The extent of the curtilage is a question of fact and circumstances. The geographical relationship and the use made of the land and buildings will be important. Curtilage is generally constrained to a small area about a building; an intimate association with land which is undoubtedly within the curtilage is required in order to make the land under consideration part and parcel of that undoubted curtilage land; and although it is not necessary for there to have been physical enclosure of the land which was within the curtilage, the land in question at least needs to be regarded in law as part of one enclosure with the house. The appropriate time for consideration of the curtilage boundary is the time the development took place, but historical associations can be used in looking for identification of the curtilage at the time of the development.[69] Current ownership may be irrelevant, for example, the large grounds which often form the curtilage of listed buildings can be in the hands of several different owners.

Class 1 The enlargement, improvement or other alteration of a dwellinghouse

This class includes the erection of any building with a floor area greater than four square metres and within five metres of any part of the dwellinghouse, but excludes the erection of a building within the curtilage of a listed building. There are restrictions on the increase in floor area and the total area of ground covered by buildings within the curtilage. In addition, there must be no increase in height beyond the height of the highest part of the roof of the original dwellinghouse. Development near either the boundary of the curtilage of the dwellinghouse or any road bounding the curtilage is limited. This class does not permit the cladding of any part of the exterior of a dwellinghouse in a conservation area.

4.21

Class 2 Any alteration to the roof of a dwellinghouse including the enlargement of a dwellinghouse by way of an addition or alteration to its roof

Planning permission is deemed to be granted for any alteration to the roof of a dwellinghouse, other than a dwellinghouse within a conservation area. The alterations cannot increase the height of any part of the dwellinghouse beyond the highest part of the existing roof. There are also limits on the extension beyond the plane of any existing roof slope (which will restrict the installation of dormer windows without planning permission) and the increase in roof area. An application for planning permission will be required if any roofing material used materially affects the external appearance of the dwellinghouse.

4.22

---

[68] *Sinclair-Lockhart's Trs v. Central Land Board*, 1951 S.L.T. 121, *per* Lord Mackintosh at p. 123. See Watchman and Young, "The Meaning of Curtilage", 1990 S.L.T. 77; Mynors, "The Extent of Listing" [1993] J.P.L. 99.
[69] *McAlpine v. Secretary of State for the Environment, The Times*, Dec. 6, 1994.

Class 3   The provision within the curtilage of a dwellinghouse of any building or enclosure, swimming or other pool required for a purpose incidental to the enjoyment of the dwellinghouse, or the maintenance, improvement or other alteration of such a building or enclosure

4.23   The erection of buildings such as garages and garden sheds, walls or fences, and swimming pools, and any subsequent maintenance, improvement or alteration, will not require planning permission.

   The building, enclosure or pool must be required for a purpose incidental to the enjoyment of the dwellinghouse, which includes the keeping of poultry, bees, pet animals, birds or other livestock. However, permitted development rights under this class do not extend to the erection, maintenance or alteration of beehives, chicken sheds and similar structures if the livestock are kept for commercial purposes and not for the domestic needs or personal enjoyment of the occupants of the dwellinghouse. Keeping up to 44 dogs in a cottage was held not to be a use incidental to the enjoyment of a dwellinghouse, notwithstanding that the dogs were kept as a hobby.[70]

   Development is not permitted by this class if it consists of a dwelling. There are also limits on the distance of the building or enclosure from any road which bounds the curtilage and from the dwellinghouse, its floor area and height, and the total area of ground covered by buildings or enclosures within the curtilage. If the land is within a conservation area or the curtilage of a listed building, permitted development rights under this class do not extend to the provision, alteration or improvement of a building with a floor area greater than four square meters.

Class 4   The provision within the curtilage of a dwellinghouse of a hard surface for any purpose incidental to the enjoyment of the dwellinghouse

4.24   Planning permission is deemed to be granted for provision of hard surfaces such as areas of tarmac for car parking and paved patio areas, other than within a conservation area or the curtilage of a listed building. The hard surface must also be for a purpose incidental to the enjoyment of the dwellinghouse (see class 3 above).

Class 5   The erection or provision within the curtilage of a dwellinghouse of a container for the storage of oil or liquified petroleum gas

4.25   This permitted development right does not apply within a conservation area or the curtilage of a listed building. In addition, there are restrictions on the capacity of the container, its height and its distance from any road bounding the curtilage. Deemed permission extends only to the provision of one container within the curtilage of a dwellinghouse.

Class 6   The installation, alteration or replacement of a satellite antenna on a dwellinghouse or within the curtilage of a dwellinghouse

4.26   The antenna must be sited so far as practicable to minimise its effect on the external appearance of the building or structure on which it is

---

[70] *Wallington, supra.*

installed. There are also restrictions on the size and height of the antenna. Development is not permitted by this class if it would result in either more than one satellite antenna on the dwellinghouse or within its curtilage, or the antenna is installed in a conservation area or national scenic area on any part of a dwellinghouse which faces on to a road.

Part 2   Sundry Minor Operations

Class 7   The erection, construction, maintenance, improvement or alteration of a gate, fence, wall or other means of enclosure

The height of any new enclosure must not exceed two metres above   4.27
ground level, or one metre if within 20 metres of a road. The height of an existing enclosure cannot be increased beyond these limits. Development is not permitted by this class if it would involve an enclosure surrounding a listed building or development within its curtilage. Permitted development rights under this class are not restricted to development within the curtilage of a dwellinghouse.

Class 9   The stone cleaning or painting of the exterior of any building or works

This permitted development right does not include stone cleaning or   4.28
painting for purposes of advertisement, announcement or direction, to which the control of advertisement regulations will apply (Chapter 9). Although the stone cleaning or painting of a listed building or building within a conservation area is also excluded, planning permission for these activities is required only if the external appearance of the building will be materially affected.[71] Painting includes the application of colour.

Part 3   Changes of Use

The Use Classes Order (UCO) provides that changes of use within   4.29
defined classes do not require planning permission (see below). A material change of use from one class to another will require permission. Part 3 of the PDO permits certain changes of use between classes without permission (see fig. 4.2).

Class 10

Permits a change of use from a use within class 2 (financial, professional   4.30
and other services), or class 3 (food and drink), from use for the sale of hot food for consumption off the premises, or for the sale or display for sale of motor vehicles to a use within class 1 (shops). From February 2, 1998, the change of use from sale or display for sale of motor vehicles to class 1 use is only permitted by the PDO if the total floor area of the building does not exceed 235 square metres.

---

[71] s. 26(2)(a).

Class 11

4.31 Permits a change of use from class 3 (food and drink) or for the sale of hot food for consumption off the premises to class 2 (financial, professional and other services).

Class 12

4.32 Permits a change of use from class 5 (general industrial) or class 6 (storage or distribution) to class 4 (business).

Class 13

4.33 Permits a change of use from class 4 (business) or class 5 (general industrial) to class 6 (storage or distribution), provided the change of use relates to no more than 235 square metres of the floor area in the building.

Part 4 Temporary Buildings and Uses

Class 14 The provision on land of buildings, moveable structures, works, plant or machinery required temporarily in connection with and for the duration of operations being or to be carried out on, in, under or over that land or on land adjoining that land

4.34 Any planning permission required for the operations must have been obtained. When the operations have been carried out, all buildings, structures, works, plant and machinery must be removed and the land on which these items were situated reinstated to its previous condition as soon as is reasonably practicable. Development is not permitted by this class in connection with mining operations.

Class 15 The use of land (other than a building or land within the curtilage of a building) for any purpose, except as a caravan site or an open air market, on not more than 28 days in total in any calendar year, and the erection or placing of moveable structures on the land for the purposes of that use

4.35 This class permits temporary uses such as rock concerts and the erection of moveable structures such as tents in connection with these uses. The use of any site for such purposes must not exceed 28 days in a calendar year. The calendar year basis applies even where an enforcement notice does not take effect until later in the year.[72]

Part 6 Agricultural Buildings and Operations

Part 7 Forestry Buildings and Operations

4.36 Planning controls over agricultural and forestry development are examined in Chapter 9.

---

[72] Attorney General's Reference (No. 1 of 1996) [1997] J.P.L. 749; [1996] E.G.C.S. 164.

Fig. 4.2   Changes of Use without Planning Permission

From class	*To class*
2 (Financial, professional and other services)	1 shops
3 (Food and Drink)	1 (shops) or 2 (Financial, professional and other services)
4 (Business)	6 (Storage or Distribution), unless the floor area involved exceeds 235 sq.m.
5 (General Industrial)	4 (Business) or 6 (Storage or Distribution), subject to 235 sq.m. limit
6 (Storage or Distribution)	4 (Business)
Sale or display for sale of motor vehicles subject to 235 sq.m. limit	1 (shops)
Hot food takeaway	1 (shops) or 2 (financial, professional and other services)

Part 8   Industrial and Warehouse Development

Class 23   The extension or alteration of an industrial building or a warehouse

4.37   The building as extended or altered must be used for the purposes of the undertaking concerned, and in the case of an industrial building, may only be used for the carrying out of an industrial process or the provision of employee facilities, or in the case of a warehouse, for storage or distribution or the provision of employee facilities. There are also restrictions on the size of the building as extended or altered, including a restriction on the increase in floor area to a maximum of 25 per cent, or 1,000 square metres, whichever is the greater. The planning authority can require an application for planning permission to be submitted if the external appearance of the premises would be materially affected by the extension or alteration.

Class 24   Development carried out on industrial land for the purposes of an industrial process consisting of

4.38   (a)   *the installation of additional or replacement plant or machinery;*
            (b)   *the provision, rearrangement or replacement of a sewer, main, pipe, cable or other apparatus; or*
            (c)   *the provision, rearrangement or replacement of a private way, private railway, siding or conveyor.*

Development is not permitted if it would materially affect the external appearance of the premises or any plant or machinery would be higher than 15 metres above ground level or the height of anything replaced, whichever is the greater.

Part 12   Development by Local Authorities

Class 30   The erection or construction and the maintenance, improvement or other alteration by a local authority of:

4.39   (a)   *any building, works or equipment not exceeding four metres in height or 200 cubic metres in capacity on land belonging to or maintained by them, being building works or equipment required for the purposes of any function exercised by them on that land otherwise than as statutory undertakers;*
            (b)   *lamp standards, refuse bins, public shelters and similar structures or works required in connection with the operation of any public service administered by them.*

4.40   *Class 31   The carrying out by a roads authority on land outwith but adjoining the boundary of an existing road of works required for or incidental to the maintenance or improvement of the road.*

Part 23   Demolition of Buildings (see above).

USE CLASSES ORDER

4.41   The 1997 Use Classes Order (UCO) came into force on February 2, 1998, replacing the 1989 Order. The main changes introduced by the new UCO are the removal of hot food takeaways from class 3 (food and drink); the deletion of classes 7–10 (special industrial groups); and the extension of class 9 (houses), previously class 14, to allow limited use as a bed and breakfast or guest house. The associated changes to the PDO are outlined below. As the changes to the UCO have resulted in a re-numbering of the use classes, the outline below cross-refers the new and former numbering.

The Scottish Office issued Circular 1/1998 explaining these changes, and updating the guidance on the operation of the UCO. In particular, fresh guidance is given on the operation of class 4 (see below).

The UCO specifies 11 classes of use. Within each class are listed uses of a broadly similar character. Provided both uses are in the same class, a change from one use to another does not involve development and, therefore, no planning permission is required for the change.[73] For example, any change from use as a post office to use for the sale of tickets will not amount to development because both uses are within class 1 (see below). Primary use is the determining factor for the provisions of the UCO and planning permission is not required where ancillary or incidental uses fall within a different class from the primary use.[74] A newsagent's shop selling hot pies at lunchtime involves uses within classes 1 and 3. If the sale of hot pies cannot be described as ancillary or incidental to the shop use, a material change of use may have occurred and planning permission be required.[75]

It should not be assumed that any change of use from one class to another automatically requires permission. There may be deemed planning permission for the change under the PDO (see above). In the absence of deemed permission, an application for planning permission is only necessary if the change of use is material.

The TCPSA declares that certain changes of use will always be material and, therefore, require planning permission (see Material Change of Use), such as subdivision of a dwellinghouse into two or more dwellinghouses,[76] which would otherwise be a change of use within class 9 (houses). In addition, a condition imposed upon a grant of planning permission can restrict changes of use notwithstanding that the change of use does not constitute development in terms of the UCO (Chapter 6).

The following uses, often described as *sui generis*, are excluded from   4.42
the provisions of the UCO and planning permission will, therefore, be required for any change to or from these uses (the character of these uses is such that the change is likely to be material):

(a)   as a theatre;
(b)   as an amusement arcade or centre, or funfair;
(c)   for the sale of fuel for motor vehicles;

---

[73] s. 26(2)(f), as amended; Town and Country Planning (Use Classes) (Scotland) Order 1997 (S.I. 1997 No. 3061), as amended by Amendment Order 1998 (S.I. 1998 No. 1196), art. 3.
[74] art. 3(3).
[75] *City of Glasgow District Council, supra.*
[76] s. 26(3)(a).

   (d) for the sale or display for sale of motor vehicles[77];
   (e) for a taxi business or for the hire of motor vehicles;
   (f) as a scrap-yard or a yard for the breaking of motor vehicles;
   (g) for the storage or distribution of minerals;
   (h) as a public house;
   (i) for any works registrable under the Alkali, etc. Works Regulation Act 1906; or
   (j) for the sale of hot food for consumption off the premises.

Where a single undertaking occupies land on a single site or on adjacent sites which are used for purposes within classes 4 and 5 (business and general industrial), those uses may be treated as if they were in a single class in considering the use of that land, provided this will not result in a substantial increase in the area used for a purpose falling within class 5 (general industrial).[78]

The 11 use classes are:

Class 1   Shops

4.43
   (a) *The retail sale of goods other than hot food;*
   (b) *as a post office;*
   (c) *for the sale of tickets;*
   (d) *as a travel agency;*
   (e) *for the sale of cold food for consumption off the premises;*
   (f) *for hairdressing;*
   (g) *for the direction of funerals;*
   (h) *for the display of goods for sale;*
   (i) *for the hiring out of domestic or personal goods or articles;*
   (j) *as a launderette or dry cleaners; or*
   (k) *for the reception of goods to be washed, cleaned or repaired;*

where the sale, display or service is principally to visiting members of the public.

The retail sale of goods within class 1 includes supermarkets, pharmacies[79] and auction houses,[80] but not bureaux de change.[81] The Scottish Office guidance states that a sandwich bar does not cease to be within class 1 merely because it sells hot drinks, or if a few customers eat on the premises.

The PDO permits change of use of some motor vehicle showrooms and premises falling within class 2 (financial, professional and other services) or class 3 (food and drink) and food takeaways to a class 1 use without planning permission.

---

[77] A change of use of a building with a floor area of 235 sq.m. or less from sale and display for sale of motor vehicles to class 1 (shops) does not require planning permission— PDO, class 10.

[78] UCO, art. 3(4).

[79] *R. v. Maldon D.C., ex p. Pattani* [1998] 1 E.G.C.S. 135.

[80] *R. v. Kensington & Chelsea LBC, ex p. Europa Foods* [1996] E.G.C.S. 5.

[81] *Palisade Investments Ltd v. Secretary of State for the Environment* [1996] 1 P.L.R. 37.

Class 2 Financial, professional and other services

Use for the provision of   4.44

    (a) financial services;
    (b) professional services; or
    (c) any other services (including use as a betting office);

which it is appropriate to provide in a shopping area and where the services are provided principally to visiting members of the public.

Thus a change of use from an estate agency to a betting office will not require planning permission, as both uses fall within class 2. Office uses which do not serve the public directly fall within class 4 (business), to avoid loss of shopfront property. Bureaux de change fall within class 2.[82] A solicitor's office will fall within class 2 where it provides services principally to visiting members of the public, whether or not by prior appointment.[83] Where a solicitor's practice is largely undertaken by telephone and written communication, it may fall within class 4 (below).

Class 2 only includes uses which are appropriate to provide in a shopping area (the equivalent English use class does not impose this requirement on financial and professional services).

In terms of the PDO, where the established use of a property falls within class 2, no planning permission is required for a change to a use within class 1 (shops). However, in consequence of the perceived desirability of preserving shop units, planning permission will be required for a change of use from class 1 to class 2. The PDO also provides that no permission is required for a change of use from class 3 (food and drink) or hot food takeaway to class 2.

Class 3 Food and drink

Use for the sale of food and drink for consumption on the premises.   4.45

This class includes restaurants, cafes and snack bars. Previously class 3 also included hot food takeaways. The 1997 UCO now excludes these from class 3 and the other use classes, with the result that a change of use from a restaurant to a hot food takeaway, or vice versa, will require planning permission. However, a restaurant whose trade is primarily in-house dining can operate a minor takeaway without requiring planning permission. Planning permission is required if a cafe is to become a public house (unlike the equivalent position in England and Wales).[84]

In terms of the PDO, a change of use from class 3 to either class 1 (shops) or class 2 (financial, professional and other services) does not require planning permission. The potential to change from a hot food takeaway to class 1 or class 2 is also preserved by the PDO, notwithstanding that a hot food takeaway no longer falls within class 3.

Class 4 Business

---

[82] *ibid.*
[83] *Kalra v. Secretary of State for the Environment* [1996] 1 P.L.R. 37.
[84] art. 3(5).

4.46   (a)   *as an office, other than a use within class 2 (financial, profes-*
                      sional and other services);
                (b)   *for research and development of products or processes;*
                (c)   *for any industrial process;*

        being a use which can be carried on in any residential area without detriment
        to the amenity of that area by reason of noise, vibration, smell, fumes, smoke,
        soot, ash, dust or grit.

        This combines non-class 2 office use and non-class 5 industrial use, often
        described as light industry.
        The Scottish Office guidance indicates that there is neither a require-
        ment for a class 4 building to be located in a residential area, nor for it
        to be physically capable of accommodating all the uses within the class.
        An application for a use within class 4 should not be refused permission
        on the grounds that the land is allocated for class 4 as a whole, or for a
        different use within the class, unless such a refusal would accord with
        development plan policy. The presumption against the use of planning
        conditions or agreements to limit future changes of use permitted by the
        UCO or PDO applies with particular force to class 4.
        Even if the building satisfies the residential amenity text in class 4,
        planning permission can still be refused on the grounds of traffic
        generation, design, density, loss of mature trees, and so on. If the
        intensification of the use leads to the development no longer satisfying
        the residential amenity test, the use is no longer a class 4 use, with the
        result that there has been a material change of use requiring planning
        permission.
        The flexibility of this class is increased by the permitted changes of use
        under the PDO from classes 5 (general industrial) and 6 (storage or
        distribution) to class 4. In addition, no permission is required for a
        change of use from class 4 to class 6 (storage or distribution) provided
        the floor area involved does not exceed 235 square metres.

        ### Class 5   General industrial

4.47   *Use for the carrying on of an industrial process other than one falling within*
        class 4 (business).

        Class 5 now includes the processes falling within the special industrial
        use classes, classes 7–10 of the previous UCO. The other legislation
        applying to these processes is now considered sufficiently comprehensive
        to control potential pollution.
        The PDO permits a change of use from class 5 to class 4 (business). A
        change to class 6 (storage and distribution) is also competent without
        permission provided the floor area involved does not exceed 235 square
        metres.

        ### Class 6   Storage or distribution (previously class 11)

        Use for storage or as a distribution centre.

4.48   An established class 6 use holds the potential of a change without
        permission to the flexible class 4 (business).

Class 7 Hotels and hostels (previously class 12)

Use as a hotel, boarding house, guest house, or hostel where no significant 4.49
element of care is provided, other than premises licensed for the sale of
alcoholic liquor to persons other than residents or to persons other than
persons consuming meals on the premises and other than a use within class 9
(houses).

No planning permission is required to change a nurses' home to a hotel use, despite such planning consequences as increased traffic, especially buses and taxis, with resultant parking difficulties, and increased cooking smells. The reference to the sale of alcoholic liquor excludes public house uses from class 7 (public houses are completely excluded from the UCO).

Class 8 Residential Institutions (previously class 13)

Use: 4.50

   (a) for the provision of residential accommodation and care to people
        in need of care other than a use within class 9 (houses);
   (b) as a hospital or nursing home;
   (c) as a residential school, college or training centre.

The Scottish Office guidance directs planning authorities to concentrate on land-use planning considerations when considering a planning application for a change of use to a use within class 8. It explains that private and voluntary residential care homes have to register with the local authority where they provide a substantial amount of care or support. Planning authorities should therefore concern themselves mainly with the impact of a proposed institution on amenity and the environment.

Class 9 Houses (previously class 14)

Use: 4.51

   (a) as a house, other than as a flat, whether or not as a sole or main
        residence, by

        (i)   a single person or by people living together as a family, or
        (ii) not more than five residents living together including a house-
              hold where care is provided for residents;

   (b) as a bed and breakfast establishment or guesthouse (not in either
        case being carried out in a flat), where at any one time not more
        than two bedrooms are, or in the case of premises having less than
        four bedrooms one bedroom is, used for that purpose.

Working at home may involve a change of use of part of the dwelling-house to use for business purposes. However, planning permission will not be required if the overall character of the use as a residence is unchanged. Factors such as increased visitors and deliveries will be relevant. A change of use to multiple occupancy involving more than five residents who are not members of a family will require planning permission.

The Scottish Office guidance explains that the single household concept provides more certainty over the planning position of small group homes, which play a major role in the Government's community care policy. Any resident care staff should be included in the calculation of the number of people accommodated. The class also includes groups of people such as students who live on a communal basis as a single household.

The 1997 UCO extends this class to include limited use as a bed and breakfast or guest house.

Class 10   Non-residential institutions (previously class 15)

4.52   *Use, not including residential use:*

   (a)   as a crêche, day nursery or day centre;
   (b)   for the provision of education;
   (c)   for the display of works of art (otherwise than for sale or hire);
   (d)   as a museum;
   (e)   as a public library or public reading room;
   (f)   as a public hall or exhibition hall; or
   (g)   for, or in connection with, public worship or religious instructions, or the social or recreational activities of a religious body.

Class 11   Assembly and leisure (previously class 16)

4.53   *Use as a:*

   (a)   cinema;
   (b)   concert hall;
   (c)   bingo hall or casino;
   (d)   dance hall or discotheque; or
   (e)   swimming bath, skating rink, gymnasium or area for other indoor or outdoor sports or recreation, not involving motorised vehicles or firearms.

DETERMINATION WHETHER PLANNING PERMISSION REQUIRED: CERTIFICATES OF LAWFULNESS OF USE OR DEVELOPMENT

4.54   With the lack of a precise definition of "development", it is often unclear whether planning permission is necessary for an operation or change of use. Such difficulties can be resolved by obtaining a formal determination from the planning authority, either in advance of the development or following its completion.

Previously an application would be made to the planning authority for a section 51 determination or an established use certificate. A section 51 determination indicated whether planning permission was required for proposed operations or change of use. Although the section 51 determination was described as good as a grant of planning permission, there had been some uncertainty surrounding its legal status. An established use certificate was conclusive evidence that the use was immune from enforcement action, but did not render the use lawful. Section 51 determinations and established use certificates granted prior to September 25, 1992 remain valid.

From that date, determinations are given in the form of Certificates of Lawfulness of Use or Development.[85] The applicant for a certificate must provide the planning authority with the information to reach its decision. The procedure cannot be used as a "fishing expedition" to obtain information from the planning authority on existing lawful uses or development, or an indication of what classes of use or development would be lawful.

This new procedure would seem to remove the possibility of arguing that a written statement by an officer is a formal determination even although no formal application had been made for such a determination. It is a well-established principle that statements by planning officers cannot bind the planning authority. Notwithstanding a statement by a planning officer that planning permission is not required for proposed work, the planning authority may take enforcement action against the work on the grounds that permission was required (Chapter 7). Under the new procedure the only way to prevent such enforcement action is to apply for a certificate.

A Certificate of Lawfulness of Proposed Use or Development   4.55
(CLOPUD) will be issued if the planning authority is satisfied that the use or operations would be lawful (presumably by reference to statute, the PDO or UCO, and case law) if begun at the time of the application. There is an irrefutable presumption that the use or operations specified in the certificate are lawful, unless the law changes before the use or operations are begun.

The Certificate of Lawfulness of Existing Use or Development (CLEUD) is a determination of the lawfulness of either any existing use of land or building, or any operations which have been carried out, or any failure to comply with a condition or limitation attached to a grant of planning permission. The lawfulness of any use or development specified in the certificate is conclusively presumed. For the first time this enables a statutory document to be obtained certifying the lawfulness of existing operational development or use as a single dwellinghouse.

A use or operation is lawful if it is immune from enforcement action (Chapter 7) and is not in contravention of the requirements of any enforcement notice or breach of condition notice which is in force (this removes the concept of established or immune development). Once the lawfulness of a use or operation has been certified, that use or operation enjoys the permitted development rights conferred by the PDO.[86]

Any person (not just the owner of the land) may apply to the planning authority for a Certificate of Lawfulness of Proposed/Existing Use or Development. A completed form similar to that for an application for planning permission is submitted, together with full supporting information. There is no requirement to give notice to persons with an interest

---

[85] TCPSA, ss. 150–155, and Town and Country Planning (General Development Procedure) (Scotland) Order 1992, arts 26–29, as substituted by 1992 Amendment Order (S.I. 1992 No. 2083).

[86] Following revocation of art. 2(3) of the PDO by Amendment No. 2 Order (S.I. 1992 No. 2084).

in the land which is the subject of the application, or neighbours. The planning authority is not obliged to publicise the application. Owners/tenants/neighbours/other interested parties will therefore not be alerted to the application unless they routinely inspect the planning register in which details of the application will be entered. Although the planning authority is not required to consult interested parties, it may choose to do so.

4.56   The fee payable is set by reference to the fees for an application for planning permission for the operation or change of use in respect of which a certificate is sought: in the case of a CLOPUD, 50 per cent of that fee, and for a CLEUD, the full fee, or a set rate, currently £95, for an application relating to a failure to comply with a condition. If an application for a CLOPUD is refused, there is no exemption from payment of the full fee for any application for planning permission which is lodged in consequence of that refusal.

The onus is on the applicant to provide sufficient information of the lawfulness to satisfy the planning authority, but not to prove the lawfulness beyond reasonable doubt. Corroboration of the applicant's evidence does not appear to be required. If there is no evidence to contradict or cast doubt upon the applicant's evidence, the Scottish Office advises that the application should not be refused, provided the evidence is sufficiently precise and unambiguous to justify the grant of a certificate on the balance of probability.[87] This leaves open the question of whether it is ever competent for the planning authority to adopt an active role to seek out information to rebut the applicant's evidence.

The origin and identity of the applicant, and the planning merits of the use or development have no relevance to the legal issues involved in the determination of the application. As a result, it may be appropriate for determination of such applications to be delegated to planning officers rather than left in the hands of the councillors sitting on the planning committee.

As the effect of a certificate is similar to a grant of planning permission, the authority will require to specify precisely the description of the use or development and the boundaries of the site, to avoid giving permission for more than is intended. The authority may modify the description of the use, operation or other matter specified in the application, presumably to avoid refusing the application. An aggrieved person could seek judicial review of the decision to issue a certificate, on the grounds that its terms are wider than the existing use.[88]

4.57   If sufficient information is provided, the authority will issue a certificate which shall conclusively presume the lawfulness of any use, operations or other matters specified in the certificate. For the purposes of certain statutes, the certificate will have effect as if it were a grant of permission. A refusal is not conclusive evidence that the use or development is unlawful and will not preclude a further application based on new evidence.

---

[87] Scottish Office Environment Department Circular 36/1992, "Planning and Compensation Act 1991—Lawful Development and Enforcement", para. 69.
[88] *R. v. Sheffield C.C., ex p. Power* [1994] E.G.C.S. 101.

It is an offence either knowingly or recklessly to make a statement which is false or misleading in a material particular or, with intent to deceive, to use any document which is false or misleading in a material particular, or to withhold material information. The planning authority may revoke a certificate without compensation if a statement was made or a document used which was false in a material particular or any material information was withheld. The possibility of revocation without compensation will limit the value of a certificate to any subsequent owner of the land.

The applicant has a right of appeal to the Secretary of State against a refusal or part refusal to issue a certificate. The 1997 Act introduced a right of appeal against a failure to determine an application within the two-month time limit.[89] The normal appeal procedures apply, with a choice of written submissions procedure or a public local inquiry (Chapter 8).

The decision of the Secretary of State on appeal may be challenged in the Court of Session (Chapter 8).[90] However, such a challenge is limited to allegations that he acted illegally and his decision on the facts is final.

---

[89] TCPSA, s. 154(1)(b) and DPO art. 28(4) as substituted.
[90] For example, *East Dunbartonshire Council v. Secretary of State for Scotland*, 1998 G.W.D. 40–2079; SPEL 71:16.

CHAPTER 5

DEVELOPMENT CONTROL II—APPLYING FOR PLANNING PERMISSION

5.01   If planning permission is required for a proposed development, an application for that permission must be made to the planning authority for the district in which the development site is located. When applying for planning permission it is easy to fall into the trap of treating the planning authority as the "enemy" to whom information should only be given as a last resort. In reality they fulfil a valuable consultative role. All but the simplest of applications for planning permission should be discussed in advance with the planning officer responsible for the area in which the development site lies. Although any indications given by the officer cannot dictate the decision eventually reached by the planning committee on the application, careful consideration should be given to his comments regarding relevant policies and possible alterations to the proposals to make the application more likely to be awarded permission. No fee can be charged for this service.[1]

The general rules governing the procedure for applying for planning permission, formerly part of the General Development Order (GDO), are now contained in the Development Procedure Order (DPO).[2] In addition to these rules, each planning authority has its own internal procedures for handling planning applications.

TYPES OF APPLICATION

5.02   Before applying for planning permission, a decision has to be made on the type of permission to be sought, as this must be indicated on the application form. This decision will be influenced by the nature of the proposed development, the planning history of the site and, to some extent, the attitude of the planning authority as indicated in pre-application consultations (see above).

(a)   Full or Detailed Planning Permission

5.03   The terms "full" or "detailed" planning permission do not appear in the TCPSA, but are used interchangeably in practice to highlight the difference between what the Act refers to as "planning permission" and

---

[1] *R. v. Richmond upon Thames B.C., ex p. McCarthy & Stone (Developments) Ltd* [1991] 3 W.L.R. 941; 1992 S.P.L.P. 35:22.
[2] Town and Country Planning (General Development Procedure) (Scotland) Order 1992 (S.I. 1992 No. 224), as amended by S.I.s 1992 No. 2083, 1993 No. 1039, 1994 Nos. 2585 and 3293, and 1996 No. 467.

"outline planning permission". An application for full or detailed planning permission is appropriate where the applicant has decided all or most of the details of the proposed development and these details can be submitted to the planning authority for its approval. If that approval is given, the development can proceed and be completed without further applications to the authority, unless permission is needed to change some of the details of the development or the permission is subject to a condition requiring the approval of the authority for some further matter. It is competent for permission to be granted in detail for part of the development and in principle for the remainder, for example where details of roadworks have been approved but the only information submitted relating to the proposed foodstore is the footprint within which it is to be built.[3]

(b) Outline Planning Permission

It is competent for outline planning permission to be granted for the carrying out of any development except a material change of use (Chapter 4).   5.04

Outline permission is sought when the applicant wishes to obtain consent to the outlines or principle of the development before drawing up a detailed scheme, thereby saving the expense of that work if outline permission is not granted. Following a grant of outline permission, a further application must be made to the authority for its approval of the detailed scheme, in compliance with the condition imposed upon every grant of outline permission requiring subsequent approval to be obtained from the planning authority for specified areas of detail, known as reserved matters (see below).

Where it is intended to sell land with the benefit of permission (the grant of permission will normally increase the value of the land and therefore its sale price), it is often advisable to obtain outline rather than detailed planning permission. A grant of outline planning permission provides a guarantee that the broad outlines of the development have been approved, leaving the purchaser free to draw up detailed proposals to his own requirements and obtain approval by submitting an application for approval of reserved matters.

An application for outline planning permission necessarily contains less detail than an application for detailed permission, but is similar in other respects. Further details and information can be requested from the applicant if the planning authority consider that in the circumstances of the case the application ought not to be considered separately from the siting, design or external appearance of the building, or the means of access thereto or the landscaping of the site.[4] The existence of uncertainties regarding matters such as noise do not necessarily prevent a grant of outline permission.[5]

---

[3] *Lothian Borders & Angus Co-operative Society Ltd v. Scottish Borders Council*, O.H. 18 December 1998, unreported.
[4] DPO, art. 4(3).
[5] *R. v. Northampton B.C., ex p. Rice & Co.* [1998] E.G.C.S. 84.

In one case, an outline application which specified the floor area committed those concerned to a development on that scale, subject to minimal adjustments for siting, design and external appearance.[6] Accordingly, matters such as traffic generation could not be reassessed during the determination of the application for approval of reserved matters.

(c) Approval of Reserved Matters

5.05   Every outline planning permission is granted subject to a condition preventing commencement of development until approval of specified reserved matters is obtained from the planning authority. If no such condition is specified, the permission is deemed to have been granted subject to such a condition.[7]

Reserved matters can be any matters concerning the siting, design or external appearance of a building, or its means of access, or the landscaping of the application site, in respect of which details were not given in the application for outline planning permission.[8] The reservation of siting and means of access was held to be unlawful where details of those matters had been given in the outline application.[9] Density, drainage and disposal of sewage, and treatment of boundary walls and fences, are matters which may be reserved for future approval within these categories.[10] Floorspace is not a reserved matter, as it is neither siting nor design.[11] A reserved matters application could not be refused on the grounds that the design provided more office floor space than was needed to make the class 4 development viable.[12]

Where an office building had been erected on part of a site for which outline planning permission had been granted for five houses, the subsequent application for approval of reserved matters was held not to be in accordance with the outline permission, as the entire development authorised by the outline permission could not be constructed with the generous plots envisaged in that permission.[13]

Application for approval of reserved matters is made in a broadly similar form to an application for full or detailed permission, with the same requirement to notify owners, agricultural tenants and neighbours (see below). The application must give particulars sufficient to identify the outline planning permission in relation to which it is made. The details submitted, and the reserved matters approval granted, cannot depart from the ambit of the outline planning permission.

The application must be submitted (but need not be granted) within three years from the date outline permission was granted, or six months

[6] *R. v. Newbury D.C., ex p. Chieveley Parish Council* [1998] E.G.C.S. 131, *The Times*, Sept. 10, 1998.
[7] TCPSA, s. 59.
[8] DPO, art. 2(1).
[9] *R. v. Newbury D.C., ex p. Chieveley Parish Council, supra.*
[10] *Inverclyde District Council v. Inverkip Building Co.*, 1983 S.L.T. 563; *cf. Tesco Stores Ltd v. North Norfolk D.C.* [1998] P.L.C.R. 183, which held that drainage is not a reserved matter.
[11] *R. v. Newbury D.C., ex p. Chieveley Parish Council, supra.*
[12] *Camden LBC v. Secretary of State for the Environment* [1993] J.P.L. 466.
[13] *Orbit Development v. Secretary of State for the Environment* [1996] E.G.C.S. 91.

from the date any earlier application for approval was refused, or six months from the date of the dismissal of an appeal against such a refusal, whichever is the latest. Moreover, only one application may be made after three years from the date outline permission was granted. The planning authority may attach a condition to the outline planning permission substituting longer or shorter periods, or specify separate periods for separate parts or phases of the development.[14] Approval may be sought in single or separate applications. However, submission of an application in respect of some, but not all, of the reserved matters, or for part only of the site, within the time limit does not prevent the remainder of the outline permission from expiring.[15] An application for approval of reserved matters which is submitted outside the time limit is treated as not made in accordance with the terms of the permission.[16] It is possible to apply to renew the permission (see Renewal of Permission below).

(d) Consent, Agreement or Approval

Planning permission is often granted subject to conditions requiring aspects of the development to meet a standard acceptable to the planning authority. The wording of such conditions will require the developer to apply to the planning authority for its approval. Such applications should identify the planning permission and the condition in terms of which approval is sought, and describe the matter to be approved. The notification requirements do not appear to apply to these applications, but the DPO provides that notice of the decision of such applications by the planning authority must be provided within two months, and gives the same rights of appeal against refusal or deemed refusal as other planning applications.[17] No application fee is payable.

5.06

(e) Variation of Planning Permission

An applicant may request the planning authority to vary the grant of planning permission. Such variation is competent provided it appears to the authority that the change sought is not material.[18] This allows minor changes to be made to the details of a development without the submission of a fresh application for planning permission. As the change is not material, the normal requirements for an application, such as notification of parties, do not apply.

5.07

(f) Retrospective Planning Permission

As a result of the complex rules governing when planning permission is required (Chapter 4), as well as public ignorance, it is inevitable that development is sometimes carried out without planning permission.

5.08

---

[14] TCPSA, s. 59.

[15] *Hunterston Development Company Ltd v. Secretary of State for Scotland*, 1992 S.L.T. 1097.

[16] s. 60(4)(b).

[17] DPO, arts 14 and 23 as amended.

[18] s. 64.

Often the omission only comes to light during the sale of land or buildings, or when the planning authority takes enforcement action (Chapter 7). In these circumstances an application may be made for permission for development already carried out, more commonly known as retrospective planning permission.[19] The procedure for submitting such an application is similar to that for an application for full planning permission. If permission is granted, it will have retrospective effect from the date on which the work or use began. This procedure may also be used where development has been carried out in breach of a condition attached to a planning permission, or has not ceased on the expiry of a temporary planning permission (see below).

(g)   Renewal of Permission

5.09   There are two different procedures for applying to renew a planning permission. Both require the application to be submitted prior to the expiry of the time limit for the commencement of development. The applicant therefore also has the option of implementing the permission by commencing the development prior to the expiry of that time limit (see Duration, below).

The first procedure is to apply for renewal of the permission.[20] This application must be submitted prior to the expiry of the time limit for the commencement of development and, for an outline permission, also the time limit for submission of reserved matters for approval. It appears that the application is determined as if it were a fresh planning application. The Scottish Office guidance advises that as a general rule such applications should be refused only where there has been some material change in planning circumstances since the original permission was granted, or there is likely to be continued failure to begin the development and this will contribute unacceptably to uncertainty about the future pattern of development in the area, or the application is premature because the permission still has a reasonable time to run.[21]

For the renewal application, there is no form to complete, and neighbour notification (see below) is not required. The only requirements are that the application be made in writing and identify the previous grant of permission, and that owners and agricultural tenants of the application site be notified. The application fee is calculated as though it is a fresh application for planning permission.[22]

The other procedure is to apply for variation of the time limit condition.[23] Unlike the renewal procedure, such an application is competent where the time limit for submission of reserved matters for approval has expired, provided the time limit for commencement of development has yet to expire.[24] If the application is submitted prior to the expiry of

---

[19] s. 33.

[20] DPO, art. 5, as amended by S.I. 1994 No. 3293.

[21] Circular 4/1998, "The Use of Conditions in Planning Permission", Annex, para 52.

[22] Circular 1/1997, "Town and Country Planning (Fees for Applications and Deemed Applications) (Scotland) Regulations 1997", para 8(e).

[23] TCPSA s. 42. See Chap. 6.

[24] *R. v. Secretary of State for the Environment, ex p. Corby B.C.* [1994] 1 P.L.R. 38.

the time limit for the reserved matters application, the acceptability of the principle of the development cannot be reviewed even if there has been a change of planning circumstances.[25] In contrast, where that time limit has expired, material changes in policy can be taken into account.[26]

(h) Duplicate Applications: Twin Tracking

Where problems in obtaining permission are anticipated, many appli-   5.10 cants submit two applications in exactly the same terms. The submission of duplicate applications allows an appeal to be lodged against the deemed refusal (see below) of one application while negotiations continue with the planning authority with a view to permission being granted for the other application. If applications are submitted on the same day by or on behalf of the same applicant for alternative schemes for development of the same site, a reduced fee is payable, calculated as the highest of the fees applicable for each option and a sum equal to half the rent.

A similar practice involves the submission of a fresh application for the same development when an appeal is lodged in respect of the original application. In most such cases, no fee is payable in respect of the duplicate application provided it is submitted within 12 months. The appeal decision may be a material consideration which the authority must take into account when deciding the application (see below). One option available to the planning authority is to refuse the application as premature until the appeal has been decided.

SUBMISSION OF APPLICATION

An application for planning permission should be lodged with the   5.11 planning authority for the area in which development is proposed.

The application is made by completing and submitting an application form (form D1), obtained from the planning authority. The completed application form should be accompanied by a plan sufficient to identify the location of the site of the proposed development and such other plans and drawings as are necessary to describe the proposed development. The application form usually specifies the number of copies of the form and associated plans and drawings required by the planning authority. Copies are requested to enable at least one copy of the application and supporting plans to be made available for public inspection. The planning authority may require the applicant to provide further information or evidence in respect of information accompanying the application, including plans or drawings.[27]

In addition to lodging the completed application form and supporting plans, the applicant must also submit signed certificates relating to notification of owners, agricultural tenants and neighbours, and enclose any fee payable for the application. These matters are discussed below.

---

[25] *Allied London Property Investment v. Secretary of State for the Environment* [1997] J.P.L. 199.

[26] *Pye v. Secretary of State for the Environment* [1998] 3 P.L.R. 72, applying *R. v. London Docklands Development Corporation, ex p. Frost* (1996) 73 P. & C.R. 199.

[27] DPO, art. 13.

Description of Proposed Development

5.12   The description of the proposed development given on the application form is important because it governs the extent of the permission sought. Ancillary documents such as plans cannot extend the description. The description is also significant because it is used in both the notices served by the applicant upon notifiable persons and newspaper advertisements, which alert parties to their opportunity to inspect the application and lodge representations.

The description must be accurate, convey the substance of what is applied for and give full and fair notice to possible objectors. A grant of planning permission for petrol stations, restaurants, car parks and a 40-bed lodge was challenged successfully by a third party on the grounds that the application, neighbour notification notices and newspaper advertisements had merely described the proposed development as a roadside petrol station, notwithstanding that the full extent of the development had been shown in the accompanying plans.[28]

Notification of Owners and Agricultural Tenants

5.13   Although the applicant seeking permission is not required to own or control the site of the proposed development nor obtain the consent of the owner of the land to the application, the benefit of any grant of planning permission attaches to the land rather than to the applicant, who will be unable to commence the development without the agreement of the landowner.

The applicant must notify the owner that an application for planning permission is being submitted for a proposed development on his land.[29] This avoids the possibility of an owner selling land without knowing its true value following a grant of planning permission. The applicant must also notify any tenant of an agricultural holding on the site, whose security of tenure may be affected by a grant of permission. Special rules apply for developments consisting of the working and winning of minerals (Chapter 9).

For these purposes the expression "owner" refers to any person who owned the land 21 days before the date of the application, and includes a tenant with a lease which still has more than seven years to run.[30] The identity of the owner or tenant may be ascertained from the valuation roll kept by the council, or from a search of the Register of Sasines or the Land Register.[31] The applicant must utilise all steps reasonably open to him for tracing the owner, but there is provision for advertisement of applications if the owner cannot be traced (see below).

Agricultural holdings are defined by the Agricultural Holdings (Scotland) Act 1949 as land used for the purposes of agriculture as a trade or business. There is no conclusive method for identifying

[28] *Cumming v. Secretary of State for Scotland*, 1993 S.L.T. 228.
[29] TCPSA, s. 35 and DPO art. 8 as substituted by S.I. 1994 No. 3293.
[30] s. 35(7). The general definition of "owner" is contained in s. 277.
[31] Members of the public can carry out searches in person at the Registers of Scotland in Edinburgh (tel: 0131 659 6111) or a professional searcher can be instructed.

agricultural tenants, other than requesting this information from the landowner or making inquiries in the locality.

The application form obtained from the planning authority will contain a copy of the prescribed form of notice to be served upon owners and tenants of agricultural holdings. The notice is intended to alert these parties to the submission of the application and their right to make representations regarding the application to the planning authority within 21 days of the date of service of the notice (an extended period may be available if the application is advertised, and many authorities will accept representations outwith specified time limits). The notice also states that the grant of permission does not affect owners' rights to retain or dispose of their property unless there is an agreement to the contrary, but that it may affect the security of tenure of a tenant of an agricultural holding.

The applicant completes the notice by filling in details of the application, including the description of the proposed development (see above). The notice is normally sent by recorded delivery post or delivered by hand (methods of serving notices are examined in Chapter 7).

Together with the completed application form, the applicant must submit a signed certificate stating, as appropriate: 5.14

(a)   whether or not any part of the application site is an agricultural holding;

(b)   that at the date 21 days before the date of the application no person other than the applicant was the owner of the site or an agricultural tenant;

(c)   that he has served notice on every person who at the date 21 days before the date of the application was the owner or an agricultural tenant of the site, setting out the name of every such person, and the address at which and the date on which each notice was served;

(d)   that he has been unable to serve notice on some or all of these persons, and has taken reasonable steps (which must be specified) to ascertain the names and addresses of the others but has been unable to do so and has given notice by local advertisement.[32]

Unless the applicant certifies that no person other than himself was the owner of the site or an agricultural tenant, the application cannot be determined until the expiry of 21 days from the last date of service of any notice referred to in the certificate or the date of publication of the advertisement, whichever is the later.[33]

The planning authority must take into account any representations submitted by a person who satisfies them that he is an owner or agricultural tenant of the application site, provided those representations are submitted within 21 days of the date of service of the notice on that person, or within 21 days of the date of the advertisement. Although no

---

[32] Prescribed form of certificates and advertisements: DPO, Scheds 1 and 3, as substituted and amended by S.I. 1994 No. 3293.

[33] DPO, art. 14(1A) as inserted by S.I. 1994 No. 3293.

limit is imposed by this part of the statutory provisions, the authority cannot take into account any part of the representations which raise non-material considerations (see below). The authority must give notice of their decision to every such person who submits representations.

A failure to notify an owner or agricultural tenant may leave a subsequent grant of permission open to challenge in judicial review proceedings (see below). In addition, it is an offence to issue knowingly or recklessly a certificate which contains a statement which is false or misleading in a material particular, with liability on summary conviction to a fine not exceeding level 5 on the standard scale (see appendix 1). Proceedings for such an offence may be brought within two years of commission of the offence rather than the normal six-month period.

Notification of Neighbours

5.15   The applicant for planning permission is also required to serve notice of submission of the application upon the owners and occupiers of land neighbouring the site of the proposed development.[34] The equivalent procedure in England and Wales is discretionary and carried out by the planning authority. The purpose of neighbour notification is to alert those who will be most affected by the proposed development of their opportunity to make representations to the planning authority regarding the application.

Neighbour notification is one of the most problematic parts of the procedure for submission of planning applications. It generates many (unjustified) complaints from members of the public mainly because of widespread public overestimation of the extent of notification required. Broadly, only those neighbours within four metres of the site, excluding the width of any road, must be notified. In urban tenement property areas this may result in identification of over 100 notifiable neighbours, but in the majority of cases only 10–20 persons will require to be notified. The complexity of the procedure makes it unpopular with applicants, not least because of the wide opportunity for errors to be made. Despite this unpopularity, the requirement for neighbour notification is an important aspect of planning applications and is unlikely to be removed.

While notification of owners and agricultural tenants is required for "any application for planning permission", the requirement for neighbour notification only extends to applications for full or detailed permission, outline permission, and for approval of reserved matters. The applicant must serve notice upon those persons holding a "notifiable interest" in "neighbouring land" who have not been notified of the application as an owner or agricultural tenant of the site of the proposed development.

The term "neighbouring land" is defined as land which is conterminous with or within four metres of the boundary of land for which the development is proposed. In most cases the boundary will be clear, but on large sites it may seem more appropriate to identify a boundary within the site. To some extent this is dealt with by the provision that

---

[34] TCPSA, s. 34 and DPO, arts 2 and 9. The Scottish Office published a Consultation Paper "Review of Neighbour Notification" in 1997 outlining options for change.

part of such neighbouring land must lie within 90 metres of any part of the development in question. Where the proposed location of the development is more than 90 metres from the boundary, neighbours should suffer minimal impact as a result of the development and there is no justification for requiring them to be notified. However, this leaves open the question of where the boundaries of a site can be drawn (and there have been instances of boundaries being redrawn to avoid notifying neighbours). The boundaries of the planning unit may be a useful guide (Chapter 4).

The best method to identify neighbouring land is by measuring the distances from a large scale Ordnance Survey map for the area (1:1250 for urban areas), as illustrated in figure 5.1. In calculating the four-metre distance, the width of any road up to a limit of 20 metres is disregarded, unless the planning authority dispense with the requirement of notification in such circumstances, either as a matter of policy or on request for an individual application. Although there are rules for identifying neighbouring land which consists of buildings divided into separate units such as tenements, the safest course must always be to notify all persons within such buildings.

Fig. 5.1   Identifying Neighbouring Land (reproduced by permission of Highland Regional Council)

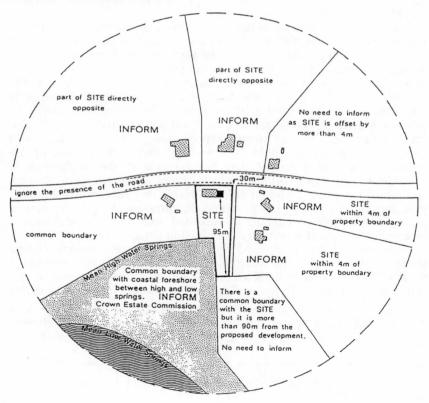

5.16   Once neighbouring land has been identified, the next step is to identify the persons holding a "notifiable interest" in the land. If the neighbouring land is entered on the valuation roll as consisting mainly of commercial premises, separate notification should be sent to each of the named owners, lessees and occupiers at the addresses given on the roll. Where the valuation roll fails to provide this information, notification should be sent to the premises of the neighbouring land individually addressed to "The Owner", "The Occupier" and "The Lessee" respectively (this procedure may also be adopted as a safety measure even where the parties are identified on the roll). In addition, it would seem advisable to send notification to any parties or addresses known to the applicant, but not specified on the roll.

For any land not entered on the valuation roll, including all residential property, separate notification should be sent addressed to "The Owner" and "The Occupier" respectively at the address of the premises on the neighbouring land.

There is provision for the application to be advertised if there are no premises on the neighbouring land to which notice can be sent. However, it may be possible to persuade the planning authority to dispense with an advertisement if the applicant can demonstrate that the notice has been sent to the notifiable party at another address. Alternatively, the authority may be requested to dispense with notification if a road runs between the site of the proposed development and the neighbouring land.

The prescribed form of notice to be served on notifiable neighbours will be included with the application form obtained from the planning authority. The applicant completes the form by specifying details of the application, including the location of the proposed development and its description (normally in the same terms as the description on the application form). The form also states that the application and supporting plans can be inspected at the offices of the planning authority or other specified locations, such as post offices in rural areas. It also informs the recipient that written representations may be lodged with the planning authority within 14 days beginning with the date of the notice (an extended period may be available if the application is advertised, and many authorities will accept representations outwith specified time limits). The completed notice, together with a location plan showing the site of the proposed development, is normally served upon the notifiable neighbours by recorded delivery letter or delivered by hand (methods of service are examined in Chapter 7).

5.17   Together with the completed application form, the applicant must submit a plan showing the location of the neighbouring land in respect of which notification has been carried out, and complete one of the certificates included with the application form which states either that[35]:

> (a)   notification has been carried out, giving the names and addresses of the persons to whom notification has been sent and their interest ("owner", "lessee" or "occupier"), with land

---

[35] DPO, arts. 4(2)(c)(iv) and 6(c)(iii) refer to art. 9(4) when the context indicates that what is meant is art. 9(5).

entered on the valuation roll and other land listed separately; or

(b) no notification is necessary because there are no notifiable neighbours; or

(c) it is not possible to carry out notification because there are no premises situated on the neighbouring land to which the notification can be sent.

As the applicant is no longer required to notify persons by name and provision is made for advertising applications if there are no premises to which a notice can be addressed, the applicant no longer has the opportunity to certify that he has taken all the steps reasonably open to him to ascertain the names and addresses of all the notifiable neighbours, but is unable to ascertain some or all of their names and addresses.

If the applicant certifies that there are no premises on the neighbouring land to which notification can be sent, or if the planning authority dispenses with neighbour notification in respect of land separated from the development site by a road and the applicant has not signed a neighbour notification certificate, the authority is required to publish notice of the application in a local newspaper.

The planning authority must not determine the application until 14 days after the date of its receipt or the date of publishing of an advertisement, whichever is the later.[36] This gives neighbours 14 days in which to lodge representations. In practice most authorities will accept representations received outwith this 14-day period.

Failure to notify a neighbour may leave a subsequent grant of permission open to challenge in judicial review proceedings (see below). In addition, it is an offence to issue knowingly or recklessly a notification, make an advertisement other than a newspaper advertisement, or supply a certificate, which purports to comply with these provisions, but which contains a statement which is false or misleading in a material particular.[37] The penalty on summary conviction is a fine not exceeding level 3 on the standard scale (see appendix 1). Proceedings for such an offence may be brought within two years of commission of the offence rather than the normal six-month period.

Error in Notification Certificates

The planning authority cannot entertain a planning application unless any statutory requirements relating to notification have been satisfied.[38] In most cases the authority will simply check that the appropriate certificates have been completed correctly. It seems unlikely that this statutory duty extends to checking the accuracy of the notification process, but this point is uncertain.

Once possible deficiencies in the notification process are drawn to its attention, the planning authority should investigate and require the

5.18

---

[36] art. 14, as amended.
[37] TCPSA, s. 34(3).
[38] ss. 34(5) and 35(4).

applicant to correct any errors. There seems no reason why an application should be rejected as invalid due to errors in the notification procedure,[39] unless the errors are so major that the whole procedure is better repeated. The objective of notification is to alert those persons whom the law perceives to have a special interest to the submission of the application and their opportunity to object to the application. The present practice of most planning authorities is to suspend consideration of the application and request the applicant to remedy defects by serving notification on overlooked persons. At the end of the further period which must be allowed for representations to be received from those persons, the application is then considered in the normal way. This practice fulfils the objective of the notification requirements and therefore seems acceptable. The alternative is for the authority to reject the application as invalid, leaving the applicant to make good the deficiency in notification and resubmit the application.

Errors in the notification process, particularly those pointed out to the planning authority prior to its decision, but not remedied, may leave a grant of permission open to challenge in the courts by a person with a notifiable interest who received no notification of the application.[40] The extent of the error required before the permission may be challenged successfully is not clear. A factual error in a certificate could be regarded as a mere irregularity which would not justify the court in striking down the planning decision. The exercise of the court's discretion may be influenced by the length of time since the grant of permission and the knowledge or otherwise of the application for permission of the person seeking to challenge that permission.[41]

Application Fees

5.19   A fee is payable for submission of most applications for planning permission.[42] This is intended to cover the administrative costs incurred by the planning authority in processing and determining applications, although fees are charged on a general scale rather than by reference to the time spent on individual applications. Most authorities provide a list of fees when dispensing application forms; not every application requires payment of a fee. A telephone call to the authority prior to submission of the application should confirm the correct fee. Failure to pay the correct fee will delay processing of the application.

PROCESSING OF APPLICATION

5.20   In the majority of cases the planning authority will decide straightforward applications in two to three months. Some authorities have a better record than others and much will depend on the development pressures

---

[39] But see *Lochore v. Moray D.C.*, 1992 S.L.T. 16, *per* Lord Cullen at p. 20 K–L; *Pollock v. Secretary of State for Scotland*, 1993 S.L.T. 1173, 1993 S.P.L.P. 38:19 (both cases were decided on other grounds).

[40] *Forrester v. Kirkcaldy District Council*, 1996 G.W.D. 21–1244, SPEL 56:74; *Bonnes v. West Lothian District Council*, 1994 G.W.D. 31–1888.

[41] *Forrester, supra*; *Main v. Swansea City Council* [1985] J.P.L. 558.

[42] Town and Country Planning (Fees for Applications and Deemed Applications) (Scotland) Regulations 1997 (S.I. 1997 No. 10).

in the district at the time. In complex cases a decision may not be received for many months or even years. The applicant has the opportunity to appeal against a deemed refusal after two months, but if the details of the proposed development are still being negotiated with the authority such an appeal is unlikely to succeed and is not an option worth pursuing, leaving the applicant with no alternative but to persevere with the application.

Each authority has its own internal procedures for processing applications, but the general outline of the procedure is similar, as illustrated in figure 5.2.

(a) Registration

On receipt of the application and any fee required, the planning 5.21 authority must send to the applicant a letter of acknowledgement in the prescribed form. This letter acknowledges receipt of the application, but states that examination of it has not been completed and a further communication will be sent if it is discovered to be invalid because statutory or other requirements have not been met. It also advises the applicant of the statutory right to appeal to the Secretary of State if the application has not been determined within two months of the date of receipt of the application as specified in the letter.

The application must comply with the statutory requirements. The correct fee must be included with the application, together with the cost of any advertisement which the applicant is required to pay (see below). The application form is checked to ensure that the appropriate certificates have been signed in connection with notification of owners, agricultural tenants and neighbours. The required number of copies of the application form and associated drawings and plans must be submitted. If the application does not meet any of these requirements, the authority must as soon as possible advise the applicant that the application is invalid. Usually, it will also advise the applicant of the steps necessary to validate the application. For the purposes of a deemed refusal appeal, the date of receipt becomes the date on which the applicant fulfils these requirements.[43]

Once the planning authority is satisfied that a valid application has been submitted the application is registered. The applicant is informed in writing of the registration date and the right to lodge an appeal to the Secretary of State if the planning authority does not decide the application within two months of that date (a deemed refusal appeal). Authorities are required to keep a register of applications for planning permission made to them and to make this register available for inspection by the public at all reasonable hours.[44] This register, commonly referred to as the planning register, must contain copies of every application not finally disposed of, together with copies of any plans and drawings submitted along with the application. Another part of the register details the progress of applications, specifying such matters as

---

[43] DPO, arts 12(6) and 14(3).
[44] TCPSA, s. 36.

the date of receipt, the decision (if any) of the authority on that application and the date of that decision, and the date of any subsequent approval given in relation to the application. Entries in the register must be made within seven days.[45] The register allows members of the public to monitor the submission and determination of applications.

Following registration, the application is allotted to a planning officer who is often named in the registration letter.

(b)   Power to Decline to Determine Application

5.22   Since September 25, 1991 planning authorities have had power to decline to determine an application prior to considering its merits.[46] This power is exercisable if, within the two years prior to submission of the application, the Secretary of State has refused a similar application either on appeal or under a reference to him, and in the opinion of the authority there has been no significant change in the development plan or in any other material considerations since his decision. This is a two-stage process: first, the authority has to decide whether as a matter of fact the application is "similar", and, secondly, whether as a matter of discretion to decline to consider it on its own merits.[47]

Applications are considered "similar" if the proposed development and the site to which the applications relate are the same or substantially similar. If the application has been revised in what appears to be a genuine attempt to take account of objections to an earlier proposal, the Scottish Office guidance states that it should not be regarded as similar. The power should be used only where the authority believes the applicant is intending to exert pressure by submitting repeated similar applications. In doubtful cases the authority should proceed to determine the application.[48]

There is no right of appeal to the Secretary of State against the decision of the planning authority to decline to determine the application in this way. Judicial review of the decision of the authority will be competent, but requires the applicant to show that the exercise of this discretionary power was illegal rather than merely wrong (Chapter 8). Provided all relevant considerations are taken into account, the courts will be unwilling to interfere with the decision made by the authority on what is essentially a factual matter. For example, where a first application concerned an "amusement centre and ancillary retail sales", and the second a reduced area for an "amusement centre/snack bar (with exclusive retail area)", the authority were entitled to have regard to the fact that the second application raised substantially the same planning considerations as the first, including being contrary to the development plan, and to refuse the second application as similar.[49]

---

[45] DPO, art. 10 and Sched. 5, as amended, and art. 11.
[46] TCPSA, s. 39.
[47] *The Noble Organisation v. Falkirk D.C.*, 1994 S.L.T. 100.
[48] Scottish Office Environment Department Circular 22/1991, "Planning and Compensation Act 1991", Annex 2.
[49] *The Noble Organisation v. Falkirk D.C.*, *supra*.

Fig. 5.2   Processing planning application

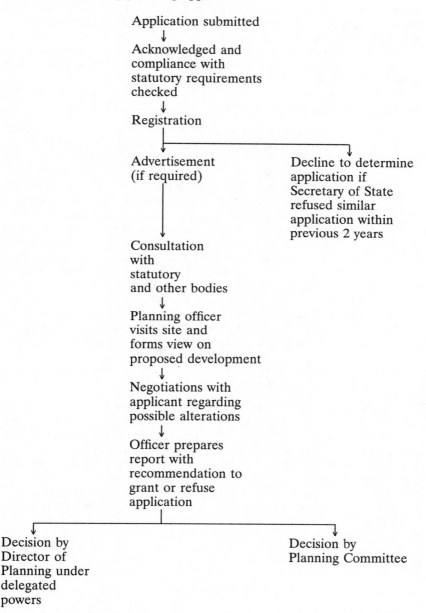

Application submitted
↓
Acknowledged and
compliance with
statutory requirements
checked
↓
Registration

Advertisement
(if required)

Decline to determine
application if
Secretary of State
refused similar
application within
previous 2 years

Consultation
with
statutory
and other bodies
↓
Planning officer
visits site and
forms view on
proposed development
↓
Negotiations with
applicant regarding
possible alterations
↓
Officer prepares
report with
recommendation to
grant or refuse
application

Decision by
Director of
Planning under
delegated
powers

Decision by
Planning Committee

(c)   Advertisement

There are several situations in which an application must be adver-   5.23
tised in a local newspaper. If the applicant certifies that he has been
unable to serve notice on some or all of the owners or agricultural

tenants of the site of the proposed development, he is required to publish an advertisement before submitting the application. Where, in the opinion of the planning authority, the proposed development would affect the character or appearance of a conservation area, or affect the setting of a listed building, the application must be advertised by the planning authority and a site notice displayed for at least seven days.[50]

An application must be advertised in a local newspaper by the planning authority, but at the expense of the applicant where[51]:

(i)   the planning authority has dispensed with the neighbour notification requirement in respect of land separated from the development site by a road up to 20 metres wide, and the applicant has not completed a neighbour notification certificate (as the DPO provides for the applicant to certify that no notification is required, this provision for advertisement if no certificate is completed seems redundant);

(ii)   the applicant seeks permission for one of the specified classes of development known as "bad neighbour development", which are considered to have such a potentially adverse effect on amenity that applications for those developments must be advertised; bad neighbour developments include public conveniences, sewage works, theatres, fun fairs, licensed premises, hot food shops and other specified leisure-related premises[52];

(iii)   the applicant certifies that there are no premises situated on neighbouring land to which neighbour notification can be sent; or

(iv)   an environmental statement is submitted in connection with a planning application (see below).

The applicant is required to pay the cost of this advertisement when submitting the application. The planning authority must publish the advertisement as soon as practicable after receipt of the application.

A single advertisement is sufficient to satisfy the requirements of all or any of the above provisions.[53] Advertisements in relation to ownership notification and conservation areas or listed buildings must state that representations may be made to the planning authority within 21 days.[54] In the other cases, a 14-day period is allowed for representations to be submitted.[55] The planning authority cannot decide the application until the expiry of the appropriate period. Where a site notice is displayed, the application cannot be determined until 21 days after the first date of display.[56]

---

[50] Planning (Listed Buildings and Conservation Areas) (Scotland) Act 1997, ss. 60 and 65.
[51] TCPSA, s. 34 and DPO, arts 12(5) and (8).
[52] App. 2 gives the full list.
[53] DPO, art. 12(7); prescribed form: Sched. 8.
[54] TCPSA, s. 35 and DPO, arts 8(1) and 14(1A) and Sched. 3; PLBCASA, ss. 60 and 65.
[55] DPO, art. 14(1).
[56] PLBCASA, ss. 60 and 65.

If the local authority itself is applying for planning permission, it is required to give notice of its intention in a local newspaper and allow for representations to be made to the authority (Chapter 9).

Before granting planning permission for a development which does not accord with the provisions of the development plan, the planning authority must advertise the application in a local newspaper and allow 21 days for representations (see below).

(d)   Consultation

Before making its decision on the application, the planning authority   5.24
is required to consult various bodies requesting their views on the proposed development.[57] In addition to these statutory consultees, it is open to the planning authority to consult with any body regarding the application, and many authorities have informal consultation processes involving civic amenity groups. Such informal practices may give rise to a legitimate expectation of future consultation (Chapter 8).

The bodies to be consulted vary depending upon the circumstances of each development. A typical development would require consultation with the roads department on access and traffic issues, the environmental health department on issues such as smells or dust, and the water authority on drainage and sewerage provision. Developments in rural areas may require consultation with Scottish Natural Heritage (Chapter 9). The Scottish Environment Protection Agency are consulted on issues such as flood risk, mining operations, sewage treatment and disposal, works to river banks or beds, and waste disposal projects.

The community council within whose area the development is to take place must be consulted if:

(i)   it informs the planning authority that it wishes to be consulted on an application for a development within its area, provided it informs the authority within seven business days from the date of dispatch by the authority to all community councils of the weekly list of applications; or

(ii)   the development is in a class or in an area in respect of which the authority and the community council have agreed in writing that the community council will be consulted; or

(iii)   it appears to the authority that the development is likely to affect the amenity of the area of the community council.[58]

Statutory consultees must be given at least 14 days to comment and the application cannot be determined until the expiry of that period. Any representations from such a body must be taken into account in deciding the application. There is an opt-out provision whereby bodies that require to be consulted can inform the planning authority in writing that consultation will not be required in respect of any case or class of case or in respect of development within a specified area.

---

[57] DPO, art. 15 specifies the bodies.
[58] DPO, art. 15(1)(n); the weekly list is provided for by art. 12(9)—both inserted by S.I. 1996 No. 467. Circular 4/1996 and PAN 47 provide further guidance.

(e) Environmental Assessment

5.25   To comply with Directive 97/11/EC, the United Kingdom law on environmental assessment is to be amended by March·14, 1999. The Scottish Office intend to issue the Environmental Assessment (Scotland) Regulations 1999 to implement the Directive and consolidate the existing law. The principal changes proposed are[59]:

(i) Deciding whether Annex II Projects require environmental assessment (known as "screening")—the proposed 1999 Regulations will introduce a system of lower level criteria above which projects will need to be considered for environmental assessment. If a project listed in Schedule 2 of the proposed 1999 Regulations is to be carried out in a sensitive area (Sites of Special Scientific Interest (SSSIs), proposed SSSIs and Nature Conservation Order sites, World Heritage Sites, scheduled monuments) or falls within the criteria listed in that schedule, environmental assessment will be required where the proposed development would be likely to have significant effects on the environment by virtue inter alia of its nature, size or location. Schedule 3 provides selection criteria to be taken into account in judging whether a project requires environmental assessment.

(ii) The developer can ask the planning authority for a written opinion of the information to be provided in the environmental statement (known as "scoping"), but is not required to do so.

(iii) Environmental statements must include an outline of the main alternative studied by the applicant and an indication of the main reasons for his choice, taking into account the environmental effects.

(iv) Where permission is granted for a development for which there was environmental assessment, the planning authority must publicise the decision and make available for public inspection a statement including the main reasons and consideration on which the decision is based.

(v) For Annex II projects, "urban development projects" will include the construction of shopping centres and car parks, sports stadia, leisure centres and multiplex cinemas, and golf courses will be added as a new class of development.

Other than these changes, the system will remain largely as outlined below.

Unless the application includes an environmental statement, the planning authority must consider whether assessment of the environmental effects of the proposed development is required.[60] Environmental

---

[59] Consultation Paper dated Nov. 20, 1998.
[60] The Environmental Assessment (Scotland) Regulations 1988 (S.I. 1988 No. 1221) as amended by S.I.s 1990 No. 526, 1994 No. 2012 and 1997 No. 1870. Circulars 13/1988, 26/1994 and 25/1997.

assessment (E.A.) is the term used to describe the process of gathering information and reporting on the environmental effects of the proposed development. The result of the process is the submission of an environmental statement which reports on the environmental impact of the proposed development (for this reason it is often referred to as an environmental impact assessment).

There is no prescribed form of environmental statement, but it must include specified information such as a description of the proposed development, comprising information about the site and the design and size or scale of the proposed development. It should report on the likely significant effects of the proposed development, direct and indirect, on human beings, flora, fauna, soil, water, air, climate, the landscape, the interaction between these effects, material assets, and the cultural heritage. Where significant adverse effects are identified, a description must be given of the measures envisaged in order to avoid, reduce or remedy those effects. Consideration may also have to be given to the use of natural resources, the emission of pollutants, the creation of nuisances, and elimination of waste. A non-technical summary must be given.

Environmental assessment is required for every Annex I project, 5.26 including crude-oil refineries, major chemical and steel works, aerodromes with runway lengths over 2,100 metres, and the permanent storage or final disposal of radioactive and other toxic waste.

Annex II projects only require E.A. if the authority considers that the proposed development is likely to give rise to *significant environmental effects*, having taken into account:

(i) whether the project is a major one of more than local importance, especially in terms of size;

(ii) whether the location of the site of the proposed development is sensitive and for that reason may have significant effects on the environment even though the development is on a smaller scale (this falls short of creating an automatic presumption in favour of E.A. for projects in designated areas such as National Scenic Areas, conservation areas and SSSIs (Chapter 9): the determining factor is whether the project is likely to give rise to significant effects on the environment of the area);

(iii) whether the project is thought likely to give rise to particularly complex or adverse effects, for example, in the discharge of pollutants.

The Scottish Office guidance suggests indicative criteria and thresholds for Annex II projects, but reminds authorities that the fundamental test remains the likelihood of significant environmental effects. There is no presumption that E.A. is not required for a development which falls below the threshold, or where there is no threshold. Examples of Annex II projects include large pig- and poultry-rearing units, ore extraction, metal processing, chemical, food, textile or rubber industry, waste disposal sites and urban development projects.

It is always open to the authority to suggest that E.A. be carried out in connection with a project which falls outwith Annexes I and II.

5.27

An applicant for planning permission, or person proposing to exercise rights under the Permitted Development Order (Chapter 4), has the option of requesting an advance ruling from the planning authority on whether E.A. is likely to be required. The authority has four weeks to reach a decision, although this period may be extended with the agreement of the developer. If no opinion is given within this time, the applicant is entitled to assume at that stage the opinion of the planning authority is that E.A. is not required, but the person proposing to exercise permitted development rights has to decide whether to ask the Secretary of State for his direction on the matter. If the authority concludes (timeously) that E.A. will be required but the applicant disagrees, the applicant may apply to the Secretary of State for a direction on whether it is required. This is effectively a right of appeal.

Where an application is submitted with no environmental statement, the planning authority has four weeks to notify the applicant that such a statement is required. If the information accompanying the application differs materially from that available when its opinion was given, the authority can require a statement even although it previously indicated that no E.A. would be required. The applicant has four weeks to indicate his intention to supply an environmental statement or apply to the Secretary of State for a direction that no statement is required, failing which the application is deemed to have been refused four weeks from the date of notification from the planning authority. There is no right of appeal in these circumstances. If the applicant agrees to submit an environmental statement, there is no time limit for submitting the statement and the time limit for a deemed refusal appeal runs from when the statement is supplied.

Where the planning authority has determined that E.A. is required or the Secretary of State has so directed, various public bodies are obliged to make available information to the applicant, including Scottish Natural Heritage, the Health and Safety Executive, and the Scottish Environment Protection Agency. These bodies are notified by the planning authority and a list of their names and addresses given to the applicant. The bodies are only obliged to provide information which is in their possession and are not required to carry out research. Confidential information may be withheld. A reasonable charge may be made for providing the information. A copy of the environmental statement must be sent free of charge to each body.

5.28   Where an application includes an environmental statement, there are additional publicity requirements. The applicant must serve notice on all notifiable neighbours prior to submitting the environmental statement. If the statement is submitted with the application, this may be combined with notification of submission of the application. In addition, the planning authority must advertise submission of the environmental statement in a local newspaper and the *Edinburgh Gazette*, at the expense of the applicant. Both the advertisement and the notice served upon neighbours must state that a copy of the environmental statement is available for public inspection and purchase at a specified address in the locality, specifying the charge (if any), and that there is a four-week period for making representations to the authority in connection with the statement.

Copies of the environmental statement must be submitted to the authority, who must place one copy on the planning register. The planning authority is given 16 weeks to determine the application, rather than the usual eight weeks. It is obliged to consult various bodies including Scottish Natural Heritage, the Health and Safety Executive, the Scottish Environment Protection Agency Authority, and the Secretary of State, allowing them four weeks to lodge representations. It is always open to the authority to request further information from the applicant. The decision on the application must be intimated to the applicant, the Secretary of State, all consultees, and the notifiable neighbours.

As the E.A. process is carried out by the applicant, many objectors to proposed developments cast doubt on the reliability of the information contained in the environmental statement. Planning authorities in appropriate cases may choose to employ an environmental consultant to comment on the environmental statement lodged with the application.

If an appeal is lodged in connection with a planning application which does not include an environmental statement, the Secretary of State may require such a statement to be lodged. The reporter hearing the appeal may apply to the Secretary of State for a direction on the matter.

Any failure to comply with the environmental assessment procedures might form grounds for a petition for judicial review seeking the quashing of a grant of planning permission. For example, the failure to require environmental assessment may be illegal,[61] although information considered during the planning process may be sufficient to overcome the lack of an environmental statement.[62] There is no requirement to give reasons why an environmental assessment was not required.[63]

DECIDING THE APPLICATION

Once the application has been processed, the planning officer normally visits the site and then prepares a report which gives details of the proposed development and its site. It also summarises the representations received, the consultation responses, the relevant provisions of the structure and local plans, and any relevant Scottish Office advice. The report ends with a recommendation of how the application should be decided. Copies of this report must be made available to members of the public, generally three clear days before the relevant committee meeting takes place.[64] The function of the report is to brief the person or persons determining the application and ensure that they are in possession of all the relevant considerations before making a decision. While the report recommends a decision, the decision-maker is not bound to follow the

5.29

---

[61] *Swan v. Secretary of State for Scotland*, 1998 S.C.L.R. 763, SPEL 69:102; *R v. North Yorkshire County Council, ex p. Brown, The Times*, Feb 12, 1999.

[62] *Berkeley v. Secretary of State for the Environment, The Times*, Mar. 2, 1998. Leave has been granted to appeal to the House of Lords.

[63] *R v. Secretary of State for the Environment, ex p. Marson*, [1998] J.P.L. 869.

[64] Local Government (Scotland) Act 1973, s. 50B and E.

recommendation. Any significant error in the report can result in the decision by the committee being invalid.[65]

Once the report has been prepared, the application can be decided. The decision-making process varies between authorities. The Director of Planning may have delegated power to decide classes of application which are considered non-contentious, with all other applications being decided by the councillors who sit on the planning committee of the authority. There are variations on this theme, and for highly contentious applications, the decision may be referred to a meeting of the full authority. Increasingly, authorities are adopting a system of circulating reports to its members in advance of the committee meeting with the direction that unless a member indicates otherwise, the application will not be discussed at the meeting and will be determined in accordance with the recommendation in the report.

It is important to identify which body within the authority will actually determine the application. If the application will be decided by the councillors, it must be considered whether the development proposals are presented in a clear and attractive fashion. The applicant may wish to brief in advance the councillors who will make the decision (not all councillors are receptive to lobbying). If the Director of Planning will make the decision, less care need be taken to avoid the use of technical terms.

What are the factors behind the decision on the application? In making a decision on the application, the authority must not fetter its discretion and each application must be individually decided on its merits. There is a presumption in favour of granting planning permission: unless there are sound planning reasons for refusing permission, it must be granted. When making its decision the authority must take into account the provisions of the development plan, all material considerations and all representations received. The application must be determined in accordance with the provisions of the development plan unless material considerations indicate otherwise (commonly referred to as the "plan-led" system). The authority may refuse planning permission, or grant permission unconditionally or subject to conditions. It may also grant permission for a development in different terms to that proposed by the application.

The decision on the application is an exercise in balancing the competing considerations. The planning authority must take into account all considerations which are both material and relevant to the application and ignore any other matters. A failure to fulfil this duty may result in an illegal decision, unless the same decision would have been reached on other valid reasons.[66] The consideration challenged need not have been the dominant reason for reaching the decision, and provided it was not insubstantial or insignificant there is no requirement to prove

[65] *Campbell v. City of Edinburgh Council*, 1998 G.W.D. 17–877; SPEL 69:99. But see *Lothian Borders & Angus Co-operative Society Ltd v. Scottish Borders Council*, O.H., Dec. 18, 1998, unreported, and *Freeport Leisure v. West Lothian Council*, I.H., Nov. 3, 1988, unreported; 1998 G.W.D. 28–1450 (O.H.).
[66] *R. v. Broadcasting Complaints Commission, ex p. Owen* [1985] Q.B. 1153.

that a different conclusion would have been reached had it not been taken into account.[67] The courts will not interfere with the decision of the planning authority on the weight to be given to each consideration.[68]

Where there is a material change in circumstances in the course of the determination of the application, the authority must take that change into account. This highlights the risk of so-called "minded to grant" decisions, which involve the authority resolving to grant permission once certain outstanding matters, normally execution of a section 75 agreement (Chapter 6), have been resolved. Such a decision gives the applicant no guarantee that permission will be granted. For example, where an authority resolved to grant permission once a section 75 agreement was concluded, it was open to that authority to refuse to enter into the agreement and not grant permission if there was a change of circumstances in the intervening period.[69]

Presumption in Favour of Development

There has always been a presumption in favour of development, deriving from government policy. In other words, the applicant for permission is under no onus to show that permission should be granted. The Scottish Office guidance states that permission should only be refused where there are sound and clearcut reasons for such a refusal even if the proposal is contrary to the development plan.[70] The applicant is not required to prove the case for the proposed development, and the onus is on the planning authority to demonstrate clearly why the development cannot be permitted.

This presumption arises from the historical background to the planning system. When the requirement for planning permission was introduced nationally in 1947, it removed the rights of landowners to do as they pleased on their land and forced them to apply to the State for permission to develop their land. It would have been draconian to require them further to demonstrate why they should be allowed to develop their land in a particular way. As a result, it has always been government policy that the State's control over development should only be exercised to prevent development where it can show good planning reasons for refusing permission.

To some extent this presumption has been modified by the introduction of the plan-led system (see below), becoming a presumption in favour of development which accords with the provisions of the development plan. However, the force of the presumption will still apply.

Development Plan

When determining a planning application the planning authority must have regard to the provisions of the development plan (Chapter 3). Following the shift to the plan-led system on March 7, 1994 when the

5.30

5.31

---

[67] *Simplex v. Secretary of State for the Environment* [1988] 3 P.L.R. 25.
[68] *Seddon Properties v. Secretary of State for the Environment* [1978] J.P.L. 835.
[69] *John G. Russell (Transport) Ltd v. Strathkelvin D.C.*, 1992 S.L.T. 1001.
[70] Circular 17/1985, "Development Control—Priorities and Procedures", para. 3; NPPG 1, "The Planning System", para. 44.

relevant provisions of the Planning and Compensation Act 1991 were brought into force, the determination requires to be made in accordance with the provisions of the development plan unless material considerations indicate otherwise.[71] This creates a presumption in favour of development proposals which are in accordance with the provisions of the development plan.

Although these provisions impose a presumption in favour of the development plan, this does not amount to a requirement that the authority decide all applications according to the terms of the plan. The authority has to decide in light of the whole plan whether the proposal accords with it, and then if there are material considerations of such weight as to indicate that the plan should not be accorded priority. The House of Lords have stated that the assessment of the facts and the weighing of the considerations remains in the hands of the decision-maker. The assessment of the considerations can only be challenged on the ground that it is irrational or perverse.[72] The law does not require a material consideration to have any special weight to overcome the presumption in favour of the development plan.[73] The material consideration must however be identified in the decision.[74]

The House of Lords' decision indicates the following approach[75]:

- The decision-maker must consider the development plan, identify any provisions in it which are relevant to the question before him and make a proper interpretation of them. His decision will be open to challenge if he fails to have regard to a policy in the development plan which is relevant to the application or fails properly to interpret it.
- He will also have to consider whether the development proposed in the application before him does or does not accord with the development plan. There may be some points in the plan which support the proposal but there may be some considerations pointing in the opposite direction. He will require to assess all of these and then decide whether in light of the whole plan the proposal does or does not accord with it.
- He will also have to identify all the other material considerations which are relevant to the application and to which he should have regard. He will then have to note which of them support the application and which of them do not, and he will have to assess the weight to be given to all of these considerations. He will have to decide whether there are considerations of such weight as to indicate that the development plan should not be accorded the priority which the statute has given to it.
- Having weighed these considerations and determined these matters he will require to form his opinion on the disposal of the application.

---

[71] TCPSA, ss. 25 and 37.
[72] *City of Edinburgh Council v. Secretary of State for Scotland*, 1998 S.L.T. 120.
[73] *St. Albans D.C. v. Secretary of State for the Environment* [1993] J.P.L. 370.
[74] *Perth and Kinross Council v. Secretary of State for Scotland*, 1998 G.W.D. 38–1976.
[75] *City of Edinburgh Council, supra.*, Lord Clyde at p. 127G–L.

- If he fails to take account of some material consideration or takes account of some consideration which is irrelevant to the application, his decision will be open to challenge. But the assessment of the considerations can only be challenged on the ground that it is irrational or perverse.
- It is undesirable to devise any universal prescription for the method to be adopted by the decision-maker. Different cases will invite different methods. It should be left to the good sense of the decision-maker, acting within his powers, to decide how to go about the task before him in the particular circumstances of each case.

Some importance thus now attaches to the decision whether the proposed development accords with the development plan.[76] This issue is discussed further in Chapter 3.

The Scottish Office advice is that determinations should depart from the provisions of relevant and up-to-date development plans only if there are compelling reasons.[77] Where plans become less relevant through the passage of time, there may be good reason for departing from the provisions of those plans. Changes in government policy may also make parts of a plan obsolete. The advice also cautions that the provisions of the plan are also an important factor in the award of expenses in appeals (Chapter 8).   5.32

The person challenging the decision has the onus of proving that section 25 has not been followed.[78] The courts have been unwilling to require decision-makers to follow the rigid pre-set formalistic order of approach taken by section 25.[79] It is not essential for the report to committee or reporter's decision letter to mention section 25 if examination of the report/letter shows that the conclusion was reached in a manner consistent with the provisions of that section.[80] Defects of presentation in the report to committee will not result in the decision on the application being quashed unless the overall effect of the report is significantly misleading.[81] If the report appears to give an incorrect view on the legal provisions, such that there is a real risk of the committee being misled as to the correct approach, their decision may be invalid.[82]

The presumption in favour of the development plan highlights the importance of making representations during the process of replacement or renewal of development plans (Chapter 3) in an attempt to ensure that the new or revised plan contains provisions favourable to envisaged development proposals or does not promote development detrimental to

---

[76] *e.g. Stirling D.C. v. Carvill (Scotland) Ltd*, 1996 S.C.L.R. 265.

[77] NPPG 1, "The Planning System", para 44.

[78] *McDonald v. Moray Council*, 1998 G.W.D. 16–819, SPEL 69:101.

[79] Lord Clyde in *City of Edinburgh Council, supra*; *Budgens Stores Ltd v. Secretary of State for the Environment* [1998] E.G.C.S. 28; *North Yorkshire County Council v. Secretary of State for the Environment*, [1996] J.P.L. 32.

[80] *Newham LBC v. Secretary of State for the Environment* (1995) 70 P. & C.R. 288.

[81] *Lothian Borders & Angus Co-operative Society Ltd v. Scottish Borders Council, supra*; *Freeport Leisure v. West Lothian Council, supra*; *R. v. Selby D.C. ex p. Oxton Farms* [1997] E.G.C.S. 60.

[82] *Campbell v. City of Edinburgh Council*, 1998 G.W.D. 17–877, SEPL 69:99.

the interest of a landowner or developer. Once a provision is enshrined in an adopted development plan it will be difficult to overcome.

The importance of development plans to the determination of planning applications is underlined by the requirement for notification and advertisement of applications contrary to provisions of development plans for which planning authorities propose to grant permission.

Other Material Considerations

5.33   In addition to the terms of the development plan, the planning authority must also take into account all other material considerations when determining an application. These considerations provide the grounds for the reasons both for granting/refusing to grant planning permission and for objecting to planning applications. It is, therefore, not surprising that what amounts to a material consideration is one of the most debated topics in planning law.

No definition of "material considerations" is provided by the legislation. As the power to determine an application for planning permission is vested in the planning authority by the TCPSA, to be material a consideration must be a planning consideration. There are many theories of planning (Chapter 1) and therefore many different answers to the question: What is "planning"? Case law is continually identifying new examples of planning considerations. Although this leads to uncertainty, it gives planning authorities a necessary degree of flexibility in the matters which they may take into account when deciding an application.

Broadly, any consideration which relates to the use and development of land is capable of being a material planning consideration.[83] The courts have provided more specific guidance, but only on a case-by-case basis. Court decisions make it possible to state whether or not certain matters are planning considerations, but do not give a general indication of what may amount to a material planning consideration.

Many of the material considerations discussed below contribute directly towards the general objective of sustainable development, which has been defined as "development that meets the needs of the present without compromising the ability of future generations to meet their own needs".[84] The objective of sustainable development can be assisted by the planning system encouraging development and investment in ways which will also help to conserve the quality of the environment for the future.[85] The NPPGs issued by the Scottish Office contain guidance on how the planning system can help to secure the objectives of sustainable development.

Specific examples of material considerations are now considered. The list is not exhaustive.

---

[83] *Per* Cooke J. in *Stringer v. Minister for Housing* [1971] All E.R. 65.
[84] Brundtland Commission 1987. The Environment Act 1995 and the Natural Heritage (Scotland) Act 1991 refer to sustainable development and sustainability, but provide no definition. The U.K. policy is contained in "Sustainable Development: The U.K. Strategy", Cm. 2426, 1994 and subsequent papers.
[85] NPPG1, "The Planning System", para 7; "Sustainable Development: The UK Strategy", Chap. 35.

(a) Suitability of Site

The suitability of the site for the proposed development is one of the 5.34
main material considerations. Instability as a result of mine workings
(the Coal Authority is a statutory consultee in areas of coal working),
tipping, or liability to flooding,[86] may make sites unsuitable for certain
types of development. Any potential contamination of the site is relevant
and authorities will require investigation of likely contaminated sites
prior to development.[87]

*(b) Appearance of the Proposed Development and its Relationship to its
Surroundings*

The decision on the application necessarily involves consideration of 5.35
the appearance of the proposed development and its relationship to its
surroundings. Relevant matters include the materials to be used; the
height, scale, massing, layout and density, in comparison to buildings in
the surrounding area; landscaping; privacy, both for surrounding properties and the occupiers or users of the proposed development; over-
shadowing; lack of natural light; noise, smell and fumes; and glare from
floodlights or headlights of vehicles.

A controversial issue is the extent to which planning authorities can
consider the design of a proposed building, which is a highly subjective
matter. The external appearance of a building can have a significant
effect on the character of an area, but architects complain that too often
planning authorities take a restrictive, conservative view towards innova-
tive design.[88]

(c) Impact

The impact of the proposed development upon the surrounding area 5.36
must be evaluated. Regard must be had to the desirability of preserving
the setting of a listed building, and of preserving or enhancing the
character and appearance of a conservation area or national scenic area
(Chapter 9). Any general loss of amenity or privacy, increases in noise
level[89] and volume of traffic, questions of safety and other potential
social costs must be considered.[90] The impact of the development on
private individuals must also be considered. For example, there may be a
resultant loss of privacy, sunlight or amenity suffered by neighbouring
proprietors, whether or not these proprietors are notifiable neighbours.
Thus material considerations may be either the public or private
interests of both the applicant and objectors.[91]

In dismissing an appeal for a major toxic-waste plant in England, the
Secretary of State took into account the deleterious effect on local

---

[86] NPPG7, "Planning and Flooding".
[87] SDD PAN 33, "Development of Contaminated Land".
[88] NPPG1, "The Planning System", paras 70–73 provide advice.
[89] Charlton Smith, "Noise Law : Planning and Construction", SPEL 63:98 and 64:120.
[90] *per* Lord Denning in *Esdell Caravan Park v. Hemel Hempstead Rural D.C.* [1965] 3 All
E.R. 737 at p. 743F.
[91] *City of Glasgow D.C. v. Secretary of State for Scotland and Bank of Scotland*, 1993
S.L.T. 1332, S.P.L.P. 38:21.

employment, investment and industry, and public fears of long-term effects on health, although the major determining factor was potential pollution of the underground acquifer.[92]

The development may result in pollution or contamination (see paragraph (m) below). Local flooding likely to be caused by the development is relevant.[93]

Justified public concern in the locality about emanations from the land as a result of its proposed development can be a material consideration. The fear and concern felt by occupants of neighbouring land was as real in relation to a proposed extension to a bail hostel as in a case involving polluting discharges, and as relevant to the reasonable use of the land.[94] In considering a claim for expenses as a part of an appeal, it was an error of law to approach the question of whether the planning authority had behaved unreasonably on the basis that genuine fears on the part of the public, unless objectively justified, could never amount to a valid ground for refusal.[95] It therefore appears that public concerns, even if not justified on scientific or other grounds, can still be a material consideration which could be used as a reason for refusing planning permission.

Even if planning permission is granted, this does not give immunity from a claim of nuisance brought by persons affected by the development.[96]

(d) Compatibility with Existing Uses

5.37   In addition to its general impact on the surrounding area, the compatibility of the proposed development with existing uses is a material consideration.[97] In one case, the effect of dust created by a proposed concrete plant on neighbouring factories manufacturing precision products and requiring clean air was a relevant factor.[98] Alternatively, existing uses may be incompatible with proposed developments such as a proposed housing development on land neighbouring an explosives factory. However, it may be proper for a planning authority to wish to encourage residential development in an area of existing industrial users.[99] While planning powers should not be used to protect commercial interests, it may be relevant to consider the degree to which the opening of a shopping centre might lead to the decay of existing centres.[1] The desirability of preserving a balance of uses may also be a material consideration.

---

[92] APP/F4410/A/89/126733 (Doncaster Incinerator Appeal).
[93] NPPG 7, "Planning and Flooding"; *W. E. Black v. Secretary of State for the Environment, The Times,* Nov. 27, 1995.
[94] *West Midlands Probation Committee v. Secretary of State for the Environment* [1998] J.P.L. 388.
[95] *Newport County B.C. v. Secretary of State for Wales* [1998] J.P.L. 377.
[96] *Wheeler v. Saunders* [1995] 2 All E.R. 697. For further information on nuisance, see Smith, Collar and Poustie, *Pollution Control: The Law of Scotland,* Chaps 2 and 10.
[97] *Collis Radio v. Secretary of State for the Environment* (1975) 29 P. & C.R. 390.
[98] *RMC Management Services v. Secretary of State for the Environment* (1972) 222 E.G. 1593.
[99] *R. v. Exeter C.C., ex p. Thomas* [1990] J.P.L. 129.
[1] *R. v. Doncaster Metropolitan District, ex p. British Railways Board* [1987] J.P.L. 444; Revised NPPG8, "Town Centres and Retailing".

It will be important to assess the degree of incompatibility. A proposed waste transfer facility was refused on the grounds that any malodorous emissions could prejudice the operation of an adjacent factory manufacturing cocoa products. This decision was quashed by the court on the grounds that no effort had been made to estimate the likely frequency of the worst case scenario, and there was no evidence that a tainting incident would sooner or later be likely to occur.[2]

A grant of planning permission for an incompatible development will not give the developer immunity from a claim of nuisance. A grant of planning permission for intensification of pig farming did not give immunity from liability in nuisance to neighbouring landowners in respect of smells inevitably caused by implementation of the permission.[3]

(e) Desirability of Retaining the Existing Use

The existing use of the site is a material consideration, such as the continuation of industrial uses which are important to the character and functioning of a city.[4] It may be desirable to continue an existing residential use in an area where there is a shortage of housing.[5] This ground would require evidence of a reasonable probability that a refusal of permission would result in the continuance of the existing use. Alternative permitted uses of the site must also be considered. The planning authority is not bound to apply a competing needs test of desirability of preserving the existing use versus the merits of the proposed new use, as this would override the presumption in favour of planning permission (see above).[6]   5.38

(f) Existence of a Better Alternative Site

The existence of a better site for the proposed development may be a material consideration as a result of characteristics of either the proposed development or its site, including whether the adverse effects of the proposed development might have a reduced impact on a specified alternative site.[7] The criteria for the materiality of the relative merits of the application site and other sites have been expressed as: the presence of a clear public convenience or advantage in the proposal under consideration; the existence of inevitable and adverse effects or disadvantages to the public, or to some section of the public, in the proposal; the existence of an alternative site for the same project which would not have those effects, or would not have them to the same extent; and a situation in which there could only be one permission granted for such a development, or at least only a very limited number of permissions. These criteria were satisfied where there were several applications for service areas along a stretch of trunk road.[8]   5.39

---

[2] *Envirocor Waste Holdings v. Secretary of State for the Environment* [1996] J.P.L. 489.
[3] *Wheeler v. Saunders, supra.*
[4] *Westminster C.C. v. Great Portland Estates* [1985] A.C. 661.
[5] *Clyde & Co. v. Secretary of State for the Environment* [1977] 1 W.L.R. 926.
[6] *London Residuary Body v. Lambeth LBC* [1990] 2 All E.R. 309.
[7] *Ynystawe, Ynforgan & Glair Gipsy Site Action Group v. Secretary of State for Wales* [1981] J.P.L. 874.
[8] *Secretary of State for the Environment v. Edwards* [1994] 1 P.L.R. 62.

If the existence of alternative sites is relevant, the planning authority is not required to determine which site is better, but only to consider the other site as an alternative.[9] Where the development on the proposed site is acceptable, planning permission should not be refused on the grounds that it would be more acceptable on an alternative site, with the possible exception of competing applications for the same development, but on different sites, in circumstances where permission can be granted for one development only.[10] If the site of the proposed development is unsuitable, the applicant may be required to demonstrate the need for the proposed development on that site. A decision that there was a strong possibility that another site would be available that would cause less harm than the current proposal was quashed where there was no evidence regarding any alternative sites.[11]

(g) Financial Viability

5.40   The cost of the proposed development is not a material consideration in itself.[12] Assessment of the financial viability of the proposed development is best carried out by the developer and most planning authorities do not have the expertise to make such an assessment. However, the planning consequences of the financial viability of the proposal can be considered.[13] Lack of financial viability results in some developments being abandoned before completion, sterilising the site against future development and leaving the authority with the problem of how the site should be managed.

There may be assertions by the applicant that no other form of development is financially viable on the site and that as a result, permission should be granted for the proposed development. Securing the retention and use of existing buildings, especially listed buildings (Chapter 9), may require the authority to permit economically viable development notwithstanding that the proposed development is not wholly appropriate.

(h) Planning Benefits

5.41   Planning benefits are used by applicants to "sweeten the pill" by offsetting the planning disadvantages of the proposed development. Such benefits may arise from the terms of the application or provisions of a planning agreement entered into between the applicant and the authority (Chapter 6). If the benefits do not amount to material considerations, the authority must ignore them when determining the application.

The law regarding the extent to which planning benefits are permissible, and therefore become material considerations, has been settled by

[9] *R. v. Royal County of Berkshire, ex p. Mangnall* [1985] J.P.L. 258.
[10] *Trusthouse Forte v. Secretary of State for the Environment* (1986) 53 P. & C.R. 293; [1986] 2 E.G.L.R. 185; *GLC v. Secretary of State for the Environment* [1986] J.P.L. 193.
[11] *Beech v. Secretary of State for the Environment* [1993] E.G.C.S. 214.
[12] *J. Murphy & Sons v. Secretary of State for the Environment* [1973] 1 W.L.R. 560; 2 All E.R. 26.
[13] *Per* Woolf J. in *Sosmo Trust v. Secretary of State for the Environment* [1983] J.P.L. 806.

the decision of the House of Lords in the *Tesco* case.[14] Their Lordships held that a benefit which has nothing to do with the development will plainly not be a material consideration. If the benefit has some connection, then regard must be had to it. The extent to which it should affect the decision is a matter entirely within the discretion of the decision-maker. In exercising that discretion, he is entitled to have regard to his established policy.[15] This decision draws a clear distinction between the question of whether something is a material consideration and the weight which it should be given: the former is a question of law, and the latter is a question of planning judgment which is entirely a matter for the planning authority.

The House of Lords also upheld the decision in the *Plymouth* case[16] that the legal validity of taking into account an offer of a planning benefit did not depend on the benefit being necessary to overcome what would otherwise be planning objections to the proposed development, although such a test could be applied as a matter of policy. Lord Hoffmann also rejected the proposition that a planning agreement must have the effect of making acceptable what would otherwise have been unacceptable. In his view, this was indistinguishable from the test of necessity rejected in the *Plymouth* case.

The consequence of the *Tesco* decision is that the courts cannot intervene in cases where there is sufficient connection between the development and the planning benefit to make it a material consideration, but the benefit appears disproportionate to the external costs of the development.

To form a material consideration, the benefits must have a planning purpose and fairly and reasonably relate to the proposed development. It is not necessary for the benefits to be required to overcome, remedy or alleviate planning objections to the proposed development. There must be a clear and direct nexus or a recognised and real relationship between the benefit and the proposed development. This nexus or relationship may be geographic, functional or financial.[17] A reasonable prospect of the benefit arising is sufficient and there is no requirement that the benefit be guaranteed, for example, through a planning agreement.[18] In determining an application for a sports facility at one site, it was a material consideration that the grant of permission would enable redevelopment of another site. The consequent benefits to the conservation area of this redevelopment outweighed the harm to important conservation interests at the site of the new sports facility.[19] In contrast, traffic management measures to be financed by the applicant were not a material consideration because there was no direct nexus between the proposed superstore and the improvements where these measures were

5.42

---

[14] *Tesco Stores Ltd v. Secretary of State for the Environment* [1995] J.P.L. 581.

[15] *R. v. South Northamptonshire D.C., ex p. Crest Homes* [1994] 3 P.L.R. 47. The Scottish Office policy is in SDD Circular 12/1996, discussed in Chap. 6.

[16] *R. v. Plymouth C.C., ex p. Plymouth and South Devon Co-operative Society Ltd* [1993] E.G.C.S. 113.

[17] *Northumberland C.C. v. Secretary of State for the Environment* [1989] J.P.L. 700.

[18] *Crawley B.C. v. Secretary of State for the Environment* [1993] J.P.L. 148.

[19] *Wansdyke D.C. v. Secretary of State for the Environment* [1992] J.P.L. 1168.

aimed at problems already in existence.[20] Offers of community benefits such as provision of a tourist information centre, a bird-watching hide and a static art feature were upheld as a material consideration in the determination of an application for a superstore development.[21]

In the *Tesco* case, as part of its superstore application Tesco had offered to pay for a new link road required to resolve traffic problems in the town centre. The Secretary of State did not consider that the road was needed to enable the store proposal to go ahead, or was otherwise so directly related to the proposed development that the store ought to be permitted without it. The offer of funding therefore failed to comply with the provisions of the government guidance. The extent to which he would take it into account would be of such a limited nature that it would not tip the balance of the arguments. Tesco appealed on the ground that by discounting the funding offer the Secretary of State had failed to take into account a material consideration. This was rejected by the House of Lords, who held that, far from dismissing Tesco's offer as immaterial, the Secretary of State had carefully weighed up its significance. His decision was not therefore open to challenge.

5.43   Policies contained in development plans seeking community benefits from applicants do not automatically render the offer (or lack of an offer) of such benefits material considerations. Benefits sought by the authority in planning conditions or agreements must be imposed for a planning purpose, be fairly and reasonably related to the proposed development, and not so unreasonable that no reasonable authority could have imposed them (Chapter 6).

The proposed development may be presented as enabling other more worthy development to proceed. The profits of the substantial office development included in the scheme for the redevelopment of the Royal Opera House, London, were to be applied to improve the Opera House and it was competent for the planning authority to take this consideration into account when granting permission contrary to the provisions of the development plan.[22] This concept of enabling development is still evolving and it is uncertain what degree, if any, of functional, geographical or physical relationship is required.

Applications for housing or other highly profitable development frequently include proposals attractive to planning authorities such as renovation of listed buildings or relocation of football grounds to modern purpose-built stadia, with the applicant stating that the more attractive element of the proposed development cannot proceed without the funds generated from the housing development.[23] If this economic or planning benefit is a material consideration, the authority must consider whether the benefit is sufficient to justify granting permission. In most

---

[20] *Safeway v. Secretary of State for the Environment* [1990] J.P.L. 759, but see *Tesco v. Secretary of State for the Environment, supra.*

[21] *R. v. Plymouth C.C., ex p. Plymouth and South Devon Co-operative Society Ltd, supra.*

[22] *R. v. Westminster C.C., ex p. Monahan* [1989] J.P.L. 107.

[23] *Brighton B.C. v. Secretary of State for the Environment* [1979] J.P.L. 173; *South Oxfordshire D.C. v. Secretary of State for the Environment* (1994) 68 P. & C.R. 551; *Worsted Investments Ltd v. Secretary of State for the Environment* [1994] E.G.C.S. 66.

cases, the applicant will require to demonstrate that there is no source for securing these benefits other than the enabling development.

(i) Economic Benefits

Economic benefits arising from the proposed development can be a material consideration.[24] It is common for applicants to point to the number of jobs which will be created if the development goes ahead. It was a material consideration that a proposed retail development would finance the relocation of a factory, safeguarding jobs which might otherwise be threatened.[25]

5.44

(j) Social Considerations

There is a social dimension to planning (Chapter 1) and some of the material considerations identified above have social elements. In so far as social considerations can be subsumed into planning considerations, these considerations will be material. In one case, the need for a period of social stability and consolidation was a good reason for refusing permission.[26] Many development plans contain policies on low-cost or affordable housing. The need for housing in a particular area is a material consideration. No sensible distinction can be drawn between a need for housing generally and a need for particular types of housing, whether or not the latter could be defined in terms of cost, tenure or otherwise. In each case the question is whether, as a matter of planning for the area under consideration, there is a need for housing which the grant or refusal of the application will affect.[27] Planning conditions requiring proportions of housing developments to be allocated to meet local authority housing needs were held to be illegal.[28]

5.45

(k) Provision of Suitable Access and Transportation

The transportation aspects of the proposed development must be taken into account.[29] If the development involves forming or altering an access to a road, or is likely to cause a material increase in the volume of traffic entering or leaving the road, the planning authority must consult the roads authority about the proposed development and take their comments into account when the application is determined (the Secretary of State is consulted if the road is a trunk road).[30] The roads authority may advise that the access from the development to the road is unsatisfactory or unsuitable, perhaps due to the dangers of turning traffic, or insufficient visibility and no possibility of visibility splays being

5.46

---

[24] *Northumberland C.C. v. Secretary of State for the Environment, supra.*
[25] *R. v. Kingston upon Hull C.C., ex p. Kingswood Development Co. Ltd* [1996] E.G.C.S. 200.
[26] *Severn Trent Water Authority v. Secretary of State for the Environment* [1989] J.P.L. 21.
[27] *Mitchell v. Secretary of State for the Environment* [1994] 2 P.L.R. 23.
[28] *R. v. Hillingdon B.C., ex p. Royco Homes* [1974] 2 All E.R. 643; *David Lowe & Sons v. Musselburgh Town Council,* 1973 S.C. 130.
[29] Draft NPPG and PAN "Transport and Planning".
[30] DPO, art. 15.

provided to preserve visibility for vehicles using the access, or the unsuitability of the road for the traffic generated by the development, or insufficient parking provision.

The planning authority is not bound to follow the advice offered by the roads authority.[31] In many cases, the roads authority response is dictated by adopted policies and the planning authority may consider that the policy is not appropriate in the circumstances of the particular development (following local government re-organisation, the same council is now both planning and roads authority, so this approach is unlikely, but can occur where the Secretary of State is the decision-maker).

(l) Sewerage, Drainage and Water

5.47   There must be provision for proper disposal of surface water and sewerage, and an adequate supply of water for the development. Permission can be refused because of inadequacies of the existing public sewers.[32] Overcapacity in the drainage system is sometimes cited as a reason for refusing planning permission. The planning authority cannot allow a policy of the sewerage authority, imposing a total embargo on further sea discharges, to dictate its decision on a planning application, although this would be a relevant factor to be taken into account when determining the application.[33]

(m) Pollution and Contamination

5.48   The likelihood of pollution as a result of the proposed development appears to be a material consideration, irrespective of the existence of other statutory powers such as integrated pollution control (IPC) under the Environmental Protection Act 1990 (EPA).[34] Public concerns, even if not justified on scientific or other grounds, may be a material consideration (see paragraph (c) above).

Noise and odour have always been important planning issues, but it seems that planning authorities should now be taking into account pollution of any type. The environmental impact of emissions to the atmosphere is a material consideration, as is the existence of the statutory pollution control regime. There will come a point when the authority is entitled to be satisfied that, having had regard to the existence of EPA controls, residual concerns over pollution matters should not constitute a reason for refusal of planning permission.[35]

Planning authorities are required to ensure that waste is recovered or disposed of without endangering human health or harming the environment.[36]

---

[31] *Castle Rock Housing Association v. Secretary of State for Scotland*, 1995 S.C.L.R. 850.
[32] *George Wimpey & Co. Ltd v. Secretary of State for the Environment* [1978] J.P.L. 773.
[33] *Ynys Mon B.C. v. Secretary of State for Wales* [1993] J.P.L. 225.
[34] Collar, "Planning, Pollution Control and Waste Management", SPEL 56:67.
[35] *Gateshead MBC v. Secretary of State for the Environment* [1994] 1 P.L.R. 85; *R. v. Bolton MBC, ex p. Kirkham* (1998) 276 E.N.D.S. 52.
[36] Waste Management Licensing Regulations 1994, reg. 19 and sched. 4.

Contamination, or the potential for it, is a material consideration.[37] Contamination may give rise to hazards, for example putting at risk people working on, or in the immediate vicinity of, the site, or affecting structural durability. It may be possible to use the planning benefit of cleaning up contaminated land to justify the grant of permission for development which would not otherwise be permitted (see Planning Benefit above).

The contents of any environmental statement submitted in association with the application must be taken into account (see below).

A planning application cannot be determined on the basis of the worst case scenario without first conducting a risk assessment exercise to determine the likelihood of that situation occurring. An appeal decision was quashed because there was no evidence that a tainting incident would sooner or later be likely to occur. The inspector who determined the appeal was held to have made no effort to estimate the likely frequency of the worst case scenario.[38]

Scottish Office policy provides guidance on how planning authorities should deal with the overlap between planning, pollution control and waste management powers.[39] In general the planning system should focus on whether the development itself is an acceptable use of the land, rather than control the process or substances involved; it should regulate the location of the development and the control of operations in order to avoid or minimise adverse effects on the use of land and on the environment; and it should secure restoration to a condition capable of the agreed after-use.[40]

Planning decisions will also have to have regard to the air quality objectives to be achieved by local authorities within their area.[41] The planning system is expected to contribute by guiding the location of new development, reducing the need to travel and promoting choice in transport. Where the objectives are unlikely to be met by December 31, 2005, the local authority concerned must designate Air Quality Management Areas (AQMA) and prepare action plans. The designation of an AQMA may have implications for planning decisions. For example, development of a site allocated in the local plan for housing which subsequently falls within an AQMA might have to be reconsidered. In contrast, a superstore development in Bath was granted permission on the grounds that air quality would not suffer because traffic would be cut elsewhere.[42]

(n)   Archaeology

The effects of the proposed development on archaeological remains   5.49
and their setting is a material consideration. Where the physical preservation *in situ* of the remains is not justified in the circumstances,

---

[37] SDD PAN 33, "Development of Contaminated Land".
[38] *Envirocor Waste Holdings v. Secretary of State for the Environment*, above n. 2.
[39] NPPG 10, "Planning and Waste Management", PAN 51, "Planning and Environmental Protection"; Draft Circular "Land Use Planning and Electro-Magnetic Fields".
[40] NPPG 10, para. 16.
[41] Environment Act 1995, Pt IV and Air Quality Regulations 1997 (S.I. 1997 No. 3043). Scottish Office Consultation Paper "Air Quality and Land Use Planning" Jan. 1997.
[42] "A breath of fresh air", *Estates Gazette*, Dec. 13, 1997.

and the development will result in the destruction of the remains, the planning authority should satisfy itself before granting permission that the developer has made appropriate and satisfactory provision for the excavation and recording of the remains.[43]

(o) Nature Conservation

5.50   In determining an application for planning permission, the authority must have regard to the desirability of conserving Scotland's flora and fauna, geological and physiographic features, and its natural beauty and amenity. The authority also has a duty to ensure that adequate provision is made for the preservation or planting of trees. Nature conservation (natural heritage) is discussed further in Chapter 9.

(p) Need

5.51   To require the landowner to show the need for a proposed development is excessive interference with rights of ownership. This is the basis for the presumption in favour of granting planning permission, now modified by the presumption in favour of development in accordance with the terms of the development plan. The need for the development only requires to be demonstrated if its detrimental effects are such that an overriding need must be shown. Thus an overriding need may require to be demonstrated for particular types of development or development in particular locations, such as in the Green Belt (Chapter 9), or where there is a better alternative site (see above).

In the same way, lack of need is not a valid reason in itself for refusing permission, unless the lack of need is relevant because of the detrimental effects of the development.[44]

(q) Creation of an Undesirable Precedent

5.52   Planning authorities are not obliged to follow their previous decisions on similar applications. However, consistency in decision-making is desirable and it is a material consideration that granting permission for the proposed development might set a precedent making it difficult for similar applications to be refused in the future.[45] A generalised concern is insufficient and there must be some evidence for this view.[46] However, it has been held that this principle should not be applied too narrowly, and that unless an inspector's reliance on the existence of an outstanding appeal in the area was in some way perverse, his finding that the present proposal would trigger similar proposals and seriously weaken the council's ability to enforce the local plan policy, was not capable of successful challenge.[47]

---

[43] Scottish Office Environment Department NPPG 5, "Archaeology and Planning", and PAN 42, "Archaeology—The Planning Process".
[44] *R. v. Hambleton D.C., ex p. Somerfield Stores Ltd* [1998] E.G.C.S. 155.
[45] *Collis Radio v. Secretary of State for the Environment, supra.*
[46] *Poundstretcher v. Secretary of State for the Environment* [1988] 3 P.L.R. 69.
[47] *Woolwich Building Society v. Secretary of State for the Environment* [1995] E.G.C.S. 114.

(r) Planning History of the Site

It is relevant to consider what development can be carried out on the 5.53
site in terms of existing permissions or by exercising permitted development rights under the PDO or UCO (Chapter 4). Grants of planning
permission for similar developments on the same site may be used to
show that the authority have conceded the principle of development of
the site.

Where an existing permission is cited as a fall back position, it is a
material consideration, and there is no general rule requiring it to be
shown that it is more likely than not that the development authorised by
that permission will ever proceed.[48]

Previous planning decisions in respect of the site cannot be followed
slavishly[49] and each application must be decided upon its merits. As a
result, there may be several grants of permission for one site which are
mutually inconsistent and conflicting.[50] Multiple implementation of
permissions in such circumstances may be problematic (see below).

Where there are two different decisions on identical applications, the
second decision is not necessarily irrational. Provided the planning
authority act rationally and take into account all material considerations,
they are not bound by their previous decisions.[51]

(s) Duplicate Applications

The outcome of an appeal may be a material consideration for the 5.54
planning authority in determining a duplicate application for the same or
a similar development. Depending upon the stage reached in the appeal
proceedings, the authority may be obliged either to delay deciding the
application until the appeal decision has been received and can be taken
into account, or to reject the application as premature. For example,
where a public local inquiry had been held and the reporter's decision
was awaited, it was unreasonable for the planning authority to grant
permission for a duplicate application as the outcome of the appeal had
become a material consideration to which the authority had to have
regard when it considered the application.[52] The stage reached in the
appeal proceedings is not conclusive.[53]

It may be competent for the planning authority to decide that the
second application is materially different from the first, and that
the outcome of the appeal is not a material consideration which they
ought to await.[54]

---

[48] *New Forest D.C. v. Secretary of State for the Environment* [1996] J.P.L. 935.
[49] *North Wiltshire D.C. v. Secretary of State for the Environment* [1992] J.P.L. 955;
Standard Securities Estates v. Secretary of State for the Environment [1992] E.G.C.S. 129;
Palm Developments Ltd v. Secretary of State for the Environment [1997] E.G.C.S. 173.
[50] *Pilkington v. Secretary of State for the Environment* [1973] 1 W.L.R. 1527 *per* Widgery
C.J. at p. 1531.
[51] *R. v. Aylesbury Vale D.C., ex p. Chaplin* [1996] E.G.C.S. 126.
[52] *Trusthouse Forte v. Perth & Kinross District Council*, 1990 S.L.T. 737.
[53] *Pickering v. Kyle & Carrick D.C.*, 1991 G.W.D. 7–361.
[54] *Henderson v. Argyll and Bute Council*, 1998 S.C.L.R. 1; SPEL 64:126.

(t)   Decisions on Similar Proposals in Respect of Other Sites

5.55   There is no concept of binding precedents in the planning system
whereby an authority might be obliged to follow the same approach
taken in a previous decision. Each application must be decided upon its
individual merits. However, previous decisions by the same authority
relating to other sites might be used to show a consistent pattern in the
application of its policies. Decisions by other authorities are unlikely to
be of assistance in this manner.

         Appeal decisions are not binding precedents, but show how the policy
of the Secretary of State has been applied. If appeal decisions showing
that planning permission is likely to be granted on appeal can be
exhibited to the planning authority, this can be a factor in its determination of the application. The desirability of avoiding losing an appeal
should not be a material consideration in itself, but is an important
administrative consideration for all authorities.

(u)   Statements of Policy

5.56   Statements of the policy of the Secretary of State contained in NPPGs
and other policy instruments are a material consideration,[55] although a
decision of the Court of Session cast a doubt on whether the planning
authority are bound to have regard to comments and observations by a
civil servant in circular.[56] The use of Scottish Office policy in final and
draft form in the determination of planning appeals appears to be
accepted by the Court of Session.[57]

         Although the advice in a NPPG has no binding or legal force, in
practice there is pressure on planning authorities to follow the provisions
of NPPGs as these represent the policy which will be applied by the
Secretary of State or his reporter when deciding an appeal. Thus
ignoring the advice within the NPPG carries with it a considerable risk of
losing any subsequent appeal.

         Guidance issued by the Department of the Environment/DETR and
the Welsh Office may be a material consideration, and is frequently
used, in the absence of Scottish Office guidance.[58]

(v)   Draft Development Plan

5.57   The provisions of draft development plans can be a material consideration.[59] However, taking into account the policies of a draft plan which
have not been adopted by the planning authority may pre-empt the
outcome of the plan-making process. An application may properly be

---

[55] *Scottish House Builders Association v. Secretary of State for Scotland*, 1995 S.C.L.R.
1039 at 1043 E–F; *J.A. Pye (Oxford) Estates v. Wychavon D.C.* [1982] J.P.L. 575; *Gransden
v. Secretary of State for the Environment* [1986] J.P.L. 519 and [1987] J.P.L. 365.
[56] *The Noble Organisation Ltd v. Falkirk D.C.*, 1994 S.L.T. 100.
[57] *e.g. Bondway Properties Ltd v. City of Edinburgh Council*, 1998 S.C.L.R. 225; SPEL
66:31; *M-I Great Britain Ltd v. Secretary of State for Scotland*, 1996 G.W.D. 22–1303; SPEL
57:93; *Dobbie v. Secretary of State for Scotland*, 1996 G.W.D. 22–1302; SPEL 57:92.
[58] 1983 S.P.L.P. 10:90 and 1984 S.P.L.P. 11:8.
[59] *R. v. City of London Corporation, ex p. Allan* (1980) 79 L.G.R. 223.

refused on the ground that the development will be likely to prejudice the outcome of the draft development plan, but all that is required is that the effect of the proposed development on the policies and proposals of the draft plan should be considered before the application is decided.[60] Provided the planning authority take into account all material considerations, it is not incompetent to grant a planning permission which pre-empts objections to the draft local plan which are due to be heard at the local plan inquiry.[61]

(w) Applicant's Personal Circumstances

Planning relates to the use of land rather than to the user.[62] The general rule is that the personal circumstances or attributes of the applicant should be ignored by the authority. For example, it is not relevant that the applicant has lived in the area for many years. However, personal circumstances may be taken into account in exceptional cases where refusal of permission would cause an applicant great hardship.[63]

5.58

A more unusual instance of personal circumstances being relevant is where outline planning permission had been granted for a retail development following a retail impact assessment which adopted a notional turnover based on floor space reflecting the average of a number of selected United Kingdom companies operating superstores. The Northern Ireland Court of Appeal held that in determining a fresh planning application by Sainsbury, it was a material consideration that the business skills and experience of Sainsbury would cause a greater retail impact. A fresh retail impact assessment should therefore have been required.[64]

The private interests of the applicant are a material consideration and it was, therefore, held to be relevant to take into account improvements in efficiency, service and staff accommodation which would result from the proposed development.[65]

(x) Prematurity

Planning permission may be refused on grounds of prematurity where the development plan is in preparation or under review (see Draft Development Plan, above). This would be competent only in respect of development proposals which are individually so substantial or likely to be so significant cumulatively, as to predetermine decisions about the scale, location or phasing of new development which ought properly to be taken in the development plan context.[66] An application may also be

5.59

[60] Young and Rowan-Robinson, *op. cit.*, p. 211.
[61] *Watson v. Renfrew D.C.*, 1995 S.C.L.R. 82, SPEL 50:68.
[62] *East Barnet Urban D.C. v. BTC* [1962] 2 Q.B. 484, *per* Parker C.J. at p. 498; *David Lowe v. Musselburgh Town Council*, 1973 S.C. 130, *per* Lord President Emslie at p. 142.
[63] *Westminster C.C. v. Great Portland Estates* [1985] A.C. 661, *per* Lord Scarman.
[64] *Re F. A. Wellworth; Re Boots, The Times*, Dec. 16, 1996.
[65] *City of Glasgow D.C. v. Secretary of State for Scotland and Bank of Scotland*, 1993 S.L.T. 1322; 1993 S.P.L.P. 38:21.
[66] *Arlington v. Secretary of State for the Environment* [1989] J.P.L. 166.

premature where an appeal decision for the same proposed development is awaited (see Duplicate Applications, above).

Non-Material Considerations

5.60   In general, the following considerations are not material and should be ignored:

(a)   the personal circumstances of the applicant (but not always, see above);

(b)   the identity of the occupier, user or developer[67];

(c)   private interests such as a landowner losing a desirable view from his property; however, it is relevant for the planning authority to take into account any loss of visual amenity (which in some respects includes loss of a view), daylight or privacy which will be caused to properties neighbouring the site of the proposed development;

(d)   moral considerations arising from developments such as sex shops, or religious objections to Sunday working;

(e)   political considerations or ideological dislike of projects such as private hospitals;

(f)   the cost of the development (contrast financial viability, see above);

(g)   title restrictions which may prevent the development from going ahead as the restrictions may be varied or discharged by the Lands Tribunal for Scotland[68];

(h)   the applicant's lack of ownership of part of the application site.[69] The planning authority's function is to decide whether or not the proposed development is desirable in the public interest. The answer to that question should not be affected by the consideration that the landowner is determined not to allow the development. However, where there are competing sites for a desirable development, difficulties of bringing about implementation on one site which are not present in relation to the other might affect the choice of site to receive permission. All other things being equal it is possible that an assembled site package would be preferable to one with unresolved ownership problems;

(i)   any other factor which indicates that there is a lack of any reasonable prospect of the development proceeding. The mere fact that a desirable condition, worded in a negative form, appears to have no reasonable prospects of fulfilment does not mean that planning permission need necessarily be refused as a matter of law.[70]

---

[67] But see *Re F. A. Wellworth*; *Re Boots, supra*.
[68] See Paisley, "Feudal Conditions and Statutory Planning Powers", 1990 S.P.L.P. 31:74.
[69] *British Railways Board v. Secretary of State for the Environment* [1994] J.P.L. 32.
[70] SDD Circular 4/1998, "The Use of Conditions in Planning Permissions", para. 38.

Overlap with Other Statutory Powers

It may be thought that planning powers should not be used to regulate 5.61
matters more properly dealt with under other specific statutory powers.
Indeed, Scottish Office policy strongly favours this view.[71] However, as a
matter of law, it is competent for planning powers to be exercised in
such circumstances provided a planning purpose is being served.

For example, the likely creation of litter as a result of a proposed
development may be a relevant planning consideration because it could
affect residential amenity.[72] A refusal of permission on the ground that
the land would be required for future road widening was held to be valid
despite the result that the authority avoided paying the compensation
which would have been due if other statutory powers had been
exercised.[73] Planning powers can be used to restrict opening hours
notwithstanding that the same power is available under the gaming
legislation.[74] The overlap between planning and integrated pollution
control powers conferred by the Environmental Protection Act 1990 may
also cause difficulties. There will come a point when the existence of
EPA controls results in residual concerns over pollution matters not
forming a valid reason for refusing planning permission (see Pollution
and Contamination, above).

Representations Received and Consultation Responses

When deciding an application for planning permission, the authority 5.62
must also take into consideration representations received timeously
under the provisions regarding notification of owners, agricultural tenants and neighbours, bad neighbour development, and the advertisement
and display of notice under the provisions applicable to development
within conservation areas (see above).[75]

Although the wording of the statute fails to qualify this requirement
by limiting the relevance of such representations to planning considerations, this qualification is implicit in the general legal requirement that
the planning authority ignores all irrelevant considerations. As a result,
the authority should only take into account representations which raise
planning considerations. Objections from neighbouring proprietors on
the grounds that the proposed development will reduce the value of their
property should therefore be ignored. However, some of the factors
giving rise to the reduction in value may be relevant planning
considerations.

It must also take into account responses timeously received from the
bodies which it was required to consult. Although there is no requirement to consider representations by other interested parties, such
representations may raise material considerations which the authority is
obliged to consider.

---

[71] *ibid.*, paras 19–22.
[72] *City of Aberdeen D.C. v. Secretary of State for Scotland*, 1993 S.L.T. 1325; [1992] 1
P.L.R. 1.
[73] *Westminster Bank v. Minister of Housing* [1971] A.C. 508.
[74] *Ladbroke v. Secretary of State for the Environment* [1981] J.P.L. 427.
[75] TCPSA, s. 38; PLBCASA, ss. 60 and 65.

The authority would be acting illegally if it ignored material considerations on the grounds that these considerations were submitted late.

Environmental Statement

5.63 The authority must also take into account the contents of any environmental statement submitted with the application, but these contents can only influence its decision in so far as they amount to planning considerations.

Fettering of Discretion

5.64 The power to grant planning permission is discretionary. Improper exercise of this discretion may render the decision illegal (Chapter 8). The planning authority must always exercise its discretion freely and each case must be considered on its merits.

Proper exercise of the discretionary power requires the decision to be made by the planning authority. Unless authorised by statute, it is not competent for the authority to delegate this power. Planning authorities are permitted by statute to delegate the power to determine a planning application to a committee or sub-committee of the authority, an officer of the authority such as the Director of Planning, or another local authority in Scotland.[76] The authority remains responsible for the decision made under delegated powers and retains the power to revoke the delegation of power.

The views of other bodies on the application may be taken into account, but the authority cannot allow these views to dictate the decision on the application as the authority would be effectively delegating its power to that body. A decision to refuse permission on the grounds of a policy of another statutory body placing an embargo on future development was therefore held to be illegal.[77]

Each application must be decided on its merits. This principle does not prevent the authority from formulating policies applicable to certain types of development (indeed, policies encourage consistent decision-making). However, the policy cannot dictate the decision, otherwise the policy has fettered the exercise of discretion.[78] The authority can apply its policy in deciding the application but the possibility of making an exception to that policy must be considered in each case.

THE DECISION

5.65 The report by the planning officer summarises the provisions of the development plan, other material considerations, and other matters to be taken into account. It recommends how the application should be determined, but the final decision rests with the decision-making body,

---

[76] Local Government (Scotland) Act 1973, s. 56, as amended.
[77] *Ynys Mon B.C. v. Secretary of State for Wales, supra.*
[78] *Lavender v. Minister of Housing* [1970] 3 All E.R. 871; *Stringer v. Minister of Housing* [1970] 1 W.L.R. 1281, *per* Cooke J. at p. 1298.

which is normally the planning committee. Written notice is given of the decision, stating the reasons for a refusal of permission or imposition of conditions upon a grant of planning permission. This notice must be accompanied by a form notifying the applicant of his rights of appeal. For the purposes of time limits for lodging an appeal, the date of the decision by the authority is the date on which the notice bears to have been signed on behalf of the authority.[79] Details of the decision must be entered into the Planning Register. Notice of the decision must also be given to any owner or agricultural tenant of the application site who submitted representations.[80]

The authority may refuse the application, or grant it unconditionally, or subject to such conditions as it thinks fit.[81] If the application is not determined within two months, the applicant may choose to lodge an appeal on the grounds that the authority is deemed to have refused planning permission. In addition, there is some scope for its decision to change the terms of the application. The various types of decision will now be explored.

(a)   Deemed Refusal

If the authority fails to determine the application within two months 5.66 of the date of its receipt, the applicant has the option of lodging an appeal on the grounds that the authority is deemed to have refused the application.[82] Such an appeal must be lodged within six months of the expiry of the two-month period. Where the authority obtains the written agreement of the applicant to an extension of the two-month period, no appeal against a deemed refusal can be lodged until the agreed extension has expired.[83]

The decision to appeal will be influenced by the costs involved in pursuing the appeal, the prospects of further delay when the authority may be close to a favourable decision, and the chances of the appeal being successful. It will be important to consider whether significant unresolved issues exist in connection with the application to render an appeal worthless. Deemed refusal appeals are sometimes used as a tactical device to pressurise authorities into granting permission on a duplicate application (see above).

(b)   Refusal

If the planning authority decides to refuse the application, the notice 5.67 of its decision must specify its reasons for that decision. The application can only be refused on planning grounds and these reasons will be drawn from the material considerations relevant to the application. The applicant has six months from the date of the notice to appeal to the Secretary of State (Chapter 8).

---

[79] TCPSA, s. 37(4).
[80] DPO, art. 8(10).
[81] s. 37(1).
[82] It is interesting to note that in the Republic of Ireland planning permission is deemed to have been granted if no decision is made within two months.
[83] TCPSA, s. 47(2) and DPO, arts 14(2) and 23(2).

(c) Resolution to Grant Permission

5.68   In the case of complex developments, it is not unusual for the planning authority to resolve to grant permission once certain matters have been resolved, most typically the execution of a section 75 agreement. The resolution, normally followed up with a "minded to grant" letter which states that the authority is minded to grant permission, does not amount to a grant of planning permission. Nor does it oblige the authority to grant permission, as any change in circumstances must be taken into account and could lead to a refusal of permission.[84] However, it may provide sufficient comfort to the applicant that permission will be granted to persuade him to resolve the outstanding matters.

(d) Conditional Grant of Permission

5.69   Strictly speaking, a grant of planning permission can never be unconditional as the conditions relating to the duration of planning permission apply to every grant of permission (see below). However, the authority may decide to grant planning permission without any other conditions attached.

The planning authority has a wide discretionary power to grant planning permission "subject to such conditions as it thinks fit" (Chapter 6). Permissions for large or complex developments may be subject to over 50 conditions. The reasons for imposing each condition must be specified in the decision letter. There are various means by which the applicant can attempt to challenge the imposition of conditions (Chapter 6). Implementation of a permission (see below) implies acceptance of the conditions. The lack of any right of appeal against a breach of condition notice (Chapter 7) emphasises the importance of ensuring that conditions are acceptable prior to implementation.

It is not unlawful for permission to be granted in detail for roadworks and in principle for development of a foodstore, where the store building is to be erected within the footprint shown on the application plan.[85]

(e) Temporary and Personal Permissions

5.70   The planning authority may grant permission subject to a condition requiring the removal of any buildings or works or discontinuance of any use of land authorised by the permission at the end of a specified period.[86] Such a temporary permission may be justified where a trial period is necessary to assess the effect of the development on the area. On expiry of the specified period, planning permission is not required for resumption of the previous use provided that use is lawful (see Lawful Development, Chapter 7).[87]

Planning permission normally enures for the benefit of the land rather than the applicant (see below). Personal permissions are grants of

---

[84] *John G. Russell (Transport) Ltd v. Strathkelvin D.C.*, 1992 S.L.T. 1001.
[85] *Lothian Borders & Angus Co-operative Society Ltd v. Scottish Borders Council, supra.*
[86] s. 41(1)(b).
[87] s. 28(2).

permission subject to conditions restricting the benefit of the permission to specified persons, often the applicant alone. It is seldom desirable to grant a personal permission but there may be exceptional circumstances where it is proposed to grant permission for use of a building for some purpose which would normally be allowed, for some compassionate or other personal grounds.[88]

(f) Outline Permission

Outline planning permission is always granted subject to a condition requiring subsequent approval of reserved matters to be obtained from the authority. The reserved matters are any matters of detail not specified in the application concerning the siting, design or external appearance of any building to which the planning permission or the application relates, or the means of access to such building, or the landscaping of the application site.[89] These reserved matters may extend to density, drainage and disposal of sewage, and treatment of boundary fences.[90] Floorspace is not a reserved matter, as it is neither siting nor design.[91]   **5.71**

In one case, an outline application which specified the floor area committed those concerned to a development on that scale, subject to minimal adjustments for siting, design and external appearance.[92] Accordingly, matters such as traffic generation could not be reassessed during the determination of the application for approval of reserved matters.

Other conditions may also be imposed on the grant of outline permission, possibly requiring submission of further details for the approval of the authority.

The existence of uncertainties regarding matters such as noise do not necessarily prevent a grant of outline permission.[93]

(g) Approval of Reserved Matters

There is a time limit specified for submission of the application for approval of reserved matters following on a grant of outline permission (see below). The reserved matters application concerns details of the development and may be refused only on grounds arising out of the reserved matters. It cannot be used by the authority as an opportunity to reconsider the principle of development which it approved by granting outline permission.   **5.72**

---

[88] SDD Circular 4/1998, para. 92.

[89] DPO, art. 2(1).

[90] *Inverclyde District Council v. Inverkip Building Co.*, 1983 S.L.T. 563; *cf. Tesco Stores Ltd v. North Norfolk D.C.*, [1998] P.L.C.R. 183, which held that drainage is not a reserved matter.

[91] *R. v. Newbury D.C., ex p. Chieveley Parish Council* [1998] E.G.C.S. 131, *The Times*, Sept. 10, 1998.

[92] *ibid.*

[93] *R. v. Northampton B.C., ex p. Rice & Co.* [1998] E.G.C.S. 84.

(h)   Grant of Planning Permission for Revised Development

5.73   In the negotiations prior to determination of the application for planning permission, it is common for the applicant to make changes to the proposals, often following suggestions by the planning officer dealing with the application. Unless these changes are material, most authorities will not suggest that the application be re-notified/re-advertised. However, this may deprive those persons whose views must be taken into account by the authority of an opportunity to give their views on what would be a different proposal, with the possible result that the permission is illegal. If there is any doubt, the safest course must always be to re-notify all parties and give fresh notice by advertisement. Where an original application sought permission for buildings of 85,000 square metres, the planning authority did not act unreasonably in treating a revisal to 15,000 square metres as not altering the substance of the application and in not re-notifying a party.[94]

It is competent for the authority to grant planning permission for a development different from that proposed in the application.[95] The test is whether the amended proposal is different in substance.[96] A grant of planning permission which reduced the size of the proposed development from 35 acres and 420 dwellings to 25 acres and 250 dwellings was upheld on the basis that the result did not differ substantially from the development proposed in the original application.[97] This suggests a test of character: does the permitted development have a substantially different character from the development proposed in the original application? For example, an amendment was material where it increased the site area by 50 per cent, brought the proposed gypsy camp significantly closer to three nearby residences and increased the number of pitches which might be accommodated.[98]

The authority may also regulate matters ancillary or incidental to the proposed development, but which do not form part of the application, such as the provision of children's play areas and public open spaces for a large housing development.[99]

(i)   Development Contrary to the Development Plan

5.74   Provided that the authority have regard to the provisions of the development plan, it is competent for planning permission to be granted for a development which is contrary to the terms of the plan. However, unless the notification requirements apply (see below), notice must have been given by advertisement in a local newspaper and any representations received in the 21 days following publication considered.[1]

---

[94] *Walker v. City of Aberdeen Council*, 1998 S.L.T. 427; SPEL 61:59.
[95] *Kent C.C. v. Secretary of State for the Environment* (1976) 33 P. & C.R. 70.
[96] *Walker, supra*; *Lothian Borders & Angus Co-operative Society Ltd v. Scottish Borders Council, supra.*
[97] *Bernard Wheatcroft v. Secretary of State for the Environment* [1982] J.P.L. 37.
[98] *Breckland v. Secretary of State for the Environment* [1992] 3 P.L.R. 89.
[99] *Britannia (Cheltenham) Ltd v. Secretary of State for the Environment* [1978] J.P.L. 554.
[1] DPO, art. 18 and Town and Country Planning (Development Contrary to Development Plans) (Scotland) Direction 1996, attached to Circulars 3/1994, 10/1996 and 4/1997. PAN 41 (revised 1997) provides guidance.

This requirement applies whether or not the proposed development is a significant departure from the development plan. Many authorities offer objectors to a departure application the opportunity to appear at a special hearing.

Planning authorities are no longer required to submit to the Secretary of State details of individual grants of planning permission contrary to an approved local or structure plan, and report departures from development plans in their statistical return.

NOTIFICATION AND CALL-IN

(a) Notification

If the planning authority proposes to grant planning permission for certain types of development, they must first notify the Secretary of State.[2] This notification procedure alerts the Secretary of State to applications which it may be appropriate for him to call in for determination.   5.75

The types of development to which this requirement applies are:

Agricultural Land: changes of use of 10 hectares or more of agricultural land within Macaulay classes 1, 2 or 3.1, where either the development would be contrary to an adopted or approved local plan, or no local plan has been adopted or approved, or an officer of the Scottish Office Agriculture, Environment and Fisheries Department has advised against granting permission, or no such officer has been consulted.

Industrial, Petrochemical and Business Developments requiring more than 100 hectares of land.

Development Affecting Large Single User High Amenity Sites, Large Industrial and Business Sites, or Large Petrochemical Sites in accordance with NPPG 2 "Business and Industry", either development of all or part of such a site, or development on a conterminous site which in the view of the planning authority would prejudice its development potential.

Oil-related Development: the construction of offshore installations or of major parts of such installations, or the fabrication of pipelines; installations or storage tanks associated with the landing and transportation of offshore oil and gas; and major installations associated with the processing of oil and gas including refineries, gas liquefaction plans, and plants for the manufacture or processing of petrochemicals.

Major Retail Development: development for the purpose of retail shopping comprising an area of 10,000 square metres or more of gross retail

---

[2] Town and Country Planning (Notification of Applications) (Scotland) Direction 1997, attached to SDD Circular 4/1997, as amended by the Directions attached to Circulars 43/1997, 15/1998 and 20/1998.

floor space (prior to October 6, 1998 the relevant area was 20,000 square metres), or where the purchases are likely to be made to a significant extent by persons resident outwith the planning authority's area, and the local authority for that area has made representations that permission should not be granted.

Development Affecting Trunk and Special Roads, and Motorway Service Areas where the Secretary of State has advised against the grant of permission or has recommended conditions which the planning authority do not propose to attach to the permission.

Development Contrary to Approved Structure and Local Plans: any development which the planning authority considers to be a significant departure from a structure plan approved by the Secretary of State, or from the provisions of a local plan approved by the Secretary of State (most local plans are not approved by the Secretary of State (Chapter 3), departures from them will not require to be notified to the Secretary of State). Circular 4/1997 advises that it is for the planning authority to judge whether a departure is significant, but that in general a significant departure will only be where it is for development on a substantial scale or if it is likely to prejudice the implementation of the strategic objectives of the plan. Unless other criteria apply, such as conflict with a SSSI, planning applications for fewer than 10 houses need not be notified to the Secretary of State.

Development in the Vicinity of Major Hazards, where there has been consultation with the Health & Safety Executive and they have advised against the grant of planning permission or recommended conditions which the planning authority do not propose to attach to the permission.

Nature Conservation: where the development affects a Site of Special Scientific Interest, a site proposed or designated as a Special Area of Conservation, an area proposed or classified under the Wild Birds Directive, or an area designated as a Wetland of International Importance (these categories are discussed further in Chapter 9), and Scottish Natural Heritage on being consulted by the planning authority has advised against granting planning permission or has recommended conditions which the planning authority do not propose to attach to the permission.

5.76 *Coastal Quarry:* capable of achieving a production output of 2 million tonnes or more per annum.

Wind Generators: where the development consists of 10 or more generators (until December 30, 1997, notification was required for one or more generators).

Scheduled Monuments and Category A Listed Buildings: where the Secretary of State has been consulted because the development may affect the site of a scheduled monument or its setting, or a category A listed building or its setting, and advised against the granting of planning permission or has recommended conditions which the planning authority do not propose to attach to the permission.

Flooding: where the Scottish Environment Protection Agency has been consulted because it appears to the planning authority that the development is likely to result in a material increase in the number of buildings at risk of being damaged by flooding, and has advised against the granting of planning permission or has recommended conditions which the planning authority do not propose to attach to the permission.

Development in which Planning Authorities have an Interest: either a financial interest, or where the development is located on land wholly or partly in their ownership or in which they have an interest. The notification requirement only applies if the proposed development does not accord with the adopted or approved local plan for the area, or has been the subject of a substantial body of objections, and if the Town and Country Planning (Development by Planning Authorities) (Scotland) Regulations 1981 do not apply to the development (see Chapter 9).

Playing Fields: development affecting any land of 0.4 hectares or more currently in use, or last used, for any pitch sports, including any adjacent tennis courts and bowling greens, and athletic tracks. The notification requirement applies where the Scottish Sports Council (SSC) have been consulted by the planning authority because the development is likely to prejudice the existing use as a playing field, or result in the loss of the playing field, or is likely to prevent its re-use as a playing field, and the SSC have advised against granting planning permission or recommended conditions which the planning authority do not propose to attach to the permission. Notification is also required where the Town and Country Planning (Development of Planning Authorities) (Scotland) Regulations 1981 apply to the development (see chapter 9).

Opencast Coal: sites greater than 500 hectares; sites greater than 100 hectares, where in the opinion of the planning authority two or more workings already exist or would exist (*i.e.* unimplemented consents or other current planning applications) within a time period of more than two years, in an area within five kilometres of the proposed site; all sites with an excavation boundary within 500 metres of an existing community or sensitive establishment; and all sites with soil and overburden mound area and/or site maintenance and administration area boundaries within 100 metres of an existing community or sensitive establishment.

Together with the notification, copies must be sent of the application and plans, any environmental statement, observations by consultees and representations received, with the authority's comments on those observations and representations and the authority's reasons for proposing to grant permission. The Secretary of State confirms the date of receipt of notification and the planning authority cannot decide the application until 28 days after that date unless the Secretary of State confirms in writing that a shorter period applies. If no response is forthcoming within the 28-day period, the authority may grant permission. The response within this period can direct that the application be referred to the Secretary of State (see Call-in, below), or further restrict the grant of planning permission for a further specified period or indefinitely.

There are separate requirements to notify the Secretary of State before granting permission for any development which includes or involves alteration or extension of a listed building unless listed building consent is required,[3] and for certain forms of development within National Scenic Areas where Scottish Natural Heritage advise against granting permission or recommend conditions other than those proposed by the planning authority (Chapter 9).

(b) Call-in

5.77   The Secretary of State has the power to direct that an application be referred to him for decision, instead of being determined by the planning authority. This process is commonly known as calling in an application. Exercise of this call-in power is not restricted to applications notified to him by the planning authority. In general, only applications which raise issues of national significance will be called in.[4]

The Secretary of State's call-in power is exercised by giving a direction to a particular planning authority or authorities generally that any application or type of application be referred to him for decision.[5] After an application is called in for decision by the Secretary of State, either the applicant or the authority may request as of right a hearing (normally a public local inquiry) before a reporter, who will prepare a report for the Secretary of State. The non-delegated appeal procedure rules apply (see Chapter 8), with some slight differences in pre-inquiry procedure. The Secretary of State serves a written statement of the reasons for the call-in within four weeks of his written notice to the planning authority that an inquiry is to be held, unless he has already provided written reasons. The decision of the Secretary of State on the called-in application is final, but may be challenged by application to the Court of Session on legal grounds only within six weeks (Chapter 8).[6]

Following the call-in of an application, the planning authority must notify the applicant of the terms of the call-in direction and of any reasons given for issuing that direction. The notice must inform the applicant of his right to request a hearing and that the decision on the application will be final.[7]

Where an application has been called-in for decision by the Secretary of State, other than the points mentioned above, the procedure for determining that application is the same as that applicable to determinations by planning authorities.

The exercise, or not, of the call-in power is significant for certain forms of development such as retailing and housing where issues of capacity may mean that only a limited number of permissions can be granted. If there are two applications in circumstances where only a

---

[3] DPO, art. 20.
[4] NPPG1, "The Planning System", para. 54.
[5] TCPSA, s. 46.
[6] ss. 46(7), 237 and 239.
[7] DPO, art. 21.

single consent can be granted, and the Secretary of State calls in only one of those applications, the planning authority can competently determine the remaining application. If the authority decides to grant that application, the called-in application will have to be refused on grounds of lack of capacity. A similar situation arises where one applicant appeals, and the Secretary of State refuses to call in the other application.

The courts have examined the legal issues arising in these situations. It was held that the Secretary of State did not act illegally in not calling in a rival application when he recalled an appeal for his determination on the grounds of its implication for a structure plan policy that was before him for decision. The Secretary of State is carrying out different statutory functions in dealing with an appeal and deciding whether to call in an application, and the same considerations do not necessarily apply. The reason given for recalling the appeal explained why that procedure had been adopted for the appeal, and did not justify a review of all relevant applications. Any prejudice caused to the appellant was inherent in the planning process because of the absence of a right of appeal against the grant of permission to a rival applicant. This decision overturned the judgment of the Outer House judge, who had held that procedural fairness required the Secretary of State to take account of the need to protect the interests of the appellant, because his decision not to call in the application was capable of resulting in substantial prejudice to the appellant and even to the pre-empting of their appeal.[8]

The Secretary of State's decision in a previous case was unlawful because in deciding not to call in the rival application he had considered the merits of the two sites and had therefore prejudged the issue and pre-empted the appeal.[9] This decision would probably have been valid if he had ignored the existence of alternative sites completely, even although this would still have effectively prejudged the outcome of the appeal.

EFFECT OF PLANNING PERMISSION

Many consequences arise from the grant of planning permission. The important legal consequences are examined below. An important practical consequence is that the permission generally increases the value of the land over which it has been granted. Once planning permission has been granted, other statutory consents, such as building warrants, may still be required before development can commence. A grant of planning permission by the Secretary of State or his reporter may prevent the local authority from refusing to grant other statutory consents or enter into necessary agreements on grounds which were determined as part of the appeal decision, such as road safety,[10] unless circumstances have

5.78

---

[8] *Asda Stores Ltd v. Secretary of State for Scotland*, 1998 S.C.L.R. 246, SPEL 66:33; O.H. decision 1997 S.L.T. 1286, SPEL 61:61; *R. v. Secretary of State for the Environment, ex p. Carter Commercial Development Ltd* [1998] E.G.C.S. 130.
[9] *Lakin v. Secretary of State for Scotland*, 1988 S.L.T. 780.
[10] *R. v. Warwickshire C.C., ex p. PowerGen plc* [1998] J.P.L. 131.

changed since that decision.[11] Planning permission does not give immunity from liability in nuisance to neighbouring landowners.[12]

(a) Enures for the Benefit of the Land

5.79   With the exception of personal permissions (see above), the grant of planning permission is not personal to the applicant or the owner of the application site, but enures for the benefit of the land on which development is permitted and is transferred with the ownership of the land.[13]

Where the impact of the proposed development may depend upon the identity of the operator, the benefit of the permission may be limited to a particular class of person, notwithstanding the lack of any condition to this effect. Where outline planning permission had been granted for a retail development following a retail impact assessment which adopted a notional turnover based on floor space reflecting the average of a number of selected United Kingdom companies operating superstores, the Northern Ireland Court of Appeal held that in determining fresh planning applications by Sainsbury, it was a material consideration that the business skills and experience of Sainsbury would cause a greater retail impact and a fresh retail impact assessment should therefore have been required.[14]

(b) Does not Prevent Future Applications

5.80   There is no obligation to commence the development permitted by a grant of planning permission. While the grant of planning permission remains unimplemented it is competent for any person including the original applicant to make further applications for planning permission in respect of the same site. A further application may seek a more favourable grant of permission for a similar development, or propose an entirely different development. The planning authority is required to consider each application on its merits, ignoring any previous grants of permission and pending applications for the same site.[15] There is no limit on the number of grants of planning permission in respect of an individual site, and the owner can select which permitted development should proceed. This can lead to problems with multiple implementation of permissions (see below).

(c) Interpretation

5.81   The wording of the decision letter granting planning permission will be given its ordinary and natural meaning.[16] It will not be construed against the interests of the authority in favour of the applicant (*contra proferentem*).[17] In general, only the document granting planning permis-

---

[11] *R. v. Cardiff C.C., ex p. Sears Group Properties*, [1998] P.L.C.R. 262.
[12] *Wheeler v. Saunders* [1995] 2 All E.R. 697.
[13] TCPSA, s. 44(1).
[14] *Re F. A. Wellworth; Re Boots, The Times*, Dec. 16, 1996.
[15] *Pilkington v. Secretary of State for the Environment* [1973] 1 W.L.R. 1527.
[16] *Wyre Forest D.C. v. Secretary of State for the Environment* [1989] J.P.L. 362.
[17] *Crisp from the Fens v. Rutland C.C.*, 1950 L.G.R. 210.

sion, and any reasons stated thereon, can be considered.[18] Other documents, such as the application form or plans, cannot be used to help interpret the permission, unless the permission refers to those documents. In determining whether a development which increased the floor space by some 45 per cent was within the terms of the outline planning permission, the court held that regard must be had to the permission. The inclusion of the application reference number in the permission was not sufficient to incorporate the application into the permission, for which words such as "in accordance with the plans and application" would be necessary.[19] Where the permission was not ambiguous, regard should not have been had to the plan attached to it and the application.[20] Similarly, it will not be competent to refer to the resolution of the authority to grant permission, except where the issue is whether planning permission was granted.

(d) Duration

Every grant of planning permission is subject to conditions requiring the commencement of the development authorised by the permission within a specified period.[21] Outline permissions are also subject to conditions requiring submission of applications for approval of reserved matters within a specified period. There are separate provisions applicable to the limit of duration of planning permission for winning and working minerals (Chapter 9). Failure to adhere to these time limits will cause the permission to expire.   5.82

In the absence of an express condition, a condition is deemed to have been imposed requiring commencement of development within five years of the date of the grant of permission. For outline permissions, the development must begin either within five years of the grant of outline permission, or within two years of the final approval of the reserved matters (or the final approval of the last reserved matter), whichever is later. In both cases, the authority may impose an express condition specifying a longer or shorter period which they consider appropriate having regard to the provisions of the development plan and to any other material considerations.

In a similar way, every grant of outline planning permission is subject to an express or implied condition requiring an application for approval of reserved matters to be made within either three years of the grant of outline planning permission, or six months of refusal of an earlier application for approval, or six months from dismissal of an appeal against such a refusal, whichever is latest. If three years from the grant of outline permission have elapsed, only one application for approval may be made. This gives the applicant a last chance to submit an acceptable application. When granting permission the authority may substitute a

---

[18] *Miller-Mead v. Minister of Housing* [1963] 2 Q.B. 196; but see *Wivenhoe Port Ltd v. Colchester B.C.* [1985] J.P.L. 396.

[19] *R. v. Secretary of State for the Environment, ex p. Slough B.C.* [1995] J.P.L. 1128, applied in *Foyle v. Secretary of State for the Environment* [1997] E.G.C.S. 65.

[20] *Springfield Minerals v. Secretary of State for Wales* [1995] E.G.C.S. 174.

[21] TCPSA, ss. 58 and 59.

longer or shorter period for the three-year period as it considers appropriate. Submission of an application in respect of some but not all of the reserved matters, or for part only of the development site, within the time limit will not preserve the remainder of the outline permission from expiry.[22]

When a development is split into distinct parts or phases, it is competent for the authority to specify separate periods for the submission of applications for approval of reserved matters for each part or phase. The requirement for commencement of development should be framed correspondingly by reference to those parts rather than to the development as a whole. In imposing such conditions, the authority must have regard to the provisions of the development plan and to any other material considerations.

5.83   For these purposes, development commences on the earliest date on which any of the following specified operations begin to be carried out[23]:

(i)   construction work in connection with the erection of a building;

(ii)   any work of demolition of a building;

(iii) digging of a trench for the foundations of a building, even although the trenches are immediately back-filled[24];

(iv)   laying any underground main or pipe to the foundations of a building or to a trench for the foundations;

(v)   any operation in the course of laying out or constructing part of a road, including marking out the route of a road with pegs[25];

(vi)   specified changes of use which constitute material development.

Any of these specified operations in respect of part of a development scheme will be sufficient for implementation of the entire scheme.[26]

Any development commenced after the grant of permission has expired in terms of these express/implied conditions will be treated as not authorised by the permission and, therefore, as a breach of planning control (Chapter 7). Similarly, application for approval of reserved matters submitted after expiry of outline permission will be treated as not made in accordance with the terms of the permission.[27] To avoid expiry of the permission, an application for renewal of the permission may be made before its expiry (see above).

In general, operations which are in breach of a condition cannot amount to a commencement of development for the purposes of complying with these time limits. For example, where a condition requires works to take place in accordance with a scheme to be agreed with the planning authority, works which proceed where no scheme has

[22] *Hunterston Development Co. Ltd v. Secretary of State for Scotland*, 1992 S.L.T. 1097.
[23] s. 27.
[24] *High Peak B.C. v. Secretary of State for the Environment* [1981] J.P.L. 366.
[25] *Malvern Hills D.C. v. Secretary of State for the Environment* (1983) 46 P. & C.R. 58.
[26] *City of Glasgow D.C. v. Secretary of State for Scotland*, 1993 S.L.T. 268.
[27] TCPSA, s. 60(4).

been agreed do not commence the development in implementation of the permission.[28] Where the drainage information included within an application for approval of reserved matters was insufficient to constitute the full drainage details required by the condition to be approved before work commenced on site, and the planning authority were not alerted to the fact that approval of the drainage matters was sought, no application under the relevant condition had been submitted and the works on site were therefore in breach of the condition.[29] If the condition has in substance been complied with and work has been carried out with the full knowledge and co-operation of the planning and highways authorities, this general principle should be applied with common sense.[30]

If there are several planning permissions for development of the site, and work has commenced, it will be necessary to determine which permission has been implemented by the commencement of development. The erection of two houses in terms of a detailed planning permission did not constitute the commencement of development in terms of earlier outline planning permissions, which had therefore expired.[31]

For development to have commenced, it is not necessary for the works to have been undertaken with the intention of carrying out the development.[32] This has been described as "colourability". It is not necessary that there is an intention to proceed with the development immediately or at a definite date.[33]

(e) Abandonment

It cannot be implied that a valid planning permission capable of being implemented has been abandoned or lost through the actions of the holder of the benefit of the permission.[34]   5.84

(f) Revocation or Modification

The planning authority has power to revoke or modify any grant of permission to such extent as it considers expedient at any time before the change of use has taken place or prior to completion of building or other operations.[35] However, instances of the exercise of this power are limited in consequence of the liability to pay compensation as a result.[36]   5.85

Once the revocation/modification order has been confirmed by the Secretary of State, only those building or other operations carried out

---

[28] *F. G. Whitley v. Secretary of State for Wales* [1992] 3 P.L.R. 72.
[29] *Tesco Stores Ltd v. North Norfolk D.C., supra.*
[30] *R. v. Flintshire C.C., ex p. Somerfield* [1998] E.G.C.S. 53.
[31] *Campbell v. Argyll & Bute D.C.,* 1997 S.C.L.R. 197, SPEL 59:15.
[32] *East Dunbartonshire Council v. Secretary of State for Scotland,* 1998 G.W.D. 40–2079, SPEL 71:16; *cf. Malvern Hills, supra.*
[33] *Tesco Stores Ltd, supra; Agecrest Ltd v. Gwynedd C.C.* [1996] E.G.C.S. 115; *cf. R. v. Arfon B.C., ex p. Walton Commercial Group Ltd* [1997] J.P.L. 237.
[34] *Pioneer Aggregates v. Secretary of State for the Environment* [1985] A.C. 132. Contrast with existing use rights (Chapter 4).
[35] TCPSA, s. 65; *Caledonian Terminal Investments v. Edinburgh Corporation,* 1970 S.C. 271.
[36] s. 76.

prior to the date of confirmation are authorised by the permission. The only procedure for challenging the validity of a confirmed order is an application to the Court of Session (Chapter 8).[37]

(g) Variation

5.86   The planning authority may vary any permission at the request of the applicant if it appears to it that the variation sought is not material.[38] This obviates the need for a fresh application and re-notification/re-advertisement, but will necessarily be limited to minor variations.

CONSEQUENCES OF IMPLEMENTATION OF PLANNING PERMISSION

5.87 The grant of planning permission is implemented on commencement of any of the specified operations (see Duration, above). Implementation prevents expiry of the permission which then endures in perpetuity, with important implications for the completion of the development and the competence of implementing other permissions for the same site.

(a) Completion of Development: Completion Notice

5.88   There is no duty or obligation to complete a development which has been commenced. As a result, sites may be sterilised from future development. The possibility that the remainder of the permission may be implemented in due course would seem to be a material considera-tion in the determination of any fresh application. The planning authority should consider imposing a condition or suggesting a planning agreement to prevent further implementation of the permis-sion, prior to granting a fresh permission.

The planning authority may serve a completion notice where it is of the opinion that the development has been commenced but will not be completed within a reasonable time.[39] The notice will only take effect if confirmed by the Secretary of State. On the expiry of the period specified in the notice no further development in terms of the permis-sion will be competent and only the development carried out by that date will be authorised by the planning permission. The effectiveness of completion notices is therefore limited to situations in which the developer has some intention of proceeding with the development. Use of completion notices is unusual.

(b) Multiple Implementation of Permissions

5.89   Difficult questions arise where a permission has been partially or fully implemented and work commences in implementation of another per-mission applicable to the same site.[40] The central question is whether it is

---

[37] s. 237.
[38] s. 64.
[39] s. 61.
[40] Collar, "Multiple Implementation of Planning Permissions" [1993] J.P.L. 627.

possible to carry out the development authorised by the permission, having regard to what was done or authorised to be done under the permission which has been implemented.[41] If the position is uncertain, an application could be made to the planning authority for a Certificate of Lawfulness of Proposed Use or Development (Chapter 4).

This test is one of physical possibility, not just of construction but also provision of the curtilage (Chapter 4) for the building identified in the application. Where two permissions authorised erection of a farmhouse, but in different locations within the same 50-acre site, their effect was that the landowner was entitled to build a farmhouse in either location for use as a farmhouse in connection with farming the 50 acres. Having built one, he could not build on the other so long as there was a farmhouse standing and used for farming the 50 acres.[42] Mere incompatibility with the other permission already implemented is insufficient.[43] The intention of the planning authority in granting permission may be thought relevant, but in interpreting planning permissions reference may only be had to the decision letter (see above).

A permission which is mutually inconsistent with an implemented permission remains in suspense (subject to time limits for implementation), until its implementation becomes physically possible.

(c) Challenge of Conditions

By implementing the permission, it might be thought that the   5.90
developer impliedly accepts the conditions attached to the permission and should not be able to challenge those conditions thereafter. However, there is no statutory bar to lodging an appeal against conditions in these circumstances. In addition, it is competent to apply for permission to develop the land without compliance with the conditions (Chapter 6).

FAILURE TO COMPLY WITH PERMISSION

If development proceeds contrary to the conditions imposed on the   5.91
planning permission, there is a breach of planning control, and the planning authority may take enforcement action (Chapter 7). Work in breach of planning conditions will not constitute a commencement of development for the purposes of preventing the expiry of the planning permission (see above).

Development which is not in accordance with the permission is also a breach of planning control, as it amounts to development without planning permission, and is therefore subject to potential enforcement action. Importantly, restrictions imposed on the development by conditions attached to the permission will not apply. A bungalow which was

---

[41] *Pilkington v. Secretary of State for the Environment* [1973] 1 W.L.R. 1527.
[42] *Ellis v. Worcestershire C.C.* (1961) 12 P. & C.R. 178. Also *Orbit Development v. Secretary of State for the Environment* [1996] E.G.C.S. 191.
[43] *Prestige Homes v. Secretary of State for the Environment* [1992] J.P.L. 842.

about 90 feet west of the permitted location was not subject to the occupancy restriction imposed by the condition attached to the planning permission.[44] As a period for enforcement of development without planning permission is only four years in contrast to 10 years from a breach of planning condition, this is an important issue.

CONSEQUENCES OF REFUSAL OF APPLICATION

(a)   Challenging the Refusal

5.92   Chapter 8 examines the procedures for challenging decisions on planning applications.

(b)   Purchase Notice

5.93   Following a refusal of planning permission, or a grant subject to conditions, the owner or lessee of land which is incapable of reasonably beneficial use may serve a purchase notice on the planning authority.[45] There is no requirement to demonstrate a causal connection between the decision on the planning application and the fact that the land is incapable of reasonably beneficial use.[46] The purchase notice must relate to the whole of the site refused planning permission.[47] If the planning authority is willing to comply with the notice, it is deemed to acquire the land compulsorily. Compensation is assessed as for compulsory purchase. If the authority refuses to comply, the notice is referred to the Secretary of State for decision. He may either confirm the notice, grant planning permission, revoke or amend conditions, or direct that planning permission be granted for an alternative development if the appropriate application is made.

---

[44] *Handoll v. Warner Goodman and Steat* [1995] J.P.L. 930.
[45] TCPSA, s. 88.
[46] *Purbeck D.C. v. Secretary of State for the Environment* (1982) 80 L.G.R. 545.
[47] *Cook v. Winchester C.C.* (1995) 69 P. & C.R. 99.

Chapter 6

DEVELOPMENT CONTROL III—PLANNING CONDITIONS AND PLANNING AGREEMENTS

Planning permission is a crude device for controlling development: 6.01
either the proposed development is acceptable or it is not. The power to
impose conditions upon the grant of permission enables the planning
authority to go beyond the adjudicative "yes/no" role by using conditions
to control the detailed aspects of developments. Therefore, the imposition of conditions can be identified as a powerful tool for promoting
flexibility within development control. However, the use of conditions is
limited by legal restrictions.

As if to emphasise the weakness of the requirement to obtain planning
permission as a development control tool, planning authorities have
further statutory powers enabling them to enter into agreements with
applicants. Controversially, these powers are often used to achieve
"planning gain". Use of these powers has increased in the past decade,
partly as a result of the restrictions placed on the use of conditions by
the requirements for legal validity.

Planning Conditions

Planning conditions may be used to provide greater control and flexibil- 6.02
ity within the development control process by virtue of their dual role:

(a) making an otherwise unacceptable development acceptable,
thereby furthering the presumption in favour of development,[1]
always subject to the limits to which conditions can modify the
proposed development (see below); or
(b) controlling the details of an otherwise acceptable application,
allowing the development to be "fine-tuned", making it more
satisfactory. In this way, a development which is generally
acceptable can be tailored to meet the needs of the surrounding locality and details such as landscaping and design settled.

There is no duty upon the planning authority to draw up and use a
condition to make an otherwise unacceptable development acceptable,
but if the application is acceptable it has a duty to consider whether
conditions can be imposed to make it more acceptable.[2] Standard lists of

---

[1] SDD Circular 4/1998, "The Use of Conditions in Planning Permissions", para. 2.
[2] *Mason v. Secretary of State for the Environment* [1984] J.P.L. 332; *Garbutt v. Secretary of State for the Environment* (1989) 57 P. & C.R. 284.

conditions may be used to achieve parity of treatment between appli-cations and to promote consistency of decisions, although the decision to impose conditions must be considered for each application on its merits.

One investigation found that many planning officers believed that conditions were imposed for their psychological impact.[3] This provides an example of what has been described as a game of bluff.[4] Applicants are willing to accept conditions which may be invalid, or at least may never be enforced, because this persuades the authority to accept the application. The authority may similarly doubt the possibility of enforc-ing the obligation in practice, but impose the condition in the hope that the applicant will accept and implement it. Research has suggested that enforcement of conditions may be minimal.[5] The introduction of the power to serve breach of condition notices (Chapter 7) may result in a higher level of enforcement and highlights the importance of drafting precise conditions.[6]

Conditions attached to planning permissions should be scrutinised and their effect considered before the permission is implemented (Chapter 5), although there is no statutory bar to an appeal against the conditions imposed once the development has commenced.

If development does not proceed in accordance with the planning permission, such as a bungalow built about 90 feet west of the permitted location, restrictions imposed on the development by conditions attached to the permission will not apply.[7] In such circumstances, there is a breach of planning control consisting of development without planning permis-sion, and not a breach of condition. The significance is that the period for enforcement action is four years in contrast to 10 years for a breach of planning condition.

Conditions cannot infer a grant of anything which goes beyond the terms of the planning permission.[8] A planning permission for clay extraction granted subject to a condition requiring the excavations to be filled in was held to be capable of granting planning permission by implication for depositing waste on the site, as the necessary importation of material from outside the site was clearly contemplated by the condition.[9]

---

[3] Booth, "Development Control and Design Quality Part 1—Conditions: A Useful Way of Controlling Design?" (1983) 54 T.P. Rev. 265.

[4] McAuslan, *Land, Law and Planning* (1974).

[5] Loughlin, *Local Needs Policy* (1984): 49 per cent of developments in one council area had failed to comply with agricultural occupancy conditions. See also Booth (above) and Peart and Rutherford, "Opencast Guidance—Opportunities for Green Policies" [1989] J.P.L. 406.

[6] e.g. *Rees v. Secretary of State for the Environment* [1994] E.G.C.S. 157, *R. v. Ealing B.C., ex p. Zainuddin* [1995] J.P.L. 925.

[7] *Handoll v. Warner Goodman and Streat* [1995] J.P.L. 930.

[8] *Paisley Mills Development Co. Ltd v. Renfrewshire Council*, 1997 G.W.D. 25–1279.

[9] *R. v. Secretary of State for the Environment, ex p. Walsall MBC* [1997] E.G.C.S. 23.

Power to Impose Conditions

In determining an application for planning permission, planning 6.03
authorities "may grant planning permission, either unconditionally, or
subject to such conditions as they think fit."[10] This power only extends to
the imposition of conditions upon land which forms part of the site of
the proposed development as identified in the application.

Without prejudice to this general power to impose conditions, there is
an additional power to attach conditions regulating the development or
use of any land under the control of the applicant (whether or not it
forms part of the application site), or requiring the carrying out of any
works on any such land, so far as appears expedient for the purposes of
or in connection with the authorised development.[11] The consequence of
this additional power is that only land which is neither within the terms
of the application for planning permission nor under the control of the
applicant is not potentially subject to a planning condition.[12] It is a
question of fact and degree whether the applicant has sufficient control
to ensure compliance with the conditions.[13]

There are also statutory powers to impose specific types of conditions.
Every permission is subject to an express or implied condition providing
for the expiry of the permission if the development authorised by the
permission is not commenced within a specified period of time (Chapter
5). A condition may be attached to a grant of temporary permission
requiring removal of buildings or works authorised by the permission, or
discontinuance of any authorised use of land, and reinstatement of the
land on the expiry of that permission.[14] Conditions may also limit the
benefit of a planning permission to a named person (a personal
permission), or specify the use of a proposed building.[15] The planning
authority has a duty to ensure that, where appropriate, conditions are
imposed upon a grant of planning permission to secure adequate
provision for the preservation and planting of trees.[16]

Validity of Planning Conditions: Legal

Planning authorities have the power to impose such conditions as they 6.04
think fit. The width of this discretionary power is limited by the
requirements for the legal validity of a planning condition which have
been formulated by the courts through a process of statutory interpretation. A planning condition must have a planning purpose, fairly and
reasonably relate to the permitted development, and not be so unreasonable that no reasonable planning authority could have imposed it.[17]

---

[10] TCPSA, s. 37(1).
[11] s. 41(1).
[12] *Birnie v. Banff C.C.*, 1954 S.L.T. (Sh.Ct.) 90.
[13] *George Wimpey v. New Forest D.C.* [1979] J.P.L. 314.
[14] TCPSA, s. 41(1)(b).
[15] s. 44.
[16] s. 159.
[17] *Newbury D.C. v. Secretary of State for the Environment* [1981] A.C. 578 at p. 607; [1980]
J.P.L. 325.

(a)   Planning Purpose

6.05   The power to impose conditions is conferred by the planning legislation and must therefore be used to achieve a planning purpose and not
an ulterior object.[18] As a result of the vagueness of the objectives of
planning (Chapter 1), it is difficult to draw the line between a "planning"
and an "ulterior" object. The TCPSA provides no guidance on the
objects of planning powers, and the courts can only provide assistance on
a case-by-case basis. As a result, there can be no precise guidelines on
the requirement for a planning purpose. However, as the examination of
material considerations has shown (Chapter 5), the scope of potential
planning matters is wide-ranging and the need for a planning purpose
should not be an onerous requirement.

Planning has been held to relate to the use of land rather than to the
user.[19] However, if the purpose of the condition relates to the use of the
land, it is valid notwithstanding that it limits categories of users.[20] Thus, a
condition limiting occupation of a dwellinghouse to agricultural workers
was valid because it was imposed to further the policy of protecting the
Green Belt.[21] Other decisions on "planning purpose" also involve
conditions imposed to further planning policies. Inclusion of a policy
within the development plan may give it the badge of "planning
purpose", although this will not always be the case.[22] For example, many
structure plans state that the area has been declared a "nuclear-free
zone".

It was held that a condition restricting the extension or connection of
water and sewerage service pipes to serve any other residential development had the valid planning purpose of prohibiting an arrangement
between landowners which would lead to excessive provision of housing.[23] An agreement requiring the developer to provide an access road to
an adjacent development site had a proper planning purpose.[24] In
contrast, a condition amounting to a requirement that a road be
constructed and dedicated to the public was invalid because it had the
ulterior purpose of requiring the developer to take on the duty of the
highway authority.[25] Similarly, conditions imposed on a housing development requiring that the houses should first be occupied by persons on
the local authority's housing waiting list were invalid because they
required the developer to assume the duty of the local authority as a
housing authority at his own expense.[26] However, the need for housing in
a particular area is a material consideration, and no sensible distinction
can be drawn between a need for housing generally and a need for
particular types of housing, whether or not the latter could be defined in

[18] *Pyx Granite v. Minister of Housing* [1958] Q.B. 554, *per* Lord Denning at p. 572.
[19] *Westminster C.C. v. Great Portland Estates* [1985] A.C. 661.
[20] *cf. David Lowe & Sons v. Musselburgh Town Council*, 1973 S.C. 130.
[21] *Fawcett Properties v. Buckingham C.C.* [1961] A.C. 636.
[22] *Westminster Renslade v. Secretary of State for the Environment* [1983] J.P.L. 454.
[23] *North-East Fife D.C. v. Secretary of State for Scotland*, 1992 S.L.T. 373.
[24] *McIntosh v. Aberdeenshire Council*, 1998 G.W.D. 6–255, SPEL 67:56.
[25] *Hall v. Shoreham-By-Sea Urban D.C.* [1964] 1 W.L.R. 240.
[26] *R. v. Hillingdon LBC, ex p. Royco Homes* [1974] 2 All E.R. 643.

terms of cost, tenure or otherwise. In each case the question is whether, as a matter of planning for the area under consideration, there is a need for housing which the grant or refusal of the application will affect.[27]

A reporter did not make an error of law in deleting a condition preventing the erection of a gate until a public right of passage had been removed, as any infringement of a legal right of passage is dealt with by other statutory and common law provisions, and accordingly this was not a relevant issue for the planning decision.[28]

Other guidance on possible planning purposes may be found in the court decisions interpreting the scope of "material considerations" (Chapter 5).

The authority may have many purposes in mind when imposing a condition. A condition might have other purposes, but must not be imposed solely to serve some other purpose or purposes.[29] This suggests that the mere presence of a planning purpose is enough. There must, however, come a point at which the planning purpose becomes subordinated to the other purposes to such an extent that it has negligible influence on the decision. Another view suggests that the purpose must be solely or primarily to achieve a planning objective.[30] Once the planning purpose becomes secondary to the other purposes then the condition is invalid. This seems the preferable view. In practice, however, planning authorities are unlikely to mention any non-planning purposes in their written reasons for imposing the condition, in an attempt to avoid any appeal against their decisions.

(b) Fairly and Reasonably Relates to Permitted Development

The condition must fairly and reasonably relate to the development authorised by the permission.[31] This is the result of the wording of the statutory power to impose conditions which links inextricably, and subordinates, this power to the decision to grant permission. Since permission is given for a specified development, any condition must also relate to that development. **6.06**

What is the meaning of "fairly and reasonably relates"? It has been suggested that a "recognised and real relationship" is required, which is a question of fact and judgment, rather than requiring the condition to be imposed to remedy some direct adverse consequence ("mischief") caused by the development. It would be enough that the condition was imposed because of matters "merely consequential" to the development. Any test is open to subjective application, and while the test of directness is capable of narrow application, the "merely consequential" test may achieve the same result as a test of directness applied broadly. Each case is determined on its facts and it is difficult to identify a consistent approach in the court decisions.

---

[27] *Mitchell v. Secretary of State for the Environment* [1994] 2 P.L.R. 23.
[28] *South Lanarkshire Council v. Secretary of State for Scotland*, 1997 S.L.T. 961, SPEL 60:34.
[29] *Newbury D.C. v. Secretary of State for the Environment* [1981] A.C. 578, *per* Lord Fraser at p. 618.
[30] Grant, *Urban Planning Law* (1981), p. 337.
[31] *Pyx Granite v. MHLG* [1958] 1 Q.B. 554, *per* Lord Denning at p. 572.

By including land within the application, the developer may be taken to admit the connection between that land and the proposed development. A more contentious issue arises where conditions are imposed on land under the control of the applicant which is not contained within the terms of the application. The statutory power to impose such conditions (see above) requires the conditions to be "expedient for the purposes of or in connection with the development authorised by the permission." This wording would appear to achieve a similar result to the "fairly and reasonably relates" test. Court decisions relating to this statutory power may therefore be used to help interpret the "fairly and reasonably relates" requirement.

Doubt has been expressed whether conditions attached to land under the control of the applicant a mile away rather than immediately adjacent to the development would be valid.[32] Geographical separation cannot be conclusive, but the directness of the relationship between condition and development must deteriorate with physical distance.[33]

Cases have affirmed conditions relating to land or buildings on the same site as the development, to the purpose of the development, and to its possible effects. Where machinery was used to process quarried stone, there was a direct relationship between the use of the machinery and the quarry development, with the result that a condition relating to the use of that machinery sufficiently related to the development.[34] As a factory extension allowed an existing building to be used more effectively, conditions controlling the use of machinery in the existing factory were valid as connected to the purpose of the permitted development.[35] A condition designed to control noise caused by air traffic fairly and reasonably related to the construction of a new terminal building required because of increased air traffic.[36]

Conditions have been struck down for failing to fairly and reasonably relate to the proposed development. A condition intended to restrict residential development elsewhere was held invalid because it did not reasonably relate to the proposed residential development.[37] A condition requiring demolition of buildings had nothing to do with the change of use for which planning permission was sought.[38] However, there was arguably an indirect connection because the continued use of the building affected the amenity of the neighbourhood. A condition regulating the killing of foxes could have been validly imposed on a grant of permission for construction of fox pens, but a condition preventing the slaughter of any animals on the premises was too remotely connected to the permitted development to be valid.[39] Similarly, a condition requiring installation of frosted glass in windows imposed when an occupancy condition was altered to allow a change of occupier was held to be

[32] *ibid.*
[33] *Peak Park JPB v. Secretary of State for the Environment* [1980] J.P.L. 114.
[34] *Pyx Granite v. MHLG, supra.*
[35] *Penwith D.C. v. Secretary of State for the Environment* (1977) 34 P. & C.R. 269.
[36] *BAA v. Secretary of State for Scotland,* 1979 S.C. 200.
[37] *North-East Fife D.C. v. Secretary of State for Scotland, supra.*
[38] *Newbury D.C. v. Secretary of State for the Environment* [1981] A.C. 578.
[39] *Gill v. Secretary of State for the Environment* [1985] J.P.L. 710.

unrelated to the development and therefore invalid, since the requirement for the glass was not brought about by the proposed occupation, but dated back to the first occupation of the building.[40] However, it could be argued that the change of use did not cause the need for the condition, but continued that need.

A condition preventing the erection of a gate until a public right of passage had been removed was held not to reasonably relate to the proposed development as any infringement of a legal right of passage is dealt with by other statutory and common law provisions.[41]

(c) Reasonableness

The imposition of a condition must be reasonable, but in the special 6.07 legal sense (referred to as *Wednesbury* reasonableness[42]). A condition will be invalid on the ground of unreasonableness only if it is so unreasonable that no reasonable planning authority would have imposed that condition.

Unfortunately the term "reasonableness" has come to be used as an umbrella term for other legal requirements which have developed, such as certainty and necessity (see below). It should be used as a residual category, for use only where a condition meets all other requirements, but demonstrates such a perverse or irrational exercise of the statutory discretion that it is illegal. The danger is that the concept of reasonableness may be stretched to the stage that it is used to interfere with the merits of the decision, enabling the court to reject a condition of which it disapproves without having to show that the condition is defective in any more specific way.

This problem may be resolved by adopting the formulation of the grounds for judicial review (Chapter 8) to restate the requirements for the legal validity of a condition as follows:

1. it must have a planning purpose;
2. it must fairly and reasonably relate to the permitted development;
3. it must be otherwise legal; and
4. it must be otherwise rational, and not "so outrageous in its defiance of logic or of accepted moral standards that no sensible person who had applied his mind to the question to be decided could have arrived at it."[43]

Matters often discussed under the heading of reasonableness, which could be relocated under the heading of legality, include contributions from the applicant, derogation from the benefit of permission, certainty, enforceability and necessity.

Where a condition required the removal of all waste from the site within 12 months of the date of the permission, but another condition

---

[40] *Elmsbridge B.C. v. Secretary of State for the Environment* [1989] J.P.L. 277.
[41] *South Lanarkshire Council v. Secretary of State for Scotland*, 1997 S.L.T. 961, SPEL 60:34.
[42] *Associated Provincial Picture Houses v. Wednesday Corporation* [1948] 1 K.B. 223.
[43] *ibid.*

required a technical assessment to examine the environmental benefits and disbenefits of the wastes remaining within the site set against those of its removal, the planning permission was quashed on the grounds that these conditions were repugnant to each other.[44]

(d) Contributions from the Applicant

6.08   A condition cannot require payment of a monetary contribution by the applicant.[45] It would also be invalid for a condition to require the applicant to provide another form of contribution, such as relinquishing land for use by the public as open space[46] or parking.[47] For these purposes it is irrelevant that the applicant has agreed: validity cannot be conferred by consent.[48]

(e) Derogation from the Benefit of Permission

6.09   Although imposition of a condition necessarily alters the development proposed by the application, there must be a limit to such alteration. Conditions cannot be used to derogate from the benefit of the permission, with the result that the nature of the development permitted is significantly different to that proposed in the application for planning permission. In other words, the planning authority cannot seek to take away with one hand what it has granted with the other. This requirement derives from the statutory wording which subordinates the power to impose conditions to the power to grant permission. Use of conditions to alter radically the proposed development would leave no opportunity for the public to give their views on what would be a substantially different proposal.

    It must always be a question of fact and degree whether a particular condition takes away the substance of the permission.[49] It is competent to impose conditions scaling down an application, but not to the extent of altering the substance of the development. A condition reducing the size of the proposed development from 35 acres and 420 dwellings to 25 acres and 250 dwellings was upheld on the basis that the result did not differ substantially from the development proposed in the original application.[50] This suggests a test of character: does the permitted development have a substantially different character from the development proposed in the original application? Conditions requiring "ancillary or incidental" development, such as the provision of children's play areas and open space in a housing development, have also been upheld.[51]

    A grant of permission on appeal seeking to restrict the benefit of a permission previously granted for development of adjacent ground was held invalid.[52]

---

[44] *R. v. Essex C.C., ex p. Tarmac Roadstone Holdings Limited* [1998] J.P.L. B23.
[45] *R. v. Bowman* [1898] 1 Q.B. 663; *Att.-Gen. v. Wilts United Dairies* (1922) 91 L.J. (K.B.) 89.
[46] *M.J. Shanley v. Secretary of State for the Environment* [1982] J.P.L. 380.
[47] *Westminster Renslade v. Secretary of State for the Environment, supra.*
[48] *Birnie v. Banff C.C.* (n. 12, *supra*).
[49] *Kent C.C. v. Secretary of State for the Environment* (1976) 33 P. & C.R. 70.
[50] *Bernard Wheatcroft v. Secretary of State for the Environment* [1982] J.P.L. 37.
[51] *Britannia (Cheltenham) Ltd v. Secretary of State for the Environment* [1978] J.P.L. 554.
[52] *North-East Fife D.C. v. Secretary of State for Scotland, supra.*

(f) Certainty

A condition must be capable of being understood so that the owner of 6.10
the burdened property can comply with it. A planning condition is only
void from uncertainty if it can be given no meaning or no sensible or
ascertainable meaning, and not merely because it is ambiguous or leads
to absurd results.[53] A Scottish judge has suggested that it would be
equally invalid to impose a condition which produced an absurd result
which was plainly not the one intended. This suggestion should be
treated with caution, as it is not supported by previous decisions and was
made in a case where the condition was void from uncertainty.[54]

The courts will take pains to find some meaning in the terms of a
condition,[55] and have refused to construe the terms of a condition
against the interest of the authority in favour of the applicant (*contra
proferentem*).[56] Thus, mere ambiguity or doubtful instances will not
render a condition invalid.[57] Even vagueness will probably not be
sufficient to invalidate a condition. Terms such as "local"[58] and "surplus
stock"[59] have been upheld even though incapable of precise definition. It
is enough that such terms can be understood and applied. It would
appear that there is effectively a presumption that a condition is certain
in its wording, and this is emphasised by the few instances of successful
challenges.[60]

Although the conditions imposed on a permission were not completely
lucid, these conditions were not invalid because they were capable of
being given a sensible and ascertainable meaning.[61] A condition imposed
under the Environmental Protection Act that "All emissions to air from
the process shall be free from offensive odour as perceived by an
authorised officer of the Agency, outside the boundary" was held valid.[62]
The court rejected the argument that the condition was void from
uncertainty, on the grounds that the language of the condition was not
ambiguous and there was nothing uncertain about what the condition
was meant to achieve.

A condition that "leisure units should be completed and equipped for
use before any shops commence trading" was challenged on the grounds
that the use of the word "should" rather than "shall" or "must"
rendered the condition invalid. It was held that there was nothing in this
point, as it was plain that in the context of the conditions the word

---

[53] *Fawcett Properties v. Buckingham C.C.* [1960] 3 All E.R. 503, *per* Lord Denning at
p. 517; [1961] A.C. 636.
[54] *Eastwood D.C. v. Mactaggart & Mickel Ltd.*, 1994 S.L.T. 38; 1992 S.P.L.P. 37:76.
[55] *Kingsway Investments v. Kent C.C.* [1971] A.C. 72.
[56] *Crisp from the Fens v. Rutland C.C.*, 1950 L.G.R. 210, *per* Singleton J.
[57] *Inverclyde D.C. v. Inverkip Building Co.*, 1983 S.L.T. 563; *cf. David Lowe & Sons v.
Musselburgh Town Council*, 1973 S.C. 130.
[58] *Alderson v. Secretary of State for the Environment* [1984] J.P.L. 429.
[59] *R. v. Wakefield MDC ex p. Pearl Assurance* [1997] E.G.C.S. 32.
[60] *Eastwood D.C. v. Mactaggart & Mickel Ltd. supra*; *David Lowe & Sons v. Musselburgh
Town Council, supra* is a doubtful authority.
[61] *City of Aberdeen Council v. Secretary of State for Scotland*, 1997 G.W.D. 33–1692,
SPEL 64:127.
[62] *Wheelan v. Seed Crushers (Scotland) Ltd*, 1998 S.C.C.R. 293, SPEL 68:76.

"should" was equivalent to "shall", and that the insistence on "shall" or "must" was over-exacting. Although one of the proposals granted permission subject to this condition did not contain a leisure component, the condition was held to mean no more than that in so far as the development contained leisure units, those units should be completed and equipped before any shops commenced trading.[63]

(g) Enforceability

6.11   There are two senses in which a condition may be unenforceable: if it requires action that is outwith the control of the applicant, or if it is too vague to form the subject of enforcement action.

A condition which requires any action that is outwith the control of the applicant is unenforceable and therefore invalid because there are no steps that the applicant can take to secure the required result. As control of air traffic was the statutory responsibility of another body, a condition specifying the direction of aircraft flights was unenforceable because the applicant was unable to meet the requirements of the condition.[64] A condition relating to land that is neither within the application nor under the control of the applicant must be unenforceable, because the applicant will have no power to ensure compliance with the condition.[65] A condition requiring access to be by way of a specified road was held invalid because the road was neither within the application site nor under the control of the applicant and in consequence there were no steps which the applicant could take to secure or ensure that all vehicles used the prescribed route.[66] On similar reasoning, a condition may be unenforceable and invalid if it relates to land within the application site, but outwith the control of the applicant.

Where it would be invalid to impose a condition requiring action outwith the control of the applicant, the same result can be achieved legitimately by using a negatively worded (or suspensive) condition (see below). The effect of such a condition is that the development cannot commence until the action is achieved. The obligation to be enforced would not be the obligation to achieve the result, but rather the lack of permission to start the development until the result was achieved. The decision to commence the development is under the control of the applicant.

The other sense of enforceability relates to the need for the meaning of a condition to be precise enough for enforcement action to be taken against any breach of its terms. Conditions that are so vague as to be incapable of definition, or physically incapable of performance, may be unenforceable. A condition requiring that the first opportunity to buy houses be given to local people was declared unenforceable because there was no indication of the method or terms upon which this opportunity was to be offered.[67] It is not enough that the condition is

---

[63] *Dumfries and Galloway R.C. v. Secretary of State for Scotland*, 1996 G.W.D. 26–1558, SPEL 58:118.

[64] *BAA v. Secretary of State for Scotland, supra.*

[65] *Birnie v. Banff C.C., supra.*

[66] *Mouchell Superannuation Trustees v. Oxfordshire C.C.* [1992] 1 P.L.R. 97.

[67] *M.J. Shanley v. Secretary of State for the Environment, supra.*

merely difficult to enforce.[68] Conditions may be valid even though breaches of the condition may be difficult to detect.[69]

A condition imposing a noise limit which did not indicate where the noise level was to be measured was unenforceable because it was impossible to ascertain whether or not it was being complied with.[70] However, the court was considering whether it was competent for the reporter to replace the condition, and not whether the condition itself was valid. In a subsequent case, legal arguments dealt with the issue of certainty and enforceability does not appear to have been raised as a separate issue.[71]

The enforceability of a condition that "leisure units should be completed and equipped for use before any shops commence trading" was challenged on the grounds that the use of the word "should" rather than "shall" or "must" rendered the condition unenforceable and invalid. It was held that there was nothing in this point, as it was plain that in the context of the conditions the word "should" was equivalent to "shall", and that the insistence on "shall" or "must" was over-exacting. Although one of the proposals granted permission subject to this condition did not contain a leisure component, the condition was held to mean no more than that in so far as the development contains leisure units, those units should be completed and equipped before any shops commence trading.[72]

If a condition can be certain enough for the applicant to understand the limits placed on his property rights, but open to challenge on the basis that it is unenforceable, it is difficult to resolve the requirements for certainty (see above) and enforceability of conditions,[73] and it has been suggested that there is no independent head of challenge to the validity of a condition relating to its enforceability.[74]

(h)　Necessity

The Court of Session has declared that an unnecessary condition is　6.12 invalid, by applying an expediency test to the imposition of all conditions irrespective of their statutory source.[75] This aspect of the decision has been criticised. (The conditions were also found invalid on the ground that they related to activities that were outwith the power of the applicants or to land that was outwith the control of the applicants and were therefore unenforceable.)

---

[68] *Chichester D.C. v. Secretary of State for the Environment* [1992] 3 P.L.R. 49.
[69] *Kent C.C. v. Secretary of State for the Environment, supra.*
[70] *Dunfermline D.C. v. Secretary of State for Scotland,* 1996 S.L.T. 89, SPEL, 52:110.
[71] *City of Aberdeen Council v. Secretary of State for Scotland,* 1997 G.W.D. 33–1692, SPEL 64:127.
[72] *Dumfries and Galloway R.C. v. Secretary of State for Scotland,* 1996 G.W.D. 26–1558, SPEL 58:118.
[73] This can be seen from the discussion in *Bromsgrove D.C. v. Secretary of State for the Environment* [1988] J.P.L. 257 of the decisions in *M.J. Shanley, supra; Penwith D.C. v. Secretary of State for the Environment* [1986] J.P.L. 432; *Bizony v. Secretary of State for the Environment* [1976] J.P.L. 306.
[74] *Chichester D.C. v. Secretary of State for the Environment, supra.*
[75] *BAA v. Secretary of State for Scotland,* 1979 S.C. 200. Only TCPSA, s. 41(1) refers to conditions being "expedient".

This concept of necessity can be criticised for taking the courts beyond questions of legality into the merits of a decision. The review jurisdiction of the courts is limited to examining the legality of a decision (Chapter 8). It is difficult to imagine an unnecessary condition that would be reprehensible enough to be illegal. If a condition is unnecessary because the application did not require it, then it should be caught by the "fairly and reasonably relates" test. The close link between the condition and the mischief caused by the development required by the concept of necessity appears to go further than the "fairly and reasonably relates" test and renders it redundant. However, the concept of proportionality, which also requires a close link between the action taken and the mischief at which it is aimed, has been rejected by a British court as going beyond the notion of *Wednesbury* reasonableness into the question of the merits of a decision.[76]

The decision can also be criticised on its facts. One condition was found to have no practical need or effect because another body had already taken action to achieve the desired result. It could be argued that the condition was harmless and no burden to the applicant, and guarded against the possibility of the action being reversed in the future. Other conditions were held unnecessary on the ground that if they were validly imposed on one permission then there was no need to duplicate them on other permissions. Duplication gives the authority greater opportunity for enforcement and adds greater force to the requirement.

It is therefore suggested that the courts should not declare conditions invalid on the basis of lack of necessity. To do so would lead to judicial intervention in the merits of a planning decision. The question of necessity should be left to the planning authority and the Secretary of State, as they can examine the issue of necessity as part of the planning merits of the condition.

In a subsequent case, the Court of Session held that a condition preventing the erection of a gate until a public right of passage had been removed was unnecessary as any infringement of a legal right of passage is dealt with by other statutory and common law provisions.[77] However, the court was considering whether it was competent for the reporter to delete the condition, and not whether the condition itself was valid.

Validity of Planning Conditions: Policy

6.13   In considering whether to impose conditions upon a grant of planning permission the planning authority is bound by the legal requirements for the validity of a condition. The authority must also have regard to the policy laid down by the Secretary of State. As this policy is used in the determination of any appeal, authorities anxious to avoid successful appeals against their decisions will give it careful consideration when applying conditions.

The Scottish Office policy is more restrictive than the legal requirements, stating that a condition must be necessary, relevant to planning,

[76] *R. v. Secretary of State for the Home Department, ex p. Brind* [1991] A.C. 696.
[77] *South Lanarkshire Council v. Secretary of State for Scotland*, 1997 S.L.T. 961, SPEL 60:34.

relevant to the development to be permitted, enforceable, precise and reasonable in all other respects.[78] The nature of the development permitted or its effect on the surroundings must call for the condition to be imposed. A greater burden is placed upon planning authorities to impose precise and clear conditions. The Secretary of State may find a condition unenforceable if breaches of the condition may be difficult to detect. The policy includes suggested models of acceptable conditions and indicates that conditions requiring the following results are not acceptable (the explanations in brackets have been added by the author).[79]

(a)   On Policy Grounds

1.   Completion of a development within a specified time limit.   6.14
2.   Delaying the commencement of development until a future date.
3.   Preventing the display of advertisements on the site (lack of planning purpose: there are separate statutory powers for control of advertisements—Chapter 9).
4.   Restricting occupation, for example, of flats, to a specified number of persons (difficult to enforce).
5.   Construction of an ancillary road by the applicant as and when required by the planning authority (vague).

(b)   On Legal Grounds

1.   That means of access shall be set back and splayed in   6.15 agreement with the roads authority, when the latter is a third party (unenforceable—actions of third party).
2.   That the land in front of the building shall be made available for future road widening (cession of land).
3.   A lay-by, having been constructed, should thereafter be assigned to the roads authority (cession of land).
4.   Loading and unloading, and the parking of vehicles, shall not take place on the road in front of the premises (enforceability—road not under control of applicant).
5.   The site shall be kept tidy at all times (certainty/ enforceability—vague).
6.   The applicant shall comply with the bye-laws and general statutory provisions in force in the district (lack of planning purpose).
7.   Furnishing shall be of a fireproof material (lack of planning purpose).
8.   Aircraft should only arrive or depart at an airfield on specified air traffic routes (lack of planning purpose—activity regulated by other statutory provisions; enforceability—outside control of applicant).

---

[78] Circular 4/1998, Annex, para. 12.
[79] Circular 4/1998, para. 1 and Circular 18/1986, App. B.

9. A shop window display to be maintained in an attractive condition (certainty/enforceability—no criterion by which it could be enforced).

The list of model conditions should be consulted for forms of condition which may achieve these results validly.

Challenge of Condition

6.16   There are several options available to the applicant for planning permission to challenge an unacceptable condition (see fig 6.1), most of which are described in more detail in Chapter 8. The acceptability of the conditions should be considered before the permission is implemented (Chapter 5).

(a)   Negotiation

6.17   Formal procedures such as appeals are expensive and time-consuming for both the applicant and the planning authority, and negotiations must be in the interests of both parties. It may be possible to persuade the planning authority to dispense with the condition, with the result that permission is granted without the condition following a fresh application, or an application for permission to develop the land without compliance with the condition is approved (see below). Additional information may be produced which was not before the authority when it made the decision to impose the condition. Developers frequently complain that authorities do not appreciate the impact of conditions, especially their adverse financial impact, and these matters could be put to the authority. If valid grounds of appeal can be shown, the authority may be willing to negotiate a compromise to avoid losing an appeal.

When negotiating, care must be taken that time limits for commencing a formal challenge do not expire. If time limits are looming, it is possible to lodge the challenge and sist (suspend) further procedure with the agreement of the authority to allow negotiations to continue. To pressurise the authority into negotiating, it may be necessary to commence formal procedures for challenge in tandem with the negotiations.

(b)   Appeal to the Secretary of State

6.18   It is competent to appeal to the Secretary of State against a grant of permission with an unacceptable condition.[80] The appeal must be lodged within six months of the decision by the planning authority. As part of the appeal, the planning merits of the condition and the facts of the case will be considered. The policy of the Secretary of State on imposition of conditions will be applied (see above). The appeal is dealt with as if it were an application for planning permission. The Secretary of State may, therefore, reverse or vary any part of the original decision, no matter what aspect is challenged. In consequence, there is a risk of losing the entire permission or being burdened with a more onerous condition.

[80] TCPSA, s. 47.

Fig. 6.1   Challenging Planning Conditions

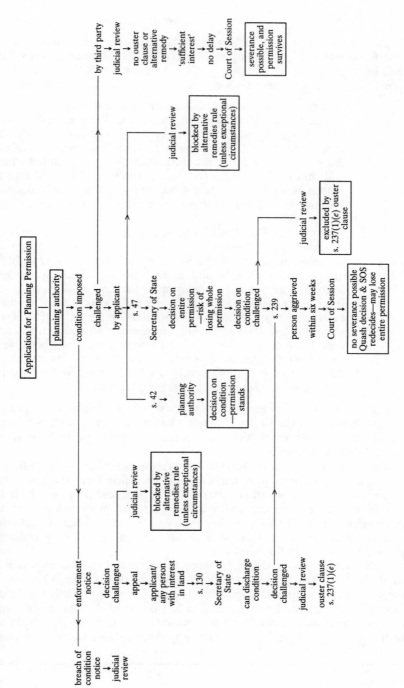

(c) Review by Court of Session

6.19   Review by the Court of Session relates to the legal validity of the condition and not its planning merits. The legal requirements for validity will be applied and not the policy of the Secretary of State. A distinction must be drawn between statutory and common-law judicial review:

1.   Statutory review is only competent for challenge of a decision by the Secretary of State on a condition.[81] It is available to any person aggrieved, but it is subject to a strict six-week time limit. The court has no power to sever the invalid condition from the remainder of the permission.[82] A successful challenge will therefore result in the permission being quashed and the matter being returned to the Secretary of State for re-decision. He may decide that without the condition, permission should be refused.

2.   An application for judicial review at common law may be used to challenge a decision to impose a condition by either the planning authority or the Secretary of State. It is available to any person with title and interest to sue. There is no pre-scribed time limit, but delay may bar any challenge. Unless there are exceptional circumstances, the existence of an alternative remedy will exclude an application for judicial review at common law. The applicant for permission therefore cannot utilise the common-law judicial review procedure because of his statutory rights of appeal to the Secretary of State against a decision by the planning authority, and review by the Court of Session of the Secretary of State's decision.

Unlike statutory review, in the exercise of its common-law judicial review jurisdiction the Court of Session has the power to sever an invalid condition with the result that the remainder of the permission stands shorn of the condition.

There is no statutory test to determine whether a condition is severable, but several approaches can be identified from the cases. It is important to decide whether severance is a practical proposition. If the invalid condition is "inextricably interconnected" with the rest of the permission, severance may be impossible.[83] However, there is no absolute requirement for textual severability and the court may redraft a permission to retain the valid part.[84]

A distinction can be drawn between fundamental conditions which go to the root of the permission, and conditions that are unimportant or incidental, superimposed or collateral to the permission. Only conditions of the latter type can be severed. This test is essentially one of substance or character: can the condition be severed without changing the nature of the grant of permission? Another approach focuses on the intentions

---

[81] s. 239.
[82] *BAA v. Secretary of State for Scotland, supra.*
[83] *R. v. Secretary of State for Transport, ex p. GLC* [1985] 3 All E.R. 300.
[84] *DPP v. Hutchison* [1990] 2 All E.R. 836.

of the planning authority, asking whether it would have granted the permission without the offending condition. If not, the condition should not be severed and the whole permission should be quashed. It may be thought that a condition which does not fairly and reasonably relate to the permitted development is likely to be severable, but even in these circumstances the courts remain reluctant to alter the permission granted by the authority and prefer to quash the entire permission.

In consequence of the need to speculate on the intention of the planning authority in imposing the condition, the courts rarely declare a condition severable. There are only three reported cases in which an invalid condition has been severed from the planning permission.[85] It is, therefore, unlikely that a successful application for judicial review at common law will result in anything other than invalidation of the whole permission.

(d) Application for Permission to Develop Land Without Compliance With Condition

An application can be made to the planning authority for permission to develop the application site without complying with the conditions subject to which the permission was granted.[86] In deciding the application, the authority can only consider the conditions and there is no risk of losing the permission. If it decides permission should be granted subject to the same conditions, the application will be refused. If the application is successful permission will be granted subject to different conditions or unconditionally.

The disadvantage of this procedure is that the application is made to the same body that imposed the condition. Powerful arguments will be required to convince it that the condition should not have been imposed or should now be discharged. Using this procedure to challenge a condition may only be an option if circumstances have changed since the condition was imposed.

(e) Ignore the Condition

The applicant may choose to ignore the condition in the hope that the planning authority will not take enforcement action. A breach of condition becomes immune from enforcement action, and lawful, after 10 years (Chapter 7). In the event that the authority serves an enforcement notice, an appeal may be lodged with the Secretary of State on the grounds that the condition ought to be discharged,[87] or an application for retrospective permission lodged. However, authorities are more likely to use the new power to serve a breach of condition notice where there is non-compliance with a condition regulating the use of land. There is no right of appeal against such a notice although it may be

6.20

6.21

---

[85] *Allnatt Properties v. Middlesex C.C.* (1964) 15 P. & C.R. 288, *R. v. St Edmundsbury B.C., ex p. Investors in Industry* [1985] 3 All E.R. 234; *Elmsbridge B.C. v. Secretary of State for the Environment* [1989] J.P.L. 277.
[86] TCPSA, s. 42.
[87] s. 130(1)(a).

possible to seek judicial review at common law on the grounds that the condition which is the subject of the notice is invalid. If attempts to challenge the enforcement or breach of condition notice are unsuccessful, failure to comply with its terms is a criminal offence. The invalidity of the condition can be raised as a defence to any prosecution for failure to comply with a breach of condition notice,[88] but not in relation to an enforcement notice offence (Chapter 7).

(f) Application for Retrospective Permission

6.22   An application for retrospective permission may be made for development which was carried out without complying with a condition subject to which permission was granted.[89] As part of the application, it would be necessary to convince the authority that there was no need for the condition. If no such application is made, the breach of condition will only become immune from enforcement action after 10 years.

Types of Conditions

6.23   In addition to the two general statutory powers to impose planning conditions, there are several more particular statutory powers relating to expiry of permission, temporary and personal permissions, specification of use, and preservation and planting of trees (see above). Many other types of planning conditions have arisen in practice. Of these, four have been examined in particular detail by the courts: those relating to occupancy, restriction of use or development, avoidance of compensation payment, and the imposition of negative or suspensive conditions.

(a) Occupancy Conditions

6.24   As a basic proposition, conditions restricting the class of potential occupiers of property appear unduly restrictive of rights of private property. Indeed, the existence of an occupancy condition will restrict the opportunities to re-sell a property and therefore reduce its value for mortgage purposes. Planning relates to the use of the land rather than to the user.[90] However, personal circumstances can be taken into account in certain cases.[91] Conditions may, therefore, be imposed which restrict occupancy to a particular occupier or class of occupier, provided the condition relates to a legitimate planning purpose.

A condition limiting occupation of a dwelling to persons employed in agriculture (agricultural occupancy condition) was validly imposed where the reason for the condition was the protection of the Green Belt from residential development.[92] Similarly, a condition restricting occupation of

---

[88] *Dilieto v. Ealing LBC* [1998] 2 All E.R. 885.
[89] s. 33.
[90] *Westminster City Council v. British Waterways Board* [1985] A.C. 676; [1985] J.P.L. 102; *David Lowe & Sons v. Musselburgh Town Council*, 1973 S.C. 130, *per* Lord President Emslie at p. 142.
[91] *Westminster City Council v. Great Portland Estates* [1985] A.C. 661, *per* Lord Scarman at p. 669H (also [1985] J.P.L. 108).
[92] *Fawcett Properties v. Buckingham City Council* [1961] A.C. 636.

commercial or industrial property to local firms was imposed to restrict the entry of new industry into the area.[93] In contrast, an occupancy condition imposed to relieve the authority of its statutory duty had no legitimate planning reason and was therefore invalid.[94]

In considering whether an occupancy condition has been complied with, the relevant issue is occupancy and not use. A property subject to an agricultural occupancy condition had been occupied from May to September as holiday accommodation, and was empty from October to April. The decision to grant a Certificate of Lawful Use on the grounds of 10 years' non-compliance with the condition was quashed on the grounds that the question of use had been improperly confused with the question of occupancy.[95]

An occupancy condition does not apply to a building which is not built in accordance with the planning permission. A bungalow which was about 90 feet west of the permitted location was held not to be subject to the occupancy restriction imposed by the condition attached to the planning permission.[96] As the period for enforcement of development without planning permission is only four years in contrast to 10 years for a breach of planning condition, this is an important issue.

The Scottish Office guidance states that occupancy conditions should only be used when the need for special planning grounds can be demonstrated, and permission would otherwise be refused. Conditions restricting the occupancy of commercial or industrial premises to local firms should not be imposed. Similarly, occupancy conditions should be imposed on housing developments only in the most exceptional cases where there are clear and specific circumstances that warrant allowing an individual house (or extension) on a site where development would not normally be permitted. Agricultural occupancy conditions may be imposed where permission is granted for a house to be built to accommodate a worker engaged in agricultural or forestry employment on a site where residential development would not normally be permitted. Although conditions should not normally be used to control matters such as tenure, price or ownership, there may be circumstances in which it will be acceptable to use conditions to ensure that some of the housing built is occupied only by people falling within particular categories of need.[97]

(b)   Restriction of Use/Development

It is competent to impose a condition restricting changes of use. This   6.25
has the effect of restricting the freedom provided by the UCO (Chapter 4), with the result that an application for planning permission may be required for any change from the permitted use. The condition may prohibit any change from the use permitted; alternatively, it may preclude specific alternative uses or restrict changes to specified classes

---

[93] *Slough Industrial Estates v. Secretary of State for the Environment* [1987] J.P.L. 353.
[94] *R. v. London Borough of Hillingdon, ex p. Royco Homes* [1974] Q.B. 720.
[95] *North Devon D.C. v. Secretary of State for the Environment* [1998] 4 P.L.R. 46.
[96] *Handoll v. Warner Goodman and Streat* [1995] J.P.L. 930.
[97] Circular 4/1998, Annex, paras 91–102.

of the UCO. For example, it may be valid to impose a condition preventing the change of use permitted by class 4 from light industrial to office use, provided the planning authority have valid planning reasons for imposing this restriction.[98]

It is similarly possible to restrict permitted development rights under the PDO.[99] For example, where permission is granted for erection of a dwellinghouse in the grounds of an existing dwellinghouse, it may be appropriate to restrict the permitted development rights which would otherwise be enjoyed by the new dwellinghouse. This would have the effect of requiring an application for planning permission to be made which would provide the planning authority with an opportunity to consider the effects of fresh development on the existing dwelling.

The Scottish Office guidance states that conditions limiting the provisions of the UCO or PDO should only be imposed in exceptional circumstances.[1] This type of condition requires to be carefully worded.[2]

(c)   Liability to Pay Compensation

6.26   Where there is a choice of statutory powers, an authority can legitimately use the power that carries no liability to payment of compensation. It is therefore competent to impose a condition for planning reasons which has the effect of avoiding the payment of compensation,[3] although avoidance of the payment of compensation is not a planning consideration.[4] The Scottish Office policy is that conditions should not be imposed in order to avoid liability to pay compensation under other legislation, but that such conditions would not be illegal if justified on planning grounds.[5]

(d)   Negative/Suspensive Conditions

6.27   Permission for a proposed development often hinges on an element outside the applicant's control, such as the provision of adequate sewerage facilities by the sewerage authority. Since the result is outwith the applicant's control, any condition requiring him to achieve that result would be unenforceable (see above). The solution is to word the condition negatively so that it provides that development will not commence until the result has been achieved. It is competent to impose such negative or suspensive conditions, often referred to as "Grampian" conditions.[6] Use of this type of condition may avoid the necessity of

---

[98] Compare *London Borough of Tower Hamlets v. Secretary of State for the Environment* [1990] J.P.L. 688 and *Camden London B.C. v. Secretary of State for the Environment* [1989] J.P.L. 613.
[99] PDO, art. 3(4); *Gill v. Secretary of State for the Environment* [1985] J.P.L. 710; "Research on the General Permitted Development Order and Related Mechanisms" (the Scottish Office, 1998), Pt 6.
[1] Circular 4/1998, Annex, para. 86.
[2] *Dunoon Developments v. Secretary of State for the Environment* [1992] J.P.L. 936.
[3] *R. v. Exeter City Council, ex p. J.L. Thomas* [1991] 1 Q.B. 471; [1990] J.P.L. 129; *cf. Hall v. Shoreham-by-Sea Urban D.C.* [1964] 1 W.L.R. 240; [1964] J.P.L. 316.
[4] *BAA v. Secretary of State for Scotland*, 1979 S.C. 200, *per* L.P. Emslie at p. 218.
[5] Circular 4/1998, Annex, paras 20 and 22.
[6] *Grampian R.C. v. Aberdeen D.C.*, 1984 S.L.T. 197.

entering into a planning agreement (see below), but is not appropriate where the development has already commenced.[7]

Until a decision of the House of Lords, it was trite law that it would be unreasonable and *ultra vires* to impose a negative condition on a grant of planning permission unless there was a reasonable prospect of the result being achieved.[8] In the absence of such a prospect, the authority would have granted a worthless permission.

In *British Railways Board v. Secretary of State for the Environment*, the House of Lords overruled the reasonable prospect test.[9] If the negative condition is appropriate in light of sound planning principles, the fact that it appeared to have no reasonable prospects of being implemented did not mean that the grant of planning permission subject to it would be unlawful. What is appropriate depends on the circumstances and must be determined in the exercise of the discretion of the planning authority determining the application. The mere fact that a desirable condition appears to have no reasonable prospect of fulfilment does not mean that planning permission has to be refused.

The practical implications of this decision are uncertain. Authorities are likely to continue to regard the lack of a reasonable prospect of fulfilment as an important factor in their decision, albeit not a determining factor. It should be noted that the case before their Lordships concerned the imposition of negative conditions to solve ownership difficulties, where it was clear that those difficulties had no relevance to the determination of the planning application. One can speculate that a different approach might be taken where the problems concern more important matters such as necessary infrastructure.

Previously the Scottish Office guidance indicated that a negative condition should only be imposed where there were at least reasonable prospects of the action in question being performed. The reasonableness of the requirement depended on the likelihood of the precondition being fulfilled within such time as to enable the development to be commenced within the time limit imposed by the permission. This advice no longer appears in the new guidance, which indicates that there is no longer a legal requirement to satisfy a reasonable prospects test, and advises planning authorities to note the ruling by the House of Lords "and its implications for a less restrictive view in the use of negative conditions".[10]

Negative conditions can also be used to control the separate phases of a large development. For example, a condition may require provision of specified infrastructure works (roads, drains, etc.) before the development or a further phase of the development commences. Such conditions ensure the provision of expensive works which the developer might be tempted to defer for many years.

---

[7] *Empress Car Co. v. Secretary of State for Wales* [1995] E.G.C.S. 22.

[8] *Norfolk House v. Secretary of State for the Environment* [1990] J.P.L. 490; *Jones v. Secretary of State for Wales* [1990] J.P.L. 907.

[9] *British Railways Board v. Secretary of State for the Environment* [1994] J.P.L. 32; [1993] 2 PLR 125, followed in *Strathclyde R.C. v. Secretary of State for Scotland*, 1996 S.L.T. 579, SPEL 55:51.

[10] Circular 4/1998, Annex, para. 38.

Negative conditions are not invalid where they relate to actions which might take place on land beyond the control of the applicant or depend on decisions taken by someone other than the planning authority.[11]

Conclusion

6.28   The court decisions on the use of the particular types of conditions discussed above do not show the expected degree of judicial concern to protect private rights of property against interference by way of conditions imposed on grants of planning permission.[12] Indeed, it seems that the courts generally favour the validity of conditions. Although the judges have developed a series of limitations on the exercise of the power to impose conditions, there are few instances where the courts have found conditions invalid. This may in part be due to the influence on the imposition of conditions of the Scottish Office/Department of the Environment guidance on the use of conditions which is often more restrictive than the legal requirements.

PLANNING AGREEMENTS

6.29   Planning agreements are contracts entered into between the landowner and planning authority (and often with other parties). Agreements can be entered into at any stage of the planning process, but most commonly arise in connection with applications for planning permission. There are several statutory powers which enable local authorities to enter into agreements with developers. The widest and, therefore, most important is the power to enter into a section 75 agreement conferred by the TCPSA (previously section 50 of the 1972 Act). Although many of the following points would apply to all forms of planning agreements, discussion will focus exclusively on section 75 agreements.[13]

It should be noted that the statutory power to enter into a section 106 obligation, which is the English equivalent of a section 75 agreement, is worded differently, partly as a consequence of differences between the land law of each legal system. Decisions of English courts relating to planning agreements must therefore be read with care.

The attraction for developers lies in the possibility of using a planning agreement to increase the likelihood of a grant of planning permission for a proposed development. This may be achieved by using an agreement to remove obstacles which would otherwise render the development unacceptable. Agreements can also be used to offer community benefits as a balance to offset the planning disadvantages of a proposed development. The development potential of a site can be

---

[11] *Strathclyde R.C. v. Secretary of State for Scotland, supra.*

[12] *cf.* McAuslan's thesis that the courts favour individual rights of private property at the expense of the public interest, thereby upholding individual challenges to the actions of planning authorities—*Ideologies of Planning Law* (1980) and article of same name (1979) 2.U.L. & P.1.

[13] Other powers include Local Government (Scotland) Act 1973, ss. 69 and 85; Roads (Scotland) Act 1984, s. 48.

unlocked through an agreement providing that the developer will undertake or pay for infra-structure improvements, such as roads and sewers, without which no development could be permitted on the site and which would otherwise be at the mercy of local government budgets. In the developer's eyes the agreement is a device to increase the likelihood of planning permission being granted. In consequence, it is essential to ensure that the planning authority may validly take into account the benefits promised in the agreement when determining the application for planning permission (see Agreements as a Material Consideration, below).

Although planning agreements are entered into voluntarily, it must be acknowledged that developers are often left with no alternative but to agree. If there are planning problems with the proposed development which can only be resolved through a planning agreement, planning permission cannot be obtained until the developer and the planning authority have negotiated the terms of the agreement. This places the planning authority in a position to dictate the terms, and possibly require the provision of planning gain. Without the agreement permission will be refused on appeal and the option of appealing to the Secretary of State against a deemed refusal of planning permission (Chapter 8) is, therefore, not available to the developer. The Secretary of State/reporter has no power to impose an agreement on the planning authority. The developer must agree terms with the authority or abandon the proposed development. However, the developer's negotiating position need not be inherently weak. Considerations such as the number of jobs which would be created by the proposed development may cause the planning authority to be anxious to avoid its abandonment. In addition, in some circumstances, the Secretary of State may be able to grant planning permission without the agreement.[14]

The English courts have recently held that it was unreasonable for a 6.30 highway authority, whose road safety objections had been fully heard and rejected on appeal, to maintain their original view and refuse to enter into an agreement with the developer.[15] However, it was not perverse for an updated assessment to be required before the agreement was concluded when the original study had been undertaken four years ago and there was evidence of changed traffic conditions in the area.[16] It is unclear how far this principle may extend. For example, it could be argued that it would be *ultra vires* for a planning authority to refuse to enter into a section 75 agreement where the Secretary of State has indicated that he is minded to grant planning permission.

For planning authorities, agreements are an alternative means of controlling developments, especially in light of the uncertainty regarding the validity of conditions (see above), and their desire to avoid successful appeals against conditions. Agreements can also be used to control matters clearly beyond the scope of conditions. For example, conditions cannot validly require payment of money or provision of infra-structure

---

[14] *e.g., Strathclyde R.C. v. Secretary of State for Scotland, supra.*
[15] *R. v. Warwickshire C.C., ex p. PowerGen* [1998] J.P.L. 131.
[16] *R. v. Cardiff City Council, ex p. Sears Group Properties,* [1998] 3 P.L.R. 55.

such as roads and sewers on land outside the application site which is not under the control of the applicant for permission, even where the work is only necessary because of the proposed development. In addition, agreements can secure a degree of flexibility of control and management of development beyond the normal range of planning permission and conditions. Other attractions are the lack of any rights of appeal, and the availability of contractual remedies for enforcement without the procedural requirements of the planning enforcement regime (Chapter 7).

The use of planning agreements is not without criticism.[17] It circumvents the formal procedures laid down for determining applications for planning permission and therefore avoids statutory protections and limitations. The lack of public scrutiny means that interests other than those of the negotiating parties may not receive proper protection. Most importantly, there is concern that the advantages (often referred to as "planning gain") accruing from the planning agreement may affect the objectivity of the authority in evaluating the planning merits of the scheme. In other words, that the process amounts to a sale of planning permission.[18] Above all, the objection is that it is precisely because conditions cannot be imposed that the applicant must "voluntarily" offer the benefit.[19] The legal restrictions placed on the use of conditions are circumvented by using planning agreements to achieve the desired objective. Criticism has focused on the use by planning authorities of agreements to secure planning gain or benefit for the community which does not form an essential part of the development.

A study of the use of section 75 agreements in Scotland found that on average considerably less than 1 per cent of planning applications are linked to agreements. It concluded that the negotiation of substantial unrelated gains seems to be uncommon, although several "relatively minor" cases were noted. At least half the authorities interviewed cited instances where the infrastructure requirement appeared to be in excess of what was strictly required for the development in question. The study concluded that there is an element of ill-considered use of agreements, especially when suspensive conditions would suffice. It recommended that planning authorities should review their use of agreements to see whether they are really required in all cases.[20]

Developers have cited more specific objections to the practice of using agreements.[21] Negotiating the terms of agreements is time-consuming and delays the grant of planning permission. Agreements often include restrictions which are contrary to Scottish Office policy and would, therefore, be overturned in any appeal against refusal of planning permission. It is common for the first developer in an area to be left with no choice but to agree to pay for the provision of infrastructure and services which are then used by subsequent developers without any

---

[17] Most recently by the Nolan Committee—SPEL 68:73 and 63:96.
[18] Loughlin, "Planning Gain—Law, Policy and Practice" (1981) 1 O.J.L.S. 61.
[19] Lichfield, "From Planning Gain to Community Benefit" [1989] J.P.L. 68.
[20] Rowan-Robinson and Durman, "Section 50 Agreements" (1992) Scottish Office.
[21] *ibid.*, para. 10.0 *et seq.*

contribution to the cost. A frequent complaint is that restrictions proposed by planning authorities for inclusion in agreements exhibit a lack of understanding of the financial aspects of development.

It is clear that there is some distrust of the use of planning agreements. Indeed, it has been suggested that authorities should review their practices with a view to utilising suspensive conditions in place of planning agreements wherever possible. Nevertheless, it must be emphasised that the power to use agreements to achieve objectives other than planning gain (as distinct from benefits related to the development) provides planning authorities with a flexible development control power. Planning agreements have a useful role to play in the planning system in the interests of planning authority and developer alike.

Scope of Section 75 Agreements

Two issues arise in any discussion of the scope of section 75 agreements: first, the limits to the power of planning authorities to enter into such agreements; and, secondly, the circumstances in which it would be illegal for the planning authority to take into account the provision of planning gain in terms of the agreement when determining an application for planning permission. Only the first issue truly concerns the scope of section 75 agreements; the second forms more a practical limit beyond which developers will be unwilling to venture although it provides scope for a rival developer to seek to reduce a grant of planning permission. It must be emphasised that it does not necessarily follow that where the provisions of an agreement cannot be validly considered when deciding an application, the planning authority must have exceeded its statutory power to enter into the planning agreement with the result that it is invalid.[22]   6.31

(a) Scope of the Statutory Power

As the term suggests, the power to enter into a section 75 agreement is conferred by statute.[23] If a planning authority exceeds the power conferred by statute, it is acting outwith its power (*ultra vires*) and, thus, illegally. The limits of the statutory power of a planning authority to enter into a section 75 agreement are therefore important.   6.32

The wording of section 75 gives planning authorities power to enter into agreements "for the purpose of restricting or regulating the development or use of the land." It is difficult to identify what limits are placed on the scope of agreements by this wording. It has been suggested that "restrict" refers to the prohibition or limitation of what is done on land, while "regulate" is more concerned with ensuring that something is done in a particular way.[24] The wording of section 75 does not permit the agreement to restrict or regulate the development or use of land, other than the land described in the agreement. Thus agreements cannot restrict off-site uses such as routes used by vehicles after leaving the site.

---

[22] *R. v. South Northants D.C., ex p. Crest Homes* [1994] 1 P.L.R. 47, Henry L.J. at 56 D–G.

[23] TCPSA, s. 75.

[24] Rowan-Robinson and Young, *Planning by Agreement in Scotland* (1989), p. 22.

This interpretation may suggest that section 75 agreements cannot require that some positive obligation be undertaken, in other words that the developer agrees to do something as opposed to not doing something. However, it has been argued that positive obligations can be included in section 75 agreements, provided that the sole or main purpose of the agreement is not to achieve the positive obligation. Thus planning authorities may require developers to pay all or part of the cost of providing sewers, roads, open spaces and so on, provided the purpose is to secure regulation of the development by ensuring that the development is adequately drained and served by roads.[25] Provision of a road was broadly interpreted as permently restricting use of the land on which the road was to be built, with the result that the restriction and not the provision of the road was the sole or main purpose of the agreement.[26] An agreement requiring the developer to provide an access road to an adjacent development site was held to have been competently entered into by the planning authority.[27] An agreement requiring demolition of a building was for the purpose of restricting or regulating the development or use of the land because it regulated or restricted the circumstances in which a new building could be built.[28]

The restrictions or regulations imposed by a section 75 agreement may be permanent or for a period prescribed by the agreement. The section 75 agreement may also contain "such incidental and consequential provisions (including provisions of a financial character) as appear to the planning authority to be necessary or expedient for the purposes of the agreement."

6.33   From this brief discussion it will be clear that the wording of the section 75 power is general and, therefore, open to interpretation. By way of comparison, the scope of the English equivalent of section 75 is more precise. A planning obligation may:

1. restrict the development or use of the land in any specified way;
2. require specified operations to be carried out in, on, under or over the land;
3. require the land to be used in any specified way; or
4. require a sum or sums to be paid to the planning authority on a specified date or dates or periodically.[29]

The first section of this chapter explored the limits on the power to impose planning conditions. Many of these limits have arisen from judicial interpretation of the statutory power. It had been suggested that if a condition would be invalid (*ultra vires*) then the same result could not be achieved through the use of a section 75 agreement.[30] This

---

[25] *ibid.*, p. 24; Circular 12/1996, "Town and Country Planning (Scotland) Act 1972 Planning Agreements", Annex 2, para. 2.
[26] *R. v. Gillingham B.C. ex p. Parham* [1988] J.P.L. 336.
[27] *McIntosh v. Aberdeenshire Council*, 1998 G.W.D. 6–255, SPEL 67:56.
[28] *Wycombe D.C. v. Williams* [1995] 3 P.L.R. 19, Alliott J. at 23B.
[29] Town and Country Planning Act 1990, s. 106.
[30] Most recently by Sir Graham Eyre, Q.C. in *Eagle Star v. Secretary of State for the Environment* [1992] J.P.L. 434 at p. 440.

implied that the same restrictions had to apply to use of agreements under section 75 as applied to conditions. The House of Lords have rejected this suggestion.[31]

Both the powers to impose planning conditions and to enter into section 75 agreements are provided by the TCPSA, so there is a common requirement of a planning purpose.[32] As any consideration relating to the use and development of land can be a planning consideration,[33] this requirement should not unduly constrain the use of agreements. An agreement requiring the developer to provide an access road to an adjacent development site was held to have a sound and proper planning purpose.[34]

Although most section 75 agreements are made in the context of applications for planning permission, agreements may be made in other situations. Unlike the power to impose conditions, the wording of section 75 does not connect the agreement to a grant of planning permission and the "fairly and reasonably relates" test therefore should not apply.[35] An agreement requiring provision of infrastructure beyond that required for the development has been upheld.[36]

While a fair and reasonable relation to the proposed development is not necessary for the agreement to be valid, some degree of relationship is necessary before the authority can take into account the terms of the agreement when determining the application for planning permission (see below).

The requirement of reasonableness or rationality is common to the exercise of all statutory discretionary powers by a public authority and applies both to conditions and agreements.[37] It may however be arguable that because a section 75 agreement is a contract this requirement should not apply.

From this brief examination, section 75 agreements appear to have greater scope than planning conditions because there is no requirement that for an agreement to be valid its provisions must "fairly and reasonably relate" to the development. This conclusion necessarily implies that section 75 agreements may be used to achieve a result that could not be legally achieved through imposition of a planning condition.[38] Indeed, this is one of the attractions of section 75 agreements in the eyes of planning authorities.

(b) Agreements as a Material Consideration

In most cases a developer enters into a section 75 agreement because 6.34
the terms of the agreement will increase the likelihood of planning permission being granted. This objective will not be attained unless the

---

[31] *Tesco Stores Ltd v. Secretary of State for the Environment* [1995] 2 All E.R. 636.

[32] *Good v. Epping Forest D.C.* [1993] J.P.L. 127.

[33] *Stringer v. MHLG* [1970] 1 W.L.R. 1281, *per* Cooke J.

[34] *McIntosh v. Aberdeenshire Council, supra.*

[35] *Good v. Epping Forest D.C.* [1994] 1 W.L.R. 376, CA.

[36] *R. v. Gillingham B.C., ex p. Parham, supra.*

[37] *R. v. Wealden D.C., ex p. Charles Church* [1989] J.P.L. 837, but this element is only included in the Lexis transcript.

[38] *Good v. Epping Forest D.C., supra.*

terms of the agreement form a material consideration in the determination of the application for planning permission (Chapter 5). If the terms are not a material consideration, it would be illegal for the planning authority to take account of them when deciding the application for planning permission. In such circumstances, the developer would still be bound by the terms of the agreement, but the authority would be bound to ignore these terms when reaching its decision on the application. Any failure to ignore the agreement when deciding the application would expose any grant of planning permission to the risk of challenge by a competing developer or concerned member of the public. Similar comments apply to the relevance of the agreement to an appeal to the Secretary of State.

Chapter 5 examines the circumstances in which the authority may take into account the agreement, which may give rise to planning benefits, when considering the application. A benefit which has nothing to do with the development will plainly not be a material consideration. If the benefit has some connection, then regard must be had to it. The extent to which it should affect the decision is a matter entirely within the discretion of the decision-maker. In exercising that discretion, he is entitled to have regard to his established policy.[39] The courts have rejected the contention that the benefit must be necessary to overcome, remedy or alleviate planning objections to the proposed development.[40]

For example, an agreement by a developer to pay for a new primary school in connection with a proposed housing development may be a material consideration as occupation of the new housing will increase the demand for school places. Much will depend upon the level of demand in comparison with the number of school places which the developer intends to fund. In contrast, the planning authority would be forced to ignore a similar agreement to pay for a school in connection with an office development when deciding the application for the office development, in consequence of the lack of connection between the need for the school and the proposed office.

As part of its superstore application Tesco offered to pay for a new link road required to resolve traffic problems in the town centre. The Secretary of State did not consider that the road was needed to enable the store proposal to go ahead, or was otherwise so directly related to the proposed development that the store ought to be permitted without it. The offer of funding therefore failed to comply with the provisions of the government guidance. The extent to which he would take it into account would be of such a limited nature that it would not tip the balance of the arguments. Tesco appealed on the ground that by discounting the funding offer the Secretary of State had failed to take into account a material consideration. This was rejected by the House of Lords, who held that, far from dismissing Tesco's offer as immaterial,

---

[39] *Tesco Stores Ltd v. Secretary of State for the Environment* [1995] J.P.L. 581.

[40] *R. v. Plymouth C.C., ex. p. Plymouth and South Devon Co-operative Society Ltd* [1993] J.P.L. 538 and (on appeal) [1993] E.G.C.S. 113; *approved in Tesco v. Secretary of State for the Environment, supra.*

the Secretary of State had carefully weighed up its significance. His decision was not therefore open to challenge.[41]

It has been held that where residential development made additional 6.35 infrastructure necessary or desirable, there was nothing wrong in the planning authority having a policy requiring major developers to contribute to the cost of infrastructure related to their development. The formula adopted by the authority, which was based on the enhanced value of the land, was not bad in law as insufficiently connecting the individual development with its associated infrastructure, as there was no suggestion that it would raise an amount disproportionate to what the developments required.[42]

Planning permission was granted for a Savacentre subject to an agreement to build a leisure centre and swimming pool. A group of local children sought judicial review of the subsequent decision to grant permission for other facilities. It was held that the planning authority had changed their policy regarding the provision of a leisure centre, and that even if the original agreement was still enforceable and the subsequent agreement was invalid, this could not affect the decision to grant planning permission.[43]

Traffic management measures to be financed by the applicant were held not to be a material consideration where there was no direct nexus between the proposed superstore and the improvements because these measures were aimed at problems already in existence.[44] However, offers of community benefits such as provision of a tourist information centre, a bird-watching hide and a static art feature were upheld as a material consideration in relation to another proposed superstore development.[45]

The conflict underlying the scope of section 75 agreements should now be apparent. The wording of section 75 and, therefore, the legal validity of planning agreements, does not require any connection between the provisions of the agreement and the proposed development, but this connection is required before the provisions may be taken into account by the planning authority in deciding the planning application normally associated with the agreement.[46] It is not necessarily outwith the powers of a planning authority to enter into a section 75 agreement which it would be forced to ignore as an irrelevant consideration when determining an application for planning permission. It is up to the developer to resist provisions which are not sufficiently connected to the development to form material considerations for the planning application.

The connection required between the benefits offered by the agreement and the proposed development before the agreement can be deemed a material consideration may seem similar to the "fairly and reasonably relates" requirement applicable to conditions. However, the

---

[41] *Tesco, supra.*
[42] *R. v. South Northants D.C., ex p. Crest Homes* [1994] 3 P.L.R. 47.
[43] *R. v. Merton LBC, ex p. Barker* [1998] J.P.L. 440.
[44] *Safeway v. Secretary of State for the Environment* [1990] J.P.L. 759.
[45] *R. v. Plymouth C.C. ex p. Plymouth and South Devon Co-operative Society Ltd, supra.*
[46] *R. v. South Northants D.C., ex p. Crest Homes* [1994] 1 P.L.R. 47, Henry L.J. at 56 D–G.

potential scope of agreements must inevitably result in a wider degree of connection than that permitted under the "fairly and reasonably relates" test, as agreements can, for example, require either contributions from developers or control off-site works on land outside the control of the developer.

(c)   Scottish Office Guidance

6.36   The Scottish Office has issued guidance on the use of planning agreements.[47] There is no right of appeal to the Secretary of State against the terms of a planning agreement. However, the guidance is an indication of the weight which will be given to the terms of a planning agreement in the course of determining an appeal to the Secretary of State against refusal of planning permission. It can, therefore, be used by developers in the course of negotiating the terms of a section 75 agreement to resist excessive demands made by the planning authority.

The guidance advises that wherever possible planning authorities should rely on planning conditions rather than using a planning agreement. It reminds planning authorities that the question of requiring a developer to enter into an agreement should only arise where it would not be appropriate to grant planning permission without the agreement. Unacceptable development should never be permitted because of unrelated benefits offered by the developer, nor should an acceptable development be refused planning permission because the developer is unwilling to offer such benefits.

The requirements of the guidance emphasise the need for a connection between the terms of the agreement and the proposed development. As a result, any agreement which accords with the guidance is likely to be a material consideration in the determination of a planning application.

The guidance also suggests the following questions regarding the reasonableness of a planning agreement:

- Is an agreement needed to enable the development to go ahead?
- In the case of financial payments, will these contribute to the cost of providing necessary facilities required as a consequence of or in connection with the development in the near future?
- Is the requirement in the agreement so directly related to the regulation of the proposed development that it should not be permitted without it?
- Will the agreement offset the loss of, or impact on, any amenity or resource which is present on the site prior to the development?

The guidance also states that planning agreements should be related in scale and kind to the proposed development. Developers should not be asked to fund improvements unless the need for those improvements

---

[47] Circular 12/1996, "Town and Country Planning (Scotland) Act 1972—Planning Agreements".

arises wholly or substantially from the proposed development. There may be wider benefits from infrastructure improvements but payments should be consistent with the scale of the proposed development. Although the need to improve, upgrade or replace infrastructure will not always arise directly from the proposed development, in some situations it will be inappropriate to grant permission for the development because it would exacerbate the situation, and the guidance acknowledges that agreements can be used in these situations to enable development to proceed.

The study on planning agreements concludes that most agreements satisfy the requirements of the guidance that the obligations contained in an agreement should arise from or deal with a consequence of the development and be in proportion to the problems which they are intended to resolve. However, the test of need ("required to enable the development to proceed") is not always strictly applied.[48]

Effect of Section 75 Agreement

(a) Relevance of Agreement to Planning Application or Appeal

The extent to which the provisions of a section 75 agreement form a material consideration in the determination of a planning application or appeal has already been discussed. There must be some relationship between the provisions of the agreement and the development proposed in the application. The absence of such a relationship may give a third party, such as a rival developer, grounds for seeking judicial review of the decision to grant planning permission.   6.37

(b) Fettering of Discretion

In accordance with the general legal principle that decision-makers must not fetter their exercise of discretionary powers conferred by statute (Chapter 5), it is not competent for a planning authority to bind itself in a section 75 agreement to grant planning permission for a specified development.[49] Assuming that the terms of the agreement are a material consideration, the authority can take into account those terms when deciding the application. However, it must also take into account all other relevant considerations, which may dictate that permission should be refused.   6.38

In a similar way, the planning authority is obliged to take into account any material changes in circumstances arising between the time of the resolution to grant permission once a planning agreement is concluded and conclusion of that agreement, and may refuse to grant permission on the basis of these changes.[50]

(c) Binding on the Land

The importance of section 75 agreements lies in the provisions allowing for recording of the completed agreement in the Register of Sasines or Land Register. Once the completed agreement has been   6.39

---

[48] Rowan-Robinson and Durman, *op. cit.*, para. 27.0 *et seq.*.
[49] TCPSA, s. 75(5); *Windsor and Maidenhead Royal Borough Council v. Brandrose* [1983] 1 W.L.R. 509.
[50] *John G. Russell (Transport) Ltd. v. Strathkelvin D.C.*, 1992 S.L.T. 1001.

recorded in the property register, its provisions bind in perpetuity the land to which it applies, applying to not only those persons who signed the agreement, but to all future parties who obtain an interest in the land notwithstanding their ignorance of the terms of the agreement, and it may be enforced against them by the planning authority.[51] In this way, it is similar to a grant of planning permission which attaches to the land rather than to the person who made the application. Other forms of planning agreements merely bind the signatories to the agreement.

The terms of the recorded agreement will not be enforceable against a third party who obtained an interest in the land in good faith prior to the agreement being recorded. This will apply whether or not the title of the third party was recorded before the recording of the agreement. This protection extends to any person who derives title from the bona fide third party. In such circumstances, the agreement will only be effective against the parties who signed it and, therefore, of little value to the authority.

Any future grant of planning permission cannot override the provisions of a section 75 agreement.[52]

(d) Enforcement of the Agreement

6.40   In the absence of any provision in the agreement regarding enforcement powers in the event of a failure to observe its terms, the agreement is treated as a contract and the normal contractual remedies are available to the planning authority without the necessity of following the enforcement procedures described in Chapter 7.[53] For example, the authority may seek a court order for specific implement of the obligations of the developer under the agreement or for interdict preventing the developer from acting contrary to the restrictions contained in the agreement, and damages. There are at least four instances of planning authorities obtaining interdict or specific implement in this manner in the sheriff court.[54] In England, a court order was granted to require demolition of a building in implement of an agreement.[55] The provisions of the agreement have to be sufficiently precise before a court order will be granted.[56]

(e) Variation and Discharge

6.41   Following recording in the property register, the provisions of the section 75 agreement bind the land in perpetuity. These provisions may be discharged or varied at any time and the appropriate legal document recorded in the property register, but only if all the parties to the agreement or their successors in title agree. If the parties cannot reach agreement on a discharge or variation, the agreement will remain

---

[51] TCPSA, s. 75(3).
[52] *R. v. Tunbridge Wells B.C., ex p. Blue Boys Developments Ltd* [1990] 1 P.L.R. 55.
[53] *Avon C.C. v. Millard* [1986] J.P.L. 211.
[54] Rowan-Robinson and Durman, *op. cit.*, para. 17.2.
[55] *Wycombe D.C. v. Williams, supra.*
[56] *e.g. R. v. Maldon D.C., ex p. Pattani* [1998] E.G.C.S. 135.

undischarged or unamended. In contrast to English law, there are no statutory provisions for applying to the planning authority for modification or discharge of the obligations in an agreement, or right of appeal to the Secretary of State against the authority's decision on such an application. In addition, the jurisdiction of the Lands Tribunal for Scotland does not extend to discharging obligations and restrictions contained in planning agreements, unlike its equivalent body in England which has such a jurisdiction in relation to pre-1992 agreements. It is, therefore, important that variation and discharge provisions be included in the agreement.

(f)   Challenge of Agreement

6.42   Unlike English law, there is no right of appeal to the Secretary of State against the terms of a planning agreement. However, the provisions of an agreement may be a relevant consideration in an appeal against the decision by the authority on an associated planning application.

It is unlikely that it will be competent for any party who signed the agreement to apply to the Court of Session for judicial review of the agreement. Having implemented an agreement, it was held that a developer could not competently apply to the court on the grounds that the council's exercise of its powers was invalid, and it was a matter of private contract law, and not an issue for judicial review, whether the obligations under the agreement had been fulfilled.[57] Although in practice many agreements are imposed upon reluctant developers who feel that they have no choice but to enter into the agreement to obtain planning permission, signature of the agreement is a voluntary act.

It may be competent for a third party to challenge the decision by the planning authority to enter into or vary an agreement or decisions by the authority based on the agreement.[58] Possible grounds of challenge are that the authority acted unreasonably or that the agreement does not serve a planning purpose or that the authority has exceeded the scope of its powers under section 75.

The Lands Tribunal for Scotland has no jurisdiction to discharge or vary the obligations contained in a section 75 agreement. The Scottish Law Commission have invited views as to whether the Lands Tribunal should be given such a jurisdiction.[59]

Drafting the Agreement

6.43   A recorded agreement applies to the land in perpetuity, thus an overly restrictive or badly drafted agreement may adversely affect the value of the land. It is important for all parties to ensure that the agreement records fully what has been agreed and that it will be effective in securing the performance of the obligations. The Scottish Office guidance includes advice to solicitors on drafting agreements.

---

[57] *McIntosh v. Aberdeenshire Council, supra.*
[58] *R. v. Merton LBC, ex p. Barker, supra; R. v. South Northants D.C., ex p. Crest Homes, supra.*
[59] Scottish Law Commission Discussion Paper No.106, "Real Burdens" (Oct. 1998).

In most cases the agreement will be drafted by the planning authority once the principal obligations have been agreed. Inevitably the draft agreement will require some revision by the developer to avoid overly burdensome restrictions or obligations.

There is no prescribed form of planning agreement. The agreement must be expressed in clear and precise terms and any ambiguities avoided. In complex agreements, an interpretation clause defining the meaning of various key phrases is useful. To be accepted for recording in the property register, a section 75 agreement must identify the parties to the agreement, the land to which the agreement applies, and the obligations agreed between the parties.

(a) Parties

6.44   The agreement will normally be entered into by the planning authority dealing with the planning application associated with the agreement, although the roads authority may be a party if the agreement provides for roads improvements.

The other principal party to the agreement is the person or persons who have sufficient legal interest in the site to bind the land. Without the signature of all such persons, the agreement cannot be recorded in the property registers and can only be enforced against the parties who have signed the agreement.

An "interest" in land must be such as to enable that person to enter into an agreement which will bind future owners of the land. Clearly the owner of the land (the infeft proprietor) has sufficient interest for this purpose. The best practice must be to enter into section 75 agreements only with persons who have a title to the land which is recorded in the property register.[60]

It would seem inadvisable to enter into a section 75 agreement with a person whose ownership is based on an executed, but unrecorded, disposition (legally described as an uninfeft proprietor). Such a person has sufficient interest to bind the land, but until the disposition is recorded in the property register there is a (slight) risk of a third party recording a title to the land before that disposition (and the section 75 agreement) is recorded, rendering any section 75 agreement recorded thereafter ineffective unless signed by that third party. Limited protection could be sought through a clause in the agreement prohibiting the party signing the agreement from selling the land prior to the recording of the agreement.

It is common for a sale of land to a developer to be agreed up to conclusion of missives, but the transfer of ownership not completed until planning permission is obtained. In such circumstances, the seller remains owner of the land until a signed disposition is delivered to the developer.[61] The only right available to the developer under concluded

---

[60] Circular 12/1996, Annex 2, paras 2 and 7. See Rowan-Robinson and Durman, *op. cit.*, para. 14.0 *et seq.*.

[61] *Gibson v. Hunter Homes*, 1976 S.L.T. 94, *per* Lord President Emslie at p. 96; but see *Sharp v. Thomson*, 1997 S.L.T. 66 (HL).

missives is the right to demand performance of the contractual obligation to convey the land to him, and this is not an interest in land.[62] Thus
a developer who has concluded missives, but has yet to complete the
purchase, cannot enter into a section 75 agreement, other than as a
consenter (see below). A person in this position may enter into an
agreement with the planning authority undertaking to complete a section
75 agreement in specified terms as soon as a disposition in his favour has
been delivered and recorded. Alternatively, in order to give sufficient
confidence for the purchase transaction to be completed the planning
authority may give an indication that planning permission will be
forthcoming if a section 75 agreement is entered into (see below).

The Scottish Office guidance suggests that a lessee under a recorded   6.45
lease may also have a sufficient interest to enter into a section 75
agreement. In such circumstances, the landlord (and the owner if this is
not the same person as the landlord) must consent to the agreement (see
below). Thus section 75 agreements are often entered into with tenants
and landlords under minerals leases in connection with applications for
permission for mineral extraction.

A section 75 agreement is not enforceable against any third party who
in good faith onerously acquired right to the land prior to the recording
of the agreement in the property registers, notwithstanding that the title
of that third party has yet to be recorded. As a result, some persons who
do not have sufficient interest to bind the land should be requested to
sign the agreement as consentors. Their signature of the agreement will
have the effect of binding them by its terms even before the agreement is
recorded in the property register.

Possible consenting parties include heritable creditors, tenants, feudal
superiors, parties with servitude rights over the site, purchasers under
concluded missives and applicants for planning permission. Any restrictions contained in the agreement may significantly reduce the value of
the land. Such a reduction in value may prejudice the interests of a bank
or other financial institution which has lent money and been granted a
security over the land. This has already occurred in England where one
financial institution withdrew from lending because the terms of an
agreement providing for "low-cost" housing would have made it difficult
to sell the property if it ever came to be repossessed by the institution.
Any heritable creditors should be asked to indicate their consent to the
agreement by signing it as consentors.

If the owner has leased part of the land and the agreement affects the
tenant's enjoyment of the land, the landlord may require the consent of
the tenant depending upon the terms of the lease. The consent of the
feudal superior or those with servitude rights over the land may be
required, depending on the provisions of the title to the land. If the
owner of the land has concluded missives for its sale, the planning
authority should consider seeking the purchaser's signature of the
agreement as a consentor. The applicant for planning permission should
sign the agreement.

---

[62] *Margrie Holdings Ltd v. Commissioners of Customs & Excise*, 1991 S.L.T. 38.

In drafting (and revising) the agreement, it should be considered whether it is necessary for all signatories to be bound under all the obligations contained in the agreement. In particular, if some parties have an interest in only part of the site, they should ensure that they are bound only by the obligations in the agreement which apply to that part.

(b)   The Land

6.46   To be accepted for recording in the property register, the planning agreement must contain a legal description of the land to which it is to apply. This description is prepared by reference to the previous title deeds, and may refer to a plan attached to the agreement. Unless the description is simple, it may be advisable for it to be contained in a separate schedule to the agreement.

(c)   The Obligations

6.47   A wide range of obligations can competently form the basis of a section 75 agreement and new examples will continue to emerge. The only legal requirements are the need for a planning purpose and a rational decision (see above).

For example, infrastructure improvements are a common subject of agreements. Developers often agree to pay the cost of the authority carrying out off-site infrastructure works in order to unlock the development potential of sites. Agreements can be used to phase-in parts of the development in conjunction with the provision of supporting infrastructure, or to prevent the construction of lucrative portions of the development ahead of parts of the development which the authority considers important to the community, for example, tying in provision of a school to occupancy of a housing development.

Following the restrictions placed on the use of occupancy conditions, agreements can be used to regulate the occupancy of sheltered homes and retirement flats or provision of low-cost housing for local people. An agreement may contain restrictions on future sale of a property, for example, prohibiting the separate sale of farm cottages or granny flats.

The agreement may revoke existing, but unimplemented, permission in return for a fresh grant of permission, or discontinue the existing use of premises once permission has been granted for the similar use of new premises. Where planning permission is granted for a replacement dwellinghouse, an agreement may be used to secure demolition of existing buildings.

Some forms of development have almost standard provisions. Agreements in connection with retail developments may limit the range of goods which may be sold. Authorities frequently require agreements for provision of restoration bonds in connection with mineral workings.

Some authorities have even used agreements to require the developer to observe a local employment or local contractor preference. However, it may be difficult to prove that such requirements fulfil a planning purpose.

It is important that the provisions of the agreement are sufficiently precise. The operation of a pharmacy within a superstore was held to fall within the terms of agreements restricting the use to the sale of food and associated household consumables and to use as a supermarket.[63]

(d) Other Matters

In addition to identifying the parties, the land and narrating the obligations, the parties should consider the desirability of including other provisions. 6.48

The developer should consider including a clause in the agreement to the effect that it will only come into force if the grant of planning permission is implemented. This avoids the situation of the developer deciding not to proceed with the development, but the land remaining subject to the agreement.

If the agreement provides for a financial contribution to be paid, the purpose of the payment should be clearly specified and an obligation placed on the recipient to expend the money for that purpose. Provision should be made for a refund if this is not satisfied, either at all or within a specified period.

The normal contractual remedies are available to enforce the provisions of the agreement, but other remedies can be specified. For example, the agreement may empower the authority to carry out work and recover the cost from the developer if the work has not been commenced or completed within a specified time. Agreements in connection with mineral workings normally provide for sums to be paid to the authority if the developer fails to carry out restoration works or goes into liquidation. These payments are guaranteed under fidelity bonds issued by banks or insurance companies.

Alternatively, the agreement may allow the authority to treat any failure to observe the terms of the agreement as a breach of planning control entitling it to use the powers conferred by the planning enforcement regime (Chapter 7). The legality of such provisions is uncertain and developers should carefully consider their position before agreeing to such a provision.

More importantly, the agreement may provide that on any breach of its terms by the developer, the authority can revoke the grant of planning permission without compensation. This would terminate the development and any change of use would have to cease. It is doubtful whether it is competent for permission to be revoked in this way, but developers should seek the deletion of such a provision during the revisal of the draft agreement. An alternative to this draconian measure is for the agreement to provide for the effect of the planning permission to be suspended until the breach of the agreement is remedied.

In connection with powers to secure compliance with the terms of the agreement, ancillary powers should be provided. For example, planning officials should be given rights of entry to monitor compliance with the terms of the agreement and for the carrying out of any works upon which the developer has defaulted. Provision should be made for the authority to reclaim the cost of carrying out such works from the developer. 6.49

---

[63] *R. v. Maldon D.C., ex p. Pattani* [1998] E.G.C.S. 135.

The agreement may provide that the planning authority is to be the sole judge of what constitutes a breach of the agreement, entitling it to exercise its enforcement powers under the agreement. Any provisions of this type, which give the planning authority complete discretion, should be resisted by the developer. An alternative is to provide for any disputes which arise in relation to the agreement to be settled through arbitration rather than legal action. An arbitration clause should be worded to include disputes relating to the interpretation as well as the level of compliance with the agreement. Careful consideration should be given to the profession from which the arbiter(s) is to be selected. The decision of the arbiter is normally declared to be final, although it may be challenged if the arbiter makes a legal error in the course of the decision. Provision should be made for payment of expenses.

If subsequent subdivision of the site is likely, the agreement should be drafted to avoid future difficulties regarding the enforcement and the distribution of obligations.

Following recording in the property register, the provisions of the section 75 agreement bind the land in perpetuity. Formal discharges of agreements or parts of agreements (which will then be recorded in the property register) should be obtained wherever possible to prevent legal difficulties arising in any future sale of the land. Positive obligations will usually be carried out shortly after the agreement is executed. Provision should be made in the agreement for a formal discharge of those obligations to be executed by the planning authority after the obligations have been carried out. In contrast, any restrictions on use will remain in force indefinitely, irrespective of any changes in circumstances. Although the provisions of the agreement may be varied or discharged with the agreement of all the parties, it is advisable for the agreement to specify procedures for its variation or discharge to protect the developer against future intransigence on the part of the authority.

In a similar way, the agreement may be drafted to include provision for reviews either at specified intervals or on the application of any party to the agreement, with a reference to an arbiter in the event of deadlock. Such provisions would avoid obsolete agreements continuing to affect land.

Timing of Agreement and Associated Planning Permission

6.50   Most section 75 agreements are entered into in the context of applications for planning permission. The planning authority will be unwilling to grant planning permission until the agreement has been executed, but the developer will be wary of entering into an agreement unless he can be certain that planning permission will be granted. Several solutions to this problem have been adopted in practice[64]:

(a)   The planning authority may resolve to grant planning permission once the agreement has been concluded (sometimes referred to as a "minded to grant" letter), often delegating to

---

[64] Rowan-Robinson and Young, *op. cit.*, p. 57.

the Director of Planning the power to grant permission once an agreement in appropriate terms has been executed. This is the most common method. There is no grant of planning permission until the decision notice is issued.[65] If there is a material change of circumstances in the period between the decision and completion of the agreement, the authority is obliged to take those circumstances into account and may refuse to grant the permission.[66] Any delay in concluding the agreement therefore risks losing the permission.

A variation on this procedure is for the application to be determined, but the decision notice left un-issued until the agreement is executed. As planning permission is only granted once the notice is issued, this method must also carry the risk of losing the permission.

(b) The other common procedure is for planning permission to be granted subject to a condition requiring the applicant to enter into an agreement. Such a condition should specify all the terms of the agreement or at least the heads of the agreement. It has been suggested that it would be illegal for a condition to require an applicant to enter into an agreement on matters outwith the legal scope of conditions.[67] There is also a danger for the authority that following a successful appeal, planning permission could be granted without the condition and, therefore, no requirement upon the developer to enter into the agreement.

Planning permission may also be granted subject to a suspensive condition providing that the grant of permission will not be effective until the agreement is executed or recorded. Alternatively, the condition could prevent commencement of development until specified works have been carried out, those works being the subject of the agreement.

(c) If the application for planning permission is not to be determined until the agreement is executed, the agreement will be expressed to be conditional on the grant (or implementation) of planning permission in the terms specified in a schedule to the agreement. This procedure will be appropriate only where the applicant has sufficient interest to enter into the agreement before planning permission is granted.

(d) The decision notice is issued on the strength of a formal undertaking by the developer to execute the agreement.

(e) The decision notice in respect of the application is incorporated into a schedule to the agreement.

Proposal for Agreement on Appeal

As most agreements are intended to remove planning disadvantages 6.51 of proposed developments which might lead to a refusal of planning permission, the inability to reach agreement with the planning authority

---

[65] *R. v. West Oxfordshire D.C.* [1986] J.P.L. 523.
[66] *John G. Russell (Transport) Ltd v. Strathkelvin D.C.*, *supra*.
[67] Rowan-Robinson and Young, *op. cit.*, pp. 58–60.

normally prevents any appeal. Although there is no duty on them to do so, reporters may encourage the parties to enter into negotiations with a view to concluding an agreement to remove an obstacle to a grant of planning permission, which cannot be removed by imposition of a condition. However, the reporter can play no part in the negotiations or specify the terms of the agreement, and the developer may be unable to reach agreement with the authority. There have been instances where permission has been granted on appeal despite the failure to conclude an agreement.[68]

The English courts have recently held that it was unreasonable for a highway authority, whose road safety objections had been fully heard and rejected on appeal, to maintain their original view and refuse to enter into an agreement with the developer.[69] However, it was not perverse for an updated assessment to be required before the agreement was concluded when the original study had been undertaken four years ago and there was evidence of changed traffic conditions in the area.[70] It is unclear how far this principle may extend. For example, it could be argued that it would be *ultra vires* for a planning authority to refuse to enter into a section 75 agreement where the reporter has indicated that he is minded to grant planning permission.

English law allows developers to sidestep unco-operative planning authorities by entering into a unilateral planning obligation to provide planning advantages.[71] This obviates the need to reach agreement with the planning authority. The obligation will have an equivalent effect to a section 75 agreement. Most importantly, it will be a material consideration during the determination of the application for planning permission and in any appeal against refusal or deemed refusal of planning permission.

There is no equivalent provision in Scots law. However, promises are enforceable contracts in Scots law. It is conceivable, if unlikely, that a developer could draw up a legal document in the form of a promise which could, depending upon its content, form a material consideration which a reluctant authority would either be forced to consider when determining an application for planning permission, or face a successful appeal.

---

[68] *e.g. Strathclyde R.C. v. Secretary of State for Scotland, supra.*
[69] *R. v. Warwickshire C.C., ex p. PowerGen plc, supra.*
[70] *R. v. Cardiff City Council, ex p. Sears Group Properties, supra.*
[71] Town and Country Planning Act 1990, s. 106A and 106B, as amended.

CHAPTER 7

DEVELOPMENT CONTROL IV—ENFORCEMENT

In order to control development effectively, planning authorities have **7.01** sanctions to enforce planning control and prevent or stop unauthorised development. These enforcement powers were strengthened following the overhaul of the statutory enforcement system by the Planning and Compensation Act 1991 (amending the TCPSA), which adopted many of the recommendations of the Carnwath Report.[1] The procedures have been simplified, tougher penalties introduced, loopholes removed, and new powers conferred upon planning authorities.

A review of the practical operation of these provisions found that attitudes to the effectiveness of the new and revised powers were very positive, but there were wide variations in their use in practice. In particular, there was very limited use of breach of condition notices, stop notices, direct action and interdict. There were continuing problems of delay in the enforcement process, principally caused by enforcement notice appeals and blatant and persistent transgression of planning control. There were also continuing difficulties with prosecution of planning offences.[2]

The incorporation of the European Convention on Human Rights into Scots law may have significant implications for planning enforcement. There has already been an unsuccessful application to the European Commission of Human Rights in the context of an enforcement notice appeal alleging a violation of the right to peaceful enjoyment of possessions and the right to a fair and public hearing within a reasonable time by an independent and impartial tribunal.[3]

Underlying Principles of Enforcement Powers

(a) Breach of Planning Control

The planning authority cannot exercise its enforcement powers unless **7.02** there at least appears to have been a breach of planning control (a stricter requirement applies to the exercise of some powers). A breach of

---

[1] Carnwath, *Enforcing Planning Control* (1989).

[2] "Review of Planning Enforcement", Scottish Office Central Research Unit 1997. Following this review, on Mar. 1, 1999 the Scottish Office issued Circular 4/1999 and PAN 54, "Planning Enforcement". This guidance supersedes circulars 8/1992 and 36/1992, which are referred to in this chapter, but the content of the guidance is broadly unchanged.

[3] *Bryan v. United Kingdom* [1996] 1 P.L.R. 47.

planning control occurs when development is carried out without first obtaining the required planning permission (Chapter 4), or contrary to any condition or limitation subject to which planning permission has been granted.[4] There is no statutory definition of "limitation". The Scottish Office guidance refers to the limitations which are imposed by the provisions for permitted development rights in the PDO (Chapter 4).[5]

(b)   Enforcement Action

7.03   Although there is a wide range of enforcement powers available to planning authorities, only service of an enforcement or breach of condition notice constitutes taking enforcement action for the purposes of preventing a breach from becoming lawful development.[6]

(c)   Lawful Development (Immunity from Enforcement Action)

7.04   A breach of planning control becomes lawful once the prescribed time limits (see below) for taking enforcement action have expired.[7] In consequence, there is no breach upon which to found enforcement action. In addition, permitted development rights under the PDO may be utilised. A Certificate of Lawfulness of Existing Use or Development may be sought from the planning authority to establish conclusively the lawfulness of the use or development (Chapter 4).

Prior to the PCA reforms, a breach of planning control became immune from enforcement action after expiry of the time limit, but could never become lawful. As a result, permitted development rights could not be exercised and, in the event of compulsory purchase, there was no right to compensation for any value attributable to the activity.

The concept of lawful development does not extend to breaches of the statutory systems applicable to listed buildings, tree preservation, or advertisement control (Chapter 9). Breaches never become immune from enforcement action under these statutory systems, but may be immune from enforcement action under the planning system where there is an overlap in the statutory controls.

(d)   Offences

7.05   A breach of planning control is not an offence in itself. In general, commission of an offence relates to a failure to comply with the requirements of a notice served by the authority in exercise of its enforcement powers against the breach. Individual offences are created in relation to each enforcement power, and are examined in the appropriate part of this chapter.

---

[4] TCPSA, s.123(1).
[5] Scottish Environment Department Circular 36/1992, "Planning and Compensation Act 1991—Lawful Development and Enforcement," para. 5.
[6] TCPSA, s. 123(2).
[7] s. 150(2).

All enforcement offences are subject to a six-month time limit for commencing summary court proceedings.[8] This period runs from the occurrence of the contravention. In the case of a continuing contravention, the six-month period runs from the last date of the contravention. There is uncertainty about the application of the six-month period to planning offences. As enforcement offences do not relate to the breach of planning control, but to the non-compliance with the terms of the notice, the offence is a single one which can be charged by reference to a single day or longer period. It is therefore arguable that the six-month period runs from the date of the expiry of the period specified in the notice for compliance with its terms, notwithstanding that the breach of planning control continues. However, it is possible that this argument only applies to a notice requiring positive action (*i.e.* something to be done). If it requires negative action, such as cessation of an activity, the failure to comply with the requirement is a continuing offence and the six-month time limit only runs from the date on which the activity ceases. This uncertainty can only be clarified by a court ruling or amendment of the law.

The PCA reforms also provide for prosecution of second or subsequent offences if the contravention of the notice continues after conviction.

Although the penalties for individual offences vary, the PCA reforms have increased the penalties to a maximum fine of £20,000 following summary conviction, or an unlimited fine after conviction on indictment. In addition, the court is directed to have regard to any financial benefit which has accrued or appears likely to accrue to the person in consequence of the offence. For example, where an enforcement notice requires use of a building for retail purposes to be stopped, the court may take into account the profits made from that retail business following expiry of the period for compliance with the requirements of the notice until conviction. There is no provision for imprisonment following conviction for an enforcement offence.

This system of enforcement offences is not without its problems. A planning authority intent on negotiating a solution to avoid the need for prosecution may fall foul of the six-month time limit. A substantial weight of corroborated evidence will be required to prove the case beyond reasonable doubt, including evidence on such prosaic matters as service of the notice upon the person charged with the offence. It is unclear whether the intent (*mens rea*) to commit the offence must be proved. A major hurdle is the apparent attitude of many procurators fiscal, who are responsible for prosecuting, and sheriffs, that planning offences are not true criminal matters. Indeed, the need to change this attitude was one of the underlying reasons for the increase in penalties for enforcement offences from £2,000 to £20,000. The hard-pressed fiscal with a heavy caseload of "real" criminal matters may decide that prosecution of an enforcement offence is not in the public interest and exercise his discretion not to prosecute. This decision is likely to be

---

[8] Criminal Procedure (Scotland) Act 1995, s. 136. Robertson, "Time-Limits for Criminal Prosecutions", SPEL 45:73.

influenced by the generally low level of fines imposed by sheriffs in the few successful cases.

Research has found that while planning authorities want to see contraveners prosecuted and convicted, fiscals want the authorities to make full use of their powers in pursuing alternative remedies before prosecution is considered as there is a risk that the court will not apply a sanction where those remedies have not been exhausted. Only about 49 per cent of cases reported by planning authorities to the fiscal resulted in prosecution. The success rate for prosecutions was 84 per cent. Six successful prosecution cases were reported in 1992–96, with the fines imposed ranging from £500–£2,000, well below the maximum fine of £20,000. In comparison, 14 successful prosecutions were reported for environmental offences, resulting in one imprisonment for six months and fines ranging from £1,500 to £15,000.[9]

ENFORCEMENT ACTION: TIME LIMITS

7.06   Enforcement action must be taken within the following time limits, otherwise the breach of planning control will become lawful development[10]:

Four-Year Time Limit

7.07   (a)   Building, engineering, mining or other operations (Chapter 4) undertaken without planning permission will become lawful development after four years from the date of substantial completion of the operations (such operations in breach of conditions or limitations are subject to the 10-year time limit). Where an embankment was substantially completed within the four-year period, an enforcement notice requiring its demolition was upheld notwithstanding that parts of the embankment had been in place for over four years.[11]

    (b)   A change of use of any building to use as a single dwelling-house will become lawful development after four years from the date of the change of use. It is irrelevant whether the building is converted into a single dwellinghouse or an existing dwellinghouse is subdivided into two or more separate dwellinghouses.[12] A house in multiple occupation with the occupants sharing facilities remains within the 10-year rule. It was held that former staff accommodation and outbuildings of a country house converted in breach of planning control into 10 self-contained units of residential accommodation for holiday lettings were used as single dwellinghouses and not as one planning unit, and were therefore subject to the four-year time limit.[13]

---

[9] "Review of Planning Enforcement", Scottish Office Central Research Unit, 1997.

[10] TCPSA, s. 124.

[11] *Ewen Developments v. Secretary of State for the Environment* [1980] J.P.L. 404.

[12] *Van Dyck v. Secretary of State for the Environment; Doncaster B.C. v. Secretary of State for the Environment* [1993] J.P.L. 565.

[13] *Moore v. Secretary of State for the Environment,* [1998] J.P.L. 877.

Ten-Year Time Limit

All other breaches of planning control become lawful development 7.08
after 10 years from the date of the breach. This will include all material
changes of use, and breaches of planning conditions, other than those
relating to change of use of a building to a single dwellinghouse. Where
a house was built about 90 feet west of the permitted location, the
occupancy condition was held not to apply, and the breach of planning
control related to development without planning permission rather than
failure to comply with the condition.[14]

This involves an extension of the four-year period which previously
applied to building, engineering, mining or other operations in breach of
conditions or limitations. As a transitional measure, any breach of
condition or limitation relating to operational development immune
from enforcement action in terms of the previous four-year limit will
continue to be immune notwithstanding that it would now be subject to
the 10–year limit.[15] The other main change is the substitution of the 10-
year time limit for most changes of use. Previously only changes of use
which had occurred prior to 1965 were immune.

Enforcement action against a change of use can require restoration of
the land to its state prior to the change, thereby undoing any incidental
operational development which may in itself not require planning
permission or be lawful development. The laying of hardcore was an
integral part of an unauthorised change of use for the parking of lorries
and enforcement action against that change of use could validly require
removal of the hardcore notwithstanding that it had been laid more than
four years previously and was therefore immune from enforcement
action in itself.[16]

Further Action Outwith Time Limits

If an enforcement notice has been served within the time limit and is still 7.09
in effect, it is competent for the planning authority to serve a breach of
condition notice in respect of the same breach of planning control,
notwithstanding that the time limit for enforcement action has expired.

Further enforcement action is also possible where the planning
authority have taken or purported to take enforcement action against
the breach within the previous four years. This extends the time limit for
a further four years to allow a planning authority to issue a fresh
enforcement or breach of condition notice where the previous notice was
withdrawn or found to be null.

Where the purpose of two enforcement notices was the same, to stop
multiple occupancy of the premises, the reporter was entitled to find that
the notices purported to relate to the same breach. The phrase in the
statute "purported to take enforcement action" clearly included
the possibility that the first notice contained some defect. The second
notice was not therefore time barred.[17] This "second-bite" provision only

---

[14] *Handoll v. Warner Goodman & Streat* [1995] 1 P.L.R. 40, [1995] J.P.L. 930.
[15] PCA, s. 36(2).
[16] *Murfitt v. Secretary of State for the Environment* [1980] J.P.L. 598.
[17] *Barn Properties v. Secretary of State for Scotland*, 1995 S.C.L.R. 113, SPEL 49:52.

applies if the previous actual or purported enforcement action was timeous, otherwise the planning authority could issue a first notice out of time, withdraw it and issue a further notice.[18]

ENFORCEMENT POWERS

7.10   All enforcement powers are discretionary and the planning authority can choose not to take enforcement action. Equally, the authority may choose to under-enforce by taking enforcement action against only part of the breach. Such decisions can only be challenged by applying to the Court of Session for judicial review on the grounds that the decision is unreasonable (in the special legal sense, see Chapter 8).[19]

The Scottish Office guidance states that in considering any enforcement action the decisive issue for the planning authority should be whether the breach of control would unacceptably affect public amenity or the use of land and buildings meriting protection in the public interest. Enforcement action should always be commensurate with the breach of planning control to which it relates.[20]

The first phase of enforcement action is likely to be service of a planning contravention notice requiring provision of further information. Planning officers may exercise rights of entry to ascertain whether there has been a breach. If a breach of planning control appears to have occurred, the person responsible for the apparent breach may be encouraged to apply for retrospective planning permission (Chapter 5) or a Certificate of Lawfulness of Existing Use or Development (Chapter 4) with a view to regularising the position. If the person refuses, or the case is serious, the authority may take further enforcement action to require the breach to be remedied.

Only service of an enforcement or breach of condition notice within the prescribed time limits prevents a breach of planning control becoming lawful development (see above).

The methods of serving notices are dealt with at the end of this chapter.

If there is failure to comply with the requirements of the notice, the planning authority may report the matter to the procurator fiscal for a decision on prosecution, or take direct action to carry out the requirements and recover the cost from the recipient of the notice (this power to take direct action only arises following failure to comply with an enforcement or wasteland notice).

Planning Contravention Notices

7.11   The power to serve a planning contravention notice was introduced by the PCA. It is intended to enable planning authorities to seek information where there is a suspected breach of planning control. The notice

---

[18] *William Boyer (Transport) Ltd v. Secretary of State for the Environment* [1996] 1 P.L.R. 103.

[19] *e.g. R. v. Flintshire C.C., ex p. Somerfield Stores* [1998] E.G.C.S. 53.

[20] Scottish Office Environment Department Circular 8/1992, "Enforcing Planning Control", para. 7.

should also encourage discussion with the planning authority by acting as a warning of enforcement action, and provide an opportunity to regularise the situation. The power to serve a planning contravention notice may in practice replace the more general power to seek information as to interests in land.[21]

A planning contravention notice may be served by the planning authority where it appears that there may have been a breach of planning control (see above) in respect of any land.[22] A mere suspicion of a breach, following upon a complaint by a member of the public, may be enough. The absence of even a suspicion of a breach is likely to invalidate the notice.[23] Service of this notice does not affect any other power exercisable in respect of any breach of planning control. It is not an essential prerequisite to enforcement action that a planning contravention notice has been served.

The notice is served on the owner or occupier or any person with another interest in the land, or any person carrying out operations on the land or using it for any purpose.

The notice may require the person on whom it is served to give information so far as he is able about any specified operations, uses or activities being carried out on the land (the requirement to specify these matters should act as an obstacle to a planning authority using the notice as a fishing expedition for information). It may also require provision of information regarding any matter relating to conditions or limitations imposed upon a grant of planning permission. These requirements are complied with by giving information in writing to the planning authority.

For example, the notice may require the person to state whether or not the land is being used for any specified purpose or any operations or activities are being or have been carried out on the land. It may also require him to state when any use, operations or activities began, and to give the name and address of any person known to him to use or have used the land for any purpose or to be carrying out, or have carried out, any operations or activities on the land. In addition, it may require any information he holds as to any planning permission for any use or operations or any reason for planning permission not being required for any use or operation. He may also be required to state the nature of his interest (if any) in the land and the name and address of any other person known to him to have an interest in the land.

The notice must inform the person on whom it is served of the likely consequences of his failing to respond to the notice, and, in particular, that enforcement action may be taken. It must also inform the person that failure to respond to the notice may result in the loss of the right to compensation following service of a stop notice (see below). The notice may also give notice of a time and place at which the authority will consider any representations which may be made in connection with the notice. This will give an opportunity for negotiation with the planning authority to avoid enforcement action.

---

[21] TCPSA, s. 272. Research suggests the s. 272 notice is still used more—"Review of Planning Enforcement", *supra*.
[22] s. 125.
[23] *R. v. Teignbridge D.C., ex p. Teignmouth Quay Co.* [1995] J.P.L. 828.

Failure to comply with a planning contravention notice within 21 days of its service is an offence carrying liability on summary conviction to a fine not exceeding level 3 on the standard scale.[24] This offence may be committed in the space of a day or over a longer period of time and a person may be convicted again if he fails to comply with the notice following conviction. It will be a defence to prove that there was a reasonable excuse for failing to comply with the requirement.

It is also an offence knowingly or recklessly to make a statement purporting to comply with a requirement of the notice, which is false or misleading in a material particular. A person convicted of this offence will be liable on summary conviction to a fine not exceeding level 5 on the standard scale.

There is no statutory right of appeal to the Secretary of State against a planning contravention notice. However, a petition for judicial review may be brought before the Court of Session alleging that the notice is invalid.[25] Alternatively, the notice may be ignored and any prosecution defended on the basis that the notice is invalid.

Rights of Entry for Enforcement Purposes

7.12 A person duly authorised in writing by the planning authority has the right to enter any land at any reasonable hour if there are reasonable grounds for entering for the purpose in question. This right of entry may be exercised to ascertain whether there is or has been a breach of planning control, determine whether and how any enforcement powers should be exercised, or ascertain whether there has been compliance with any requirement imposed as a result of the exercise of enforcement powers.[26] The right of entry extends to neighbouring land, whether or not it is in the same ownership or occupation. Where admission is sought to a dwellinghouse, 24-hours' notice of the intended entry must be given to the occupier. Where admission has been refused, or a refusal is reasonably apprehended, or the case is one of urgency, a warrant authorising entry may be issued by a sheriff.

The land should be left as effectively secured against trespassers as when entry was taken. Compensation is payable for any damage caused. It is an offence to disclose details of manufacturing processes or trade secrets obtained while exercising the right of entry, other than in the course of duty. It is an offence wilfully to obstruct exercise of the right of entry, punishable on summary conviction by a fine not exceeding level 3 (see Appendix 1).

Enforcement Notices

7.13 Service of an enforcement notice prevents a breach of planning control becoming lawful development (see above) and therefore is one of the main enforcement powers (the other being the power to serve a breach of condition notice). Service of an enforcement notice may be combined with a stop notice (see below).

---

[24] s. 126. App. I contains details of the standard scale for fines.
[25] *R. v. Teignbridge D.C., supra.*
[26] ss. 156–158. The list of powers in s.156(1)(b) does not include interdict.

Enforcement notices remain the main enforcement power used by planning authorities, with some 200–300 issued each year. There is concern about the scope for delaying the effects of an enforcement notice by utilising the right of appeal to the Secretary of State against the notice, particularly if the right to have the appeal heard at a public inquiry is exercised. There are some 70–90 enforcement notice appeals each year, with a success rate of approximately 25 per cent in the period 1992–96.[27]

(a) Power to Serve Enforcement Notice

An enforcement notice may be issued by the planning authority where 7.14 it appears that there has been a breach of planning control and that it is expedient to issue the notice, having regard to the provisions of the development plan and to any other material considerations (Chapter 5).[28] The authority therefore has the discretion to ignore a breach of planning control, or under-enforce (see below). In deciding whether to issue a notice, the authority must act in accordance with the provisions of the development plan unless material considerations indicate otherwise.[29]

The Secretary of State also has a default power to serve an enforcement notice.[30]

One enforcement notice may be served in respect of several breaches of planning control.[31] Following service of an invalid enforcement notice, the authority may serve a fresh notice, subject to the prescribed time limits (see above).[32]

Planning authorities now have the power to withdraw an enforcement notice, or waive or relax any requirement of such a notice.[33] In particular, the time limit for taking steps to comply with the notice may be extended. This power to vary or withdraw may be exercised whether or not the notice has taken effect. The planning authority is required to give notice of the variation or withdrawal to every person served with a copy of the enforcement notice, and to any person who would be served with a copy if the notice was re-issued. Withdrawal of an enforcement notice will not prejudice the power of the planning authority to issue a further notice within the prescribed time limits (see above).

(b) Effect of Enforcement Notice

The enforcement notice must specify the date upon which it will take 7.15 effect. Any appeal against the enforcement notice must be lodged prior to that date. Lodging an appeal prevents the notice taking effect until the appeal has been determined or withdrawn.

---

[27] "Review of Planning Enforcement", Scottish Office Central Research Unit, 1997.
[28] s. 127.
[29] s. 25. See Chap. 3.
[30] s. 139.
[31] *Valentina of London Ltd v. Secretary of State for the Environment* [1992] J.P.L. 1151.
[32] *R. v. Wychavon D.C. and Secretary of State for the Environment* [1992] J.P.L. 753.
[33] TCPSA, s. 129.

Once the enforcement notice comes into effect, it will apply permanently to the land (unless withdrawn), even if there has been full
compliance with its requirements. Thus any requirement to discontinue a
use will operate as a permanent restriction, and any resumption of the
discontinued use will be in contravention of the notice and, therefore, an
offence. In particular, any reinstatement or restoration of buildings
demolished or altered in compliance with an enforcement notice, will be
in contravention of that notice notwithstanding that its terms are not apt
for this purpose. A person who carries out such reinstatement or
restoration shall be guilty of an offence and liable on a summary
conviction to a fine not exceeding level 5 on the standard scale
(Appendix 1).

The notice will cease to have effect in so far as it is inconsistent with a
planning permission granted after the service of the notice for any
development carried out before the grant of the permission (*i.e.* retrospective permission).[34] To avoid uncertainty, it would be advisable for
the notice to be withdrawn or varied when the permission is granted.

In certain limited circumstances, compliance with the terms of an
enforcement notice results in a deemed grant of planning permission.
Where the planning authority chooses to under-enforce by requiring only
partial remedying of the breach of planning control and all the requirements of the enforcement notice have been complied with, planning
permission is deemed to have been granted in respect of any construction of buildings or carrying out of activities in respect of which the
authority could have taken enforcement action. In addition, where an
enforcement notice requires construction of a replacement building and
all the requirements of that notice have been complied with, planning
permission is deemed to have been granted in respect of that
construction.[35]

There are various offences which may be committed once an enforcement notice has taken effect. The owner of the land, or lessee under a
lease with at least three years still to run, commits an offence if the
period specified in the enforcement notice for complying with its
requirements has expired without those requirements being satisfied in
full.[36] In contrast to the previous law, this offence also includes any
failure to cease a specified activity. It is a defence for the owner to show
that he did everything he could be expected to do to secure compliance
with the notice. This permits financial and physical incapacity to be
taken into account.[37] If the occupier is preventing the owner from
carrying out work required by an enforcement notice, a sheriff may issue
a warrant authorising the owner to go onto the land and carry out the
work.[38]

It is also an offence for any other person who has control of or an
interest in the land to carry on, or cause or permit to be carried on, after

---

[34] ss. 137 and 138; *Creswell v. Pearson* [1997] J.P.L. 860.
[35] ss. 128(13) and (14).
[36] s. 136.
[37] *Kent C.C. v. Brockman* [1996] 1 P.L.R. 1.
[38] s. 135(5).

the end of the period for compliance any activity which an enforcement notice requires to be ceased. Occupiers, lessees and other persons (conceivably even heritable creditors) may therefore be guilty of an offence. However, only the owner/lessee can be prosecuted for failing to take the active steps required by the notice, such as demolition of a building. The liability of other parties is confined to failing to cease an activity which the notice required to be discontinued.

The offences may be committed in the course of a single day or any longer period. A person may be convicted of a second or subsequent offence if he continues the failure to comply with the requirements of the notice following conviction. It is a defence that the person was unaware of the existence of the notice, but only if that person was not served with a copy and the notice was not contained in the register of enforcement notices which must be kept by the planning authority (see below).[39] Summary prosecution for these offences must commence within six months (see above).

The decision to prosecute and the choice of summary or solemn   7.16
procedure lies with the procurator fiscal. On summary conviction, a fine not exceeding £20,000 may be imposed (previously £2,000), but an unlimited fine may be imposed following conviction on indictment. In determining the level of fine, the court must have regard to any financial benefit which has accrued or appears likely to accrue to the person in consequence of the offence. For example, where an enforcement notice requires use of a building for retail purposes to be stopped, the court may take into account the profits made from that retail business following expiry of the period for compliance with the requirements of the notice. The court must also have regard to the means of the offender.[40] There are few reported cases dealing with sentencing.[41]

If the steps detailed in the enforcement notice have not been taken within the specified period, the planning authority may take those steps, including action to discontinue a use, and recover any expenses reasonably incurred from the person who is then the owner or lessee of the land.[42] It is an offence to obstruct the authority from taking such steps. If that person failed to exercise his right to appeal to the Secretary of State against the notice (see below), he is prevented from disputing the validity of any such action taken in accordance with the notice by the authority. The planning authority is also given the power to sell any materials removed by it from the land, unless claimed by the owner within three days. Where the owner, lessee or occupier incurs expenses for the purpose of complying with an enforcement notice or reimburses the expenses of the planning authority, these sums may be recovered from the person by whom the breach of planning control was committed.[43]

---

[39] s. 147.
[40] Criminal Procedure (Scotland) Act 1995, s. 211(7); *R. v. Browning* [1996] 1 P.L.R. 61.
[41] *McPhee v. Wilson*, 1994 G.W.D. 22–1383; *Rogerglen v. Vannet*, 1994 G.W.D. 30–1835; *McKnight v. Houston*, 1995 G.W.D. 4–227.
[42] s. 135.
[43] s. 135(4).

It was held not to be unreasonable for a planning authority to take direct action to demolish a building notwithstanding a pending appeal to the Court of Appeal in relation to the decision to dismiss the enforcement notice appeal. The authority had concluded that the appeal had little chance of success, which was not unjustified.[44]

Only two planning authorities have used the direct action power to any significant extent. The principal reason for the reluctance to use the power stems from concerns about the likelihood of recovering the costs involved. One of these main user authorities achieved approximately a 35 per cent success rate in recovering its costs.[45]

(c) Service of Enforcement Notice

7.17	Copies of the notice must be served in the required manner on the following persons within 28 days after its date of issue and at least 28 days before the date on which it is to take effect:

(i) the owner of the land, which includes a lessee under a lease with at least three years left to run[46];

(ii) the occupier of the land—whether a person is an occupier is a question of facts and circumstances, and squatters have been considered occupiers by virtue of the length of their occupation[47]; and

(iii) any other person having an interest in the land which the planning authority believes is materially affected by the notice, for example, heritable creditors and landlords.

Thus the enforcement notice is directed against the persons who may have the power to secure the result required by the notice and all other parties who have an interest in the land which requires that they be made aware of the notice. The latter parties may have the ability to force the former to comply with the terms of the notice, for example, through the terms of a lease. A planning contravention notice may be used to establish the identity of these parties (see above).

In an appeal to the Secretary of State against an enforcement notice, any failure to serve the notice on the appellant or another person may be disregarded if no substantial prejudice has been caused by the failure to serve. An enforcement notice was not null where the failure was the result of a mistaken belief that another party served with the notice was the owner.[48] In contrast, failure to serve an enforcement notice on a person known by the authority to be the owner of the land rendered the notice null.[49] If a failure to serve renders the notice null, the planning authority can serve a fresh enforcement notice on all parties, subject to the prescribed time limits.

[44] *R. v. Chiltern D.C., ex p. Dyason* [1997] E.G.C.S 147.
[45] "Review of Planning Enforcement", Scottish Office Central Research Unit, 1997.
[46] s. 277(1).
[47] *Scarborough B.C. v. Adams* [1983] J.P.L. 673.
[48] *R. v. Greenwich LBC, ex p. Patel* [1985] J.P.L. 851.
[49] *McDaid v. Clydebank D.C.*, 1984 S.L.T. 162, [1984] J.P.L. 579, but see the compulsory purchase case of *Martin v. Bearsden & Milngavie D.C.*, 1987 S.L.T. 300.

Details of the notice should also be recorded in the register available for public inspection. Failure to do so may create a defence to any prosecution (see above).

(d) Content of Enforcement Notice

Prior to the PCA, the requirements governing the content of enforce- 7.18 ment notices were a happy hunting ground for lawyers seeking to challenge notices. The overhauled system is designed to reduce the legal complexity surrounding the content of enforcement notices, coupled with increased powers for planning authorities and reporters on appeal to vary or correct notices. As a result of these changes, much of the previous case law on the content of enforcement notices must now be treated with caution. However, the courts are still prepared to take a restrictive approach to the interpretation of enforcement notices in appropriate cases.[50]

There is no prescribed form of enforcement notice, but each notice must state the following[51]:

(i) the matters which appear to the planning authority to constitute the breach (or breaches) of planning control, but only in sufficient detail or with sufficient precision to enable the recipient to know what these matters are;

(ii) whether the breach consists of carrying out development without the required planning permission, and/or failing to comply with any condition or limitation attached to a grant of planning permission: thus the notice need only identify the general nature of the alleged breach;

(iii) the steps required to be taken or the activities which must cease in order to wholly or partly remedy the breach or remedy any injury to amenity which has been caused by the breach: this is considered in detail below;

(iv) the date on which the notice is to take effect, which must be at least 28 days after the last date of service of the enforcement notice[52];

(v) the period at the end of which any steps are required to have been taken or any activities ceased; different periods may be specified for different steps or activities; and

(vi) the reasons why the planning authority considers it expedient to issue the notice, and a description of the precise boundaries of the land to which the notice relates, by reference to a plan or otherwise. The enforcement notice must be accompanied by an explanatory note giving prescribed information as to the right of appeal.[53]

A failure to include any of this information could render the notice a nullity and of no effect (see below).

---

[50] *e.g. Browning v. Tameside MBC* (1998) 75 P. & C.R. 417.
[51] TCPSA, s. 128. Model enforcement notices are attached to Circular 8/1992, Apps 2–4.
[52] s. 127(3)(b).
[53] Town and Country Planning (Enforcement of Control) (No. 2) (Scotland) Regulations 1992 (S.I. 1992 No. 2086), regs 3 and 4.

In most cases, the land to which the notice is directed will be the planning unit (Chapter 4) within which the alleged breach has taken or is taking place. However, the notice may be validly directed against a greater or lesser area than the planning unit.[54] The only requirement is that the area involved be sufficiently identified to tell the recipient what he has done wrong and what he must do to remedy that wrong.

Remedying the breach will involve making the developer comply with the terms and conditions of any planning permission by discontinuing any use of the land or by restoring the land to its condition before the breach took place, or remedying any injury to amenity which has been caused by the breach. The steps should not strike at an activity which is not part of the breach. An enforcement notice requiring discontinuation of a retail use went too far as it prevented continuation of the ancillary retail use attached to the previous main agricultural use.[55] The steps may include reversal of any development integral to the breach, notwithstanding that the development would not require planning permission in its own right or is lawful.[56] Where an enforcement notice required discontinuance of multiple occupancy of a dwellinghouse, the notice could not require the restoration of its use for single family occupation.[57]

The required steps may include the alteration or removal of any buildings, the carrying out of building or other operations, or the modification of contours of a deposit of refuse or waste materials by altering the gradient of its sides. The notice may specify restrictions on the carrying on of activities on the land. If the breach of planning control consisted of demolition of a building, the notice may require construction of a replacement building as similar as possible to the demolished building. Once the replacement building has been constructed in compliance with the enforcement notice, planning permission is deemed to have been granted for its construction.

Care will still require to be taken to describe precisely the steps to be taken to remedy the breach, and avoid exceeding what is necessary for this purpose, particularly in light of the potential criminal liability attached to the notice. Requiring the installation of "satisfactory soundproofing of a compressor and for all possible action to be taken to minimise the effects created by acrylic paint" was held to be hopelessly imprecise.[58] An enforcement notice requiring removal of stone from the foreshore was invalid because it was impossible to tell from the notice which of the stone was to be removed.[59] Instances where rights under the PDO have been exceeded require careful consideration.[60]

In addition to the discretion to ignore a breach of planning control and not serve an enforcement notice, the authority may decide to under-enforce by serving an enforcement notice requiring only partial remedy-

[54] *Rawlins v. Secretary of State for the Environment* [1990] 1 P.L.R. 110.
[55] *Mansi v. Elstree Rural D.C.* (1964) 16 P. & C.R. 153.
[56] *Murfitt, supra.*
[57] *Barn Properties Ltd, supra.*
[58] *Metallic Protectives v. Secretary of State for the Environment* [1976] J.P.L. 166.
[59] *McNaughton v. Peter McIntyre (Clyde) Ltd*, 1981 S.P.L.P. 15.
[60] Att.-Gen.'s Ref. (No. 1 of 1996) [1997] J.P.L. 749; [1996] E.G.C.S. 164.

ing of the breach. This allows the authority to take a practical view of what can be achieved through issuing an enforcement notice. Under-enforcement is not without consequences. If an enforcement notice could have required the removal of any buildings or cessation of activity, but the authority chose to under-enforce, as soon as the requirements of the enforcement notice have been complied with planning permission is deemed to have been granted for the development consisting of the construction of the buildings or carrying out of the activities.[61] Thus an ill-considered enforcement notice will prevent any future enforcement action. Planning authorities must therefore be sure to identify the full extent of breaches of planning control prior to issuing an enforcement notice.

(e) Nullity and Invalidity of Enforcement Notice

There is a distinction between a notice which is null, and one which is invalid. Where there is an obvious flaw in the notice, it is null and of no effect; if there is an underlying flaw which can only be proved on the facts, the notice is invalid but has effect until it is quashed. As a result, if on appeal to the Secretary of State the notice is found to be null, the appeal should be dismissed because there is no notice to appeal against.   7.19

Grounds of nullity have been identified by the courts. A notice which fails to specify the required information (see Content of Enforcement Notice, above) is likely to be null.[62] For example, if the notice fails to specify the date upon which it is to take effect, it cannot take effect, and must therefore be null. The failure to specify the steps required to remedy the breach renders the notice a nullity.[63] A notice which is hopelessly ambiguous and uncertain might also be a nullity.[64] Mistaken allegations of fact do not render a notice null.[65] It has been held that an enforcement notice which was not served on a person known to the planning authority to be the owner of the land rendered the notice a nullity, but this decision is likely to have been influenced by the expiry of the time limit for any appeal to the Secretary of State prior to the owner becoming aware of the notice, and is unlikely to be given wide application.[66]

A notice which has no obvious flaws is not a nullity, but may be shown to be invalid on proof of the facts. Where development without planning permission is alleged and it is found that no permission is required, the notice is invalid and may be quashed.[67] The following statutory grounds of appeal to the Secretary of State relate to issues of validity:

---

[61] TCPSA, s. 128(13). Permission is not granted if the notice is a nullity—*Tandridge D.C. v. Verrechia* [1998] E.G.C.S. 32.

[62] *Miller-Mead v. Minister of Housing* [1963] 1 All E.R. 459, Upjohn L.J. at p. 470G.

[63] *Tandridge D.C. v. Verrechia, supra,* unsuccessfully argued in *Barn Properties Ltd v. Secretary of State for Scotland, supra.*

[64] *Miller-Mead v. Minister of Housing, supra,* Upjohn L.J. at p. 470I.

[65] *Miller-Mead v. Minister of Housing, supra,* Diplock L.J. at p. 479D.

[66] *McDaid v. Clydebank D.C., supra;* but see *Martin v. Bearsden & Milngavie D.C. and R. v. Greenwich LBC, ex p. Patel, supra.*

[67] *Miller-Mead v. Minister of Housing, supra,* Upjohn L.J. at p. 470G.

(i)   the matters stated in the notice have not occurred;

(ii) these matters do not amount to a breach of planning control;

(iii) at the date when the notice was issued no enforcement action could be taken against the breach of planning control;

(iv) copies of the enforcement notice were not served as required by the TCPSA.

The distinction between nullity and invalidity is important. A notice which is null cannot be the foundation for any further enforcement action or prosecution, even if the recipient has not submitted an appeal against the notice. In contrast, an invalid notice remains valid until it is quashed. The validity of an enforcement notice on the grounds outlined above can only be challenged in an appeal to the Secretary of State.[68] Issues of validity, such as allegations that the planning authority has acted in bad faith and been motivated by immaterial considerations, cannot be raised as a defence to a prosecution, but could be the subject of a petition for judicial review in so far as the allegations do not fall within the grounds of appeal to the Secretary of State.[69] There is also scope for the Secretary of State to amend an invalid notice as part of the appeal proceedings, for example by exercising his power to correct any defect, error or misdescription in the notice.[70]

(f) *Appeal Against Enforcement Notice*

7.20   At any time before the date specified in the notice on which it will take effect, any person served with a copy of the notice or any other person having an interest in the land may appeal to the Secretary of State against the enforcement notice.[71]

Lodging an appeal prevents the enforcement notice coming into force on the date specified in the notice.[72] As a result, until the enforcement notice is upheld on appeal there is no requirement to take the steps specified in the notice to remedy the breach of planning control. Exercise of the right of appeal may therefore provide a further period for negotiation to resolve any dispute between the planning authority and the landowner, during which the alleged breach may continue. Most authorities would prefer to agree a solution, thereby avoiding the necessity of continuing with an appeal. Submission of an appeal would also provide sufficient time to lodge an application for retrospective planning permission or apply for a Certificate of Lawfulness of Existing Use or Development.

7.21   The right of appeal is open to abuse by persons seeking to continue a profitable activity, which is in breach of planning control, for as long as possible. Appeals may take up to a year to be determined. Such abuses can be prevented by the planning authority serving a stop notice with the enforcement notice, with the effect that the use or operation is pro-

---

[68] s. 134; *Barrie v. Lanark D.C.*, 1979 S.L.T. 14.

[69] *R. v. Wicks* [1997] 2 All E.R. 801.

[70] *Barn Properties Ltd v. Secretary of State for Scotland, supra.*

[71] TCPSA, ss. 130–133.

[72] s. 131(3).

hibited from continuing pending determination of the appeal. Most authorities are reluctant to serve stop notices because of the potential liability to pay compensation. Alternatively, an interdict could be sought to prevent the activity from continuing, but the authority could be liable to pay damages if the interdict was wrongfully obtained (see below).

The grounds of appeal are[73]:

(i) planning permission ought to be granted in respect of the breach of planning control constituted by the matters specified in the notice, or the condition or limitation concerned ought to be discharged;

(ii) the matters stated in the notice have not occurred;

(iii) these matters do not amount to a breach of planning control, including development which has become lawful because no enforcement action has been taken within the prescribed time limits (see above);

(iv) at the date when the notice was issued no enforcement action could be taken against the breach of planning control: this either refers to lawful development or to the time limit for further enforcement action (see above);

(v) copies of the enforcement notice were not served as required by the TCPSA;

(vi) the requirements of the notice exceed what is necessary to remedy any breach of planning control or to remedy any injury to amenity which has been caused by any such breach;

(vii) any period specified in the notice for compliance with its requirements falls short of what should reasonably be allowed.

An appeal is lodged by giving written notice of appeal to the Scottish Office Inquiry Reporters (referred to as SOIR),[74] before the date specified in the enforcement notice as that on which it is to take effect. The appeal will have been lodged timeously if the notice was sent in a properly addressed and pre-paid envelope posted in sufficient time for it to be delivered before that date in the ordinary course of the post (overturning a court ruling that the effective date is the date of receipt and not the date of posting).[75]

There is no prescribed form of notice of appeal and a short letter 7.22 stating the appellant's wish to appeal to the Secretary of State against the enforcement notice will be sufficient. A written statement of the grounds of appeal and a brief statement of supporting facts may be submitted at the same time as the notice of appeal or not later than 14 days after being requested by SOIR.[76] The appeal may be dismissed if the appellant fails to comply with this time limit.[77] The appellant will also be requested to indicate whether he wishes the appeal to follow the

---

[73] s. 130(1).
[74] 2 Greenside Lane, Edinburgh EH1 3AG, tel: 0131 244 5649, fax: 0131 244 5680.
[75] s. 130 (2).
[76] Town and Country Planning (Enforcement of Control) (No. 2) (Scotland) Regulations 1992, reg. 5.
[77] s. 132(3)(a).

written submissions procedure or be heard at a public inquiry (Chapter 8). Both the appellant and the planning authority have an absolute right to request a public inquiry.

By lodging an appeal, the appellant is deemed to have made an application for planning permission and a fee must be paid to SOIR accordingly. This requirement applies whether or not one of the grounds of appeal is that planning permission ought to be granted, but if that is one of the grounds the appeal and application will lapse if the fee is not paid within the period specified in a written notice from the SOIR to the appellant. No fee is payable if, prior to service of the notice, an application for planning permission for the development remains undetermined or an appeal has been lodged against the decision of the planning authority on such an application.[78]

The planning authority must submit a statement within 28 days of receiving notification of the appeal from SOIR, and send a copy to the appellant. This statement includes a summary of the response of the authority to each ground of appeal and will indicate whether the authority would be prepared to grant planning permission for the matters alleged to constitute a breach of planning control. If the authority fails to submit the statement within the time limit, the Secretary of State may proceed with the appeal and quash the enforcement notice.[79]

In determining an appeal against an enforcement notice, the Secretary of State has power to[80]:

(i) correct any defect, error or misdescription in the notice, or vary its terms, if he is satisfied that the correction or variation will not cause injustice to the appellant or the planning authority (previously this power was limited to correcting any non-material informality, defect or error)[81];

(ii) disregard the failure to serve a copy of the notice on any person, if neither the appellant or that person has been substantially prejudiced by this failure;

(iii) give directions to give effect to his decision on the appeal, including directions for quashing the notice;

(iv) grant planning permission in respect of any of the matters stated in the enforcement notice as constituting a breach of planning control;

(v) discharge any condition or limitation subject to which planning permission was granted, and substitute any other condition or limitation;

(vi) grant permission for such other development on the land to which the enforcement notice relates as appears appropriate; and

(vii) determine whether on the date on which the appeal was made, any existing use of the land, operations, or any matter constituting a failure to comply with a condition or limitation

[78] s. 130(7) and (8), and Town and Country Planning (Fees for Applications and Deemed Applications) (Scotland) Regulations 1997, reg. 10.
[79] s. 132(3)(b).
[80] ss. 132 and 133.
[81] *e.g. Barn Properties Ltd, supra.*

attached to a grant of planning permission, were lawful, and grant a Certificate of Lawfulness of Existing Use or Development accordingly.

In considering whether to grant planning permission, the Secretary of 7.23 State must have regard to the provisions of the development plan, so far as material to the subject-matter of the enforcement notice, and to any other material considerations. His decision must be in accordance with the provisions of the development plan unless material considerations indicate otherwise.[82] In substituting a new noise level condition without affording the parties an opportunity to express their views as to the acceptable noise level at whatever point might appropriately be specified as the measurement point, a reporter was held to have acted contrary to the principles of natural justice.[83] In deciding whether to grant permission for the erection of a wall, it was a material consideration that there were rights under the PDO to erect a fence which amounted to a valid planning permission.[84]

The statutory grounds of appeal do not include the manner of the exercise of the planning authority's discretion to take enforcement action, and this should not be considered in the determination of the appeal.[85] It is competent for the notice to be upheld where there is no longer any breach of planning control once the appeal is determined, if the situation might change and the notice would prevent such change.[86]

Aside from the grounds of appeal, the Secretary of State may find that the enforcement notice is a nullity. If the notice is a nullity, it does not exist and there is no notice upon which to determine the appeal (see above).

Where an appeal against an enforcement notice is upheld on the grounds that the matters stated in the notice do not amount to a breach of planning control, this is a conclusive determination which cannot be re-opened in subsequent proceedings.[87]

Any person aggrieved by the decision of the Secretary of State on appeal may challenge the validity of that decision in the Court of Session.[88] This right of challenge is subject to a six-week time limit from the date of the decision letter. The court is only concerned with the validity (or legality) of the decision and will not interfere with its merits (Chapter 8). The decision must therefore be challenged on the grounds that it is null or invalid as outwith the powers (*ultra vires*) of the Secretary of State. For example, the Secretary of State may have misused his statutory powers by failing to take into account a relevant factor.

As part of an appeal to the Court of Session it is competent to seek interim suspension of the decision of the Secretary of State, for example,

[82] ss. 133(4) and 25.
[83] *Dunfermline D.C. v. Secretary of State for Scotland*, 1996 S.L.T. 89.
[84] *Nolan v. Secretary of State for the Environment*, 1998 E.G.C.S. 7.
[85] *Parkes v. Secretary of State for Scotland*, 1998 G.W.D. 6–292, SPEL 67:55; *Tarn v. Secretary of State for Scotland*, 1997 G.W.D. 9–394, SPEL 62:81.
[86] *Parkes, supra.*
[87] *Hammond v. Secretary of State for the Environment* [1997] J.P.L. 724.
[88] TCPSA, s. 239.

to prevent the enforcement notice from taking effect. It is unclear whether the statutory provision that the notice "shall be of no effect pending the final determination or the withdrawal of the appeal"[89] extends to an appeal to the Court of Session. Although a decision of the English Court of Criminal Appeal indicates that this provision does apply, the relevant statutory provisions in England are different.[90]

(g)   Challenge of Enforcement Notice in the Courts

7.24   Any person aggrieved by the decision of the Secretary of State on an appeal against an enforcement notice may challenge the validity of that decision in the Court of Session (see above).

The availability of the right of appeal to the Secretary of State against an enforcement notice will in most instances mean that judicial review procedure will not be appropriate for challenging the legality of the notice. There is a statutory prohibition on any legal challenge to the validity of a notice where the grounds of challenge fall within the grounds of appeal to the Secretary of State (see above). This extends to a challenge to an anticipated enforcement notice.[91] However, it may be possible to raise judicial review proceedings on the grounds that the notice is null or invalid on other grounds, such as that it was beyond the powers of the authority to issue the notice.

The invalidity of the notice cannot be raised as a defence to a prosecution if the alleged invalidity falls within the grounds of appeal to the Secretary of State. Even if the statutory prohibition does not apply, it may be appropriate for the alleged invalidity to be challenged by judicial review rather than in the criminal courts.[92]

Stop Notices

7.25   The PCA reforms also amended the provisions relating to stop notices. For example, in special circumstances, a stop notice can now take effect immediately upon service; and a stop notice can prohibit use of residential caravans. After four years, an unauthorised use cannot be prohibited by service of a stop notice. The circumstances in which compensation will be payable following service of a stop notice are more restricted. Finally, the penalties for ignoring a stop notice have been increased. There is a very low use of stop notices, with almost half of the planning authorities serving no stop notices in the period 1992–96, and only two authorities making regular use of the stop notice powers. The principal reason appears to be concerns about liability for compensation.[93]

(a)   Power to Serve Stop Notice

7.26   The power to serve a stop notice may be exercised only in association with service of an enforcement notice, where the planning authority considers it expedient that any activity (or ancillary or associated

---

[89] s. 131(3).
[90] *R. v. Kuxhaus* [1988] 2 All E.R. 705.
[91] *Barrie v. Lanark D.C.*, 1979 S.L.T. 14.
[92] *R. v. Wicks, supra.*
[93] "Review of Planning Enforcement", Scottish Office Central Research Unit, 1997.

activity), which the enforcement notice requires to be ceased, should cease before the expiry of the period for compliance with the enforcement notice.[94] A stop notice may be served at the same time as the enforcement notice or at any time thereafter until the enforcement notice takes effect. Lodging an appeal against an enforcement notice will prevent that notice from taking effect, leaving the planning authority with the option of serving a stop notice. Scottish Office guidance states that planning authorities should ensure that the requirements of a stop notice prohibit only what is essential to safeguard amenity or public safety in the neighbourhood, or to prevent serious or irreversible harm to the environment in the surrounding area.[95]

The effect of a stop notice is to prohibit the carrying out of the activity on the land to which the enforcement notice relates or on any part of the land specified in the stop notice. The stop notice can also require cessation of activities which are ancillary to or associated with the activity struck at by the enforcement notice, in other words, activities associated with (but not part of) the breach of planning control.

The stop notice may prohibit some but not all of the activities which the enforcement notice requires to cease, or particular aspects of a single activity. It may also require cessation of activity on part but not all of the land specified in the enforcement notice. This ability to under-enforce by selecting which of the activities specified in the enforcement notice should be prohibited by the stop notice enables the planning authority to prevent a clear breach of planning control from continuing, pending an appeal against the enforcement notice, but avoid liability to pay compensation for preventing an activity which is less obviously a breach.

A stop notice cannot prohibit use of any building as a dwellinghouse. However, the restriction on prohibiting use of a residential caravan has been removed. A stop notice also cannot prohibit any use carried out (whether continuously or not) for more than four years prior to the date of service of the notice. In calculating the four years, no account is taken of any period during which the use was authorised by planning permission, such as a temporary permission. This four-year rule applies to uses and does not extend to building, engineering, mining or other operations or the deposit of refuse or waste materials.

The effect of serving a stop notice underlines the limitations of enforcement notices. An enforcement notice takes at least 28 days to come into effect and provides a further period for compliance with its terms, during which time the breach of planning control may continue. Lodging an appeal to the Secretary of State against the enforcement notice suspends its effect until the determination or withdrawal of the appeal. Service of a stop notice prevents the breach of planning control from continuing until the enforcement notice comes into effect.

Stop notices have their own limitations. A stop notice has a negative 7.27 character and can only be used to prohibit activity rather than to achieve positive action or remedy the breach of planning control. As the effect of a stop notice is limited to requiring complete cessation of an activity,

---

[94] TCPSA, s. 140. The Secretary of State can also serve a stop notice—s. 142.
[95] Circular 8/1992, Pt II, para. 71.

stop notices cannot be used to keep an activity within reasonable
bounds. In addition, unlike an interdict, a stop notice cannot be used to
prohibit a threatened breach: it can only be served with or after an
enforcement notice once there appears to have been a breach of
planning control. The usefulness of the power to serve a stop notice is
reduced further by the potential liability for compensation (see below).

A stop notice ceases to have effect once the period for compliance
with the enforcement notice has expired and an offence is thus committed for non-compliance with the terms of the enforcement notice. It
also ceases to have effect if the enforcement notice to which it relates is
withdrawn or quashed on appeal. Where the enforcement notice
is varied so that it no longer relates to an activity prohibited by the stop
notice, the stop notice will cease to have effect in relation to that activity.
A stop notice is not invalidated by any failure to serve the enforcement
notice on all parties, provided the planning authority shows that it took
all reasonably practicable steps to effect proper service.[96]

The stop notice may be withdrawn at any time by the planning
authority without prejudicing its power to serve a fresh notice. Withdrawal is effected by giving notice to all persons served with a copy of
the stop notice and displaying this notice in place of any site notices.[97]
There is no statutory power to vary a stop notice.

It is an offence for a person to contravene, or cause or permit
contravention of, the provisions of a stop notice after a site notice has
been displayed or the notice has been served on him.[98] This offence may
be committed in the course of a day or a longer period of time.
Continued contravention of the stop notice following conviction is also
an offence. It will be a defence for the accused person to prove that the
stop notice was not served on him and that he had no reasonable cause
to believe that the activity was prohibited by the stop notice. Display of a
site notice (see below) may be an important factor in determining
reasonable cause. The decision to prosecute and the choice of procedure
rests with the procurator fiscal, with liability to a fine not exceeding
£20,000 on summary conviction and an unlimited fine following conviction on indictment. In determining the level of fine the court will have
regard to any financial benefit which has accrued or appears likely to
accrue to the person in consequence of the failure to comply with the
stop notice.

(b)   Service of Stop Notice

7.28   A stop notice may be served on any person who appears to the
planning authority to have an interest in the land or be engaged in
activities which constitute or involve the breach of planning control
alleged in the enforcement notice.[99] In comparison, the enforcement
notice is served on the owner and occupier of the land. The stop notice

---

[96] s. 141.
[97] s. 140(9).
[98] s. 144.
[99] s. 140(8).

may be served at the same time as the enforcement notice or at a later date before the enforcement notice takes effect.

The planning authority may also display a site notice on the land, stating the requirements of the stop notice, the persons on whom it has been served, and the consequences of contravening the stop notice.[1] Display of a site notice may widen the categories of persons against whom prosecution for contravening the notice may be successful (see above).

(c) Content of Stop Notice

There is no prescribed form of stop notice,[2] but it must specify the date upon which it is to take effect.[3] In normal circumstances, this date must be between three and 28 days after the date of service. However, a stop notice may take earlier effect if the planning authority considers that there are special reasons why an earlier date should be specified. The Scottish Office guidance gives as an example the need to protect areas of great landscape value or conservation areas from harmful operational development.[4] For the notice to take earlier effect in this way, the authority must serve a statement of these special reasons along with the notice. There is no longer a requirement that the stop notice refer to and enclose a copy of the enforcement notice.

7.29

As penal consequences arise from a stop notice, its terms must be strictly construed, and it is not permissible to look at the enforcement notice associated with the stop notice in order to ascertain what is prohibited.[5]

(d) Challenge of Stop Notice

There is no statutory right of appeal to the Secretary of State or the Court of Session against a stop notice. However, a petition for judicial review may be brought before the Court of Session alleging that the notice is invalid on legal grounds (Chapter 8). Failure to follow the Scottish Office guidance is unlikely to be sufficient for a successful judicial review.[6] It may be difficult to obtain an interdict to prevent service of a stop notice or to suspend its effect pending the decision of the court, as there is a right to compensation if the stop notice is eventually quashed.[7] An alternative but risky option to applying for judicial review is to ignore the notice and defend any prosecution on the basis that the notice is invalid.

7.30

---

[1] s. 141(3).
[2] Circular 8/1992, App. 5 contains a model stop notice.
[3] s. 140(7).
[4] Circular 8/1992, Pt II, para. 76.
[5] *R. v. Dhar* [1993] 2 P.L.R. 60.
[6] *R. v. Elmbridge B.C., ex p. Wendy Fair Markets Ltd* [1995] J.P.L. 928.
[7] *Central R.C. v. Clackmannan D.C.*, 1983 S.L.T. 666; contrast *Shanks & McEwan v. Gordon D.C.*, 1991 S.P.L.P. 32:15.

(e) Compensation and Stop Notices

7.31   The potential liability to pay compensation has acted as a deterrent to
use of stop notices. Compensation is payable where a stop notice has
ceased to have effect (see above) in the following circumstances[8]:

   (i)   the enforcement notice is quashed on appeal as invalid, other
         than on the ground that planning permission ought to be
         granted for the activity or the condition or limitation dis-
         charged; or
   (ii) the enforcement notice is varied to omit the requirement to
         cease the activity prohibited by the stop notice; or
   (iii) the enforcement notice is withdrawn, other than in conse-
         quence of a grant of planning permission by the planning
         authority for the development to which the notice relates; or
   (iv) the stop notice is withdrawn.

Following the PCA reforms, no compensation will be payable where the
stop notice prohibits any activity which at any time when the stop notice
is in force constitutes or contributes to a breach of planning control.
Thus, even if the enforcement notice fails, the ludicrous situation will not
arise of the planning authority being liable to pay compensation for
prohibiting an activity which is a breach of planning control. The right to
compensation is also excluded where any loss or damage suffered could
have been avoided if the claimant had provided information sought
under statutory powers, such as a planning contravention notice (see
above), or had otherwise co-operated with the planning authority when
responding to the notice. Finally, no compensation is payable if either
the planning authority decides to grant planning permission and, therefore, withdraws the enforcement notice, or the Secretary of State, in
determining the appeal, decides to grant planning permission and so
quashes the enforcement notice.
        Compensation may be claimed by a person who had an interest in the
land to which the stop notice related when it was served. There is no
requirement that the person must have been served with a copy of the
notice. Interests in land will include those of an owner or occupier and
possibly other parties such as lessees and heritable creditors who had a
legal interest in the land.
        Compensation is payable in respect of any loss or damage directly
attributable to the prohibition contained in the notice, including any sum
payable in respect of a breach of contract caused by taking action
necessary to comply with the prohibition. The initial claim for compensation in respect of a stop notice must be submitted within six months, but
will be valid for 20 years.[9] Except in so far as may be otherwise provided
by any regulations, any question of disputed compensation can be
referred to and determined by the Lands Tribunal.

---

[8] TCPSA, s. 143.
[9] *Holt v. Dundee D.C.*, 1990 S.L.T. (Lands Tr.) 30.

Breach of Condition Notice

The Carnwath Report recommended that there should be a remedy to   7.32
enforce a condition without enabling the merits to be reopened in an
enforcement notice appeal. This recommendation has led to the introduction of the breach of condition notice, which joins the enforcement
notice as the other main form of enforcement action which prevents a
breach of planning control from becoming lawful development.[10]

In the period 1992–96 over 300 breach of condition notices were
served. There are wide variations between planning authorities in the
extent of use of these notices. However, the lack of clarity of conditions
is often the reason why a breach of condition notice is not served. Where
a notice has been served, there has been a 73 per cent compliance rate.[11]

As a result of the lack of a right of appeal against a breach of
condition notice, a grant of planning permission should not be implemented until consideration has been given to the appropriateness of any
conditions attached to the permission. Any purchase of land should
involve careful scrutiny of planning conditions and warranties should be
obtained from the seller that no conditions have been breached.

(a)   Power to Serve Breach of Condition Notice

A breach of condition notice may be served by the planning authority   7.33
where there is non-compliance with any of the conditions or limitations
regulating the use of land imposed upon a grant of planning permission.[12] Thus, a notice may be served only if there is actual non-
compliance (an objective test), whereas an enforcement notice may be
served where it "appears" to the authority that there has been a breach
of planning control (a subjective test). This suggests that more proof will
be required before the breach of condition notice may be served.

The Scottish Office guidance states that the decisive issue should be
whether public amenity or the use of land or buildings meriting
protection in the public interest is unacceptably affected. A breach of
condition notice should only be served where the condition is legally
valid, satisfies the criteria for imposition of conditions (Chapter 6), and
has clearly been breached on the available evidence.[13] In dismissing an
application for judicial review of a decision not to take enforcement
action, the court acknowledged that although there had not been strict
compliance with the terms of a condition, it had in substance been
complied with.[14]

The planning authority has power to withdraw the notice without
prejudicing its power to serve a fresh notice within the prescribed time
limits. There is no specific power to vary the notice. However, the time
limit for compliance may be extended.

---

[10] Carnwath, *supra*.

[11] "Review of Planning Enforcement", Scottish Office Central Research Unit, 1997.

[12] TCPSA, s. 145.

[13] Circular 36/1992, "Planning and Compensation Act 1991, Lawful Development and
Enforcement" paras 9 and 24.

[14] *R. v. Flintshire C.C., ex p. Somerfield Stores* [1998] E.G.C.S. 53.

(b) Effect of Breach of Condition Notice

7.34   In contrast to an enforcement notice, a breach of condition notice comes into effect on the date of service. If, after the period allowed for compliance has expired, any of the conditions specified in the notice are not complied with and the steps specified in the notice have not been taken or the activities have not ceased, the person served with a copy of the notice is in breach of its terms and guilty of an offence. It is not clear whether compliance with the terms of the notice has the effect of discharging the notice, or whether a breach of condition notice has a similar effect to an enforcement notice and will remain in force to catch any future breaches following compliance.

    Where a condition prevented occupation of a dwelling until a sewage treatment plant was installed, and the breach of condition notice required installation of the plant, no offence was committed when occupation commenced without installation of the plant, as cessation of use was not a step specified in the notice.[15]

    Any person found guilty of such an offence shall be liable on summary conviction to a fine not exceeding level 3 on the standard scale (Appendix 1). This offence may be committed in the course of a day or over a longer period. Further offences will be committed if there is non-compliance with the notice following conviction. It will be a defence to prove that all reasonable measures were taken to secure compliance with the conditions specified in the notice, or that the accused no longer had control of the land where the notice was purportedly served upon him as the person having control thereof.

    A breach of condition notice will cease to have effect where the condition is discharged, or so far as the notice is inconsistent with a subsequent grant of retrospective planning permission.[16] However, this will not affect liability for a previous failure either to comply or to secure compliance with the notice.

    There is no provision enabling the planning authority to take the steps specified in a breach of condition notice and recover its expenses from the person served with the notice.

(c) Service of Breach of Condition Notice

7.35   The breach of condition notice may be served upon any person who is carrying out or has carried out the development, or who has caused or permitted another to do so. In the case of conditions regulating the use of the land, the notice may be served upon the person who has control of the land. Thus, unlike an enforcement notice which is served on the owner and occupier, the objective seems to be that a breach of condition notice is served upon the person responsible for the breach of condition or the person who can secure compliance with the condition. It also seems that the planning authority has an element of discretion in deciding the person(s) to be served with a breach of condition notice.

---

[15] *Quinton v. North Cornwall D.C.* [1994] C.L.Y. 4315.
[16] TCPSA, s. 137.

The example given by the Scottish Office guidance is a condition requiring completion of a landscaping scheme in association with a housing development. This type of condition does not regulate the use of land. Thus a breach of condition notice cannot be served upon the individual homeowners (it would be possible to serve enforcement notices), but must be served upon the original developer.

(d) Content of Breach of Condition Notice

The notice must specify the planning permission to which it relates, 7.36 the conditions which have not been complied with (which need not be all the conditions), and the steps which the authority consider ought to be taken, or the activities which the authority considers ought to cease, to secure compliance with these conditions. The period for compliance must be at least 28 days from the date of service of the notice, as specified in the notice.

It may be within the discretion of the planning authority to ignore non-compliance with some or all of the conditions imposed upon a grant of planning permission. However, unlike the power to serve an enforcement notice, the statutory wording does not explicitly permit service of a breach of condition notice requiring partial and not full compliance with a condition.

(e) Challenge of Breach of Condition Notice

There is no statutory right of appeal to the Secretary of State or the 7.37 Court of Session against a breach of condition notice. It will therefore be impossible to challenge the merits of the notice, but may be possible to challenge its validity. An invalid notice could be ignored and its invalidity raised as a defence to any prosecution for non-compliance with its terms.[17] Alternatively, a petition for common-law judicial review may be submitted to the Court of Session on the ground that the notice is beyond the powers (*ultra vires*) of the planning authority to serve (Chapter 8). The Court of Session may refuse a petition for judicial review on the ground that the statutory procedures for challenging conditions should have been utilised (Chapter 6). Invalidity of the notice will not prevent the planning authority serving a fresh notice within the prescribed time limits. Where the conditions had not been breached, the decision to issue a breach of condition notice was based on an error of law and was accordingly flawed.[18]

The option of negotiating with the planning authority must always be borne in mind. Negotiations may lead to submission of an application for planning permission without compliance with the condition (Chapter 5).

Interdict

Following the PCA reforms, planning authorities have a statutory 7.38 power to seek interdict from the sheriff court or the Court of Session to restrain or prevent any actual or apprehended breach of planning

---

[17] *Dilieto v. Ealing LBC* [1998] 2 All E.R. 885.
[18] *R. v. Ealing LBC, ex p. Zainuddin* [1995] J.P.L. 925.

control.[19] Interdict is a court order requiring an activity to be stopped or preventing an activity from starting. It has a negative character and is not appropriate for requiring an activity or works to be carried out, unlike injunctions in England and Wales which can have negative ("stop") and positive ("do") requirements. Breach of interdict amounts to contempt of court and may result in a fine and/or imprisonment.

It is irrelevant to the exercise of this power that the authority has exercised or proposes to exercise other enforcement or planning powers. Interdict can, therefore, be used in conjunction with other enforcement action, for example, to prevent the lodging of an appeal from delaying the requirement of an enforcement notice to cease an unauthorised activity. This power may be used to avoid the potential liability for compensation which follows service of a stop notice in such a situation (see below). However, planning authorities should note that interim interdict is granted *periculo petentis*, with the result that there will be liability to pay compensation in the form of damages if the interim interdict is later proved to be excessive. An interdict may be sought in circumstances where a stop notice cannot be served, such as before there has been an actual breach of planning control, or after an enforcement notice has come into effect.

Application for interdict may be made to either the sheriff court or the Court of Session. The choice of court will depend on factors such as the seriousness of the case, convenience and cost. The court may grant such interdict as it thinks appropriate for the purpose of restraining or preventing the breach.[20] Refusal of the application for interdict will continue to be within the discretion of the court. For example, it is possible that the court may refuse to grant an interdict in circumstances where a stop notice could be served, on the grounds that the more specific power provided by Parliament should be exercised, especially since it carries provisions for payment of compensation.

Where a caravan site was being used in breach of planning conditions, the sheriff granted interim interdict to the planning authority preventing the landowners from permitting caravans, keeping caravans, or residing in caravans on their land, and from wilfully obstructing the council from exercising their power to take direct action to enforce an enforcement notice. The balance of convenience favoured the grant of interim interdict as there was no colourable argument that the defenders had the right to do what they were alleged to have been doing. Although the defenders might have a justifiable sense of grievance at the way in which they had been treated, this was not a relevant consideration to the grant of interdict.[21]

In an odour nuisance case, the Court of Session refused to grant an interim interdict to prevent the sewerage authority from operating the sewage treatment plant adjacent to the premises occupied by a manufacturing company, on the grounds that the balance of convenience did not

[19] s. 146.
[20] *City of London Corporation v. Bovis Construction* [1989] J.P.L. 263 shows the circumstances in which the courts in England and Wales will grant an injunction.
[21] *Perth & Kinross Council v. Alexander Lowther*, 1996 SPEL 58:119.

favour the granting of the interdict, which would result in untreated sewage overflowing into nearby watercourses.[22]

Although injunction is a wider remedy, useful principles can be drawn 7.39 from English cases. Weight should be attached to the overall conduct of the person against whom the injunction is sought and evidence of such matters as co-operation or disregard of the law and serious personal hardship should be taken into account.[23] The possibility of planning permission being granted in the future has been held not to be a legitimate reason for refusing an injunction, and it was not a defence that the respondents would comply with the law if a suitable alternative site were found for their caravans.[24] An injunction was granted notwithstanding that there had been an unsuccessful prosecution for failure to observe an enforcement notice relating to the same breach.[25] An injunction was granted restraining a householder from permitting structural alterations to his house or additions to its exterior without planning permission, following the erection of a replica spitfire and other items.[26] It has been observed that in withholding an injunction the court would be giving temporary planning permission for the continuation of an activity for which the planning authority had consistently refused permission.[27]

Although breach of interdict amounts to contempt of court and could result in imprisonment, it is up to the court to determine how to deal with the breach. In a case involving caravans, the court refused imprisonment, as the council had a statutory duty to provide accommodation for gypsies and no alternative accommodation had been found. Taking the mitigating factors into account, the court decided to show compassion.[28]

Interdicts are rarely sought as planning authorities are concerned about the costs involved. However, in 1992–96, 90 per cent of interdicts sought were granted.[29]

Notice Requiring Proper Maintenance of Land

The planning authority has power to serve a notice (previously 7.40 referred to in the 1972 Act as a "waste land notice") where it appears that the amenity of any part of its district or of an adjoining district is adversely affected by the condition of any land or buildings within the district. Unlike the other enforcement powers, this power may be exercised in the absence of a breach of planning control. The notice is served on the owner, lessee and occupier of the land or building, and requires specified steps to be taken to abate the adverse effect. The

[22] *Barr & Stroud Ltd v. West of Scotland Water Authority*, 1996 G.W.D. 36–2126, SPEL 62:83. *cf. City of Glasgow Council v. Cannell*, 1998 G.W.D. 33–1722, SPEL 71:15 (listed building control).
[23] *Harborough D.C. v. Wheatcroft* [1996] J.P.L. B128.
[24] *Hambleton D.C. v. Bird* [1995] 3 P.L.R. 8.
[25] *South Hams D.C. v. Halsey* [1996] J.P.L. 761.
[26] *Croydon LBC. v. Gladden* [1994] 1 P.L.R. 30 [1994] J.P.L. 723.
[27] *Runnymede B.C. v. Harwood* [1994] 1 P.L.R. 22 [1994] J.P.L. 723.
[28] *Guildford B.C. v. Smith* [1994] J.P.L. 734; also *Waverley B.C. v. Marney* (1995) 93 L.G.R. 86.
[29] "Review of Planning Enforcement", Scottish Office Central Research Unit, 1997.

effect of the notice is similar to an enforcement notice. An appeal against the notice may be submitted to the Secretary of State at any time until the notice takes effect. Failure to comply with the requirements of the notice is not declared to be an offence. If the required steps are not taken, the only sanction available to the authority is to enter the site and take those steps itself, recovering the costs of doing so from the owner or lessee of the site.[30]

Discontinuance Order

7.41   The planning authority has power to require discontinuance of any use of land, alteration or removal of any buildings or works, or to impose conditions on the continuance of a use of land.[31] This power is exercised in the interests of the proper planning of its area (including the interests of amenity). Regard must be had to the development plan and to any other material considerations, and the decision made in accordance with the provisions of the development plan unless material considerations indicate otherwise.[32] The order will not take effect until confirmed by the Secretary of State.[33] There is provision for a hearing to be held at the request of the owner, lessee or occupier of the land, or any other person affected by the order. If the order is confirmed, there is a right to compensation for depreciation of the value of an interest in land, or disturbance in the enjoyment of the land.[34] The cost of carrying out works in compliance with the order can also be recovered from the planning authority. It is an offence not to comply with the order.[35] If any step required by the order has not been taken within the period specified in the order, the planning authority may enter the land, take the required step and recover their reasonable expenses from the owner of the land.[36]

OTHER ENFORCEMENT MATTERS

Service of Notices

7.42   Service of a notice is achieved by delivering it to the person, by leaving it at their usual or last known place of abode, or by sending it by recorded delivery or registered mail to that address. Where the valuation roll shows a person to have an interest in the land, the notice should be served at the address on the roll for that person. Service on companies is effected by delivery to the secretary or clerk of the company at its registered or principal office, or by registered letter/recorded delivery

---

[30] TCPSA, s. 179.
[31] s. 71.
[32] s. 25.
[33] s. 72.
[34] s. 83.
[35] s. 148.
[36] s. 149.

addressed to the secretary or clerk at that office. If the planning authority is unable to identify after reasonable enquiry the persons entitled to service, the notice may be addressed to "the owner", "the lessee", or "the occupier" of the land and served as above. If any part of the land is unoccupied, the notice may be addressed to "the owners and any lessees and occupiers" and affixed in a conspicuous manner to some object on the land, but must be served upon any person who has given to the authority an address for service.[37]

Register of Notices

Prescribed details of every section 179 notice (notice requiring proper maintenance), enforcement notice, breach of condition notice, and stop notice, served in relation to land in its district must be entered by the planning authority into a register as soon as practicable and, in any event, within nine days. The register must be available for public inspection at all reasonable hours. Provision is made for removal of entries following withdrawal of a notice, a decision on appeal to quash the notice, or its reduction by the Court of Session.[38]

7.43

Personal Bar

There are certain limited circumstances in which the planning authority will be personally barred from exercising its enforcement powers (the equivalent principle in English law is estoppel).

7.44

Where an appeal has been upheld on the substantive issues, the legal principle of *res judicata* (finality of determination) applies and it is not open to the planning authority to serve fresh notices alleging similar breaches of planning control based on the same facts and circumstances.[39] However, this principle does not prevent service of a fresh notice within the time limits where a previous notice was quashed on procedural grounds or as a nullity.[40]

The other instance in which personal bar may be an issue is where a planning officer indicates that planning permission is not required for a proposed development. The problem is whether such a statement can personally bar the planning authority and prevent it from taking enforcement action against the development, which has commenced without permission in reliance upon this indication. Previously it could be argued that where the authority had delegated powers to the officer to make decisions on its behalf, a written statement in this form amounted to a section 51 determination which bound the authority. With the replacement of the formal procedure for obtaining Certificates of Lawfulness of Proposed Use or Development (CLOPUD) for the informal section 51 determinations, there is no longer a mechanism for obtaining informal but binding decisions. In the absence of delegated

---

[37] s. 271.
[38] ss. 147 and 181 and Enforcement No. 2 Regulations 1992, reg. 7 (*supra*).
[39] *Thrasyvoulou v. Secretary of State for the Environment* [1990] 2 A.C. 273; *Hammond v. Secretary of State for the Environment* [1997] J.P.L. 724.
[40] *R. v. Wychavon D.C.* [1992] J.P.L. 753.

powers, statements by its planning officers do not bind the authority.[41] However, in a recent decision the ostensible or apparent authority of the officer to make the decision prevented the authority from taking enforcement action.[42] In light of this uncertainty, it is clearly unsafe to rely upon any assurances from planning officers regarding the need for planning permission and consideration should be given to applying for a CLOPUD.

---

[41] *Western Fish Products v. Penwith D.C.* [1981] 2 All E.R. 204.
[42] *Camden LBC v. Secretary of State for the Environment* [1993] J.P.L. 1049; *Postermobile plc v. Brent LBC*, *The Times*, Dec. 8, 1997. See also Chap. 8—Sue for Negligence or Breach of Contract.

CHAPTER 8

CHALLENGE OF PLANNING DECISIONS

Prior to embarking on a challenge of a planning decision, it is essential   8.01
to identify the result that is sought and determine which, if any,
procedure could achieve this result. For example, despite a successful
judicial review petition, the Secretary of State or planning authority in
re-deciding the matter may be free to reach the same decision, provided
the decision is taken in the correct manner. Judicial review is, therefore,
not always the most appropriate procedure for challenging decisions.

Other relevant factors in deciding which procedure to use include the
existence of time limits and the availability of the remedy in
the circumstances. The degree to which professional assistance will be
necessary, with the resultant cost implications, will be an important
consideration. None of the procedures discussed in this chapter necessarily require such assistance, and indeed some are deliberately informal
to avoid intimidating non-professionals, but many persons will be
unwilling to act without professional advice. The likelihood of a successful challenge using the procedure must also be assessed.

This chapter concentrates upon the options available to a person who
wishes to challenge a decision upon a planning application, either at first
instance or on appeal. However, procedures for challenging the exercise
of other planning powers share the same general characteristics.

Following the incorporation of the European Convention on Human
Rights into United Kingdom law, it should be noted that the European
Court has held that the system of planning appeals in this country
complies with the requirement imposed by the Convention for a fair and
public hearing by an independent and impartial tribunal.[1]

NEGOTIATION

Chapter 5 commenced with a reminder of the importance of consulting   8.02
the planning authority for its views in advance of submitting a planning
application. It is equally advisable to explore the possibility of negotiating a solution with the planning authority before formally challenging a
decision. Formal procedures are expensive and time-consuming for both
challenger and planning authority, and each should recognise the
importance of compromise and avoidance of appeals.

If valid grounds of challenge can be shown, the planning authority may
be willing to negotiate a compromise. Alternatively, the authority may be

---

[1] *Bryan v. U.K.* [1996] 1 PLR 47.

willing to give an informal indication that a revised proposal may be successful. Such an indication would enable submission of a fresh application for planning permission rather than a challenge to the original decision. Additional information not before the planning authority at the time of the decision may also provide scope for negotiation.

The procedures to commence a challenge may begin during negotiations to place more pressure on the planning authority to agree a compromise. However, such action carries the risk that the authority will withdraw from further negotiations. Whatever tactics are employed, care must be taken to ensure that any time limit for commencing the challenge does not expire. If necessary, a challenge can be commenced to prevent expiry of the time limits while the negotiations continue. If negotiations will be lengthy, the parties can agree that the challenge be sisted (suspended) in the meantime. Applicants who anticipate difficulties in obtaining planning permission often submit duplicate applications, permitting them to lodge an appeal in connection with one application while continuing negotiations with the authority on the other application (Chapter 5).

As a result of the inability of the planning authority to revoke a grant of planning permission without paying compensation or re-determine the matter in the absence of a fresh planning application, for all practical purposes negotiation with the authority is not a worthwhile option for third parties wishing to challenge a decision on a planning application. Such parties may, however, wish to seek reassurance on future decisions or that compliance with conditions attached to a grant of permission will be monitored and enforcement action taken against any breaches.

APPEAL TO THE SECRETARY OF STATE

8.03 Applicants for planning permission have a statutory right of appeal to the Secretary of State in respect of the decision on their application by the planning authority. There are rights of appeal to the Secretary of State in connection with other forms of planning decisions. Unless otherwise stated, these follow a similar procedure. In most cases, the power of the Secretary of State to determine appeals has been delegated to full-time qualified officials known as reporters (equivalent to the inspectors in England and Wales).[2] The Secretary of State retains the power to recall for decision exceptional or important cases within the classes of delegated appeals. These cases, together with non-delegated appeals, are decided by the Secretary of State after consideration of the report made by the reporter who heard the appeal. The administration of planning appeals is handled by the Scottish Office Inquiry Reporters (SOIR).

---

[2] TCPSA, Sched. 4; Town and Country Planning (Determination of Appeals by Appointed Persons) (Prescribed Classes) (Scotland) Regulations 1987 (S.I. 1987 No. 1531), as amended.

Availability

The applicant (and no other person) has a right of appeal to the   8.04
Secretary of State against:

(i)   a refusal of permission by the planning authority, or against
      any conditions imposed on the grant of permission (pro-
      cedures for challenging planning conditions are examined in
      Chapter 6);

(ii) a refusal by the planning authority of an application for any
      consent, agreement or approval required by a condition
      imposed on a grant of planning permission, or against any
      conditions imposed on such consent, agreement or approval;

(iii) a refusal by the planning authority of an application for any
      approval required under any development order (for example,
      the Permitted Development Order, Chapter 4), or against any
      conditions imposed on such approval; and

(iv) a deemed refusal of permission, where the planning authority
      has failed either to notify the applicant of its decision on the
      application, or give notice that it has exercised its power to
      decline to determine the application, or that the application
      has been called in by the Secretary of State for decision
      (Chapter 5).[3]

Time Limit

The notice of appeal must be lodged within six months of[4]:   8.05

(i)   the notice of the decision of the planning authority on the
      application; or

(ii) in the case of a deemed refusal, the expiry of two months from
      the date of receipt of the application (four months if the
      application includes an environmental statement), or
      the expiry of any extended period agreed upon in writing by
      the applicant and the planning authority. The date of receipt
      of the application is the date by which the following have been
      lodged: any fee for the application together with the cost of
      any advertisement payable by the applicant, the certificates
      required in connection with the application and any details
      required under the Permitted Development Order.[5] This will
      often be earlier than the date of registration.

This time limit is absolute and any appeal lodged late will be rejected as
invalid.

Grounds of Challenge

In most appeals to the Secretary of State there is essentially only one   8.06
ground of challenge: that planning permission ought to be granted for
the proposed development. It would be competent but inadvisable for

---

[3] s. 47.
[4] Town and Country Planning (General Development Procedure) (Scotland) Order 1992
(DPO), art. 23, as amended.
[5] DPO, art. 14, as substituted.

the appellant to do no more than state this ground. The Secretary of State (or his reporter) has power to deal with the application afresh, as if it had been made to him in the first instance.[6] The planning merits of the application may, therefore, be assessed without any further input from the appellant other than the information which appears in the planning application. This is the inevitable result of the presumption in favour of development (Chapter 5), which is the usual starting point for grounds of appeal.

It is advisable for the appellant to expand on the reasons why planning permission ought to be granted to ensure that all the relevant points are put before the reporter. Rather than rely on the presumption in favour of development, the appellant may wish to stress the reasons why permission should be granted for the proposed development, by reference to the material considerations outlined in Chapter 5. Alternatively, or in addition, the appellant can argue that the reasons given by the planning authority for its decision are wrong, based on erroneous information, or insufficient to overcome the presumption. There is no single correct approach, but all the grounds of appeal must be stated on the form before the appeal is submitted.

Unlike a challenge in the courts, the grounds of appeal may involve discussion of the planning merits of the application and other factual matters. The planning merits of a proposed development stem from the provisions of the development plan and other material considerations (Chapter 5). Appropriate reference can therefore be made to relevant law, policies in the structure and local plans, any other relevant policies of the planning authority, and the advice given to planning authorities by the Secretary of State through circulars and other documents (Chapter 2). The report to the planning committee on the application, prepared by the planning officer and obtainable by members of the public through the access to information rules, is a useful starting point for gathering this information. The complexity or importance of the proposed development will dictate how much reference to such documents is required.

Initial Procedure

8.07   The appeal is lodged by submitting the following documents to SOIR within the six month time limit:

(i)   The notice of appeal in the form of a completed Form P/PPA, copies of which are provided by SOIR on request. The appellant is required to send a copy of the notice to the planning authority at the same time and, thereafter, the appellant and the authority are required to copy all correspondence with SOIR to each other.[7]

(ii)   A copy of the application which is the subject of the appeal and documents submitted along with it, including the certificate relating to notification of owners and agricultural tenants, and any neighbour notification certificate (Chapter 5).

[6] TCPSA, s. 48(1).
[7] DPO, art. 23(3) and (6).

(iii) A copy of the decision notice informing the applicant of the decision of the authority on the application, unless the appeal is against a deemed refusal.

(iv) Copies of all other relevant correspondence with any planning authority.

(v) A certificate relating to notification of owners and agricultural tenants in respect of the appeal, in the form of completed Forms 1 to 4 (supplied with Form P/PPA). By completing Form 1, the appellant certifies that at the time of submitting the appeal and within the previous 21 days nobody except the appellant was the owner of the site of the proposed development and none of the site formed part of an agricultural holding. Form 2 states that notice has been served on the owners and/or agricultural tenants named therein. Form 3 states that all reasonable steps (specifying these steps) have been taken to find out the names and addresses of the owners and/or agricultural tenants but without success, other than those named on whom notice has been served, and that notice of the appeal has been published in a local newspaper in the form of Notice No. 2 (supplied along with Form P/PPA). Form 4 is used for minerals cases. Notice is given to owners and agricultural tenants by serving a completed copy of Notice No. 1 (also supplied along with Form P/PPA) in the ways described in Chapter 7. This notice alerts these persons to their opportunity to make representations to the Secretary of State about the appeal within 21 days of the date of service. As any representations which they made in connection with the application which is the subject of the appeal will be forwarded to the SOIR by the planning authority and considered by the Secretary of State/reporter, it may not be necessary for them to lodge further representations. Unlike submission of planning applications, there is no requirement to notify neighbours, but any representations lodged by neighbours in connection with the application will be forwarded by the planning authority and considered as part of the appeal.

(vi) An indication that the applicant wishes the appeal to be determined on the basis of written submissions or by a hearing, which in the vast majority of cases will be in the form of a public local inquiry (see below). If the appellant opts for the written submissions procedure, a full statement of his case should be submitted along with the notice of appeal.

Many of these items may need to be obtained from the planning authority. If the time limit is looming, the appeal should be lodged along with an explanation that the papers are being sought from the planning authority.

Either the appellant or the planning authority is entitled to require 8.08 that the appeal be the subject of a hearing or public inquiry.[8] In other words, the appellant's choice of written submissions procedure can be

---

[8] TCPSA, s. 48(2).

overridden by the planning authority exercising its right to ask for a hearing or public inquiry to be held. Even if both parties opt for the written submissions procedure, the Secretary of State may require that a hearing or public inquiry be held, perhaps because of the complexity of the matter or the degree of public interest (the provisions empowering the Secretary of State to set up a special inquiry in the form of a Planning Inquiry Commission have never been exercised). Once the written submissions procedure has begun, it is still open to either party or the reporter to request that a hearing or public inquiry be held. During the course of a hearing or public inquiry, it is competent for the parties to agree that, thereafter, the appeal be disposed of on the basis of written submissions.

It is for the Secretary of State to decide whether the right of each party to be heard should be met by a public inquiry or hearing. The hearings procedure is simpler and quicker. Hearings may be appropriate where there is likely to be limited third party interest in the proposal or the areas to be considered are relatively narrow or straightforward. In practice, provision will usually be made for parties to be heard at a public inquiry if either the appellant or planning authority wish. In appropriate cases the alternative of a hearing will be suggested.[9]

The determining issues in selecting which appeal procedure to request are the complexity and importance of the issues involved, any dispute as to the facts, and the suitability of written submissions for deciding these issues. It may also be relevant that the written submissions procedure is quicker. The target is for 80 per cent of planning permission appeals delegated to reporters for decision to be determined within 25 weeks for written submissions procedure and 48 weeks for public inquiries. In 1997–98, 79 per cent of written submission cases and 67 per cent of public inquiry cases achieved this target.[10] If the applicant is paying for professional advice or assistance, written submissions procedure will also be considerably cheaper.

Of the planning permission appeals delegated to reporters for decision, those determined in 1997–98 by written submissions had a 31 per cent success rate, compared to a 62 per cent success rate where there was a hearing or public inquiry. It is suggested that the difference can be explained by appellants taking a much more realistic view of the prospects of success before deciding to proceed by inquiry, perhaps because of the greater amount of preparatory work required by the new inquiries procedure rules.[11]

Written Submissions Procedure

8.09   The written submissions procedure is available for most forms of planning appeals[12] and is used in the vast majority of appeals (approximately 90 per cent in 1997–98). It is quicker, simpler and cheaper than

---

[9] Circular 17/1998, "Planning and Compulsory Purchase Order Inquiries and Hearings: Procedures and Good Practice", para. 24 and Annex F, Code of Practice for Hearings.

[10] Inquiry Reporter's Unit Review of the Year 1997–1998.

[11] *ibid.*

[12] Town and Country Planning (Appeals) (Written Submission Procedure) (Scotland) Regulations 1990 (S.I. 1990 No. 507). Guidance is given in Circular 7/1990, "Written Submissions Procedure", which is under review.

the public inquiry procedure. Instead of the appeal being heard in a courtroom style setting of a public inquiry, the arguments are presented in written form and the decision reached on the basis of these submissions and a site visit.

The written submissions procedure is based around a timetable for lodging documents. Interestingly, the requirement is for documents to be sent rather than received within the specified time limits. Although there is provision made for late submissions to be excluded from consideration when deciding the appeal, there is normally some leeway allowed. Indeed lack of resources often results in planning authorities lodging submissions late. The Secretary of State has the power to extend the time limits at the request of either party, and can set later time limits in particular cases. Any failure to comply with the procedural rules which causes substantial prejudice may result in the decision being quashed by the Court of Session. In addition, the rules of natural justice apply.

(a) Notification

Within 14 days of receiving either the notice of appeal or an indication 8.10 of the applicant's choice of the written submissions procedure, if this is not included in the notice, the planning authority must give notice of the appeal to those persons or bodies notified or consulted by the authority (other than by newspaper advertisement), and who made representations in connection with the application. The authority must also serve notice on any other persons who lodged representations or, if a large number of representations were received, the authority may advertise the appeal in a local newspaper.

The notice/advertisement must state the name of the appellant and the address of the appeal site, describe the application, and explain that the representations submitted in connection with the application will be considered by the Secretary of State, unless the person requests otherwise in writing within 14 days of the date of receipt of the notice. It must also state that any written representations in relation to the appeal must be sent to the Secretary of State within 14 days of receipt of the notice or date of publication of the advertisement.

(b) Appeals Questionnaire

Within the same 14-day period, the planning authority is also required 8.11 to send a completed appeals questionnaire to SOIR, and a copy to the appellant. The questionnaire seeks confirmation from the authority of its agreement to the use of written submissions procedure and information on consultation responses and representations received in connection with the application. It is returned by the planning authority together with copies of all documents relating to the case and which are referred to in the completed questionnaire, other than any confidential written representations. These documents will normally include the planning officer's report to the committee on the application, and copies of all consultation responses and representations received.

(c) Written Submissions

Unless the planning authority elects to treat the questionnaire and 8.12 supporting documents as its written submissions, the authority is required to send its written submissions to SOIR, and a copy to the appellant, within 28 days of receipt of the notice of appeal, or the applicant's choice of written submissions procedure.

Any interested party may make written submissions within 28 days of the date of the receipt of the appeal by the Secretary of State. Copies of these submissions will be sent by SOIR to the appellant and planning authority, both of whom will be given 14 days to lodge any response.

(d) Further Procedure

8.13   The appellant has 14 days from receipt of the authority's written submissions to lodge a response with SOIR, sending a copy of the response to the authority. The authority will normally be given an opportunity to respond, although this is not provided for in the procedure rules.

(e) Site Visit

8.14   Although there is no provision in the rules, the reporter determining the appeal will usually visit the site of the proposed development accompanied by the appellant and a representative of the authority. The date of this visit will be arranged with them by SOIR. If other parties have made representations in relation to the appeal, they will be notified of the site visit. The purpose of the site visit is for the reporter to view the physical characteristics of the site and surrounding area and seek clarification from the parties in relation to any of these characteristics mentioned in their submissions. The site visit is not a forum for discussing the grounds of appeal or making statements in support of or against the appeal, and the reporter will intervene to stop any such discussion or statement.

(f) Decision

8.15   Following the site visit, the decision of the reporter on the appeal will be issued. Copies of the decision letter are sent to the appellant, planning authority and any parties who lodged representations in relation to the appeal.

Where there have been significant delays on the part of one or both parties in lodging their submissions, the reporter has the power to ignore any written submissions sent outwith the relevant time limits. If the authority fails to send its written submission/questionnaire within the time limit, the appeal may be determined on the basis of the applicant's grounds of appeal alone, provided written notice of the intention of the reporter to so determine the appeal has been given to the appellant and the authority.

(Further information is given below on the role of the reporter, undue delay, the appeal decision, withdrawal of appeals, and expenses.)

Hearings

8.16   The right of a party to be heard is normally met by holding a public inquiry. However, in appropriate cases, SOIR will suggest the alternative of a hearing before a reporter. The hearings procedure is simpler and quicker. The Scottish Office guidance indicates that a hearing will not be appropriate if more than a few members of the public are likely to be present; if the appeal raises complicated matters of policy; if there are likely to be substantial legal issues raised; or if there is a likelihood that extensive cross-examination will be needed to test the opposing cases. It is for the Secretary of State to decide whether the right of each party to be heard should be met by a public inquiry or hearing, and parties will be given the opportunity to comment on any proposal to hold a hearing. The non-statutory procedure for hearings is contained in a Code of Practice.[13]

(a) Written Statements

Within four weeks of the date on which it is decided that there is to be   8.17
a hearing, the appellant and planning authority provide written statements containing full particulars of the case they wish to make at the
hearing and a list of any documents to which they intend to refer. Where
appropriate, the reporter may request third parties to lodge written
statements. Parties send copies of their statements to each other. Any
comments on other parties' statements should be submitted within two
weeks of receipt of the statement.

(b) Documents

Copies of documents are to be submitted to the reporter and the other parties at least four weeks before the hearing is due to start.

(c) Notice of Arrangements for Hearing

The aim is for the hearing to take place within 12 weeks of the date on which it is decided that there is to be a hearing. SOIR will give not less than four weeks' notice to the parties of the arrangements for the hearing. The parties will be sent a copy of the Code of Practice and a note of the topics that the reporter has decided should be considered at the hearing. Parties will also be informed where and when they can inspect copies of any statements and documents that will be referred to during the hearing.

(d) Hearing

At the hearing the reporter will summarise his understanding of the relevant issues and indicate those matters where further explanation or clarification is required. Parties can refer to other aspects which they consider relevant, provided adequate prior notice and particulars have been given.

In contrast to a public inquiry, the hearing takes the form of a discussion which the reporter leads. The written material circulated by the parties will not normally be read out. Parties may present their case

---

[13] Circular 17/1998, "Planning and Compulsory Purchase Order Inquiries and Hearings: Procedures and Good Practice", Annex F.

through an agent or advisor, but the Code indicates that legal representation should not normally be necessary. The appellant will usually be asked to start the discussion. Those participating in the hearing will have the opportunity to comment on other parties' submissions. Although there is no cross-examination as such, questions can be asked throughout the proceedings, but should be directed through the reporter. There is no formal closing submission, but the appellant will be allowed to make final comments.

In the absence of the accusatorial procedures of an inquiry, the reporter has an inquisitorial burden to investigate the facts, and failure to take the necessary steps to inform himself of the case could mean that the decision is invalid because the appellant was not given a fair hearing.[14]

(e) Site Visit

The reporter will decide whether there should be an accompanied visit to the site. If appropriate, he may decide to allow further limited discussion of relevant matters on the site before formally closing the hearing.

(f) Decision

A formal decision letter determining the appeal will be issued by the reporter and copied to all those who took part in the hearing.

Public Local Inquiry

8.18   Where complex or contentious issues are involved, or there is a dispute on the facts, it is more appropriate for the appeal to be heard at a public local inquiry. Such an inquiry must be held if either party requests it unless SOIR decide a hearing is more appropriate (see above). Even if both parties request that the appeal be decided by written submissions, the Secretary of State may insist that a public local inquiry be held because of the complexity of the matter or the degree of public interest. At a public local inquiry the issues are presented through the giving of evidence by and cross-examination of witnesses.

All public inquiries are based on the principles of natural justice, broadly defined as openness, fairness and impartiality. The Court of Session may quash the decision if there has been a failure to comply with the procedural rules which has caused substantial prejudice or a breach of natural justice (see below). Compliance with the rules does not necessarily prevent a breach of natural justice.

There are several general principles underlying the public local inquiry procedure. Appellants should give full public explanation of their proposals and planning authorities should discuss the proposals thoroughly with appellants and with objectors to improve public understanding, open the way to compromise and avoid the need for an inquiry. As much written evidence as possible should be circulated in advance of

---

[14] *Dyason v. Secretary of State for the Environment* [1998] J.P.L. 778.

the inquiry, and the use of surprise evidence for tactical advantage is discouraged. Repetitious cross-examination during the inquiry should be avoided. The reporter conducting the inquiry is not confined to the role of the silent listener and may seek any clarification he deems necessary or direct questions to issues not adequately covered in the evidence. Above all, the procedure adopted at the inquiry should be as informal as possible.

There are different rules applicable to public local inquiries for planning appeals which are delegated by the Secretary of State to reporters for decision[15] and for appeals which are decided by the Secretary of State after considering the report prepared by the reporter.[16-17] Most forms of appeals are now delegated to reporters for decision, although the Secretary of State retains the power to recall any delegated case for his own decision.

The detailed procedures laid down in both sets of rules are broadly similar until the close of the inquiry, as examined below. The procedure commences once the planning authority receives notification that there is to be a public local inquiry. Correspondence from SOIR will normally inform parties of what is expected of them.

The current inquiry procedure rules were introduced in 1997, with minor amendments in 1998. A number of measures were introduced to improve the efficiency and effectiveness of the process while maintaining the basic requirements for openness, fairness and impartiality. Some of the procedures had already become accepted practice at inquiries prior to the introduction of the new rules. The main features of the new rules are: in appeal cases, planning authorities are now required to submit a completed appeals questionnaire to SOIR; pre-inquiry meetings are on a statutory footing; there is a timetable requiring cases to be disclosed at an earlier stage, and in particular documents and precognitions are circulated earlier in the procedure; summaries of evidence are presented at the inquiry rather than precognitions being read in full; the reporter's powers to direct proceedings are clarified, particularly the power to restrict the giving of evidence which is irrelevant or repetitious; and, in Secretary of State cases, there is no longer the opportunity for the first part of the report of the inquiry to be circulated to parties in draft for comment.

(a) Procedure: Preliminary Information

Notification of the appeal is sent to the planning authority by SOIR. 8.19
The planning authority must return a completed appeals questionnaire to SOIR within two weeks, together with all documents referred to in the questionnaire, and send copies of the questionnaire and documents to the appellant.

---

[15] Town and Country Planning Appeals (Determination by Appointed Persons) (Inquiry Procedure) (Scotland) Rules 1997 (S.I. 1997 No. 750), as amended by Amendment Rules 1998 (S.I. 1998 No. 2312). Circular 17/1998, "Planning and Compulsory Purchase Order Inquiries and Hearings: Procedures and Good Practice".

[16-17] Town and Country Planning (Inquiries Procedure) (Scotland) Rules 1997 (S.I. 1997 No. 796) as amended by Amendment Rules 1998 (S.I. 1998 No. 2311), Circular 17/1998, *supra.*

Once the decision has been taken to hold an inquiry, SOIR must send notice of this to the planning authority, and copies to the appellant and those persons who submitted representations in connection with the application (referred to as a "statutory party"). The date of this notice (referred to as "the relevant date") is used to calculate the timetable for the exchange of written material prior to the inquiry.

(b) Notification of Identity of Reporter

8.20   In delegated cases, SOIR give written notice to the appellant, the planning authority and the statutory parties, informing them of the name of the reporter appointed to hear the appeal (the rules for Secretary of State cases do not provide for such notice to be given). If a replacement reporter is appointed close to the date of the inquiry, it will be sufficient for this reporter to announce his own name and the fact of his appointment at the inquiry.

For major and/or complex cases, one or more reporters may be appointed to assist the reporter (an assistant reporter is normally appointed where an inquiry is expected to last more than a month). It is also competent for a suitably qualified assessor to sit with the reporter at the inquiry and advise him on matters involving complex or technical issues.

(c) Pre-Inquiry Meetings

8.21   Reporters have a general power to hold pre-inquiry meetings. It is common practice in complex or multiple cases for these meetings to be held. This provides an opportunity for agreement to be reached on practical arrangements for matters such as accommodation, dates and sitting times, likely duration and order of cases, clarification of issues and areas of uncertainty that require to be addressed, matters for agreed statements, arrangements for preparation, presentation and distribution of documents and precognitions, and document numbering. No discussion of the merits of the case is permitted. The procedure meeting is open to the public and notice will be given of the meeting by newspaper advertisement.

In Secretary of State cases, the Secretary of State may decide to hold a pre-inquiry meeting. If he decides to hold such a meeting, this must be intimated in the notice sent to the parties confirming that an inquiry is to be held. Where the inquiry is into an application referred to the Secretary of State, *i.e.* called in by him, he must also serve a statement of the matters about which he particularly wishes to be informed for the purposes of his consideration of the application, and set out in this statement any view expressed to him in writing by a government department or local authority. A pre-inquiry meeting called by the Secretary of State will normally take place not later than 16 weeks after the relevant date, *i.e.* the date of the notice that an inquiry is to be held. Where the Secretary of State does not hold a pre-inquiry meeting, the reporter may hold one if he thinks it desirable.

(d) Notification of Inquiry

SOIR put forward suitable dates for the holding of the inquiry and 8.22
liaise with the appellant and the planning authority to reach agreement
on the dates and anticipated length of the inquiry. For major inquiries,
these details are decided at the pre-inquiry procedure meeting.

The Scottish Office guidance indicates that the discussion of dates will
normally be limited to one month. The appellant and planning authority
will each be permitted only one refusal of a date offered before SOIR
proceed to fix a date, time and place for the inquiry. If one or both
parties refuse the first date offered, and it is clear that they are not
prepared to consider an alternative date acceptable to SOIR, SOIR may
proceed to fix the date of the inquiry before the discussion period has
expired. The guidance makes it clear that the non-availability of parties'
first choice of legal or expert advisers or technical witnesses will not be
accepted as a basis for delaying the start of the inquiry. It also states
that once a date has been fixed it will be changed only for exceptional
reasons.

In delegated cases, the start date of the inquiry will be no later than 24
weeks after the relevant date, *i.e.* the date of the notice that an inquiry is
to be held. In Secretary of State cases the start date must be within the
same period or no later than eight weeks after any pre-inquiry meeting
held by the Secretary of State. In both delegated and Secretary of State
cases, if it is considered impracticable to comply with these timescales,
the earliest practicable date shall be fixed for the start of the inquiry. Not
less than four weeks' written notice of the date, time and place of the
inquiry must be given to the appellant, the planning authority, all
persons who have submitted statements of case, all parties who submitted representations in relation to the application, and any other person
who has lodged and not withdrawn objections in relation to any matter
in question at the inquiry. This notice period can be reduced with the
agreement of the appellant and the planning authority.

The accommodation in which the inquiry is held is normally arranged
by SOIR and located within the district in which the appeal site is
situated.

SOIR usually arranges for publication of notice of the inquiry in an
advertisement in a local newspaper circulating in the district within
which the appeal site is situated. The reporter also has the power to
require the planning authority to publish notices of the inquiry in local
newspapers, to serve notice of the inquiry on specified persons or classes
of persons, or post notices of the inquiry in conspicuous places near to
the appeal site.

(e) Preparation for a Public Local Inquiry

The preparatory work for a public local inquiry is greater than that for 8.23
a written submissions appeal, mainly because more complex appeals will
always be heard at an inquiry. The adoption of the new inquiry
procedure rules in 1997 increased the advance disclosure requirements
(see below), thereby requiring parties to prepare their cases earlier in the
procedure.

Selecting witnesses is an important consideration. It is common for
expert evidence to be given by a planning witness, who may be a

planning consultant or perhaps a landscape architect. Roads engineers are often called as expert witnesses to give evidence on traffic issues. There are a myriad of other possible expert witnesses, depending upon the nature of the development and its proposed location. It will be clear from the grounds of refusal which aspects of the proposed development may require expert evidence. The appellant is not required to call expert witnesses and is free to limit his case to the evidence which he will give himself, as he benefits from the presumption in favour of development and is under no obligation to prove his case (although this should not be relied upon in practice).

Expert witnesses are entitled to express their professional opinion on the issues involved in the appeal which are within the area of their expertise.[18] However, this can be a double-edged sword. During cross-examination an expert witness can be asked for his professional opinion on a point, and will be forced to voice this opinion even if it is contrary to the case being pursued by the party who called the witness to give evidence. Questioning during the cross-examination of an expert witness may therefore provide support for the opposing case.

The planning authority will normally call the planning officer who dealt with the application (or his superior) as the main witness. However, if the decision reached on the application was contrary to that recommended by the planning officer in the report on the application (Chapter 5), the Royal Town Planning Institute (RTPI) advises the officer to refuse to appear as a witness as this would involve supporting a decision contrary to his recommendation. In the absence of a planning officer, one option is to call a member of the planning committee as a non-expert witness.

(f) Statements to be Served Pre-Inquiry

8.24   It is a general principle of the inquiry procedure that there should be advance circulation among the parties of the written statements of their cases, the precognitions of witnesses, and the documents to be founded on.

The adoption of the new inquiry procedure rules in 1997 increased the advance disclosure requirements, thereby requiring parties to prepare their cases earlier in the procedure. Previously, the only advance disclosure required by the rules was the appellant's grounds of appeal, the planning authority's written statement of observations which had to be submitted at least 28 days before the start of the inquiry, and the exchange of documents (productions) 10 days before the inquiry. Copies of precognitions were only circulated immediately prior to each witness giving evidence.

This has been replaced by a timetable for submission which commences with the notification that an inquiry is to be held. The date of that notice is referred to as the relevant date, and the deadlines for submission of outline statements and statements of case run from that date. The time limits for submission of documents and precognitions are counted back from the start of the inquiry.

---

[18] J Watchman, "An Expert's Obligations", SPEL 54:25.

The outline statement is a written statement in which the party gives advance notice of the likely principal lines of argument to be presented at the inquiry. It is not intended to be a rehearsal of the case to be presented at the inquiry. It should include a list of documents which the party intends to put in evidence. If possible, it should also include an estimate of how long it will take to present that party's case, the likely number of witnesses to be called, the issues which they are likely to speak to and details of any special studies which have been or are being prepared.

Outline statements will not always be required. In delegated cases the reporter may require the appellant, the planning authority or any other person who has notified an intention or a wish to appear at the inquiry to serve an outline statement on the reporter, the appellant, the planning authority and such other persons. The time limit for submission can be fixed by the reporter. In Secretary of State cases, the appellant and the planning authority are required to submit outline statements where the Secretary of State has called a pre-inquiry meeting. Their outline statements must be submitted to the reporter and each other not later than eight weeks after the relevant date, or such other date as the reporter thinks fit. Any other person who has notified an intention or a wish to appear at the inquiry may be required to serve an outline statement on the reporter, the appellant, the planning authority, and any other person submitting an outline statement, not later than four weeks after being so required, or by such other date as the reporter thinks fit. Where the Secretary of State does not call a pre-inquiry meeting, and the reporter decides to hold such a meeting, the reporter may require the appellant, the planning authority or any other person who has notified an intention or a wish to appear at the inquiry to serve an outline statement on the reporter, the appellant, the planning authority and such other persons within a time limit specified by the reporter.

The Scottish Office guidance indicates that an outline statement is most likely to be requested where the position of a party is unclear. For example, where an appeal has been submitted against a deemed refusal, a statement may be requested where the grounds of appeal are unacceptably brief, or the views of the planning authority are not known.

The statement of case contains full particulars of that party's case to be presented at the inquiry and must be accompanied by a list of the documents to which reference will be made. It should also include an estimate of how long it will take to present that party's case, the likely number of witnesses to be called, the issues which they are likely to speak to and details of any special studies which have been or are being prepared. The planning authority's statement should include a list of conditions that it would wish to see imposed on any approval that may be given, and a summary of the points which it wishes to be covered by a section 75 or other agreement. If a party intends to refer the inquiry to an alternative site, this should be intimated in the statement of case (for relevance of alternative sites, see Chapter 5). 8.25

The appellant and planning authority are required to submit their statements of case to SOIR within eight weeks of the relevant date, or not later than four weeks after the close of the pre-inquiry meeting, and send copies to the other parties required to lodge a statement. Other parties who have indicated an intention to appear at the inquiry may be asked to submit a statement of case within four weeks of receipt of notification of this requirement, and in any event not later than four weeks before the start of the inquiry.

Any party required to submit a statement of case may request the reporter to make a direction restricting the circulation of copies of his statement of case. The reporter may make such a direction if he considers it expedient to do so, having regard to the length of the statement of case and the number of persons on whom it would otherwise require to be served. The effect of the direction is to limit circulation of copies of the statement to SOIR, the appellant and the planning authority. The person who successfully sought the direction is also required to give notice to all the other persons on whom service would otherwise have been required stating the time and place at which the statement of case may be inspected, and afford to those persons a reasonable opportunity to inspect and, where practicable, take copies of the statement.

If any party considers that another party's statement of case is incomplete or inadequate, this should be drawn to the reporter's attention, but it is for the reporter to decide whether to request additional information.

An amended statement of case should be submitted where any party intends to put forward a case materially different from that set out in his statement of case, or considers that different conditions should be imposed to those suggested by the planning authority, or is required by the reporter to provide further information about matters contained in the statement of case. No time limit is specified, but amended statements of case should be circulated as soon as the need for such action becomes apparent. The preparation of amended statements of case is not encouraged by the Scottish Office guidance, and risks a claim for expenses by other parties.

8.26   Documents which are to be referred to in evidence were previously known as productions. These can include plans, maps and diagrams, photographs, models, tape recordings and video cassettes. Copies normally require to be circulated to the reporter and the other parties at least four weeks before the inquiry is due to start, and should have been identified in the outline statement/statement of case. The documents submitted can be edited to exclude irrelevant matters. Each document should have an identifiable reference number. The usual practice is to use an alpha-numeric reference, incorporating the party's name: COL1, COL2, etc. The planning authority is responsible for producing core documents, such as statements of government policy in NPPGs, structure and local plans, etc. Any agreed statements should be submitted as documents, but not precognitions and closing submissions.

Precognitions are full written statements of the evidence to be given by each person who proposes to give evidence at the inquiry. A precognition generally starts by identifying the person giving evidence and narrating any relevant qualifications and experience. The evidence in the precognition can consist of facts and expert opinions relating to the case deriving from the witness's own professional or local knowledge. The evidence must be relevant to the subject-matter of the inquiry, not repetitious, and should not stray beyond the issues stated in the outline statement/statement of case. Reference should be made to the relevant documents lodged, giving the appropriate reference number. For ease of reference, the precognition should have page numbers and numbered paragraphs. The precognition should not include new information not contained in the documents circulated. If such information is to be presented, a submission will need to be made to the reporter seeking his consent. Depending on the nature of the information, it may be excluded, or the inquiry may be adjourned to allow the other parties to consider it.

Precognitions of all witnesses should be circulated at least two weeks before the start of the inquiry, or by such other date as the reporter may specify. Where the precognition exceeds 2,000 words, it must be accompanied by a summary. Copies of the precognitions and summaries must be sent to SOIR, the appellant, the planning authority and the other parties required to lodge a statement.

The Scottish Office guidance discourages the use of supplementary precognitions. Where these are necessary, for example because new material comes to light or policies are amended, they should be prepared and circulated as soon as possible, and preferably before the start of the inquiry.

The planning authority must afford to any person who so requests a reasonable opportunity to inspect, and, where practicable, take copies of any statement of case, documents, precognition or summary sent to or by them. The statement of case submitted by the planning authority should specify the time and place at which the opportunity will be afforded.

The reporter has a general power to vary the time limits for submission of statements of case, documents and precognitions, on the application of any party. There does not appear to be any provision for varying the time limit for submitting outline statements.

(g) *Participants in the Inquiry*

Public local inquiries are open to the public. However, only certain   8.27
persons are permitted to participate in the inquiry. Those entitled to participate are: the appellant, the planning authority, a representative of the Secretary of State (where he gave a direction affecting the application) or government department (where the department's view is referred to in the planning authority's statement), any local authority, any person who has submitted a statement of case, any person who submitted representations in relation to the application, and any other person on whom notice of the inquiry was given. In non-delegated appeals, any person who has lodged an objection in respect of the appeal which has not been withdrawn is entitled to participate in the inquiry. In both delegated and non-delegated appeals, any other person may appear at the inquiry at the discretion of the reporter.

Persons may appear on their own behalf or be represented by a solicitor, advocate or any other person. The reporter may allow one or more persons to appear on behalf of a group of persons who have a similar interest in the matter.

(h)   Procedure at Inquiry

8.28   Apart from the requirements imposed by the rules, the procedure adopted at the inquiry is at the discretion of the reporter. The emphasis should be on informality. At the commencement of the inquiry the reporter must state the procedure which he proposes to adopt. The reporter will also normally ask the persons attending the inquiry to identify themselves and state whether they intend to participate. If any person entitled to appear at the inquiry fails to do so, it is within the discretion of the reporter to proceed with the inquiry.

The reporter may refuse to permit the giving or production of evidence, cross-examination or the presentation of any other matter, which he considers to be irrelevant or repetitious. Subject to that power, the appellant, the planning authority and any person who submitted a statement of case are entitled to call evidence, cross-examine persons giving evidence and make closing statements. Any other person appearing at the inquiry may do so only to the extent permitted by the reporter.

The usual format for an inquiry is a morning session between 10 a.m. and 1 p.m., followed by an afternoon session from 2 p.m. until 4.30 p.m. This timing may vary to avoid breaks in the evidence of a witness. More frequent breaks may be taken during long inquiries. Participants are normally free to enter and leave the room when the inquiry is sitting. It is normal for a long inquiry not to sit on a Monday.

The evidence on behalf of the appellant is normally heard first. This is followed by the evidence of the other parties in such order as the reporter may determine. If the planning authority is the only other principal party, it is customary for the authority's evidence to follow that of the appellant, with the evidence of third parties heard last. Hearing the evidence in this order has the benefit that all the detailed evidence has been presented before members of the public give evidence. The procedure rules provide for closing statements to be made in the same order, with the appellant having the right to reply to the closing statements made by the other parties, although closing statements are often made in reverse order, enabling the appellant to respond during his closing statement to the closing statements made by the other parties.

Evidence is given through testimony of witnesses, who may be experts or lay people involved in the matter which is the subject of the appeal. A person participating in the inquiry may give evidence as a witness. It is normal practice for each witness to give evidence by reading their precognition, copies of which were circulated to the other parties at least two weeks before the start of the inquiry (see above). The rules provide that only the summary precognition shall be read out at the inquiry unless the reporter permits or requires otherwise. He may agree to parts of the full precognition being read out where complex technical evidence has to be explained or where a response is necessary to rebut evidence from the opposite side.

8.29   Once the evidence of the witness has been heard (what lawyers refer to as the examination-in-chief), the other parties participating in the inquiry are given the opportunity to cross-examine the witness. The witness can be cross-examined on any point in the full precognition or summary and on any relevant matter within his knowledge. Cross-examination is not limited to matters covered in examination-in-chief and may include matters favourable to the case of the party cross-examining the witness. Cross-examination is normally restricted to opposing parties, although a witness on behalf of a supporting party may be cross-examined either to clarify matters raised or where parts of the witness's evidence are hostile to the cross-examining party. Cross-examination is used to clarify issues, highlight areas of agreement, and undermine the credibility of the evidence by exposing weakness or flaws. Expert evidence may be undermined by exposing incomplete research or faulty conclusions. The reporter may prohibit further cross-examination of a witness which would lead to undue repetition.

Following cross-examination by the other parties, the reporter will normally ask any questions he might have, although he can do this at any time. The witness may then be re-examined by the party on whose behalf the witness is giving evidence. Re-examination cannot be used to introduce matters which were not raised in the course of the witness's evidence or cross-examination. The purpose of re-examination is to clear up difficulties or ambiguities which arose during the cross-examination, and repair any flaws in the evidence. The next witness is then called and the procedure repeated.

The rigid evidential rules applicable to court procedures do not apply to inquiries. Witnesses are not normally put on oath. Corroboration of evidence is not required. Hearsay evidence, such as a report of a conversation which the witness did not hear but which was reported to him, or written evidence from a person who is not called as a witness, will be admissible even though it cannot be tested by cross-examination.[19] Comments can be made which are not supported either by documentary evidence or any expertise or experience claimed by the witness. However, less weight may be attributed to such evidence as a result.

The reporter has the discretionary power to require appearance of witnesses or production of evidence, either on the request of any party or of his own accord. However, any person may refuse to answer a question or produce evidence on the ground of the legal rules relating to privilege or confidentiality. The reporter may administer oaths and examine witnesses on oath and may accept, in lieu of evidence on oath by any person, a statement in writing by that person.[20]

The reporter must not require or permit the giving or production of any 8.30 written or oral evidence which would be contrary to the public interest. This may include information relating to the estimated profitability of the proposed development.[21] A representative of the Secretary of State or government department cannot be required to answer a question which is, in the reporter's opinion, directed to the merits, as opposed to the facts, of government policy. Such a question should be disallowed by the reporter as Parliament is the proper forum for raising such questions. However, this principle should not preclude discussion at the inquiry of

---

[19] *T.A. Miller v. Minister for Housing and Local Government* [1968] 1 W.L.R. 992.
[20] TCPSA, s. 265.
[21] *Wordie Property Co. Ltd v. Secretary of State for Scotland*, 1984 S.L.T. 345.

whether a policy should be departed from in the particular circumstances of the appeal.

Any evidence is admitted at the discretion of the reporter, who may direct that documents tendered in evidence be made available for inspection by any person entitled or permitted to participate in the inquiry and that facilities be provided for taking or obtaining copies. The reporter may take account of any written representations or statements received by him before the inquiry from any person, subject to disclosure at the inquiry and circulation in advance, where practicable. The reporter may allow any party to alter or add to the statement of case or any list of documents accompanying the statement, so far as may be necessary to determine the questions in controversy between the parties. However, the reporter must give the appellant or planning authority, and other parties who submitted a statement of case, an adequate opportunity to consider such fresh observations or document.

By applying in writing to SOIR not later than 14 days prior to the inquiry, any of the persons entitled to appear may require the appearance of a representative on behalf of the Secretary of State, where he has given a direction affecting the application, or a government department, where the statement of case by the planning authority includes the written views of the department. An application may be made to the reporter to require the appearance of a representative of a local authority where the statement of case by the planning authority includes the written views of that local authority. The representative will state the reasons for the direction or view expressed, and give evidence and be subject to cross-examination in the same way as other witnesses.

The reporter may adjourn the inquiry and provided the date, time and place of the adjourned inquiry are announced before adjournment, no further notice shall be required.

(i)   Site Inspection

8.31   The reporter may make an unaccompanied inspection of the site of the proposed development at any time, without giving notice to persons entitled or permitted to participate in the inquiry. It is usual for an accompanied site inspection to be carried out at a suitable time during or after the inquiry (such an inspection can be required by either the appellant or planning authority). The date and time of this inspection is announced by the reporter during the inquiry. Any party to the inquiry is entitled to accompany the reporter on the inspection, and the suitability of the date and time are usually confirmed with all these parties. It is within the discretion of the reporter to proceed with the inspection if any of these parties is not present at the time appointed.

The purpose of the accompanied site inspection is to enable the reporter to clarify, in the presence of the parties, the physical characteristics of the site. It is not an opportunity to place evidence before the reporter or for a discussion of the issues, and the reporter will intervene to prevent either of these situations from continuing.

(j)   Procedure after Close of Inquiry

8.32   The determination of most planning appeals is delegated by the Secretary of State to the reporters. In these delegated appeals, the reporter prepares his decision letter after the close of the inquiry. In making a decision on the appeal, the reporter may take into consideration any new evidence not raised at the inquiry which he considers to be material. The new evidence may include expert opinion on a matter of fact or any new issue of fact, other than a matter of government policy. Notification of the substance of the new evidence or of the new issue of fact must be given to the appellant, the planning authority and any party who submitted representations in relation to the application and appeared at the inquiry, giving them an opportunity within three weeks to make written representations and/or request the re-opening of the inquiry. Even if there is no request from the parties, it is within the discretion of the reporter to re-open the inquiry, if he thinks fit. The procedure for giving notice of the date, time and place of the re-opened inquiry is the same as for the original inquiry, except the minimum period of notice is reduced to three weeks.

In Secretary of State cases, the reporter makes a report in writing to the Secretary of State which includes his findings-in-fact, his conclusions and his recommendations or reasons for not making any recommendations. The reporter is not required to make a finding-in-fact on every disputed issue.[22] In exceptional circumstances the reporter may consider evidence presented after the inquiry has closed, but only after parties have been given an opportunity to comment on it either in writing or at a re-opened inquiry. Under the previous inquiry procedure rules, any party could require the first part of the report, containing the brief summary of evidence and the findings-in-fact, to be circulated to the parties for comment. This procedure enabled the reporter to make amendments following consideration of these comments, but has now been dispensed with. The second part of the report contains the reporter's reasoning and recommendations. This two-part division led to much litigation on the questions of whether a matter was a finding-in-fact or a conclusion/recommendation, and whether the findings-in-fact provided sufficient foundation for the recommendations.[23] The full report is submitted to the Secretary of State who will use it to decide the appeal. The Secretary of State is not bound to follow the recommendation made by the reporter.[24]

After submission of the report, if the Secretary of State differs from the reporter on a finding-of-fact or proposes to take into consideration any new evidence or any new issue of fact, other than a matter of government policy, which was not raised at the inquiry and as a result disagrees with the reporter's recommendation, he must notify the appellant, the planning authority, and persons who submitted representations in relation to the application and participated in the inquiry, of his disagreement and the reasons for it. An opportunity must be given for them to make written representations within three weeks. In the case of new evidence or issue of fact, the parties have the right to require the

---

[22] *London & Clydeside Properties v. City of Aberdeen D.C.*, 1984 S.L.T. 50.
[23] Young and Rowan-Robinson, *Scottish Planning Law and Procedure* (1985) p. 503 *et seq.*
[24] *e.g. London & Midland Developments v. Secretary of State for Scotland*, 1996 G.W.D. 14–861; SPEL 55:52.

re-opening of the inquiry. Even in the absence of such a request, the Secretary of State may re-open the inquiry if he thinks fit. The procedure for giving notice of the date, time and place of the re-opened inquiry is the same as for the original inquiry, except the minimum period of notice is reduced to three weeks. Even if the new evidence does not persuade the Secretary of State to disagree with the recommendation, the rules of natural justice may still require him to provide the parties with an opportunity to lodge representations in respect of that evidence. However, the courts have indicated that the Secretary of State is entitled to decide that any new material does not affect his conclusions on the case.[25]

(k) Notification of Decision

8.33   The decision on the appeal, made by either the reporter or the Secretary of State, and written reasons for that decision are notified to the appellant, the planning authority, all persons who submitted representations in relation to the application, and any person who participated in, or was represented at, the inquiry and asked to be notified. Any of the persons notified of the decision may apply in writing to the Secretary of State within six weeks of notification for an opportunity to inspect any documents listed in the notification and the Secretary of State is required to give the opportunity accordingly.

The written reasons should be proper, intelligible and adequate. They should deal with the substantial points raised in the appeal and enable the reader to know what conclusion the decision-maker has reached on the principal controversial issues, and understand on what grounds the appeal has been decided. The degree of particularity required will depend entirely upon the nature of these issues. Decision letters should not be construed as if they were Acts of Parliament and should be read as a whole. The central question is whether the deficiency of the reasons given has caused substantial prejudice.[26]

Where a report of the inquiry is to be submitted to the Secretary of State for his determination, SOIR expect the report to be submitted within either a minimum of six weeks from the close of the inquiry or three times the duration of the inquiry, whichever is longer. In 80 per cent of cases the Secretary of State's decision should normally be issued within two months of receipt of the report. In delegated cases, where the reporter decides the case, 80 per cent of decisions should normally be issued within 48 weeks of receipt of the appeal (in 1997–98, 67 per cent of planning permission appeal cases achieved that target, compared to around 50 per cent in the previous year).

[25] *Dobbie & Co. Ltd v. Secretary of State for Scotland*, 1996 G.W.D. 22–1302, SPEL 57:92; *M-I Great Britain Ltd v. Secretary of State for Scotland*, 1996 S.L.T. 1025; SPEL 57:93; *Bolton MBC v. Secretary of State for the Environment* [1995] E.G.C.S. 94, *The Times*, May 25, 1995.
[26] *J. Sainsbury plc v. Secretary of State for Scotland*, 1997 S.L.T. 1391, SPEL 63:108; *Save Britains Heritage v. Secretary of State for the Environment* [1991] 2 All E.R. 10; *Wordie Property Co. Ltd v. Secretary of State for Scotland, supra.*

Reporter's Role

The reporter is the master of the procedure at the inquiry, and is 8.34
frequently called upon to make rulings during the inquiry. He is entitled
to adopt an interventionist role and ask witnesses questions, rather than
merely note the evidence brought out during examination. Reporters
have a much more active role in hearings than in inquiries (see above).
Following the conclusion of the inquiry or hearing or the exchange of
written submissions, the reporter either determines the appeal or makes
recommendations to the Secretary of State on how the appeal should be
decided. In reaching these conclusions, the reporter is entitled to make
use of his planning experience and expertise. A reporter was entitled to
refuse to grant planning permission on road safety grounds contrary to
the views of the Director of Highways.[27] In common with the planning
authority, the reporter is obliged to take account of all material
considerations and not merely those raised by the parties at the inquiry
or in their written submissions.[28] However, where the reporter identifies
a planning issue which he considers may be material to the decision on
the appeal, but which has not been addressed by either party, the
reporter is not entitled to reach a conclusion on that issue and found
upon it as a factor material to his determination of the appeal, without
giving the parties an opportunity of commenting on it.[29] The weight to be
attached to the material put before him is a matter for the reporter and
he is not bound to accept evidence presented by a party even though it is
not contested.[30]

The decisions of the courts on challenges to reporters' decisions
emphasise the breadth of the reporter's powers, and hence the narrow-
ness of the courts' power to intervene, and give considerable leeway in
interpreting their decision letters.[31] It is relatively rare for a reporter's
decision to be successfully challenged. Between 1993 and 1997, of the 71
decisions by reporters challenged in the Court of Session, only 20
challenges were successful.[32]

Undue Delay

If the appellant appears to be responsible for undue delay in the 8.35
progress of the appeal, whether by the written submission procedure,
hearing or public local inquiry, the Secretary of State/reporter may give
the appellant notice at any time before or during the determination of
the appeal that it will be dismissed, unless the appellant takes specified
steps for the expedition of the appeal within a specified time limit.[33] For

---

[27] *Castle Rock Housing Association v. Secretary of State for Scotland*, 1995 S.C.L.R. 850.
[28] But see *Anwar v. Secretary of State for Scotland*, 1992 S.C.L.R. 875.
[29] *Anduff Holdings v. Secretary of State for Scotland*, 1992 S.L.T. 696; *cf. Ladbroke Racing Ltd v. Secretary of State for Scotland*, 1990 S.C.L.R. 705.
[30] *Narden Services v. Secretary of State for Scotland*, 1993 S.L.T. 871.
[31] For example, *City of Edinburgh Council v. Secretary of State for Scotland*, 1998 S.L.T. 120; *City of Glasgow Council v. Secretary of State for Scotland*, 1997 S.C.L.R. 711; *Parkes v. Secretary of State for Scotland*, 1998 G.W.D. 6–292.
[32] Inquiry Reporters Unit Review of the Year 1997–1998.
[33] TCPSA, s. 48(8).

example, the notice may require the appellant to agree an inquiry date. The Secretary of State/reporter has a discretionary power to dismiss the appeal if these steps are not taken within the time limit. As planning authorities would then have the power to decline to determine any similar application within the next two years (Chapter 5), appellants should comply with these notices.

Appeal Decision

8.36   The appeal may be allowed or dismissed, and any part of the decision of the planning authority may be reversed or varied, irrespective of what aspect of the decision is challenged.[34] However, an opportunity to make representations must be given to the planning authority and appellant if the Secretary of State/reporter proposes to reverse or vary any part of the decision to which the appeal does not relate.

Before embarking on an appeal against a condition or part of the decision of the planning authority, the disappointed applicant will have to consider the risk of either losing the entire permission, or being burdened with a more onerous condition. This situation has given rise to a practice of making duplicate planning applications (Chapter 5). This enables the decision on one application to be appealed in the knowledge that it is possible to fall back on the decision on the second application if the appeal is unsuccessful.

If planning permission could not have been granted by the planning authority or could not have been granted without the conditions imposed by it, the Secretary of State may decline to determine the appeal or to proceed with the determination.[35]

The Secretary of State/reporter may intimate to the parties, before issuing the decision letter, that he is minded to grant planning permission if a section 75 agreement is concluded (Chapter 6). This gives the parties an opportunity to enter into such an agreement, but this will require the co-operation of the planning authority which may be unforthcoming, given the expectation that the appeal will be dismissed if no agreement can be put in place. Recent English case law suggests that a planning authority which refuses to enter into an agreement in these circumstances may be acting *ultra vires*.[36]

Withdrawal of Appeal

8.37   An appeal may be withdrawn in writing at any time prior to issue of the decision letter. However, if the appeal is withdrawn at a late stage the appellant may become liable to pay the expenses of the planning authority.

Expenses

8.38   Unlike court cases, expenses do not follow success and the parties involved in a planning appeal are normally expected to meet their own expenses. An award of expenses will only be made if there has been

---

[34] s. 48(1).
[35] s. 48(7).
[36] *R. v. Warwickshire C.C., ex p. PowerGen* [1998] J.P.L. 131, but see *R. v. Cardiff City Council, ex p. Sears Group Properties*, [1998] 3 P.L.R. 55.

unreasonable behaviour which has caused the party applying for the award to incur unnecessary expense, either because it should not have been necessary for the case to come before the Secretary of State for determination or because of the manner in which the party against whom the claim is made has conducted his part of the proceedings.[37]

What amounts to unreasonable behaviour will depend on the circumstances of each case. Appellants risk an award of expenses against them if the planning authority can show that the proposed development is contrary to a policy in an approved or adopted development plan which is both up to date and consistent with Scottish Office guidance, and the appellant produces no substantial evidence to support the contention that there are material considerations which might justify an exception to the policy. Planning authorities risk an award of expenses against them by applying policies which are out of date or inconsistent with Scottish Office guidance and not substantiating sound reasons for refusal on appeal.[38]

Some of the other examples given in the Scottish Office guidance of unreasonable behaviour on the part of the planning authority include failing to give complete, precise and relevant reasons for refusal of an application; reaching its decision without reasonable planning grounds for doing so; refusing an application because of local opposition, where that opposition is not founded upon valid planning reasons; refusing an application where it is clear from the decision on an earlier appeal against the refusal of a similar application that no objection would be seen to a revised application in the form submitted; and failing to take account of relevant statements of government policy in departmental circulars or of relevant precedents of which the planning authority was aware.

Unreasonable behaviour on the part of the appellant may include pursuing an appeal in circumstances where there is no reasonable likelihood of success, for example as a result of a previous appeal decision in respect of a similar development on the same site; withdrawing the appeal without giving sufficient time for reasonable notice of the cancellation of the inquiry to be given to the parties; and deliberately unco-operative behaviour, including refusing to explain the grounds of appeal or refusing to discuss the appeal.

Unreasonable behaviour on the part of either party may include introducing a new matter at a late stage in the proceedings; refusing either to supply adequate grounds of appeal, or to co-operate in settling agreed facts or supplying relevant information all of which unnecessarily prolongs the proceedings; failing to comply with the requirements of any statutory procedural rules (account will be taken of the extent to which an appellant has taken professional advice); and failure to comply with procedural requirements to the serious prejudice of the other party and leading to the adjournment of the inquiry (an award may be made relating to the extra expense arising from the adjournment).

---

[37] ss. 265(9) and 266; SDD Circular 6/1990, "Awards of Expenses in Appeals".
[38] NPPG 1, "The Planning System", para. 45.

8.39   In exceptional circumstances, such as unreasonable conduct at a public inquiry which causes unnecessary expense, awards of expenses may be made in favour of or against parties other than the appellant and planning authority. In general, third parties will not be eligible to receive expenses where unreasonable behaviour by one of the main parties relates to the substance of that party's case.

Application for expenses should be made to the reporter prior to conclusion of the hearing or inquiry, to enable the reporter to hear the parties' arguments on the application. In the case of an appeal by written submissions, application may be made at any time until submission of the party's final written submission. The decision on the application for expenses will be taken on the basis of a further exchange of written submissions. In either procedure, later applications will only be entertained if good reason can be shown for not submitting the application earlier.

Once a full or partial award of expenses has been made, the parties must agree the amount of expenses incurred in relation to the appeal. If they fail to agree, the matter is referred to the Auditor of the Court of Session for decision. A decision to award expenses can only be challenged by judicial review.[39]

In 1997–98, 126 requests for awards of expenses were made, 86 of which were by applicants/appellants against planning authorities, and the remainder by planning authorities against applicants/appellants. Nineteen per cent of the claims by applicants/appellants were upheld, and 43 per cent of those by planning authorities. This is generally in line with previous years, although the success rate of claims by planning authorities is rising.[40]

CHALLENGE IN THE COURT OF SESSION—REVIEW PROCEEDINGS

8.40   The Court of Session in Edinburgh has jurisdiction to hear challenges of planning decisions or actions, either by way of the statutory review procedure or under its common-law (non-statutory) judicial review procedure.

Although an application for review is often referred to as an appeal, there are important legal differences between review by the Court of Session and an appeal decided by the Secretary of State. In deciding an appeal, the Secretary of State has the power to declare the original decision wrong, whether as a matter of policy or on the merits of the case, and substitute his own decision in place of that originally reached. In essence, the appeal involves a rehearing and re-decision of the application. In contrast, the Court of Session, as a review body, has no power to rule on the merits or correctness of the original decision. The judges can only decide whether or not the decision was made in a legal manner, and have no power to intervene where a "wrong" decision has been made in a legal manner. Even where a decision is held to be illegal

[39] *City of Aberdeen v. Secretary of State for Scotland*, 1993, S.L.T. 1149.
[40] Inquiry Reporters Unit Review of the Year 1997–1998.

and quashed, the Court of Session has no power to substitute its own decision and must refer the case back to the decision-maker for a fresh decision to be reached. At this stage it is open to the decision-maker to reach the same decision, but in a legal manner. A successful challenge in the Court of Session may, therefore, be a pyrrhic victory.

Unlike a public local inquiry (see above), a challenge by review procedure will be subject to the legal rules of evidence and procedure common to all court actions.

Common law petitions for judicial review are heard by a single judge in the Outer House, with a right to appeal (reclaim) to the Inner House and thereafter the House of Lords. Challenges under the statutory review procedure are heard by three judges in the Inner House, but the Rules of Court were amended in 1996 to provide for such challenges to be remitted to a single Outer House judge, with a right to reclaim to the Inner House against the decision of that judge.[41] The case may be remitted by the court at its own instance, after hearing the parties, or on the motion of any of the parties to the case. There is a right to reclaim from the decision of the Inner House to the House of Lords.

STATUTORY REVIEW

The term statutory review is used here to denote the review powers of the Court of Session conferred by the TCPSA. 8.41

Types of Challengeable Decision

There is a statutory right of challenge in the Court of Session against orders[42]: 8.42

    (a)   revoking or modifying planning permission (Chapter 5);
    (b)   requiring discontinuance of use or alteration or removal of buildings or works (Chapter 7);
    (c)   prohibiting resumption of or suspending the winning and working of minerals (Chapter 9);
    (d)   tree preservation orders (Chapter 9);
    (e)   defining areas of special control of advertisements (Chapter 9); and
    (f)   revocation of listed building consent (Chapter 9).

The right of statutory challenge in the Court of Session also extends to decisions by the Secretary of State/reporter in connection with:

    (a)   a called-in application for planning permission (Chapter 5);
    (b)   a planning appeal, including appeals against waste-land notices (Chapter 7), enforcement notices (Chapter 7), and listed building enforcement notices (Chapter 9), and against the refusal or partial refusal of a Certificate of Lawful Use or Development (Chapter 4);

---

[41] Rule of Court 41.45.
[42] s. 239 and Planning (Listed Buildings and Conservation Areas) (Scotland) Act 1997, s. 58.

    (c) confirmation of a completion notice (Chapter 5);

    (d) an application for hazardous substances consent (Chapter 9);

    (e) an application for consent under a tree preservation order or advertisement control regulations, or relating to any certificate or direction under any such order or regulations, whether his decision is made on appeal or on an application referred to him for determination in the first instance (Chapter 9);

    (f) confirmation or refusal to confirm a purchase notice or listed building purchase notice (Chapters 5 and 9); and

    (g) an application for listed building consent referred to him for decision or on an appeal (Chapter 9).

The statutory review procedure also extends to challenges relating to both structure and local plans.[43] These challenges share many of the characteristics discussed below, but the particular issues involved are examined in Chapter 3.

Standing—Persons who may Challenge

8.43   Standing (*locus standi*) is the legal term used to describe the classes of person who have a legal right to challenge a decision. If a person has no standing in connection with the court action, the court will refuse to consider his challenge.

The statutory review procedure can be used by the planning authority directly concerned with one of the decisions/orders specified above, and by any person "aggrieved" by the decision/order.[44] In the absence of any statutory definition, it is impossible to identify all the instances of when persons can be aggrieved. It is clear, however, that mere dissatisfaction is not enough and some connection to the decision or order will be required, most commonly through participation in the process leading up to that decision or order. Persons who can be "aggrieved" by an appeal decision include persons who have been given notice of a public local inquiry in connection with the appeal, have submitted observations to a public local inquiry and who would have been entitled to participate in the inquiry.[45] Where adjacent proprietors, the planning authority which decided the application, and the regional council, as water and drainage authority, had participated in a public local inquiry, they were held to be persons aggrieved.[46] In an appeal against an agricultural occupancy condition, "person aggrieved" included the owner of the access to the appeal site.[47]

Most recently, the Court of Session has taken a broad approach to the question of when a person is aggrieved. A third party who had not objected to an application was held to be a person aggrieved by the appeal decision in relation to the application in the exceptional circum-

---

[43] s. 238.

[44] s. 239(1) and (2); Young, "Aggrieved Persons in Planning Law", 1993 S.L.T. (News) 43.

[45] *Strathclyde R.C. v. Secretary of State for Scotland (No. 2)*, 1990 S.L.T. 149 at p. 154E.

[46] *North-East Fife D.C. v. Secretary of State for Scotland*, 1992 S.L.T. 373.

[47] *Bannister v. Secretary of State for the Environment* [1994] 2 P.L.R. 90.

stances where the application and newspaper advertisement failed to give full notice of the proposed development and deprived the third party of his opportunity to make representations.[48]

To identify persons aggrieved, some assistance may be sought from the decisions on title and interest for the purposes of common-law judicial review (see below), and on "persons aggrieved" for challenges to local plans (Chapter 3).

Time Limits

Application to the Court of Session for statutory review of an order or   8.44
action must be made within six weeks from the date on which the order is confirmed or the action taken.[49] In relation to a decision of the Secretary of State/reporter, the period commences from the date on which the letter recording the decision is typed, signed and date-stamped, and not when notification of the decision is received by the parties.[50] Christmas day and bank holidays are included within the six-week period.[51]

Grounds of Challenge

The validity of the order or action can be challenged on either of two   8.45
grounds[52]:

(a)   that the order or action was not within the statutory powers; or

(b)   that the interests of the challenger have been substantially prejudiced by a failure to comply with any of the relevant requirements in relation to that order or action.[53] This is a reference to the requirements of the TCPSA and the Tribunals and Inquiries Act 1992, and any rules made under those Acts, including the statutory procedures applicable to planning appeals.

Interpretation of these grounds has proved a problem for the courts. However, it is now accepted that under the first ground of challenge,[54]

"the court can interfere with the Minister's decision if he has acted on no evidence; or if he has come to a conclusion to which, on the evidence, he could not reasonably come; or if he has given a wrong interpretation to the words of a statute; or if he has taken into consideration matters which he ought not to have taken into account, or vice versa; or has otherwise gone wrong in law."[55]

---

[48] *Cumming v. Secretary of State for Scotland*, 1993 S.L.T. 228.
[49] TCPSA, s. 239(3).
[50] *Griffiths v. Secretary of State for the Environment* [1983] 1 All E.R. 439; J.P.L. 237.
[51] *Stainer v. Secretary of State for the Home Department* [1994] J.P.L. 44.
[52] TCPSA, s. 239(1)(a) and (b).
[53] s. 239(5)(b).
[54] *Ashbridge Investments v. Minister of Housing* [1965] 1 W.L.R. 1320, *per* Lord Denning at p. 1326.
[55] *Per* Forbes J. in *Seddon Properties v. Secretary of State for the Environment* [1978] J.P.L. 835.

This wide approach has been summarised into a checklist of four principles known as the Ashbridge formula:

(a)   The decision-maker must not act perversely. In other words, the decision may be overturned if the court considers that no reasonable person in the position of the Secretary of State, properly directing himself on the relevant material, could have reached the conclusion which he did reach.

(b)   He must not take into account irrelevant material or fail to take into account that which is relevant. Provided the Secretary of State/reporter takes account of a matter, the court will not interfere with the weight he gives to that matter in the decision, partly because the court has no opportunity to hear the witnesses or re-examine the evidence.

(c)   He must abide by statutory procedures.

(d)   He must not depart from the principles of natural justice.

In addition, in non-delegated appeals (see above) to differ from the reporter in a finding-of-fact, the Secretary of State must have sufficient material.[56]

The Secretary of State/reporter must give proper and adequate reasons for the decision, which are clear and intelligible and deal with the substantial points which have been raised.[57] The decision letter should not be subjected to the rigorous interpretation appropriate to the determination of the meaning of a contract or statute.[58]

The Ashbridge formula closely corresponds to the common-law grounds for judicial review. The first ground of statutory challenge will, therefore, be used to review all errors of law which are reviewable under the common-law judicial review procedure (see below).

As a result of the width of the first ground of challenge, the second ground is only likely to be used where there is a procedural defect which does not amount to an error of law and is, therefore, not reviewable under the first ground (or the common-law judicial review procedure), such as breach of a non-mandatory procedural requirement[59] or failure to give reasons as required by statute or regulations.[60] For a successful challenge under the second ground, the interests of the challenger must have been substantially prejudiced as a result of the failure to comply with the relevant requirements.[61] It seems that any defect in procedure which is more than a technical or insignificant defect will be assumed to have caused substantial prejudice.[62] It is not necessary for the challenger

---

[56] *Coleen Properties v. MHLG* [1971] 1 W.L.R. 433.

[57] *J. Sainsbury plc v. Secretary of State for Scotland*, 1997 S.L.T. 1391; SPEL 63:108.

[58] *e.g. Parkes v. Secretary of State for Scotland*, 1998 G.W.D. 6–292, *City of Glasgow D.C. v. Secretary of State for Scotland and William Hill (Scotland) Ltd*, 1992 S.C.L.R. 453; S.P.L.P. 36:56.

[59] For discussion of mandatory and directory requirements, see *London & Clydeside Estates v. Aberdeen D.C.* [1980] 1 W.L.R. 182, *e.g. per* Lord Hailsham L.C. at p. 189H; *James v. Secretary of State for Wales* [1966] 1 W.L.R. 135, *per* Lord Denning M.R. at p. 142.

[60] *Wordie Property Co. Ltd v. Secretary of State for Scotland*, 1984 S.L.T. 345.

[61] *Ampliflaire v. Secretary of State for Scotland*, 1998 G.W.D. 8–405, SPEL 68:77.

[62] *Wordie Property Co. Ltd, supra*, per Lord President Emslie at p. 356.

to show that the decision would have been different if the statutory requirements had been complied with—"the loss of a chance of being better off" will be enough to constitute substantial prejudice.[63] Where a local plan was challenged on the grounds that there was a lack of reasoned justification for taking no account of the possible implementation of a planning permission for a site, there was no substantial prejudice to the landowner as there was no imminent risk that the permission would expire and the balance of convenience was therefore against ordering interim suspension of the local plan.[64]

Two significant recent decisions of the House of Lords illustrate the approach of the courts to challenges to planning decisions. In each, their Lordships held that, provided the decision-maker took the relevant factors into account (in one case the development plan policies and in the other the relevant planning benefits offered by the applicant), the weight to be given to those factors was a matter for the judgment of the decision-maker, and the courts should only intervene where the decision reached was irrational or perverse.[65] The success rate of legal challenges is low. For example, between 1993 and 1997 only 20 of the 71 challenges against decisions by reporters were successful.[66]

Powers of the Court

The Court of Session has the power to suspend, by interim order, the operation of the order (except a tree preservation order) or action which is the subject of challenge until the final determination of the proceedings.[67]   8.46

If the court determines that the order or action in question is not within the powers of the Act or that the interests of the applicant have been substantially prejudiced by a failure to comply with any of the relevant requirements, it has the discretion to quash that order or action.[68] The court may decide not to quash the order or action on the grounds that the same decision would have been reached in any case, or that the decision was correct but for the wrong reasons.[69] With the exception of tree preservation orders and orders designating areas of special control under the advertisement control regulations, the court has no power to quash only part of the whole order or action.[70]

Following the quashing of a decision, the matter is referred back to the decision-maker for a fresh decision to be reached. Where a fundamental error of law has been made, it may be necessary to start the decision-making process afresh.[71] Any new evidence or circumstances

---

[63] *Hibernian Property v. Secretary of State for the Environment* (1973) 27 P. & C.R. 197, *per* Browne J. at p. 218.

[64] *Mackenzie's Trs v. Highland R.C.*, 1994 S.CL.R. 1042.

[65] *City of Edinburgh Council v. Secretary of State for Scotland*, 1998 S.L.T. 120; *Tesco Stores Ltd v. Secretary of State for the Environment* [1995] 2 All E.R. 636.

[66] Inquiry Reporters Unit Review of the Year 1997–1998.

[67] TCPSA, s. 239(5)(a). *e.g. Mackenzie's Trs v. Highland R.C.*, *supra.*

[68] s. 239(5)(b).

[69] *Glasgow D.C. v. Secretary of State for Scotland*, 1982 S.L.T. 28.

[70] *BAA v. Secretary of State for Scotland*, 1979 S.C. 200.

[71] *Kingswood D.C. v. Secretary of State for Environment* [1988] J.P.L. 248.

which have arisen in the meantime, such as the adoption of different policies, must be considered and new arguments can be raised by the parties. However, a fresh start may not always be required. For example, if the challenger has not been given an opportunity to make representations on a point, it may be sufficient to give the challenger that opportunity and to allow the other parties an opportunity to comment on those representations.

The powers of the court expose the limitations of statutory review proceedings for challenging planning orders or actions. Even if the decision is challenged successfully, the court may refuse to exercise its discretionary power to quash the decision. If the court quashes the decision, it is open to the decision-maker to reach the same decision as before, but in a legal manner. It is, therefore, possible that the challenger may be able to achieve nothing more than obtaining further time for negotiation.

Expenses

8.47   Unlike planning appeals (see above), the successful party in the Court of Session will normally be awarded his expenses against the other party (expenses follow success). Before commencing court action, the challenger must consider whether, if his challenge is unsuccessful, he can afford to pay the costs incurred by the other party (or parties) in relation to the court action. However, the costs of preparing for court action and the danger of liability to pay the costs of a successful challenger may persuade the decision-maker to negotiate a compromise.

JUDICIAL REVIEW

In addition to the statutory review jurisdiction discussed above, the Court of Session has a common-law supervisory jurisdiction to review decisions of inferior courts, tribunals and other administrative and public bodies to ensure that they do not exceed or abuse their statutory jurisdiction, powers or authority. This jurisdiction also allows the court to insist upon standards of rationality and fairness of procedure (for example, the rules of natural justice), in addition to what is expressly required by statute. In the exercise of this jurisdiction, as with statutory review, the court acts as a review body and cannot substitute its own decision for the decision which is challenged (the distinction between review and appeal procedure is discussed above).[72]

The supervisory jurisdiction of the court is exercised through decisions on petitions for judicial review. This judicial review procedure offers a quick decision on the challenge, and a wider range of remedies than is available to the court under the statutory review procedure. However, there are limitations on the availability of judicial review procedure. If there is a statutory remedy available to the challenger, judicial review may be excluded as a result of a statutory ouster clause or the duty to

[72] *West v. Scottish Prison Service*, 1992 S.L.T. 636.

exhaust a statutory remedy. Any person seeking to use judicial review procedure must also establish that they have sufficient standing to challenge the decision and that they have not delayed in making their challenge.

Types of Decision

Planning is a statutory function, with powers conferred upon planning 8.48 authorities and the Secretary of State by statute and exercised for the public benefit. Planning decisions are, therefore, a prime example of decisions which are susceptible to judicial review under the common-law supervisory jurisdiction. In general, all forms of planning decisions, orders and actions are susceptible to judicial review, although a petition for judicial review must always satisfy the restrictions examined below.

However, a petition for judicial review of a planning agreement has been dismissed as incompetent, as the petitioner, having entered into the agreement and implemented its terms, could not competently apply to the court on the grounds that the planning authority's exercise of its powers was *ultra vires*. It was a matter of private contract law whether the obligations under the agreement had been fulfilled.[73]

Ouster Clauses: Exclusion of Judicial Review

Where provisions in Acts of Parliament have sought to oust com- 8.49 pletely the jurisdiction of the court by precluding the courts from entertaining a challenge at any time (such provisions are known as ouster clauses), the courts have been willing to resist the exclusion of their judicial review powers and find jurisdiction to hear the challenge. In contrast, where a statutory review procedure offers the courts a limited opportunity to review the decision, the courts have accepted restrictions on their common-law jurisdiction. This latter approach has been consistently taken by both the Scottish and English courts towards challenges of planning decisions.

As well as providing a statutory review procedure, the TCPSA states that the orders and actions which may be challenged under that procedure cannot be questioned in any other legal proceedings.[74] As a result, any common-law judicial review proceedings to question the validity of such an order or action will not be competent, whether or not the six-week time limit for commencement of statutory review proceedings has expired.[75] For these purposes, it is irrelevant that the challenger had no knowledge of the matter complained of during that six-week period.[76]

Duty to Exhaust Alternative Remedies

Even in the absence of an ouster clause, the existence of a statutory 8.50 procedure to challenge a decision may exclude any petition for judicial review of that decision.[77] The well-established principle that failure to

---

[73] *McIntosh v. Aberdeenshire Council*, 1998 S.C.L.R. 435, SPEL 67:56.
[74] TCPSA, s. 237(1).
[75] *Pollock v. Secretary of State for Scotland*, 1993 S.L.T. 1173; 1993 S.P.L.P. 38:19.
[76] *Martin v. Bearsden & Milngavie D.C.*, 1987 S.L.T. 300.
[77] See generally, Collar, "Judicial Review: The Significance of an Alternative Remedy" (1991) J.L.S.S. 299.

exercise a statutory remedy bars resort to the common-law supervisory jurisdiction of the Court of Session, is incorporated into its rules governing judicial review procedure.[78] As a result, judicial review procedure is generally unavailable where there is a statutory right of appeal.[79]

This strict position means that any petition for judicial review will be incompetent where a statutory remedy exists. For example, the applicant for planning permission has a statutory right of appeal against the decision of the planning authority on the application. Thus, any challenge attempted under judicial review procedure would be incompetent as the applicant must first exhaust the statutory remedy. Third parties have no statutory right to challenge the decision of the authority and are, therefore, free to apply for judicial review. An extreme example of the strictness of this position is that judicial review of the decision to serve a stop notice is incompetent, notwithstanding the lack of a statutory means of appealing, on the grounds that there is a right to compensation for loss due to the stop notice.[80]

An exception is made to this duty to exhaust all alternative remedies in "exceptional circumstances".[81] The extent of this exception is uncertain and the decisions of the court on this point very much depend upon the facts and circumstances of each case. The seriousness of the alleged illegality and the effectiveness of the statutory procedure to remedy the illegality may be important factors. However it is clear that the "exceptional circumstances" test creates a strong presumption in favour of exhaustion of the statutory remedy.

Standing

8.51   The petitioner must have standing, or title and interest to sue, before the court has jurisdiction to hear the challenge. As a general rule, title and interest is a preliminary matter which should not be determined by favourable or adverse decision on the merits of the case (there is no Scottish equivalent of the English procedure for seeking leave to apply for judicial review, which requires the court to reach a preliminary conclusion on the merits of the case). The obvious illegality of the decision sought to be challenged will not relieve the petitioner of the requirement to show title and interest to challenge the decision.

Title has been described as "some legal relation which gives him [the challenger] some right which the person against whom he raises the action either infringes or denies."[82] Where a decision by the Secretary of State on another appeal pre-judged an appeal by the petitioners, their title to seek judicial review of that decision was derived from their pending appeal.[83] The existence of a statutory right of objection against a

---

[78] Rule of Court 58.3(2).
[79] *Bellway Homes v. Strathclyde R.C.*, 1979 S.C. 92; 1980 S.L.T. 66.
[80] *Central R.C. v. Clackmannan D.C.*, 1983 S.L.T. 666; *Earl Car Sales v. Edinburgh D.C.*, 1984 S.L.T. 8. *Cf. Shanks & McEwan v. Gordon D.C.*, 1991 S.P.L.P. 32:15.
[81] Collar, above n. 77.
[82] *D. & J. Nichol v. Dundee Harbour Trs*, 1915 S.C. (H.L.) 7, *per* Lord Dunedin at p. 12.
[83] *Lakin v. Secretary of State for Scotland*, 1988 S.L.T. 780.

decision seems to confer title to sue in respect of that decision.[84] Thus, the lack of any statutory right of objection against a decision by a regional council to call in an application meant that the petitioners had no title to challenge that decision.[85] While previously neighbours had no title to challenge a grant of planning permission,[86] the introduction of the neighbour notification process, which gives notifiable neighbours a statutory right of objection to planning applications, gives notifiable neighbours title to sue.[87] Third parties now have a greater statutory role in the planning process and this will give such persons more extensive title to challenge decisions. It seems that any person who lodges an objection to an application for planning permission may have title to challenge a decision relating to that application.[88] The court has stated that there seems no reason, in principle, why an individual should not sue to prevent breach by a public body of a duty owed by it to the public,[89] and that the concept of title should not be limited to a statutory right of appeal.[90]

In addition to title to sue, the petitioner must also establish "interest". This requirement was formerly described as relating to the petitioner's "pecuniary right and his status",[91] but could now be described as "sufficient interest".[92] It seems certain that, depending upon the circumstances of the case, the following parties will have sufficient interest: the applicant for permission, the planning authority and notifiable neighbours. Other third parties may have sufficient interest, but pressure groups cannot expect to prove a legal interest merely by alluding to the objects and work of the group.[93] This must surely raise a question mark over the rights of third party groups, such as amenity and conservation societies, to challenge planning decisions by petition for judicial review, unless they have a statutory right of objection. (However, a statutory right of objection could arise merely through the newspaper advertisement of the application, see Chapter 5.) A competing developer who sought to challenge the grant of reserved matters approval for a rival leisure development did not have interest to sue.[94]

The English courts have indicated that lodging an objection to a planning application does not *per se* give sufficient interest for the purpose of seeking judicial review of a grant of planning permission.

[84] *Black v. Tennent* (1899) 1 F. 423.
[85] *Bellway Homes v. Strathclyde R.C., supra.*
[86] *Simpson v. Edinburgh Corporation*, 1960 S.C. 313. See also Chap. 5.
[87] *Pollock v. Secretary of State for Scotland (supra); Lothian Borders & Angus Co-operative Society Ltd v. Scottish Borders Council*, O.H., 1999 G.W.D. 6–316.
[88] *Pickering v. Kyle & Carrick D.C.*, 1991 G.W.D. 7–361; *Trusthouse Forte (U.K.) Ltd v. Perth & Kinross D.C.*, 1990 S.L.T. 737; *James Aitken & Sons (Meat Producers) v. City of Edinburgh D.C.*, 1990 S.L.T. 241.
[89] *Wilson v. IBA*, 1979 S.L.T. 279.
[90] Per Lord Clyde in *Scottish Old Peoples Welfare Council, Petrs*, 1987 S.L.T. 179.
[91] *Swanson v. Manson* (1907) 14 S.L.T. 737 at p. 738.
[92] Per Lord Clyde in *Scottish Old Peoples Welfare Council Petrs, op. cit..*
[93] e.g. *Scottish Old Peoples Welfare Council Petrs, supra.; cf, R. v. Secretary of State for the Environment, ex p. Greenpeace* [1994] 4 All E.R. 352.
[94] *Bondway Properties Ltd v. The City of Edinburgh Council*, 1998 S.C.L.R. 225, SPEL 66:31.

Where the applicants for judicial review lived over four miles from the site, to which the public had no access, and were well provided with local facilities for the activities which they carried out on the site, it was held that they had failed to establish an interest above that possessed by the public in general in seeing public duties properly performed.[95]

When considering standing for these purposes, the decisions relating to persons aggrieved in relation to standing for statutory review should be of general assistance. These were discussed earlier in this chapter.

Time Limits

8.52   There is no Scottish equivalent to the (broadly) three-month time limit for making an application for judicial review to the English courts. As a result, the right to challenge a decision by judicial review is only extinguished by prescription after 20 years, but may be barred within the 20-year period by *mora*, taciturnity and acquiescence.[96]

The essence of the plea of *mora*, taciturnity and acquiescence is that, by reason of delay, the petitioner has abandoned his right of challenge and is personally barred from seeking to challenge the decision by way of judicial review. Whereas the time limit for statutory review may expire anyway before the petitioner is aware of reasons for challenging the decision, the plea of *mora*, taciturnity and acquiescence requires knowledge on the part of the petitioner. However, it must be emphasised that, even if the delay does not bar judicial review, the court may exercise its discretion to refuse to overturn a decision if substantial hardship or prejudice, or detriment to good administration might be caused by the delay involved.

There is little case law on this plea, but it seems that it has three elements: the petitioner must have knowledge of the decision and why it is unsatisfactory to him, but not necessarily knowledge of legal grounds of challenge; he must delay challenging the decision after gaining this knowledge; and finally (although this element may not be essential), he is silent in the face of actions by other parties on the faith of the validity of the decision.

While a delay of 10 months barred a petition for judicial review in one case,[97] in another a delay of seven months was not immediately fatal even although the applicants had been aware of the grounds of challenge during the whole of that period and there had been substantial actions on the part of the planning authority and the developer on the strength of the validity of the decision.[98] A five month delay in challenging a planning permission did not prevent a petition proceeding where no prejudice appeared to have arisen from the delay.[99] In a non-planning case, the court allowed a petition to proceed notwithstanding that it was submitted around seven months after the decision which was challenged.

---

[95] *R. v. North Somerset Council, ex p. Garnett* [1997] J.P.L. 1015.

[96] See generally Collar, "Mora and Judicial Review", 1989 S.L.T. (News) 309 and "Mora and Judicial Review—Some Further Thoughts", 1992 S.L.T. (News) 335.

[97] *Hanlon v. Traffic Commissioner,* 1988 S.L.T. 802.

[98] *Pickering v. Kyle & Carrick D.C.,* 1991 G.W.D. 7–361.

[99] *Lothian Borders & Angus Co-operative Society Ltd v. Scottish Borders Council, supra.*

The court noted that the petitioners had pursued matters with the decision-maker and others immediately after the decision was made, and that the decision-maker had not been prejudiced by any lapse of time.[1] In a case decided on other grounds, the judge indicated that a petition seeking reduction of a planning agreement submitted seven years after it had been entered into by the petitioner and the planning authority would have been refused on the basis of *mora*, taciturnity and acquiescence, due to the absence of any proper explanation for the delay, the fact that the petitioner had had legal advice and representation throughout the process, and the petitioner's awareness of the planning permission granted for an adjacent development in reliance on the agreement.[2]

These decisions may indicate a general reluctance to disqualify a 8.53 challenge at the first hurdle before the merits of the case have been discussed. However, the only safe course for potential challengers is to seek legal advice as soon as they are aware that a decision is unsatisfactory. Legal advisors must ensure that a petition for judicial review is lodged as soon as possible thereafter.

It is important to ensure that the matters complained of are brought to the attention of the decision-maker as soon as possible. Where a petition for judicial review challenged the boundaries of proposed designated areas and the consequent validity of a planning permission, the petitioners' failure to raise these issues during the planning application process, and seek to have the determination of the application delayed, amounted to *mora*.[3]

Where there is a delay between the decision to grant permission and the issue of that permission, for example while a section 75 agreement is concluded, it is generally thought that it is the issue of the permission which should be challenged.[4]

Grounds for Judicial Review

The grounds for judicial review are based upon *ultra vires* (literally 8.54 "beyond powers") conduct, where the decision-maker has acted illegally by acting outwith its powers. The grounds for judicial review frequently overlap and new grounds are always developing. Indeed, it is often difficult to identify the particular grounds at issue in a court case. Traditionally, the grounds for judicial review were classified under three heads: jurisdiction, discretion and natural justice, but have recently been re-classified under the heads of illegality, irrationality, and procedural impropriety.[5]

(a) Illegality

The decision-maker must understand the law that regulates its 8.55 decision-making power and give effect to it. This includes the need to keep within its jurisdiction and not act outwith its statutory powers, the

---

[1] *Swan v. Secretary of State for Scotland*, 1998 S.C.L.R. 763; SPEL 69:102.
[2] *McIntosh v. Aberdeenshire Council*, 1998 S.C.L.R. 435; SPEL 67:56.
[3] *WWF - UK v. Scottish Natural Heritage*, 1998 G.W.D. 37–1936.
[4] *R. v. East Dorset C.C., ex p. Mattos* [1998] J.P.L. 300.
[5] *Per* Lord Diplock in the GCHQ case—*CCSU v. Minister for the Civil Service* [1985] A.C. 374 at pp. 410–411.

need to avoid acting in bad faith, and the requirement that any statutory discretionary power be exercised properly.

Many planning powers are discretionary and seem to confer unfettered power upon decision-makers. However, limits to the exercise of these powers have been developed by the courts, allowing them to intervene to prevent abuse of discretionary powers. For example, when determining applications for planning permission, planning authorities have the statutory power to impose "such conditions as they think fit". Although the wording of this statutory power would seem to give authorities absolute discretion, the courts have evolved a series of legal restrictions on the exercise of this power (Chapter 6).

Each individual exercise of discretion must be free and not prejudged. It is well-established that each planning application must be decided upon its individual merits. The concept of precedent, whereby the planning authority is bound to act in accordance with previous similar decisions, has no place in planning law (although consistency in decision-making is encouraged by the Scottish Office). Similarly, the decision-maker may formulate a policy for dealing with future decision-making, but the possibility of making an exception to that policy must be considered in each case, otherwise the policy has fettered the exercise of discretion. Thus although planning applications must be determined according to the policies expressed in development plans, provision is made for material planning considerations in individual cases to overcome this presumption (Chapter 5). In addition, unless authorised by statute, the decision-maker must not delegate its discretion and must always make the final decision itself (Chapter 5). A planning authority cannot bind itself in a section 75 agreement to grant planning permission (Chapter 6).

8.56   Discretionary powers must also be exercised reasonably, in the special legal sense of *Wednesbury* reasonableness.[6] This requires the decision-maker to take into account all material considerations and ignore all irrelevant matters or ulterior motives. Powers conferred by the planning legislation must, therefore, be exercised for a planning purpose, otherwise an ulterior motive has been taken into account. For example, the discretionary power to impose conditions upon a grant of planning permission was illegally exercised when a condition was imposed upon a housing development requiring that the houses should first be occupied by persons on the council's housing waiting list, because the power was exercised to require the developer to assume the duty of the council at his own expense.[7]

The court will quash the decision only if the consideration which was ignored or the irrelevant factor which was taken into account influenced the decision, and the same decision would not have been reached for other valid reasons.[8] However, the consideration need not have been the dominant reason for the decision; provided it was not an insignificant or insubstantial factor in the decision reached, there will be no requirement

---

[6] *Associated Provincial Picture Houses v. Wednesbury Corporation* [1948] 1 K.B. 223.
[7] *R. v. Hillingdon London B.C., ex p. Royco Homes* [1974] 2 All E.R. 643.
[8] *R. v. Broadcasting Complaints Commission, ex p. Owen* [1985] Q.B. 1153.

to prove that a different conclusion would have been reached had it not been taken into account.[9]

The House of Lords have emphasised that, provided the decision-maker takes the relevant factors into account, the weight to be given to those factors is a matter for the judgment of the decision-maker, and the courts should only intervene where the decision reached is irrational or perverse.[10]

It appears that misinterpretation of a provision of the development plan can be an error of law.[11] However, the courts are likely to intervene only if the interpretation adopted is perverse.[12] The interpretation and application of Scottish Office guidance is also a matter for the judgment of the decision-maker.[13] If the decision-maker decides not to follow that guidance, sufficient reasons must be given.[14]

Where reports had been lodged by consultants acting for the applicants and objectors, and these reports contained conflicting views regarding the applicable law, the Director of Planning should have advised the planning committee on the correct view of the law and approach to be taken. Since his report appeared to favour the wrong approach, there was a real risk that the committee were misled as to the correct approach. The report also materially misrepresented the facts in respect of the reduction between the previous and present proposals. Since the report appeared to place importance on the comparison between those proposals, it was likely that the committee took into account irrelevant considerations concerning the extent of the reduction.[15]

Where a reporter incorrectly held that a building was not listed, this was an error of law and his decision on this issue was quashed.[16]

(b) Irrationality

"Irrationality" is defined as: 8.57

"a decision which is so outrageous in its defiance of logic or of accepted moral standards that no sensible person who applied his mind to the question to be decided could have arrived at it."[17]

Previously this formed part of the concept of *Wednesbury* reasonableness: "a conclusion so unreasonable that no reasonable authority could

---

[9] *Simplex v. Secretary of State for the Environment* [1988] 3 P.L.R. 25.

[10] *City of Edinburgh Council v. Secretary of State for Scotland*, 1998 S.L.T. 120; *Tesco Stores Ltd v. Secretary of State for the Environment* [1995] 2 All E.R. 636.

[11] Lord Clyde, *City of Edinburgh Council v. Secretary of State for Scotland, supra*, at p. 127G–L. *e.g. Rafferty v. Secretary of State for Scotland*, 1998 G.W.D. 16–818; *Greater Glasgow Health Board v. Secretary of State for Scotland*, 1996 S.C.L.R. 808.

[12] *R. v. Derbyshire C.C., ex p. Woods* [1998] Env.L.R. 277.

[13] *Freeport Leisure v. West Lothian Council*, I.H., Nov. 3, 1998, unreported; *Bondway Properties Ltd v. City of Edinburgh Council*, 1998 S.C.L.R. 225.

[14] *Scottish House Builders Association v. Secretary of State for Scotland*, 1995 S.C.L.R. 1039, SPEL 52:109.

[15] *Campbell v. City of Edinburgh Council*, 1998 G.W.D. 17–877, SPEL 69:99.

[16] *City of Edinburgh Council v. Secretary of State for Scotland*, 1998 S.L.T. 120; SPEL 65:11.

[17] *CCSU, supra, per* Lord Diplock at p. 410G.

ever have come to it."[18] The requirement for such an extreme degree of unreasonableness should act as a safeguard to prevent the court from interfering with the merits of a decision.

Where the planning authority has refused an earlier application for the same site, it is not necessarily irrational for them to grant a subsequent identical application.[19] One judge observed that while there might be grounds for thinking that the view formed by the decision-maker was surprising, that did not mean that it was perverse.[20]

(c) Procedural Impropriety

8.58   The supervisory jurisdiction allows the court to insist on standards of procedural fairness beyond what is expressly required by statute. Judicial review on this ground does not relate to the content of the decision, rather to the manner in which it was reached. The decision is tainted by a flaw in the decision-making process. Judicial development of this area of the law has given rise to suggestions that there is a duty to act fairly.[21] The degree of procedural fairness required varies depending upon the circumstances of each decision. For example, an oral hearing cannot be demanded in every circumstance.

Included under the head of "procedural impropriety" are failures to observe statutory procedural rules, and breaches of the rules of natural justice, which form a procedural code implied by the common law and supplementing any statutory provisions. There are two limbs to the rules of natural justice: the right to be heard and the rule against bias.

8.59   The right to be heard (*audi alteram partem*) includes the right to have the opportunity to present your case and know the basis of the case presented by the other side, as well as the right to a fair hearing—each party should have a "fair crack of the whip".[22] Some planning authorities give applicants the opportunity either to respond formally to objections made to a proposed development or to amend the application to counter the objections. It may be arguable that such an opportunity must be offered to ensure that the applicant is given a fair hearing. Similarly, if the application is amended, but not to such an extent that the planning authority require a fresh application to be submitted, there may be a duty to inform all those who lodged objections to the original application of the amendments and allow them to make further representations.[23] The law has not evolved to the extent that definite limits may be expressed. The only safe course is for the planning authority to assess at each stage in the progress of the application whether it has acted fairly in respect of all parties. In one case, by representing to the councillors determining the application that the outstanding problem had been

---

[18] *Associated Provincial Picture Houses, supra.*
[19] *R. v. Aylesbury Vale D.C., ex p. Chaplin* [1996] E.G.C.S. 126.
[20] *Wyre Forest D.C. v. Secretary of State for the Environment* [1995] E.G.C.S. 115.
[21] *Per* Lord Roskill in GCHQ case (n. 5, *supra*) at p. 414; *Lakin v. Secretary of State for Scotland*, 1988 S.L.T. 780.
[22] *Fairmount Investments v. Secretary of State for the Environment* [1976] 2 All E.R. 865.
[23] *Lochore v. Moray D.C.*, 1992 S.L.T. 16; *cf. Walker v. City of Aberdeen Council*, 1997 S.C.L.R. 425.

resolved, without drawing attention to the representations maintained by an objector, the planning officers had not allowed a fair opportunity for the objections to be considered.[24] There was a breach of natural justice where a reporter imposed a replacement noise condition without giving the parties an opportunity to express their views as to the acceptable noise level.[25]

In the context of planning appeals, the right to be heard extends to the right to request a hearing or public local inquiry (see above). In a hearing, a failure by the reporter to take the necessary steps to inform himself of the case could mean that the appellant is not given a fair hearing.[26] The written submissions procedure (see above) provides a good example of the procedures necessary to ensure that each party is given a fair hearing. Where an appeal was determined on issues not raised by either party and no opportunity was offered for submissions to be made by the parties on these issues, there was held to be a breach of natural justice.[27]

The other limb to natural justice is the rule against bias (*nemo judex in re sua*). Mere suspicion of bias influencing the decision may be sufficient for the decision to be declared illegal[28]: justice must not only be done, but be seen to be done. An example of this principle can be seen in the non-statutory code of conduct whereby any councillor who has an interest, financial or otherwise, in a planning application, should declare the existence of the interest and take no part in the discussion and determination of that application. This system is voluntary and individual councillors must decide whether their interest in the application is sufficiently close to warrant self-disqualification. Inevitably, in smaller communities it is more difficult to avoid conflicts of interest arising and this may have to be recognised when assessing suspicion of bias. There may be a suspicion of bias where a councillor is a business competitor of the applicant and, therefore, has an interest in the failure of a business-related planning application, although the courts have ruled that it would be going too far to say that this necessarily disqualifies him.[29] There was no real danger of bias where a councillor with a pecuniary interest in a development was present when the decision was made, but had declared his interest, vacated his chair and taken no part in the discussions or voting.[30] Involvement with the local Conservative Association or membership of the rugby club on whose land the development was proposed was held to be insufficient to invalidate the decision.[31] Where predisposition in favour of a proposal arose from performance of other council duties of a councillor, this did not of itself prevent the councillor

8.60

---

[24] *Castelow v. Stirling D.C.*, 1992 G.W.D. 19–1139.

[25] *Dunfermline D.C. v. Secretary of State for Scotland*, 1996 S.L.T. 89; SPEL 52:110.

[26] *Dyason v. Secretary of State for the Environment* [1998] J.P.L. 778.

[27] *Anduff Holdings v. Secretary of State for Scotland*, 1992 S.L.T. 696.

[28] *Steeples v. Derbyshire C.C.* [1984] 3 All E.R. 468; *Simmons v. Secretary of State for the Environment* [1985] J.P.L. 253.

[29] *R. v. Holderness B.C., ex p. James Roberts Developments Ltd, The Times*, Dec. 22, 1992.

[30] *R. v. Bristol C.C. ex p. Anderson* [1998] P.L.C.R. 314.

[31] *R. v. Secretary of State for the Environment, ex p. Kirkstall Valley Campaign Ltd* [1996] 3 All E.R. 304; SPEL 55:55.

from sitting on the planning committee, provided the councillor did not have a closed mind and considered the proposal on its planning merits.[32]

The rule against bias does not prevent the grant of planning permission for development of land owned by the planning authority, even in circumstances where the authority has agreed to lease the land to the applicant if the planning application is successful.[33] Special procedural rules apply to proposals for development by the planning authority (Chapter 9).

The reporter hearing a planning appeal must also avoid creating any suspicion of bias. A conversation between a reporter and officials of the planning authority following the close of an inquiry created such a suspicion and, therefore, amounted to a breach of natural justice.[34] Allegations of such conduct might justify the exceptional step of requiring the reporter to appear as a witness before the court.[35] Where the reporter and both parties indulged in a drink after the inquiry, it was considered inadvisable for the reporter to remain for a fresh drink after the departure of one party, although there was no breach of natural justice.[36] Similarly, there was doubtful wisdom in a reporter lunching with and travelling to the site visit with a planning authority witness, even with the consent of the appellant.[37]

8.61   As part of the requirement for procedural fairness, the law protects legitimate expectations. A legitimate expectation is normally equated with a right to be heard or a duty to consult, although the concept is wider.[38] Legitimate expectations can be created by promise or by an established practice which it is reasonable to expect will continue. If a planning authority undertakes to consult a person on a planning application or has always consulted that person on similar applications, that person may have a legitimate expectation of being consulted prior to determination of the application. Failure to fulfil that expectation may result in a challengeable decision. It is unfortunate that diligent planning authorities, which consult widely to gauge public reaction to planning proposals, may create enforceable legitimate expectations of consultation, whilst authorities which rarely consult any persons other than statutory consultees will avoid creating such expectations.

If the decision-maker creates an express legitimate expectation that a policy will be followed, then the policy cannot be changed without giving an opportunity to discuss this change to those with the expectation. However, the courts have rejected the argument that this could extend to a legitimate expectation that the Secretary of State would follow previous indications of policy and grant planning permission.[39] The

---

[32] *R. v. Hereford and Worcester C.C., ex p. Wellington Parish Council* [1996] J.P.L. 573.
[33] *R. v. St. Edmundsbury B.C., ex p. Investors in Industry* [1985] 3 All E.R. 234; *cf. Steeples v. Derbyshire C.C., supra.*
[34] *Simmons v. Secretary of State for the Environment, supra.*
[35] *Jones v. Secretary of State for Wales,* (1995) 70 P. & C.R. 211.
[36] *Cotterell v. Secretary of State for the Environment* [1991] J.P.L. 1155.
[37] *Fox v. Secretary of State for the Environment* [1993] J.P.L. 448.
[38] *R. v. Secretary of State for the Home Department, ex p. Ruddock* [1987] 2 All E.R. 518.
[39] *R. v. Secretary of State for the Environment, ex p. Barratt (Guildford)* [1990] J.P.L. 25.
See also *R. v. Great Yarmouth B.C., ex p. Botton Bros Arcades* [1988] J.P.L. 18.

expectation does not prevent a change in policy, but merely requires the decision-maker to consult with the person holding the legitimate expectation before making the change and to allow representations to be made regarding the change.[40] An appeal decision was quashed on the ground of unfairness where, by reason of the decision-maker's inconsistency in the interpretation and application of his policy, a person dealing with him had been taken by surprise and had had no adequate opportunity to meet the new approach before the relevant decision was made.[41]

Legitimate expectation is a developing area of the law and the courts have yet to issue a judgment explaining its limits in planning. Clearly much will depend on the circumstances of individual cases. From recent decisions, it seems that legitimate expectations overlap with the duty of fairness. Where applicants for planning permission failed to carry out their legal duty to notify a neighbour of the application, the neighbour drew this to the attention of the planning authority and indicated that he wished to object to the application, but reserved the statement of his reasons until he had been properly notified. The applicants then submitted an amended application in respect of which the neighbour was not notifiable and for which the planning authority granted permission two days later. This grant of planning permission was declared illegal because the planning authority had prejudiced the legitimate expectation of the neighbour of being able to lodge an objection against the application.[42]

An applicant, whose appeal against refusal of planning permission was pending, sought to challenge the Secretary of State's decision not to call in another superstore application. The court held that the applicant had been deprived of its legitimate expectation of having its appeal determined at a public local inquiry and the Secretary of State had pre-judged the issue and pre-empted the appeal. In considering the merits of the alternative site, which was the subject of the applicants' appeal, the Secretary of State failed to give them a fair hearing and, therefore, acted illegally.[43] The decision would probably have been valid if the Secretary of State had ignored the existence of alternative sites completely, even although this would have effectively prejudiced the outcome of the applicant's appeal. This is supported by the decision in a subsequent case that any prejudice caused to the appellant was inherent in the planning process because of the absence of a right of appeal against the grant of permission to a rival applicant, and that the Secretary of State did not act illegally in not calling in a rival application when he recalled an appeal for his determination.[44]

Where a previous application for residential development of the same site had been treated as a major one, with consequent procedural

8.62

---

[40] *R. v. Secretary of State for Health, ex p. United States Tobacco International Inc.* [1992] 1 Q.B. 353.
[41] *Barnet Meeting Room Trust v. Secretary of State for the Environment* [1993] J.P.L. 739.
[42] *Lochore v. Moray D.C.*, *supra*.
[43] *Lakin Ltd v. Secretary of State for Scotland*, *supra*.
[44] *Asda Stores Ltd v. Secretary of State for Scotland*, 1998 S.C.L.R. 246; SPEL 66:33.

implications, this did not constitute a regular practice which the local residents could reasonably have expected to continue.[45]

Persons who had lodged objections to a finalised local plan unsuccessfully argued that a decision to grant planning permission which effectively pre-judged their objections unfairly deprived them of their legitimate expectation of having their objections considered at a local plan inquiry. The court held that the planning authority could competently grant planning permission provided the objections were taken into account in the determination of the planning application.[46]

In response to a letter from the planning authority objectors confirmed their intention to speak at the committee meeting and asked for confirmation of the date and time of the meeting. The objectors did not provide their telephone number. No contact was made by the planning authority. The meeting took place in the absence of the objectors, who challenged the grant of permission on the grounds that they had been given a reasonable expectation. The court held that although the leaflet provided by the planning authority to the objectors could be read as placing the onus on the objectors to obtain the information about the meeting, the leaflet had to be read through the eyes of the objectors, and the authority should have informed them by letter of the date, time and place of the meeting.[47]

As the concept of legitimate expectation demonstrates, the boundaries of the grounds for judicial review are continually developing.

Procedure

8.63   An application for judicial review is made by petition to the Court of Session. There is a special accelerated procedure intended to promote flexibility and rapid decisions where required.[48] The requirement that the petition be signed by an advocate or solicitor acts as a practical (rather than a legal) obstacle to lay persons representing themselves (referred to as party litigants) in a judicial review case.

Powers of the Court

8.64   The discretionary powers of the Court of Session under judicial review procedure are wider than its statutory review powers (see above). In addition to quashing an illegal decision, either in whole or in part, judicial review procedure allows the court to prevent an illegal decision being made or restrain illegal conduct (by interdict), to force a body to carry out a stated duty (by specific implement), to declare the true legal position (make a declaration), and to award damages.[49] It also has power to make any interim order which it thinks fit, pending determination of the action.[50]

---

[45] *Campbell v. City of Edinburgh Council*, 1998 G.W.D. 17–877; SPEL 69:99.
[46] *Watson v. Renfrew D.C.*, 1995 S.C.L.R. 82; SPEL 50:68.
[47] *R. v. Alnwick D.C., ex p. Robson* [1997] E.G.C.S. 144.
[48] Rule of Court 58, first introduced in 1985. See St Clair and Davidson, "Judicial Review in Scotland" (1986) Chap. 2.
[49] Rule of Court 58.4.
[50] *e.g.* interim interdict—*Bonnes v. West Lothian D.C.*, 1994 G.W.D. 31–1888.

Expenses

The normal rule of expenses following success applies: the successful 8.65
challenger will normally obtain an order of expenses against the
decision-maker, while the unsuccessful challenger will be liable to pay
the costs of the other parties involved in the court action, in addition to
his own.

OTHER METHODS OF CHALLENGE

Ombudsman

Complaints relating to decisions and actions of planning authorities on 8.66
planning applications can now be made direct to the Commissioner for
Local Administration in Scotland (known as the ombudsman).[51] The
jurisdiction of the Commissioner is limited. There is a 12-month time
limit from the day on which the complainer first had notice of the
matters alleged in the complaint. If there is a legal remedy available, the
Commissioner will investigate the matter only if, in the circumstances, it
is not reasonable to expect the complainer to resort to that remedy.
There must be "maladministration" leading to "injustice". Although the
Commissioner has substantial powers of investigation, there is no power
to enforce his/her decisions or recommendations. However, recommendations for compensation or redress are frequently implemented by
planning authorities.

Sue for Negligence or Breach of Contract

Planning authorities are subject to the ordinary law of delict and 8.67
contract. Thus, where an individual has suffered harm as a consequence
of either the unlawful actions or the omissions of a public official or
public body, an action for damages may be available. However, the
current trend is to deny any liability in negligence of public authorities
for the exercise of their statutory powers.[52] Where a person fails to fulfil
the conditions of a section 75 agreement, the normal remedies for a
breach of contract will be available to the other parties to the agreement
(Chapter 6).

European Law

European Community law has already introduced the environmental 8.68
assessment procedure (Chapter 5) and several statutory designations
protecting areas of land (Chapter 9). The Maastrict Treaty recognises
the competence of the Community (now the European Union) in

---

[51] Local Government (Scotland) Act 1975, Pt III, as amended. The Commissioner can
be contacted at 23 Walker Street, Edinburgh EH3 7HX.
[52] *R. v. Hounslow LBC, ex p. Williamson* [1996] E.G.C.S. 27; *Tidman v. Reading B.C.*
[1994] 3 P.L.R. 72; *Ryeford Homes v. Sevenoaks D.C.* [1990] J.P.L. 36; 1989 S.P.L.P. 27:53;
cf. Lambert v. West Devon B.C., The Times, Mar. 27, 1997; *Welton v. North Cornwall D.C.*
[1997] 1 W.L.R. 570.

relation to planning and land-use policies. As the role of the European Community in planning law increases, there is the prospect of an individual bringing a case before the European Court of Justice alleging a failure to fulfil Community obligations in relation to planning. The British courts already rule on matters of European law.[53]

Human Rights

8.69   It is already possible for an individual to bring a case involving planning law before the European Court on Human Rights, for example alleging a breach of Article 8 of the European Convention on Human Rights: "Everyone has the right to respect for his private and family life, his home and his correspondence."[54] However, if planning powers are exercised in the public interest and in accordance with the law, any petition is unlikely to be successful. A petition alleging that procedures for planning appeals violated the Convention was dismissed on the grounds that the jurisdiction of the courts over reporters' decisions ensured that there was the fair and public hearing by an independent and impartial tribunal required by the Convention.[55] Enforcement notices requiring removal of gypsy caravans did not contravene the Convention, as the reasons relied on by the planning authority were relevant and sufficient to justify the interference with the gypsies' rights under Article 8.[56]

The Human Rights Act 1998 incorporates the European Convention into Scots law from January 2000.[57] The Scottish Parliament will not be able to legislate contrary to the Convention. The Act will also require the courts to interpret all legislation (Acts of Parliament and Statutory Instruments) so as to be compatible with the Convention so far as it is possible to do so. It will be unlawful for a public authority to act in a way which is incompatible with Convention rights, unless the authority could not have acted differently, or was giving effect to legislation which could not be interpreted so as to be compatible with the Convention. The victim of such an unlawful act by a public authority will have the right to raise a legal action against the authority and to seek damages. It has been suggested that the Act will lead to more emphasis on the protection of the individual in planning decisions; make it more difficult for authorities to avoid taking enforcement action; and make it more difficult for the Secretary of State to resist requests to call in controversial planning applications.[58]

---

[53] *e.g. WWF - U.K. v. Scottish Natural Heritage*, 1998 G.W.D. 37–1936; *Swan v. Secretary of State for Scotland*, 1998 S.C.L.R. 763; SPEL 69:102.

[54] Evans and Watchman, "European Convention on Human Rights and Fundamental Freedoms—A New Dimension to Planning Law?" (1981) S.P.L.P. 65; (1983) S.P.L.P. 44.

[55] *Bryan v. U.K.* [1996] 1 P.L.R. 47; [1996] J.P.L. 386.

[56] *Buckley v. U.K.* [1996] J.P.L. 1018.

[57] Holligan, "The Human Rights Bill and Planning: An Introduction", SPEL 70:121; articles in *JPL*, Apr. 1998.

[58] Corner, "Planning, Environment and the European Convention on Human Rights", 1998 J.P.L. 301.

CHAPTER 9

PARTICULAR CONTROLS

The provisions of Acts examined in the previous chapters generally have 9.01
universal application. The TCPSA and related Acts also contain particular controls which apply to items of special significance, such as listed
buildings, or to designated areas, such as conservation areas, or to
specific forms of development, such as mineral extraction, or to classes
of developers, such as the Crown and planning authorities. The following
examination of these often complex controls necessarily takes the form
of an overview rather than a complete and detailed exposition.

LISTED BUILDINGS

The Secretary of State has the power to compile lists of buildings of 9.02
special architectural or historic interest, referred to as listed buildings.[1]
There are currently some 43,000 listed buildings in Scotland. Historic
Scotland is the executive agency of the Scottish Office with responsibility
for listed buildings.[2]

The term "building" includes any structure or erection, and items such
as telephone boxes and bridges have been designated as listed buildings.
Any object or structure fixed to the listed building, or which falls within
its curtilage and has formed part of the land since before July 1, 1948, is
treated as part of the building.[3] The primary test of what is listed is the
circumstances of the site at the date of statutory listing.

Determining whether an object or structure is fixed to the building
depends on the degree to which it can be said to be annexed to the
building and the purpose for which it was put there.[4]

There is no statutory definition of "curtilage", but this term broadly
includes any land or building used for the comfortable enjoyment of the
listed building or serving its purpose in some necessary or reasonably
useful way, although not marked off or enclosed in any way (Chapter 4).
A listed building may, therefore, include stables, mews blocks or garden
walls within its grounds, notwithstanding that these have passed into
separate ownership since the date of listing, but not buildings erected
within its curtilage since July 1, 1948. Importantly, listing covers the

---

[1] Planning (Listed Buildings and Conservation Areas) (Scotland) Act 1997, s. 1(1).
[2] Contact at Longmore House, Salisbury Place, Edinburgh, tel: 0131 668 8600.
[3] s. 1(4).
[4] R. v. Secretary of State for Wales, ex p. Kennedy [1996] 1 P.L.R. 97, [1996] J.P.L. 645.

interior as well as the exterior of the building irrespective of whether the list contains a detailed interior description.

The courts can quash a decision where the list has been misconstrued, for example where the decision-maker has erroneously decided that a building is not listed.[5]

It is open to planning authorities or any person or body to suggest to the Secretary of State/Historic Scotland that a building be listed. When considering whether to list a building, the Secretary of State may take into account not only the building itself, but also the contribution of its exterior to the architectural or historic interest of any group of buildings of which it forms part.[6] He may also consider the desirability of preserving any feature of the building on the ground of its architectural or historic interest. Before compiling or approving the list, persons or bodies with special knowledge or interest in buildings of architectural or historic interest must be consulted. There is no right of appeal against listing, but representations can be made to the Secretary of State. Listed buildings may be removed from the list, either following representations by an interested party or the demolition or alteration of the building.

Listed buildings are divided into three non-statutory categories according to merit:

A   buildings of national or international importance; either architectural or historic, or fine, little-altered examples of some particular period, style or building type;

B   buildings of regional or more than local importance; or major examples of some period, style or building type which may have been altered;

C   buildings of local importance; lesser examples of any period, style or building type, whether as originally constructed or altered; and simple, traditional buildings, which group well with categories A or B or are part of a planned group, such as an estate or an industrial complex.

(The previous C category has been phased out.)
These categories have no legal effect, but are used as a guide to the importance of the listed building and might, therefore, suggest the degree of difficulty which may be anticipated in obtaining listed building consent in relation to the building.

After the list has been compiled and approved, a copy of the relevant part is deposited with the planning authority, which is responsible for serving notice on the owner, lessee and occupier of the building intimating its listing. Copies of the list of such buildings must also be made available for public inspection.

---

[5] *City of Edinburgh Council v. Secretary of State for Scotland*, 1998 S.L.T. 120; SPEL 65:11.

[6] Further principles of listing are specified in para. 1.8 of the Memorandum of Guidance on Listed Buildings and Conservation Areas (new ed. 1998) published by Historic Scotland. See also draft NPPG18 "Planning and the Historic Environment".

Listed Building Control

(a)   Listed Building Consent

Listed building consent is required in advance for demolition of a   9.03
listed building or its alteration or extension in any manner which would
affect its character as a building of special architectural or historic
interest.[7] A substantial structure erected close to the façade of the
building may so affect its character or appearance that it constitutes an
alteration or extension.[8] Whether works are demolition or alteration is a
question of fact in each case, but the demolition of part of a listed
building is an alteration and not a demolition.[9] The need for listed
building consent is not satisfied by a grant of planning permission, nor an
express or deemed consent under the control of advertisement regulations. It is an offence to carry out demolition or such works without
listed building consent, or to fail to comply with conditions attached to
such a consent (see below). An application may be made for retrospective consent to authorise works already done.[10] Unlike planning permission, a failure to obtain listed building consent can never become
immune from enforcement action through the passage of time.

The requirement for consent extends to objects or structures which are
fixed to a listed building, or come within its curtilage and have done so
since before July 1, 1948. In consequence, buildings which were originally ancillary to the listed building, but are now under separate
ownership, can continue to be regarded as listed buildings on the basis of
location within the curtilage of the principal building.

It is important to note that, unlike planning permission, consent may
be required for internal alterations to a listed building irrespective of
whether the internal features are described in the listing.

There are guidelines for identifying whether works affect the character
of a listed building and, therefore, require consent.[11] For example, stone
cleaning and proposals to replace traditional windows with modern
forms of glazing will usually require listed building consent. Staircases,
chimney pieces, panelling, doors and door furniture, dadoes, plaster-
work and other interior features can all form part of the character of the
listed building, and any changes to these items may require consent. The
opinion of the planning authority on the need for consent should be
sought in advance of any works.

Listed building consent is not required (although it may be necessary
to obtain planning permission)[12]:

1.   if the building is an ecclesiastical building used for ecclesiastical purposes (other than wholly or mainly as a residence for a
minister);

---

[7] PLBCASA, ss. 6 and 7.
[8] *Ampliflaire Ltd v. Secretary of State for Scotland*, 1998 S.C.L.R. 565; SPEL 68:77.
[9] *Shimizu v. Westminster City Council* [1997] 1 All E.R. 481 [1997] J.P.L. 523.
[10] s. 7(3).
[11] Memorandum of Guidance, *supra*, App. 1.
[12] PLBCASA, ss. 54, 55 and 74.

2. if the building is included in the schedule of monuments (scheduled monument consent is required instead);
3. for the erection of a modern free-standing building in the curtilage of a listed building, or for works to objects or structures which have been within its curtilage only since July 1, 1948 and are not physically attached to the building[13]; or
4. for works by the Crown to listed Crown buildings.

9.04   Application for listed building consent is made to the planning authority, on the form obtainable from the authority. It is not competent to apply for consent in principle (referred to as outline consent), and full details of the proposed works must be given in the application. If planning permission is also required for the work (Chapter 4), application for both consents is normally made on the same form. The applications can be processed simultaneously, but separate decisions must be issued.

When applying for listed building consent, the applicant is required to complete a certificate stating either that he is the owner of the building or any part of the building to which the application relates, or has served notice of the application on the owner(s) named in the certificate or, despite taking specified steps, has been unable to trace any or all of the owners (Chapter 5). Copies of the form of notice to be served upon the owners are included with the application form obtained from the planning authority. In the event that any or all of the owners cannot be traced, the applicant must publish notice of the application in a local newspaper.[14] In contrast to planning applications, there is no form of neighbour notification for listed building consent applications.

The planning authority must advertise the application in both a local newspaper and the *Edinburgh Gazette*, and display a site notice for at least seven days. The advertisement and site notice must include a description of the works and name a place where plans of the works can be inspected. The application cannot be determined until 21 days after the date of the advertisement or the posting of the notice. In contrast to planning applications, the authority is not obliged to consult appropriate bodies for their views, although this may be done as a matter of good practice.

In determining the application, the authority must take into account any representations relating to the application received during the 21-day period and, in particular, any representations made by a person who satisfies them that he is owner of part of the building. Special regard must be paid to the desirability of preserving the building or its setting or any features of special architectural or historic interest which it possesses.[15] Scottish Office policy specifies a presumption in favour of preservation of listed buildings, and continuation of their original use wherever possible, and requires evidence that every possible attempt has

---

[13] But see *Amplifaire Ltd v. Secretary of State for Scotland, supra.*
[14] Town and Country Planning (Listed Buildings and Buildings in Conservation Areas) (Scotland) Regulations 1987 (S.I. 1987 No. 1529), reg. 6. These Regulations are due to be updated.
[15] PLBCASA, s. 14(2).

been made to find a suitable alternative use.[16] However, exceptions to this rule may be justified by the special circumstances of the site.[17] Planning authorities are directed to be flexible in dealing with applications for changes of use of listed buildings. Where application is made for the alteration or extension of any listed building, planning authorities should always seek to preserve the architectural integrity of the building and encourage its restoration where some of that integrity has been lost.

In most cases the authority may not grant consent without notifying the Secretary of State/Historic Scotland, who have 28 days to consider calling in the application for their own decision (but can extend this period indefinitely by giving notice to the authority). The date of the grant of listed building consent by the authority is the date on which the decision notice bears to have been signed.

Listed building consent may be granted subject to conditions. In the absence of any express conditions, a grant of listed building consent is deemed to be subject to a condition requiring commencement of the works authorised by the consent within five years (three years in the case of pre-1980 consents). If the works have not commenced within that period, the consent expires.[18] Other conditions may reserve specified minor details of the work for subsequent approval of the planning authority; preserve particular features of the building; require the making good, after the works are completed, of any damage caused to the building by the works; or provide for the reconstruction of the building or any part of it following the execution of any works, with the use of original materials so far as practicable and with specified alterations to its interior. It is also competent for the authority to impose a condition preventing demolition of the listed building until it is satisfied that the site will be redeveloped in accordance with a current planning permission, either through a section 75 agreement (Chapter 6) and/or the placing of contracts for redevelopment work.[19] Any person with a legal interest in a listed building may apply to the planning authority for variation or discharge of conditions attached to a grant of listed building consent.[20]

9.05

Where consent has been granted for demolition of a listed building, work cannot commence until at least three months after the Royal Commission on the Ancient and Historical Monuments of Scotland has been notified by the applicant (the appropriate form should be sent to the applicant by the planning authority along with the grant of consent). The Commission must either have been given access to record the building, or have stated in writing that its recording is complete or that it does not wish to record it.[21]

The applicant has a right of appeal to the Secretary of State against[22]:

---

[16] Memorandum of Guidance, *supra*, para. 2.10 *et seq.*
[17] *Save Britains Heritage v. Secretary of State for the Environment* [1991] 1 W.L.R. 153.
[18] PLBCASA, s. 16.
[19] s. 15.
[20] s. 17.
[21] s. 7(2).
[22] s. 18.

1. a refusal of listed building consent or of approval of subsequent details required in terms of a condition attached to the original grant of consent, or the grant of consent or approval subject to conditions;
2. a refusal of an application to vary or discharge conditions, or any fresh conditions imposed following such an application; and
3. a failure of the planning authority to determine the application, or give notice that the application has been called in by the Secretary of State, within two months of the date of receipt of the application or any extended period agreed in writing with the applicant (known as a deemed refusal appeal).

The appeal must be submitted within six months of notice of the decision or expiry of the two-month period.[23] The wording of the regulations leaves it uncertain whether the six-month period runs from the date of the notice or the date on which it is received. The procedure is similar to that for planning appeals described in Chapter 8. In addition to the normal grounds of appeal, the appellant may allege that the building is not of special architectural or historic interest and, therefore, ought not to be listed. In determining the appeal, the Secretary of State may reverse or vary any part of the decision by the authority, whether the appeal relates to that part or not, and may deal with the application as if it had been made to him in the first instance. As part of the appeal decision, the Secretary of State can also "de-list" the building by removing it from the list.[24]

The Secretary of State's decision on the merits of the appeal or called-in application is final. However, the legality of the decision may be challenged in the Court of Session under the statutory review procedure, but only within six weeks of the decision (Chapter 8).

(b) Enforcement

9.06 Where there is a failure to obtain listed building consent, the planning authority may serve a listed building enforcement notice, and/ or may seek interim interdict.[25]

A listed building enforcement notice may be served where it appears to the planning authority, or the Secretary of State, that any works have been or are being executed to a listed building in contravention of the requirement to obtain listed building consent, or of the conditions attached to a consent. In making its decision, the authority has regard to the effect of the works on the character of the building as one of special architectural or historic interest.[26] A failure to obtain listed building consent can never become immune from enforcement action through passage of time, unlike work carried out without planning permission.

The notice specifies the alleged contravention and the steps required, within a given period, either to restore the building to its former state, or

[23] Listed Buildings Regulations (no. 14, *supra*.), reg. 8.
[24] PLBCASA, ss. 19 and 20.
[25] *City of Glasgow Council v. Cannell*, 1998 G.W.D. 33–1722.
[26] ss. 34 and 41.

to bring it to the state in which it would have been if the terms and conditions of any listed building consent for the works had been complied with. Alternatively, where it appears to the authority that complete restoration of the building to its former state is undesirable or not reasonably practical, the notice can specify steps to alleviate the effects of works executed without listed building consent, in a manner acceptable to it. The notice must specify the date upon which it is to take effect, and the period within which the steps are required to be taken. Different periods may be specified for different steps.

A copy of the listed building enforcement notice is served on the current owner, lessee and occupier of the building and on any other person who has an interest in the building which, in the opinion of the planning authority, is materially affected by the notice. (Methods of service are discussed in Chapter 7.) Details of the building in respect of which the notice has been served must be entered in a list available for public inspection.

Withdrawal of the notice by the planning authority is competent at any time, whether or not it has taken effect, and without prejudice to its power to serve another. The authority may also waive or relax any requirement of the notice and, in particular, extend any period for taking the steps specified in the notice. Notification of its withdrawal, or any waiver or relaxation of its terms, must be given to every person served with the notice.

The owner of the land is guilty of an offence if at the end of the period for compliance with the notice, any step required to be taken in terms of the notice has not been taken.[27] Such an offence may be charged by reference to any day or longer period of time. It is a defence to show that everything was done that could be expected to secure that all the required steps were taken, or that the owner was not served with a copy of the notice and was not aware of it. On summary conviction, there is liability to a maximum fine of £20,000, and to an unlimited fine following conviction on indictment. In determining the level of fine the court shall in particular have regard to any financial benefit which has accrued or appears likely to accrue to the person in consequence of the offence. Following conviction, further offences are committed if there is a continuing failure to take any step.

If the steps required by the listed building enforcement notice have not been taken within the specified period, the planning authority may enter the land and take those steps, recovering any expenses reasonably incurred in this process from the person who is then the owner or lessee of the land. Such expenses are deemed to have been incurred on behalf of the person who carried out the unauthorised works, but there is no specific provision for recovery from that person. It is an offence to wilfully obstruct the exercise of this right of entry.[28]

Any person on whom the notice was served or any other person having an interest in the building to which it relates may lodge an appeal to the Secretary of State against the notice.[29] Such an appeal follows a

---

[27] s. 39.
[28] s. 38.
[29] s. 35.

similar procedure to an appeal against a planning enforcement notice (Chapter 7) and prevents the requirements of the notice from coming into force pending determination or withdrawal of the appeal. Written notice of the appeal must be lodged with SOIR before the notice takes effect (on the expiry of the period specified in the notice), or sent in a properly addressed and pre-paid envelope posted at such a time that, in the ordinary course of post, it would be delivered before that date.

9.07 The grounds of appeal are:

1. that the building is not of special architectural or historic interest;
2. that the matters alleged to constitute a contravention of the requirements to obtain listed building consent, or of the conditions of a consent, do not involve such a contravention;
3. that those matters (if they occurred) do not constitute such a contravention;
4. that the works were urgently necessary in the interests of safety or health or for the preservation of the building, and it was not practicable for this purpose to carry out repairs or works for affording temporary support or shelter, and that the works were limited to the minimum measures immediately necessary;
5. that listed building consent ought to be granted for the works, or any relevant condition of such consent which has been granted ought to be discharged or different conditions substituted;
6. that the notice was not served in accordance with the statutory provisions;
7. that the requirements of the notice exceed what is necessary for restoring the building to its condition before the works were carried out;
8. that the period specified in the notice as the period within which any steps required thereby are to be taken falls short of what should reasonably be allowed;
9. that the steps required by the notice to be taken would not serve the purpose of restoring the character of the building to its former state;
10. that the steps specified exceed what is necessary to bring the building to the state it would have been in if the listed building consent had been complied with;
11. that the steps specified exceed what may reasonably be required to alleviate the effects of works executed without listed building consent.

In the course of the appeal, the Secretary of State may correct any defect, error or misdescription in the notice, or vary its terms, provided he is satisfied that the correction or variation will not cause injustice to the appellant or planning authority. He may also disregard a failure to serve the notice on any person where that person has not suffered material prejudice as a result. In deciding the appeal, the Secretary of State may either quash the notice and grant listed building consent for the works to which the notice relates, or discharge any condition subject to which such consent was granted and substitute any other condition, whether more or less onerous, or uphold the notice. In addition, he may de-list the building by removing it from the list of buildings of special architectural or historic interest. The legality of the decision of the Secretary of State on the appeal may be challenged in the Court of Session using the statutory review procedure (Chapter 8).

(c) Offences

It is an offence to carry out demolition or works which require listed   9.08 building consent without obtaining such consent, or to fail to comply with conditions attached to a consent. It is a defence to show that the works were urgently necessary in the interests of safety or health or for the preservation of the building, and that it was not practicable to secure these interests by repair works or works providing temporary support or shelter, that the works were limited to the minimum measures immediately necessary and written notice justifying the need for the works was given to the planning authority as soon as reasonably practicable.[30] A person guilty of such an offence is liable on summary conviction to imprisonment for up to six months and/or a maximum fine of £20,000, and for conviction on indictment up to two years' imprisonment and/or an unlimited fine. In determining the level of fine to be imposed, the court is directed to have regard to any financial benefit which has accrued or appears likely to accrue to that person in consequence of the offence.[31]

Failure to comply with a listed building enforcement notice is also an offence (see above), together with doing or permitting to be done any act, other than that authorised by a grant of planning permission and/or listed building consent, which causes or is likely to result in damage to a listed building with the intention of causing such damage (see below).

Other Consequences of Listing

(a) Permitted Development

The permitted development rights conferred by the Permitted   9.09 Development Order (Chapter 4) apply more restrictively to listed buildings, with the result that planning permission is required for a wider scope of activities. For example, permitted development rights for painting the exterior of a building do not apply to listed buildings, with the result that planning permission will be required for the painting work if the external appearance of the listed building will be materially affected as a result of that work.[32]

(b) Protection of Setting

If the planning authority considers that the setting of a listed building   9.10 would be affected by a development for which an application for

---

[30] *Secretary of State for Scotland v. Highland Council*, 1998 S.L.T. 222; SPEL 63:104.
[31] s. 8.
[32] Town and County Planning (General Permitted Development) (Scotland) Order 1992, Sched. 1, class 9(2) and TCPSA, s. 26(2)(a).

planning permission has been made, the application should be advertised in a local newspaper and a site notice displayed for at least seven days, and 21 days allowed for representations to be lodged. When deciding whether to grant planning permission for such a development, the planning authority must take into account any representations received following the advertisement and site notice.[33]

The Scottish Office guidance suggests that development within the curtilage (Chapter 4) should always be regarded as affecting the setting unless the curtilage is very large and the new building will not be visible in any principal view either from or of the listed building. New buildings outwith the curtilage which restrict or obstruct views of the listed building or rise above and behind it so that its silhouette can no longer be seen against the sky from the more familiar viewpoints should also be regarded as affecting the setting, as should development which blocks long-appreciated views of important architectural landmarks.[34]

In considering whether to grant permission for a development which affects a listed building or its setting, the authority must have special regard to the desirability of preserving the building or its setting or any features of special architectural or historic interest which it possesses.[35]

(c)   Intimation of Notices

9.11   Where a building owned, leased or occupied by the planning authority has been listed, various statutory notices, orders or proposals relating to demolition or the carrying out of works affecting the building must be intimated in writing to the Secretary of State. Written intimation may be dispensed with in cases where public safety requires demolition or other work to be carried out without delay, but intimation, even if initially oral, must be given as soon as possible before commencement of the demolition or works.[36]

(d)   Offences

9.12   It is an offence to carry out demolition or works without listed building consent, or contrary to the conditions of a consent (see above). It is also an offence to do or permit to be done any act, other than that authorised by a grant of planning permission and/or listed building consent, which causes or is likely to result in damage to a listed building (other than those buildings exempted from the provisions relating to listed building consent), with the intention of causing such damage. On summary conviction a person guilty of such an offence is liable to a fine not exceeding level 3 on the standard scale (Appendix 1). Following conviction, a further offence is committed by failure to take such reasonable steps as may be necessary to prevent any damage or further damage resulting from the offence, with a maximum fine of one-tenth of level 3 for each day on which the failure continues.[37]

---

[33] PLBCASA, s. 60 and TCPSA, s. 37(3).
[34] Memorandum of Guidance, *supra*, App. 1, para. 10.1.0.
[35] PLBCASA, s. 59. Guidance is given in draft NPPG, "Planning and the Historic Environment".
[36] s. 56.
[37] s. 53.

(e) Urgent Works for Preservation

If it appears to the planning authority (or the Secretary of State) that   9.13
any works are urgently necessary for the preservation of a listed building,
it may execute those works after giving not less than seven days' written
notice to the owner of the building.[38] This power does not extend to an
ecclesiastical building in ecclesiastical use, other than a minister's
residence, or to a scheduled monument. The works may include erection
of scaffolding for support or a temporary roof covering. If the building is
occupied, works may be carried out only to those parts which are not in
use. Scottish Office guidance encourages planning authorities to exercise
these powers at an early stage when relatively inexpensive works can halt
deterioration of a building and greatly improve its chances of economic
re-use.[39]

A similar power may be applied by direction of the Secretary of State
to an unlisted building in a conservation area which should be preserved
to maintain the character or appearance of the conservation area.

Notice may also be given to the owner rendering him liable to pay the
expenses of these works unless within 28 days of the date of the notice
he lodges an objection with the Secretary of State on the grounds that
some or all of the works are unnecessary for the building's preservation,
that temporary arrangements for support or shelter have continued for
an unreasonable length of time, or that the amount specified in the
notice is unreasonable, or that recovery of it would cause him hardship.
The Secretary of State considers the justification for such an objection
and gives notice of his decision to the owner and the planning authority,
if it carried out the works, together with a statement of the reasons for
the decision and the amount recoverable.[40]

(f) Repairs Notices and Compulsory Purchase

A repairs notice may be served at any time on the owner of a listed   9.14
building by the planning authority or the Secretary of State specifying
the works considered reasonably necessary for its proper preservation,
and explaining the effect of the compulsory purchase provisions.[41] The
notice may be withdrawn at any time, by serving notice of the withdrawal
upon any person served with a copy of the notice.

Compulsory purchase proceedings can be initiated two months after
service of a repairs notice, even if the building was demolished following
service of the notice. The Secretary of State may authorise compulsory
purchase if he is satisfied that reasonable steps are not being taken for
properly preserving the listed building, and that it is expedient to make
provision for its preservation and to authorise its compulsory purchase
for that purpose.[42] The compulsory purchase order may include any land
required for preserving the building or its amenities, or for giving access

---

[38] s. 49.
[39] Memorandum of Guidance, *supra*, para. 3.18.
[40] PLBCASA, s. 50.
[41] s. 43.
[42] s. 42.

to it for its proper control or management. This compulsory purchase power does not extend to an ecclesiastical building in ecclesiastical use, other than a minister's residence, or to a scheduled monument. Any person with an interest in the building has 28 days after service of a compulsory purchase order to apply to the sheriff for an order prohibiting further proceedings upon it. Such an order will only be granted if the sheriff is satisfied that reasonable steps have been taken to preserve the building.

Where the planning authority or the Secretary of State is satisfied that the building has been deliberately allowed to fall into disrepair for the purpose of justifying its demolition and the development of the site, a direction may be made for the payment of minimum compensation, which ignores the redevelopment value of the land.[43]

(g) Listed Building Purchase Notices

9.15   A listed building purchase notice may be served on the planning authority by the owner or lessee where the land has become incapable of reasonably beneficial use in its present state and listed building consent has been refused, granted subject to conditions, revoked or modified.[44] The notice has the effect of requiring the authority to purchase the interest in the land. The procedure is similar to that for planning purchase notices (Chapter 5).

(h) Rights of Entry

9.16   The planning authority has the right to enter land in specified circumstances in connection with listed buildings,[45] including to ascertain whether work is being carried out without listed building consent, or contrary to a condition attached to a consent, and whether the building is being maintained in a proper state of repair. Entry to land which is occupied cannot be demanded as of right unless 24 hours' notice of the intended entry has been given to the occupier. A warrant authorising entry may be sought from a sheriff if admission to the land has been refused or a refusal is reasonably apprehended, or the case is one of urgency.

Building Preservation Notices

9.17   Service of a building preservation notice extends the protection afforded to listed buildings to an unlisted building, on a temporary basis, while the Secretary of State considers whether it should be listed. This notice may be served where it appears to the planning authority that the building is of special architectural or historic interest and is in danger of demolition or alteration in such a way as to affect its character. It is not competent to serve a building preservation notice in respect of an ecclesiastical building in use for ecclesiastical purposes, other than a

---

[43] s. 45.
[44] s. 28.
[45] ss. 76–78.

minister's residence, or a scheduled monument.[46] While the notice is in force, the building is treated as a listed building, except that an act causing or likely to cause damage to the building will not be an offence.

The notice states that the building appears to be of special architectural or historic interest and that the planning authority has requested the Secretary of State to consider listing it, and explains its effect. The notice comes into force as soon as it has been served by the planning authority on the owner, lessee and occupier of the building. In urgent circumstances personal service may be dispensed with and the notice takes effect once it has been affixed conspicuously to some object on the building. The notice remains in force for six months from the last date of service, but is discharged within this period by the listing of the building or written notification to the planning authority from the Secretary of State that he does not intend to list the building.

If the Secretary of State decides not to list the building the notice is discharged and this decision must be intimated forthwith to the owner, lessee and occupier of the building by the planning authority. Following a decision not to list the building, the planning authority cannot serve another building preservation notice in respect of the building within the following 12 months. Any enforcement proceedings will lapse, although liability will remain for non-compliance with a listed building enforcement notice committed while the notice was in force.

If the building preservation notice ceases to have effect without the building becoming listed, any person who at the time when the notice was served had an interest in the building shall be entitled to be paid compensation by the planning authority in respect of any loss or damage directly attributable to the effect of the notice.[47]

CONSERVATION AREAS

The planning authority has a duty to determine periodically which parts 9.18 of its district are areas of special architectural or historic interest, the character or appearance of which it is desirable to preserve or enhance. Such areas should be designated as conservation areas.[48] The Secretary of State has a reserve power to intervene and designate a conservation area. Notice of the designation, and any variation or cancellation of a designation, is given to the Secretary of State and advertised in the *Edinburgh Gazette* and a local newspaper. Individual owners and occupiers of property within the area do not require to be notified. No formal confirmation of the designation is required from the Secretary of State. The authority must compile and make available for public inspection a list of particulars of conservation areas within its district. There are almost 600 conservation areas in Scotland.

[46] s. 3.
[47] s. 26.
[48] s. 61(1).

Conservation Area Consent

9.19   Conservation area consent is required for demolition of a building in a conservation area, with exceptions including[49]:

1. a listed building (listed building consent will be required);
2. an ecclesiastical building in ecclesiastical use, other than a minister's residence;
3. a scheduled monument (scheduled monument consent will be required);
4. a building (but not a part of a building) with a total cubic content not exceeding 115 cubic metres;
5. any gate, wall, fence or railing which is less than one metre high where abutting a road used by vehicular traffic or an open space, or two metres high in any other case; and
6. any building required to be demolished in terms of a discontinuance order or enforcement notice, or by virtue of a condition of a planning permission or provision of a section 75 agreement.

Consent may only be required where the whole building is to be demolished.[50]

Consent is obtained from the planning authority. The procedure for applying for consent and the powers of enforcement are the same as those applicable to applications for listed building consent (see above). In considering the application, the planning authority must pay special attention to the desirability of preserving or enhancing the character or appearance of the conservation area (see below). If the site is to be redeveloped, consent should in general only be given where there are acceptable proposals for the new building or the development of the cleared site.

A number of the provisions applicable to listed building control (see above) are applied to conservation area consent.[51] Conditions similar to those for listed building consents may be imposed upon the grant of conservation area consent. If consent is granted for demolition of the building, the Royal Commission on the Ancient and Historical Monuments of Scotland must be given an opportunity to record the building. Enforcement action may be taken against any failure to obtain conservation area consent, and there is a right of appeal to the Secretary of State in respect of that action. It is an offence to demolish a building without the required conservation area consent.

---

[49] The full list of exceptions appears in PLBCASA, ss. 66 and 67, and Direction, "Exemption from Demolition Control in Conservation Areas", attached to SDD Circular 17/1987, "New Provisions and Revised Guidance relating to Listed Buildings and Conservation Areas", Annex IV.

[50] Memorandum of Guidance, *supra*, para. 4.27, presumably in light of *Shimizu v. Westminster City Council, supra*; Brainsby and Carter "Shimizu: Part II—The Implications for Conservation Area Controls" [1997] J.P.L. 603.

[51] Listed Buildings and Buildings in Conservation Areas Regulations, (*supra*) reg. 13.

Permitted Development Rights

Under the Permitted Development Order (Chapter 4) permitted 9.20 development rights for development in conservation areas are restricted, with the result that planning permission is required for a wider range of development. For example, permitted development rights for painting the exterior of a building do not apply to buildings situated in conservation areas, with the result that planning permission will be required for the painting work if the external appearance of such a building will be materially affected as a result of that work.[52] Further restrictions may be placed on permitted development rights within conservation areas by the use of article 4 directions (see below).

Planning Applications—Preservation of Character and Appearance

If the planning authority believes that a proposed development would 9.21 affect the character or appearance of a conservation area, the application must be advertised in a local newspaper and a site notice displayed for at least seven days. Any comments received within 21 days of the advertisement or display of the notice must be taken into account when the application is determined.[53]

In addition, the planning authority must pay special attention to the desirability of preserving or enhancing the character or appearance of a conservation area when exercising its planning powers in relation to any buildings or land in that area, including the determination of planning applications.[54] This will include looking at such matters as scale, bulk, height, materials, colour, vertical or horizontal emphasis and design,[55] and must be the first consideration for the authority.[56] The character or appearance of a conservation area is preserved not only by a positive contribution to preservation, but also by development which has a neutral effect and leaves the character or appearance unharmed.[57] Where a development simultaneously causes both enhancement and some detriment, the detrimental effect is a material consideration.[58] This requirement may lead planning authorities to insist on applications for detailed rather than outline planning permission for development within conservation areas.

Protection of Trees

With some exceptions, it is an offence to cut down, top, lop, uproot, 9.22 wilfully damage or wilfully destroy a tree in a conservation area, even if it is not protected by a tree preservation order, unless the planning

---

[52] Town and Country Planning (General Permitted Development) (Scotland) Order 1992, Sched. 1, class 9(2) and TCPSA, s. 26(2)(a).
[53] PLBCASA, s. 65 and TCPSA s. 37(3).
[54] PLBCASA, s. 64. *Campbell v. City of Edinburgh Council*, 1998 G.W.D. 17–877; SPEL 69:99.
[55] Memorandum of Guidance, *supra*, para. 4.40.
[56] *Bath Society v. Secretary of State for the Environment* [1991] 1 W.L.R. 1303.
[57] *South Lakeland D.C. v. Secretary of State for the Environment* [1992] 2 A.C. 141.
[58] *Bath Society v. Secretary of State for the Environment, supra.*

authority was given six weeks' notice of the proposed work or consented to it (see below).

Urgent Works for Preservation

9.23　　The Secretary of State may direct that the power to undertake works which are urgently necessary for the preservation of a listed building be extended to apply to a building in a conservation area, if satisfied that its preservation is important for maintaining the character or appearance of the area.[59] If the building is occupied, works may be carried out only to those parts which are not in use.

Proposals for Preservation and Enhancement

9.24　　There is a duty placed on planning authorities to formulate and publish proposals for the preservation and enhancement of conservation areas.[60] There is some criticism that planning authorities largely ignore this duty and use the conservation area designation as a device to achieve greater control over development.

Article 4 Directions

9.25　　The requirement for conservation area consent only applies to demolition of certain classes of buildings (see above). The planning authority can achieve greater control over development within a conservation area (and elsewhere) by means of an article 4 direction.[61] The effect of such a direction is to remove permitted development rights under the Permitted Development Order (Chapter 4) for specified classes of development, with the result that planning permission must be obtained from the planning authority for those classes of development. The direction may apply to specified classes of development within a conservation area or other geographical areas or any particular development within a class, other than a small list of developments which cannot be restricted by an article 4 direction.

An article 4 direction may be made by the planning authority (or the Secretary of State), if it is satisfied that it is expedient to restrict permitted development rights in this way. In most cases the direction must be submitted to the Secretary of State for approval. Notice of the direction made or approved by the Secretary of State is published by the planning authority in the *Edinburgh Gazette* and at least one local newspaper.[62] The notice must specify any particular geographical area affected by the direction and contain a concise statement of the effect of the direction and name a place where a copy may be inspected. In the case of a direction specifying any particular development, notice must be

---

[59] PLBCASA, s. 68.

[60] s. 63.

[61] Town and Country Planning (General Permitted Development) (Scotland) Order 1992, art. 4. For information on the use of article 4 Directions, see "Research on the General Permitted Development Order and Related Mechanisms" (Scottish Office Development Department, 1998), p. 32 *et seq.*

[62] *ibid.*, art. 5.

served on the owner and occupier of the land affected. The direction comes into force on the date of publication of the first notice or date of service on the occupier or, if there is no occupier, on the owner. There is a right to compensation if an application for planning permission is refused and a development cannot proceed which but for the direction would not have required permission.[63]

An article 4 direction made by a planning authority may be cancelled without the approval of the Secretary of State, although a notice must be published or served on the owner and occupier affected by the cancelled direction.

WORLD HERITAGE SITES

The United Nations Education, Scientific and Cultural Organisation (UNESCO) designates World Heritage Sites. Scotland currently has two World Heritage Sites: Edinburgh's Old and New Towns, and St Kilda. A further eight sites were proposed in a government consultation paper issued in August 1998: the Cairngorm Mountains, the Flow Country of Sutherland and Caithness, the Forth Rail Bridge, New Lanark, the Dallas Dhu Distillery in Forres, Abbotsford (Sir Walter Scott's home), the dry stone tower of Mousa Broch in Shetland, and Stirling Castle and the upper town of Stirling. 9.26

There are no additional statutory controls relating to World Heritage Sites, but the designation is likely to be a material consideration in the determination of applications.[64]

TREES

The planning authority has a duty when granting planning permission to ensure that adequate provision is made for the preservation or planting of trees.[65] This duty is normally discharged by imposing appropriate conditions upon the grant of permission, or making tree preservation orders. 9.27

Tree preservation orders (TPOs) may be made by the planning authority where it appears expedient in the interests of amenity to make provision for the preservation of trees, or woodlands in the district.[66] The TPO will specify the particular tree, groups of trees or woodlands to which it applies and include a map showing their position. It may also provide for the prohibition of the cutting down, topping, lopping, uprooting, wilful damage, or wilful destruction of the trees without the consent of the planning authority, which consent may be given subject to conditions. A TPO can secure the replanting, in a specified manner, of any part of a woodland area which is felled in the course of forestry

---

[63] TCPSA, s. 77.
[64] Draft NPPG, "Planning and the Historic Environment", para 16.
[65] s. 159.
[66] s. 160.

operations. Where planning permission is granted subject to conditions requiring the planting of trees it is possible for a TPO to take effect from the time when those trees are planted. Nothing in a TPO prohibits the uprooting, felling or lopping of any tree if this work is urgently necessary in the interests of safety or is necessary for the prevention or abatement of a nuisance, provided written notice of the proposed work is given to the planning authority as soon as may be after the necessity for the operation arises, or if such work is carried out in compliance with any obligation imposed by or under any Act of Parliament.

The making of the TPO must be advertised and a copy of the order and map made available for public inspection. Notice must be served on the owners, lessees and occupiers of the land affected by the TPO,[67] and on any person known by the planning authority to be entitled either to work any minerals in the land by surface working or to fell any of the trees affected by the TPO. A period of 28 days from date of service must be allowed for representations to be made to the planning authority.[68] The TPO does not take effect until it is confirmed by the planning authority, which must take into account any representations received. It is competent for the TPO to be confirmed subject to modifications. Following its confirmation, the TPO is recorded in the Register of Sasines or the Land Register (the property register) by the planning authority, thereby becoming enforceable against all subsequent owners of the land on which the trees stand.

In cases of urgency, a TPO may take effect immediately without previous confirmation.[69] In these circumstances, the TPO specifies the date on which it takes effect provisionally and it continues in force for six months or until its confirmation, whichever is the earlier date.

Where a tree protected by a TPO is removed, uprooted or destroyed in contravention of the TPO, the owner of the land must plant another tree of an appropriate size and species in the same place as soon as reasonably possible.[70] The TPO will apply to the new tree as it applied to the original tree.[71] This replanting obligation also applies where the uprooting or felling is authorised only as being urgently necessary in the interests of safety. In the case of trees in a woodland, it is sufficient to replace the trees with the same number of trees either on or near the land on which the trees previously stood or on such other land as may be agreed with the planning authority. It is possible to apply to the planning authority to dispense with the requirement to replant trees.

The protection conferred by a TPO extends to trees in conservation areas which are not the subject of a TPO, with exceptions. These include the uprooting, felling or lopping of a tree not exceeding 75 millimetres or the uprooting or felling in a woodland of a tree having a diameter not

---

[67] *Knowles v. Chorley B.C.* [1997] E.G.C.S. 141.
[68] Town and Country Planning (Tree Preservation Order and Trees in Conservation Areas) (Scotland) Regulation 1975 (S.I. 1975 No. 1204), as amended by Amendment Regulations in 1981 (S.I. 1981 No. 1385) and 1984 (S.I. 1984 No. 329).
[69] TCPSA, s. 163.
[70] s. 167.
[71] *Brown v. Cooper*, 1990 S.C.C.R. 675.

exceeding 100 millimetres where this is done to improve the growth of other trees, the diameter being measured over the bark at a point 1.5 metres above ground level.[72]

In any prosecution relating to trees in conservation areas which are not the subject of a TPO, it will be a defence to prove that notice of the intention to do the act was served upon the planning authority and the authority consented to the work, or six weeks was allowed for them to respond before the work was carried out (there is a two-year time limit from giving such notice to do the work). The six-week period is intended to give the authority time to consider making a TPO. The planning authority must keep a register of such notices and make it available for public inspection. The replanting obligation applies.

The planning authority has the power to serve a notice on the owner of the land requiring him to plant a tree or trees of specified size and species within a specified period, in enforcement of the general replanting obligations or any conditions of a consent given under a TPO requiring replanting.[73] The notice must be served within two years of the date on which the failure to comply came to the knowledge of the authority. The notice takes effect after the expiry of the period specified in the notice, which must be at least 28 days from the date of service, unless the person on whom notice is served has appealed to the Secretary of State.[74] The procedure for such an appeal is similar to appeals against enforcement notices (Chapter 7).

The grounds of appeal are that:

1. the replanting obligation or the conditions of a consent given under a TPO have been complied with;
2. in the circumstances of the case the replanting obligation should be dispensed with;
3. the requirements of the notice are unreasonable in respect of the period or the size or species of trees specified therein;
4. the planting of a tree or trees in accordance with the notice is not required in the interests of amenity or would be contrary to the practice of good forestry;
5. the place on which the tree(s) is required to be planted is unsuitable for that purpose.

There is provision for recovery of the expenses incurred by the owner in complying with the notice from any person responsible for the cutting down, destruction or removal of the original tree or trees.[75] If the steps required by the notice are not taken, the planning authority has the power to enter the land and take those steps. It is an offence to obstruct wilfully the exercise of this power.[76]

It is an offence to cut down, uproot or wilfully destroy a tree, or wilfully damage, top or lop a tree in such a manner as to be likely to

---

[72] s. 172; Tree Preservation Order Regulations (n. 68, *supra*) reg. 11.
[73] s. 168(1).
[74] The grounds of appeal are specified in s. 169.
[75] s. 170(4).
[76] s. 170.

destroy it, in contravention of a TPO or where the tree is situated in a conservation area.[77] Following summary conviction a fine not exceeding £20,000 may be imposed, and an unlimited fine if convicted on indictment. In determining the amount of the fine the court is directed to have regard to any financial benefit which has accrued or appears likely to accrue to the offender in consequence of the offence. Any other contravention of a TPO, for example damaging a tree short of destruction, is an offence punishable on summary conviction by a fine not exceeding level 4 of the standard scale (Appendix 1).

ADVERTISEMENT CONTROL

9.28   The display of advertisements is restricted and regulated by a separate set of controls.[78] No advertisement may be displayed without an express consent granted either by the planning authority or the Secretary of State, or a deemed consent. As with a grant of planning permission, the consent attaches to the site rather than to the applicant, and can be utilised by future persons with an interest in the site. Planning permission is deemed to have been granted for the display of an advertisement which is in accordance with the advertisement control requirements.[79]

The advertisement control provisions are under review. A Scottish Office consultation paper issued in March 1998[80] included proposals to abolish special areas of control, the addition of national flags of any country to the classes of advertisements exempt from control, changes to the deemed consent classes, the introduction of neighbour notification (Chapter 5) for advertisement consent applications, and the restriction of the right of appeal against the determination of such applications from six to two months.

Definition of "Advertisement"

9.29   An advertisement is defined to include any word, letter, model, sign, placard, board, notice, awning, blind, device or representation, whether illuminated or not, in the nature of an advertisement, announcement or direction, and which is employed wholly or partly for that purpose. This includes anything used or designed or adapted principally for use, for the display of advertisements, such as a hoarding or similar structure, or a balloon. Anything employed wholly or partly as a memorial or as a railway signal is excluded.[81] This definition should embrace any form of advertisement, and remove any doubt that canopies installed at shops carrying manufacturers or brand names are subject to advertisement control.[82] Similarly, anything designed or adapted principally for use as

---

[77] ss. 171 and 172. *Brown v. Cooper, supra.*

[78] TCPSA, ss. 182–187; Town and Country Planning (Control of Advertisements) (Scotland) Regulations 1984 (S.I. 1984 No. 467) as amended by Amendment Regulations 1992 (S.I. 1992 No. 1763).

[79] s. 184.

[80] "Review of Advertisement Control in Scotland" SODD, March 1998.

[81] s. 277(1); Control of Advertisement Regulations (n. 78, *supra*), reg. 2(1), as amended.

[82] *Glasgow D.C. v. Secretary of State for Scotland*, 1989 S.L.T. 256.

an advertisement is controlled, which will include hoardings, rotating panels, gantry or pylon signs, and free-standing structures, such as drums. Items used to draw attention to a business, such as national flags displayed on flagpoles and searchlights, can therefore be advertisements.[83]

Advertisement control does not apply to advertisements[84]:

1. displayed within a building (with some exceptions);
2. on or in a vehicle normally employed as a moving vehicle, except during periods when it is being used primarily for the display of advertisements;
3. incorporated in and forming part of the fabric of a building (which does not necessarily include advertisements affixed or painted on the building), unless the building is used principally for the display of advertisements or a hoarding or similar structure;
4. displayed on land wholly or mainly enclosed by a hedge, fence, wall or similar screen and not readily visible from outside or from any part of the enclosed land over which there is public right of way or public access: this includes any railway station together with its yards and forecourts whether enclosed or not, but not public parks, public gardens or other land held for the use or enjoyment of the public, or any railway line;
5. displayed on or consisting of a balloon flown at a height of more than 60 metres above ground level;
6. displayed on or consisting of a balloon, provided the site is not within an area of special control (see below), a conservation area (see above), or other area designated for the purpose of conserving the natural beauty and amenity of the countryside, for example a national scenic area (see below): no more than one such advertisement may be displayed at any one time on the site, and the site may not be used for the display of such advertisements on more than 10 days in total in any one calendar year, irrespective of which part of the site is used or who is using it for this purpose; and
7. displayed on an article for sale or on the container or dispenser in or from which an article is sold, provided the advertisement is not illuminated and does not exceed 0.1 square metre in area.

Deemed Consent

There are six classes of advertisements for which consent is deemed to be granted without application to the authority, provided the specified conditions relating to matters such as height and area are observed (but other statutory consents may still be required).[85] Reference must be made to the statutory provisions for full details, but these classes are: 9.30

---

[83] *Taylor v. Secretary of State for Scotland*, 1997 S.L.T. 535; SPEL 59:15; *Great Yarmouth B.C. v. Secretary of State for the Environment* [1996] E.G.C.S. 158.
[84] Control of Advertisement Regulations (n. 78, *supra*), reg. 3.
[85] reg. 10 and Sched. 4.

I   Functional advertisements of local authorities, community councils, statutory undertakers and public transport undertakers.

II   Advertisements relating to the land on which they are displayed (including identification and direction signs, and advertisements in relation to business on the premises where the advertisement is displayed).

III   Advertisements of a temporary nature (including for sale boards, and builders' signs on sites).

IV   Advertisements displayed on business premises (including references to the goods sold or services provided, and the name and qualification of the person carrying on the business).

V   Advertisements within buildings (if not exempt from advertisement control).

VI   Iluminated advertisements (displayed on business premises wholly with reference to the business, goods sold or services provided, and qualifications of the person carrying on the business).

Deemed consent also extends to advertisements relating specifically to elections, statutory advertisements, and traffic signs. There is also deemed consent for advertisements on sites used for the display of advertisements on August 16, 1948. The deemed consent for such sites does not necessarily expire if the use of the site for advertising is interrupted, and is not extinguished by an application for express consent.[86]

In addition to the conditions attached to each class of deemed consent and the standard conditions applicable to the display of all advertisements (see below), deemed consent is subject to an implied condition preventing siting or display of an advertisement so as to obscure or hinder the ready interpretation of any road traffic sign, railway signal or aid to navigation by water or air, or so as otherwise to render hazardous the use of any road, railway, waterway (including coastal waters) or airfield.[87]

There are several ways in which deemed consent can be lost or removed. Where there is deemed consent for display of an advertisement, submission of an application for express consent removes the right to display the advertisement with deemed consent, irrespective of whether the application is successful.[88] The Secretary of State has the power to remove deemed consent for the display of advertisements of a specified class or description in any particular area or in any particular case.[89]

It is also open to the planning authority to require discontinuance of the display of an advertisement with deemed consent (other than

---

[86] *Parker v. Secretary of State for Scotland*, 1998 S.L.T. 299; SPEL 63:103.
[87] reg. 6 and Sched. 1.
[88] reg. 10(2) and (3). But see *Parker v. Secretary of State for Scotland*, *supra*.
[89] reg. 11.

election and statutory advertisements and traffic signs), by serving a discontinuance notice, where it considers it expedient to do so to remedy a substantial injury to the amenity of the locality or a danger to members of the public.[90] The notice is served upon the person who himself, or by his servant or agent, undertakes or maintains the display of the advertisement, and on the owner, lessee and occupier of the land on which it is displayed. It specifies the advertisement or the site to which it relates, the period within which the display or use of the site is to be discontinued, and the reasons why the authority considers it expedient, in the interests of amenity or public safety, that the display or use of the site should be discontinued. The notice takes effect on the date specified therein, which must be not less than 28 days after the date of service. The authority may withdraw the notice at any time until it takes effect, or, where no appeal is pending, vary its terms to extend the period before it takes effect (in contrast to most other enforcement powers, where the right to withdraw or vary a notice has been extended beyond the time when the notice takes effect).

There is a right of appeal to the Secretary of State against a discontinuance notice. Submission of an appeal prevents the notice from taking effect until the appeal has been determined. Written notice of appeal must be lodged within 28 days from the date of service of the notice.[91] The procedure is similar to that for enforcement notice appeals (Chapter 7). The Secretary of State may dismiss the appeal, quash the notice, or vary its terms in favour of the appellant.

Express Consent

In the absence of deemed consent for the display of an advertisement, an application for express consent must be submitted to the planning authority on the form available from the authority.[92] A register of the particulars of all such applications must be maintained for public inspection by the authority. The decision of the authority on the application must be notified to the applicant within two months from either the date of receipt or any longer period agreed in writing with the applicant. If consent is refused or granted subject to conditions other than the standard conditions (see below), written reasons must be given for the decision. 9.31

Unlike normal planning powers, advertisement control can only be exercised in the interests of amenity and public safety.[93] Consent cannot be refused because the planning authority consider the advertisement to be unnecessary or offensive to public morals, and any consent granted cannot limit or restrict the subject matter, content or design of the advertisement. In the interest of amenity, the authority may determine the suitability of the use of the site for the display of advertisements in light of the general characteristics of the locality, including the presence

---

[90] reg. 14.
[91] reg. 21(3).
[92] reg. 5.
[93] reg. 4.

of any features of historic, architectural, cultural or similar interest. The presence of existing advertisements in the locality should be ignored. On the grounds of public safety, the authority should have regard to the safety of persons who may use any road, railway, waterway (including coastal waters), dock, harbour or airfield which is likely to be affected by the proposed advertisement display. In particular, it should consider whether the display is likely to obscure or hinder the ready interpretation of any road traffic sign, railway signal or aid to navigation by water or air. The authority should also have regard to any material change of circumstances likely to occur within the period for which the consent is required, and any other material factor.

Consent may be granted subject to the standard conditions (see below) and such additional conditions as the authority thinks fit, or refused (but only on the grounds of amenity and/or public safety). Consent may be granted for display of a particular advertisement or specify the use of a particular site for the display of advertisements in a particular manner, by reference to the number, siting, size or illumination of the advertisements or the structures intended for such display, or the design or appearance of any such structure. A temporary consent may be granted, with a condition requiring removal of the advertisement following expiry of a specified period. Retrospective consent may be granted for the display of advertisements begun prior to the date of application or for the retention of advertisements displayed prior to the application.

Where the application relates to display of an advertisement within one of the deemed consent classes (see above), consent cannot be refused or more restrictive conditions imposed, unless required to prevent or remedy a substantial injury to the amenity of the locality or a danger to members of the public.

9.32   Consent may be granted for the temporary display on unspecified sites within the authority's district of placards, posters or bills relating to the visit of a travelling circus, fair or similar travelling entertainment.[94] Such a consent is subject to a set of conditions which apply in addition to the standard conditions. There is no right of appeal against the decision of the planning authority on an application for this form of consent.

Every grant of express consent expires after five years, or such other period as is specified in the consent.[95] This time limit may be specified as running from the date of commencement of the display of the advertisement or from a date not later than six months after the date consent is granted, whichever is the earlier. The consent may be renewed at any time within six months before its expiry. Unless prohibited by a condition or where an application for renewal is refused, the display may continue after the time limit by virtue of a deemed consent on the same terms and conditions, subject to service of a discontinuance notice (see above).[96]

An express consent may be revoked or modified by the planning authority on grounds of amenity or public safety, but only before the

[94] reg. 27.
[95] reg. 18.
[96] reg. 19.

display of the advertisement commences or building or other operations involved in the display have been completed. The confirmation of the Secretary of State is required. A written claim for compensation may be served upon the authority within six months after confirmation of the revocation or modification order.[97]

Following a refusal of express consent or grant subject to conditions, the applicant has a right of appeal to the Secretary of State within six months from receipt of the decision. There is also a right of appeal against a deemed refusal, where the authority has failed to notify its decision within two months of the date of receipt of the application, or any longer period agreed with the applicant.[98] The appeal procedure is similar to planning appeals, except that no provision is made for using the written submissions procedure (Chapter 8). Advertisement consent appeals have been delegated by the Secretary of State to reporters for decision, although some advertisement appeals may continue to be decided by the Secretary of State.[99] The Secretary of State/reporter may allow or dismiss the appeal, or reverse or vary any part of the decision by the authority whether or not the appeal relates to that part, dealing with the application as though it was made to him in the first instance. The decision on the merits of the appeal is final, but its legality may be challenged in the Court of Session using the statutory review procedure (Chapter 8), subject to a six-week time limit.

Standard Conditions

The display of all advertisements is subject to implied conditions 9.33 requiring, to the reasonable satisfaction of the planning authority[1]:

1. maintenance in a clean and tidy condition of the advertisement (other than an election notice) and the land upon which it is displayed;
2. maintenance in a safe condition of any hoarding, similar structure or sign, placard, board or other device used principally for displaying the advertisement;
3. removal of the advertisement when required under the regulations;
4. advance permission for display of the advertisement (other than statutory advertisements) to be obtained from the owner of the land or other person entitled to grant permission.

Areas of Special Control

The planning authority has the power to designate Areas of Special 9.34 Control, within which stricter standards of advertisement control apply.[2] This power is exercised in the interests of amenity, having regard to the

---

[97] regs 22 and 23.
[98] regs 20 and 21.
[99] Town and Country Planning (Determination of Appeals by Appointed Persons) (Prescribed Classes) (Scotland) Amendment Regulations 1989 (S.I. 1989 No. 577).
[1] Control of Advertisements Regulations (n. 78, *supra*), reg. 6 and Sched.1.
[2] reg. 8. The procedure is described in Sched. 2.

general characteristics of the area, including the presence of any feature of historic, architectural or cultural interest. The designation must be approved by the Secretary of State, who has indicated that it is not normally enough for the area to be a conservation area (see above), but that this stricter control is wholly appropriate in rural areas. Once the area comes into operation, advertisements already displayed in the area (with some exceptions) may continue to be displayed for a further six months or for the remainder of the term of any express consent, whichever is longer, and then for a further two months, after which the advertisement must be removed unless express consent is granted for its continued display.[3]

Enforcement

9.35   An enforcement notice may be served by the planning authority where it appears that any advertisement has been displayed without the necessary consent, or without compliance with a condition or limitation attached to a consent, whether express or deemed.[4] Unlike planning control, a breach of advertisement control can never become immune from enforcement action.[5] The notice is served upon the owner, lessee and occupier of the land and on any other person known to the authority to be displaying the advertisement. The notice requires specified steps to be taken, within a given period, to restore the land to the condition it was in before the display began or to secure compliance with the condition or limitation. In addition, it may specify as an alternative steps to be taken to bring the display up to an acceptable condition. The notice takes effect on the date specified in the notice which must be 28 days from the date of the latest service of the notice, or seven days in certain limited circumstances. Any provision in the notice requiring the use of land to be discontinued operates as a permanent restriction, notwithstanding compliance with the notice. The resumption of that use after its discontinuance will, therefore, be in contravention of the notice. Similarly, where the notice requires either demolition or alteration of buildings or works, the notice will strike at any reinstatement of those buildings or works, notwithstanding that its terms are not apt for this purpose.

Where any of the steps required by the notice have not been taken within the specified period, the planning authority may enter the land and take those steps (other than discontinuance of any use), recovering its expenses from the owner or lessee of the land.[6] The validity of this action cannot be disputed by any person who failed to exercise his right of appeal to the Secretary of State (see below). Any sums incurred by the owner, lessee or occupier in complying with the enforcement notice, or in payment of the expenses of the planning authority in taking the steps required by the notice, may be recovered from the person by whom the display was carried out.

---

[3] reg. 9(3)(c).
[4] reg. 24.
[5] *Torridge D.C. v. Jarrad* [1998] J.P.L. 954.
[6] reg. 26.

At any time prior to the notice taking effect, any person on whom the notice is served may appeal in writing to the Secretary of State, indicating the grounds of appeal and stating the facts on which it is based.[7] The notice has no effect until the appeal is either determined or withdrawn. The appeal procedure is similar to the procedure for planning enforcement appeals except that there is no provision for use of the written submissions procedure (Chapter 7). The grounds of appeal are that:

1. the matters alleged in the notice do not constitute a display of an advertisement without the necessary consent or a failure to comply with any condition or limitation;
2. the notice was not served as required;
3. the specified period for compliance with the notice falls short of what should be reasonably allowed;
4. the steps required by the notice exceed what is necessary for its purpose.

In the course of the appeal the Secretary of State may correct any non-material informality, defect or error in the notice, and disregard any failure to serve the notice if neither the appellant nor the person served with the notice have been substantially prejudiced by that failure. In determining the appeal, the notice may be quashed or its terms varied in favour of the appellant.

Offences

Display of an advertisement in contravention of advertisement control **9.36** is an offence, with a maximum fine on summary conviction of level 3 on the standard scale (Appendix 1), with a further offence carrying a fine of one-tenth of level 3 for each day during which the offence continues after conviction. The persons liable for such an offence are the owner and occupier of the land upon which the advertisement is displayed, or the person whose goods, trade, business or other concerns are publicised by the advertisement. It is a defence to show that the advertisement was displayed without the knowledge or consent of the accused person.[8] If the contravention of advertisement control consists of a failure to observe any condition relating to maintenance of the advertisement or its site, or to the unsatisfactory removal of the advertisement, a person whose goods, trade, business or other concern is publicised by the advertisement only commits an offence if he has failed to comply with the requirements of an enforcement notice served on him.[9]

Power to Remove or Obliterate Placards and Posters

The planning authority has the power to remove or obliterate any **9.37** placard or poster displayed in its area in contravention of advertisement control, unless it is displayed within a building to which there is no

---

[7] reg. 25.
[8] TCPSA, s. 186(3) and 4.
[9] reg. 7(2).

public right of access.[10] This power is aimed at the nuisance caused by flyposting.

Where the placard or poster identifies the person who displayed it or caused it to be displayed, the authority must give that person written notice of its intention to remove or obliterate it on expiry of a period specified in the notice which must be not less than two days from the date of service of the notice. This notice period is intended to give an opportunity to convince the authority that the placard or poster is not displayed in contravention of advertisement control. Written notice is not required if the placard or poster does not give the address of the person and the authority does not know it and is unable to ascertain it after reasonable inquiry. There is a right of entry onto the land at any reasonable time, provided the land is unoccupied and it would be impossible to exercise the power without entering it.

ENTERPRISE ZONES AND SIMPLIFIED PLANNING ZONES

9.38   Enterprise Zone (E.Z.) and Simplified Planning Zone (SPZ) schemes are intended to encourage development to take place where it is needed to promote regeneration and economic activity. This objective is achieved through the grant of planning permission, in advance, for forms of development specified in the scheme (some schemes permit all forms of development with specified exceptions), thus avoiding the need to submit an application and providing developers with a degree of certainty. In addition, E.Z.s offer a range of fiscal benefits, typically including exemptions from local authority rates and greater capital allowances for capital expenditure incurred on construction, extension or improvement of industrial and commercial buildings. There are no automatic fiscal benefits from a SPZ scheme. Both forms of scheme have been criticised for encouraging existing businesses in the area to relocate within the zone, rather than attracting fresh employment.

An E.Z. is prepared by the planning authority and designated by order of the Secretary of State.[11] SPZs are promoted by the planning authority.[12] Proposals for an E.Z. or SPZ are advertised, giving the public an opportunity to lodge representations. In the case of an SPZ, there is provision for a public local inquiry to be held to consider any objections received, although there is no longer a requirement to hold an inquiry. The Secretary of State has powers to require the authority to consider modifications to the proposed SPZ, and to call in the proposals for his decision. An SPZ scheme ceases to have effect 10 years after the date of its adoption or approval. No application for planning permission will be

---

[10] TCPSA, s. 187.

[11] Local Government, Planning and Land Act 1980, s. 179 and Sched. 32, as amended. TCPSA, ss. 55 and 56.

[12] TCPSA, ss. 49–54 and Sched. 5; Town and Country Planning (Simplified Planning Zone) (Scotland) Regulations 1995 (S.I. 1995 No. 2043). See "Research on the General Permitted Development Order and Related Mechanisms" (Scottish Office, 1998), Part 8, and Circular 18/1995, "Simplified Planning Zones".

required where a development authorised by a planning permission under the SPZ scheme has commenced within the 10-year period.

The grant of permission by E.Z. and SPZ schemes is subject to the provisions of the Conservation (Natural Habitats, etc.) Regulations (see below). In addition, the grant of permission by an SPZ scheme does not remove the need for environmental assessment (Chapter 5).

NATURAL HERITAGE

The term "natural heritage" includes plants and animals, landforms and geology, and natural beauty and amenity.[13] In the exercise of all statutory functions, including planning, the Government, local authorities and public bodies are required to have regard to the desirability of conserving Scotland's flora and fauna, geological and physiographical features, and its natural beauty and amenity.[14] Scottish Natural Heritage is the agency responsible for advising the Government and local authorities on natural heritage issues.[15] 9.39

Natural heritage issues are closely linked to the objective of sustainable development, which has been defined as "development that meets the needs of the present without compromising the ability of future generations to meet their own needs" (Chapter 5). Following the Earth Summit in Rio in 1992 the United Kingdom signed the Biodiversity Convention. The UK Biodiversity Action Plan sets national targets, and Local Biodiversity Action Plans are being prepared.[16] Another product of the Earth Summit is Agenda 21, which is a worldwide programme of action to achieve a more sustainable pattern of development. Agenda 21 places emphasis on the need for all sectors of society to participate in the formation of effective national strategies for sustainable development. The UK's sustainable development strategy and the EU Environmental Action Programme are linked closely to the principles of Agenda 21.

Also highly relevant is the precautionary principle, which recognises that preventative action may be justified even where the scientific evidence is less than conclusive. The Scottish Office guidance indicates that the precautionary principle should be applied in circumstances where the impacts of a proposed development are uncertain, but there are good scientific grounds for believing that significant irreversible damage could occur to natural heritage interests of international or national significance.[17]

Development plans must contain natural heritage policies (Chapter 3). Impacts on, or benefits for, natural heritage will be a material consideration in the determination of planning applications. The planning authority must consult Scottish Natural Heritage in relation to certain planning

---

[13] NPPG 14, "Natural Heritage", para. 1.
[14] Countryside (Scotland) Act 1967, s. 66 (as amended).
[15] Natural Heritage (Scotland) Act 1991 outlines its role. Its head office is 12 Hope Terrace, Edinburgh EH9 2AS, tel: 0131 447 4784. Website: www.snh.org.uk.
[16] NPPG 14, paras 4 and 18.
[17] NPPG 14, paras 80–82.

applications. The environmental assessment process includes consideration of the effects of a proposed development on flora and fauna, soil,
water, air, climate and the landscape (Chapter 5).

There are also a series of statutory natural heritage designations which
restrict the development or use of land, some of which have their origins
in European Union or international treaties.[18] This chapter outlines the
provisions relating to Natural Heritage Areas and National Scenic Areas,
Sites of Special Scientific Interest (SSSIs), Nature Conservation Orders,
and Special Areas of Conservation. Other environmental or nature
conservation designations have less direct planning consequences, and
the sites affected are often also designated as SSSIs. These designations
include:

9.40 **Areas of Great Landscape Value**, which are declared in development
plans and have no statutory force.

Environmentally Sensitive Areas (ESAs), which are designated by the
Secretary of State after consultation with Scottish Natural Heritage,
under the Agriculture Act 1986.[19] Within ESAs, agreements may be
made with farmers and crofters regarding use of environmentally
friendly methods in return for financial payments.

Green Belts, which are designated in development plans. Their purpose
is to prevent urban sprawl (see below).

Local Nature Reserves, which are declared by local authorities in
conjunction with Scottish Natural Heritage under the National Parks and
Access to the Countryside Act 1949.

National Nature Reserves (NNRs), which are declared by Scottish
Natural Heritage under the National Parks and Access to the Countryside Act 1949 and the Wildlife and Countryside Act 1981.

Ramsar Sites, which are designated by the Secretary of State under the
Ramsar Convention on Wetlands of International Importance.

Regional Parks and Country Parks, which are designated by local
authorities under the Countryside (Scotland) Act 1981.

Special Protection Areas (SPAs), which are designated by the Secretary
of State to comply with the E.C. Directive on the Conservation of Wild
Birds 1979. SPAs and Special Areas of Conservation (SACs) (see below)
are intended to form a European network of protected areas, known as
Natura 2000. SPAs are protected by the Conservation (Natural Habitats,
etc.) Regulations 1994 (discussed in relation to SACs below). The
boundaries of SPAs must be selected using ornithological criteria, and
economic requirements should not be taken into account.[20] However, in

---

[18] "Natural Heritage Designations in Scotland: A Guide" (Scottish Office, 1998).
[19] Circular 17/1997, "Environmentally Sensitive Areas".
[20] *R. v. Secretary of State for the Environment, ex p. RSPB* [1996] J.P.L. 844.

drawing the boundaries a discretion has to be exercised, and the scientific exercise to be undertaken does not require that all contiguous or linked qualifying habitats or species populations have to be included, and existing circumstances such as the presence of skiing facilities can be taken into account.[21]

World Heritage Sites, which are listed by the World Heritage Committee of UNESCO (see above) and can include natural habitats and features.

There are also statutory provisions relating to trees (see above) and species protection.[22]

The Government intends to introduce legislation in the Scottish Parliament to create National Parks in Loch Lomond and the Trossachs by April 2001 and the Cairngorms by April 2002.[23]

Natural Heritage Areas and National Scenic Areas

The power to designate Natural Heritage Areas (NHAs) has super- 9.41 seded the National Scenic Area designation (NSAs).[24] As a result, no new NSAs will be created but existing ones will continue, although some may be transformed into NHAs. The statutory controls in respect of NSAs remain in force. The introduction of national parks may supersede the NHA designation.

NHAs may be designated by the Secretary of State for Scotland on the recommendation of Scottish Natural Heritage. Such areas should be appropriate for special protection because of their outstanding value to the natural heritage of Scotland, including its flora and fauna, geological and physiographical features, natural beauty and amenity.

Scottish Natural Heritage is preparing the detailed criteria which will be used to identify appropriate areas, and no sites have yet been selected. In recommending areas for NHA designation, Scottish Natural Heritage must consult with such people as it thinks fit, and should take into account actual or possible ecological and other environmental changes to the natural heritage of Scotland; the needs of agriculture, fisheries and forestry; the need for social and economic development; the need to conserve sites and landscapes of archaeological or historical interest; and the interests of owners and occupiers of the land, and of local communities.

Notice of the proposal to designate an area as an NHA must be advertised in the *Edinburgh Gazette* and a local newspaper. Any representations received within three months must be considered by the Secretary of State. Notice of the making of the designation must also be given in the same manner.

---

[21] *WWF-UK Ltd v. Scottish Natural Heritage*, 1998 G.W.D. 37–1936, *The Times*, 20 Nov., 1998.

[22] See Reid, "Nature Conservation Law".

[23] Speech by Secretary of State for Scotland, Feb. 2, 1999; SNH, "National Parks for Scotland: Scottish Natural Heritage's Advice to Government" (1999). The exercise of planning powers will be a key issue.

[24] Natural Heritage (Scotland) Act 1991, s. 6.

Although the NSA designation has now been superseded by the power to designate NHAs, the statutory controls applicable to NSAs remain in force.[25] NSAs are areas of outstanding scenic value and beauty in a national context, designated by the Secretary of State as appropriate for special protection (similar to the Areas of Outstanding Natural Beauty in England and Wales). There are currently 40 NSAs. Planning authorities must maintain a list available for public inspection of NSAs within their district.

When any planning powers are exercised with respect to any land within NSAs, including the determination of applications for planning permission, special regard must be paid to the desirability of preserving or enhancing the character or appearance of the area. This requirement also applies to NHAs.[26] The character or appearance is preserved not only by a positive contribution to preservation, but also by development which has a neutral effect and leaves the character or appearance unharmed.[27]

To provide planning authorities with an opportunity to review development proposals, planning permission must be obtained for the following types of development within an NSA, which would otherwise have benefited from permitted development rights[28]:

1. erection for agricultural or forestry purposes of all buildings and structures over 12 metres high (permitted development rights have since been removed for all agricultural buildings over 12 metres high, see below);
2. construction of vehicle tracks for agricultural or forestry purposes except forestry tracks which are part of an approved afforestation scheme; and
3. all local authority roadworks outside present road boundaries costing more than £100,000.

As an additional safeguard, where the planning authority proposes to grant permission for the forms of development listed below within an NSA, it must consult Scottish Natural Heritage.[29] If Scottish Natural Heritage advise against granting permission or recommend conditions other than those proposed by the planning authority, the authority must send details of the application to the Secretary of State. The authority cannot grant planning permission for the development until 28 days (or any longer or shorter period specified by the Secretary of State) have

---

[25] *ibid.*, s. 6(9).

[26] TCPSA, s. 264.

[27] *South Lakeland D.C. v. Secretary of State for the Environment* (n. 57, *supra*); *Bath Society v. Secretary of State for the Environment* (n. 56, *supra*).

[28] Town and Country Planning (Restriction of Permitted Development) (National Scenic Areas) (Scotland) Direction 1987, attached to SDD Circular 9/1987, "Development Control in National Scenic Areas"; display of advertisements on or consisting of a balloon within an NSA will require advertisement consent—Town and Country Planning (Control of Tethered Balloon Advertisements in National Scenic Areas) (Scotland) Direction 1984, attached to SDD Circular 10/1984.

[29] Town and Country Planning (Notification of Applications) (National Scenic Areas) (Scotland) Direction 1987, attached to Circular 9/1987.

elapsed from the date notified to it by the Secretary of State as the date of receipt of the details of the application. This period provides the Secretary of State with an opportunity to call in the application for his own decision.

This consultation requirement applies to:

1. schemes for five or more houses, flats or chalets except those within towns and villages for which specific proposals have been made in an adopted local plan;
2. sites for five or more mobile dwellings or caravans;
3. all non-residential developments requiring more than 0.5 hectares of land;
4. all buildings and structures over 12 metres high, including agricultural and forestry developments;
5. vehicle tracks, except where these form part of an approved afforestation scheme; and
6. all local authority roadworks outside present road boundaries costing more than £100,000.

Sites of Special Scientific Interest

Sites of Special Scientific Interest (SSSIs) are areas of land designated as being of special interest by reason of any of their flora, fauna or geological or physiographical features.[30] There are 1,446 SSSIs in Scotland, covering 11.6 per cent of Scotland's land area. Aside from the planning consequences, the main result of the designation of land as an SSSI is the prohibition of carrying out a range of operations without the consent of Scottish Natural Heritage. The operation of the SSSI system is under review.[31]   9.42

Where planning permission is sought for a proposed development which may affect an SSSI (this does not require the development site to be within or adjacent to the SSSI), the planning authority must consult Scottish Natural Heritage and consider any representations made by them in determining the application.[32] Scottish Natural Heritage's views form part of the material considerations in the determination of the application (Chapter 5), but are not binding on the planning authority. However, if the authority decides to grant permission contrary to Scottish Natural Heritage's recommendation, it must notify the Secretary of State.[33] Thereafter the authority cannot grant permission until the expiry of 28 days from the date of receipt by the Secretary of State, giving him an opportunity to call in the application for decision (Chapter 5), or issue a direction restricting the grant of permission.

There is no statutory duty incumbent on the planning authority to protect an SSSI similar to the duty applicable to conservation areas or

---

[30] Wildlife and Countryside Act 1981, s. 28 (as amended).

[31] Speech by Secretary of State for Scotland, Feb. 2, 1999; Scottish Office Consultation Paper "People and Nature: A New Approach to SSSI Designations in Scotland", Sept. 1998.

[32] Town and Country Planning (General Development Procedure) (Scotland) Order 1992, art. 15(g).

[33] Town and Country Planning (Notification of Applications) (Scotland) Direction 1997, attached to Scottish Office Development Department Circular 4/1997.

NSAs/NHAs requiring special consideration to be given to preserving or enhancing the character or appearance of the area. It is also interesting to note that the restrictions on permitted development rights within SSSIs are limited to electricity cables and mineral exploration (Chapter 4). Agricultural and forestry development within SSSIs does not require planning permission, but may require to be notified to Scottish Natural Heritage as a potentially damaging operation (only grants of planning permission following an application to the planning authority provide exemption from the potentially damaging operation provisions, see below).

Designation of an SSSI commences with Scottish Natural Heritage serving a preliminary notice of its intention to notify the site on the planning authority in whose district the land is situated, every owner and occupier of that land, and the Secretary of State. The notice specifies the flora, fauna, geological or physiographical features by reason of which the land is of special interest, and any operations (known as "potentially damaging operations") which seem likely to damage that flora or fauna or those features. Until the notice ceases to have effect, it is an offence to carry out these operations without consent (see below). The notice must also specify at least a three-month period for lodging representations or objections in connection with the proposed designation. The notification ceases to have effect after nine months, unless Scottish National Heritage serve notice confirming the notification.

9.43   If no agreement can be reached for the withdrawal of a representation or objection lodged by any owner or occupier relating to the flora, fauna or features specified in the notice (but not the potentially damaging operations), the matter is referred to an independent advisory committee which has been appointed by the Secretary of State. Scottish Natural Heritage must then consider (but need not follow) the advice of the committee before determining whether to confirm the notification.[34] The committee also has power in some circumstances to advise Scottish Natural Heritage in respect of existing SSSIs.

Following confirmation by Scottish National Heritage of the notification of the land as an SSSI, notice is served upon the owners and occupiers and the planning authority, and the notification is registered in the Land Register for Scotland or recorded in the Register of Sasines (so that any new owner will be aware of the notification as a result of the usual searches carried out before purchase). There is no right of appeal, but it may be possible to apply for judicial review of the decision (Chapter 8).

During the preliminary notification period of up to nine months, and after service of the notice confirming the notification of the land as an SSSI, it is an offence for the owner or occupiers of any land which has been so notified to carry out, or cause or permit to be carried out, any potentially damaging operation. Liability does not extend to a contractor carrying out work on the land, even where the contractor received notification of the designation by virtue of the ownership of another part

---

[34] NHSA, s. 12.

of the site.[35] It is a reasonable excuse that the operation was authorised by a grant of planning permission (but not a deemed grant of planning permission for the exercise of permitted development rights), which may pre-date the notice by several years, or that it involved emergency work and Scottish Natural Heritage were informed as soon as reasonably practicable after the event.

This prohibition from carrying out potentially damaging operations is lifted if either the work is done in accordance with a management agreement, or written consent to the proposed operation is obtained from Scottish Natural Heritage, or four months have expired from the giving of notice to Scottish Natural Heritage.[36] Thus, at most, operations can only be delayed for four months without agreement.

Management agreements between Scottish Natural Heritage and the owners and occupiers of land included in an SSSI involve the owners and occupiers agreeing to refrain from carrying out potentially damaging operations or to take positive action to safeguard the scientific interest of the site. Scottish Natural Heritage may agree to make financial payments in return for such a management agreement.

Nature Conservation Orders

A Nature Conservation Order is made by the Secretary of State for the purpose of securing the survival of particular kinds of plant or animal on a site, to comply with an international obligation, or to conserve flora, fauna, geological or physiographical features in a site.[37]   9.44

Nature Conservation Orders have a broadly similar effect to the SSSI designation, but with some differences. A Nature Conservation Order takes effect immediately on being made by the Secretary of State and can, therefore, be used where there is an urgent need for protection. In addition, the restrictions on potentially damaging operations apply to any person, whether or not authorised by the owner or occupier. Finally, the prohibition on carrying out potentially damaging operations applies for three months after giving notice to Scottish Natural Heritage, which can extend this period by offering either to enter into a management agreement or to acquire the land (in which case the three-month period is extended to the date of the agreement, or three months from the date of rejection or withdrawal of the offer, or is replaced by a 12-month period, whichever period last expires). Alternatively, Scottish Natural Heritage can make a compulsory purchase order.

Compensation is payable by Scottish Natural Heritage for depreciation in the value of land which is part of an agricultural unit, resulting from a Nature Conservation Order. Compensation is also available for abortive expenditure, loss or damage where the three-month time limit for potentially damaging operations is extended.[38]

The consultation and notification requirements applicable to applications for planning permission which may affect an SSSI do not appear

---

[35] *Southern Water Authority v. Nature Conservancy Council* [1992] 1 W.L.R. 775.
[36] Wildlife and Countryside Act 1981, s. 28(6) (as amended to increase original three-month period to four months).
[37] *ibid.*, s. 29(1).
[38] *ibid.*, s. 30.

to extend to sites which are subject to Nature Conservation Orders. In practice, consultation and notification are likely to occur.

Notice of the making of the Nature Conservation Order is advertised and served on every owner and occupier of the land affected. At least 28 days must be allowed for representations or objections to be made. A public local inquiry or other hearing is held to consider any objections which are not withdrawn. In light of the representations and objections, and the report of any inquiry or hearing, the Secretary of State considers whether the order should remain in effect, or be amended or revoked. Any person aggrieved by the decision has six weeks to challenge its validity in an application to the Court of Session, on the grounds that it is not within the statutory powers of the Secretary of State or that the statutory requirements have not been complied with (Chapter 8).[39] Once confirmed, the Order is recorded in the Register of Sasines or registered in the Land Register.

If notice of potentially damaging operations is served in advance of an inquiry into objections to the order, but no action is taken in response to the notice, the operations become lawful and free from restriction after expiry of the three-month period. In such circumstances, Scottish Natural Heritage must respond to the notice (even with a view to extending the three-month period), notwithstanding that such action may seem premature until the conclusion of the inquiry. In one case where, by the time of the inquiry, operations were lawful and free from restriction under an order which was primarily intended to avoid damage from those operations, the subsequent inability of the order to control the operations and, therefore, its uncertain efficiency, was a material consideration which should have been taken into account at the inquiry.[40]

Special Areas of Conservation

9.45	Special Areas of Conservation (SACs) are designated by the Secretary of State under the Habitats Directive. A list of potential SACs has been prepared for the Secretary of State by Scottish Natural Heritage (SNH) for agreement with the European Commission. Many SACs will also be designated as SPAs (see above). The boundaries of SACs must be drawn up on the same principles applicable to SPAs.[41]

The Conservation (Natural Habitats, etc.) Regulations 1994[42] implement the provisions of the Habitats Directive. The Regulations impose an obligation on the Secretary of State and SNH to exercise their functions so as to secure compliance with the requirements of the Directive, and a more general obligation on every public authority to have regard to the requirements of the Directive in the exercise of their functions.

---

[39] *ibid.*, Sched. 11.

[40] *North Uist Fisheries Ltd v. Secretary of State for Scotland*, 1992 S.L.T. 333; S.P.L.P. 36:59.

[41] *R. v. Secretary of State for the Environment, ex p. RSPB, supra*, and *WWF-UK Ltd v. Scottish Natural Heritage, supra.*

[42] S.I. 1994 No. 2716 as amended by S.I. 1997 No. 3055. See Circular 6/1995.

The Regulations apply to every "European site", which are SACs, SPAs, sites of Community importance designated by the European Commission under the Habitats Directive, and potential SACs awaiting designation. The Secretary of State must compile and maintain a register of European sites, and the Secretary of State and SNH must keep copies of the register available for public inspection at all reasonable hours and free of charge. The Secretary of State must notify SNH of the inclusion of a site in the register, or any amendment or deletion to the register, and SNH must give notice to every owner or occupier of land within the site. SNH must also give notice to the planning authority, who must keep available at their principal office for free public inspection a register of all the European sites of which they have been given notice.

Landward European sites are likely to already be SSSIs (see above). Under the Regulations, the existing notification as a SSSI may be amended, including changes to the list of potentially damaging operations which must be notified to SNH. If the proposed operation is likely to have a significant effect on the site (either alone or in combination with other plans and projects), SNH may give consent only after having ascertained that the operation will not adversely affect the integrity of the site. If there is a risk of operations being carried out without SNH's consent, the Secretary of State may make a special nature conservation order, with the result that the operations specified in the order can only be carried out with the consent of SNH or in accordance with the terms of a management agreement. SNH can enter into a management agreement with any owner, lessee or occupier of a European site or land adjacent thereto.

SNH must review the compatibility of existing SSSI consents with the conservation objectives of each European site. Existing consents may be withdrawn or modified, but this will not affect anything done in reliance on the consent before the modification or withdrawal takes place.

The Regulations affect all authorities undertaking or giving consent, permission or other authorisation for a plan or project, and not just planning authorities. Where a project is likely to have significant effect on a European site, and is not directly connected with or necessary to the management of the site, permission can only be granted if the project will not adversely affect the integrity of the site. This restriction can be overcome if the project must be carried out for imperative reasons of overriding public interest. These reasons may relate to human health, public safety or beneficial consequences of primary importance to the environment. In some circumstances, the reasons may be of a social or economic nature. Existing decisions have to be reviewed in light of the Regulations, unless the development has been completed. This provision does not require an absolute guarantee that the integrity of the site will not be adversely affected. The authority must identify the foreseeable potential risks and put in place a legally enforceable framework to prevent them from materialising.[43]

Where permission is granted by general development order, such as the Permitted Development Order (Chapter 4), the development cannot

---

[43] *WWF-UK Ltd v. Scottish Natural Heritage, supra.*

proceed if it is likely to have a significant effect on a European site and is not directly connected with or necessary to the management of the site, until written approval is obtained from the planning authority. If development has commenced, it cannot continue until written approval is obtained. The planning authority cannot issue an approval unless the project will not adversely affect the integrity of the site. An application can be made to SNH for their opinion whether the development is likely to have a significant effect. Their opinion is conclusive.

The Regulations also introduced new requirements for the contents of structure and local plans (Chapter 3).

AGRICULTURE AND FORESTRY

9.46   Agricultural use and development traditionally enjoyed widescale exemption from the need for planning permission. This exemption is gradually being eroded, most recently following incidents of sheds being erected in inappropriate positions next to dwellinghouses. The further extension of planning powers over agriculture and forestry has been suggested as an issue for consideration by the Scottish Parliament.[44]

Agricultural Use

9.47   A change from any use to agricultural use, or between different agricultural uses, does not require planning permission,[45] although any associated building or other work is considered separately and may require permission (see below). Thus, no planning permission is required for pigs to be introduced onto land, but it is only once this agricultural use has been established that piggeries can be constructed without planning permission.[46] Fish farming is an exception to this rule, as the placing of fish cages in inland waters requires planning permission,[47] enabling planning authorities to exercise control over the visual and environmental impact of fish farms.

Provided the primary use is agricultural, no planning permission is required for ancillary uses, such as the sale of farm produce to the public on a farm. However, if produce is bought in for sale, the retail element may become a separate use in its own right and, therefore, require planning permission (Chapter 4 discusses primary and ancillary uses in more detail).

Agricultural uses include horticulture, seed or fruit growing, dairy farming, breeding and keeping livestock for the production of food, wool, skins or fur (which includes fish farming) or for use in the farming of land, the use of land as grazing, meadow, or osier land, market gardens or nursery grounds, and the use of land for woodlands (where that use is ancillary to the farming of land for other agricultural

---

[44] Consultation Paper "Land Use Planning under a Scottish Parliament" (Scottish Office, January 1999).
[45] TCPSA, s. 26(2)(e).
[46] *Joan Jones v. Stockport MBC* [1984] J.P.L. 274.
[47] TCPSA, s. 26(6).

purposes).[48] The courts have declared that agricultural use includes the use of land for allotments, grazing horses, fox and mink farming, but not for keeping and boarding cats and dogs, installation of an egg-vending machine, keeping of animals in transit, wholesale slaughtering of animals, and the breeding and training of horses for show-jumping.[49] Wine-making is not an agricultural use because the processing of the fruit is not growing or cropping.[50]

Building and Other Work

Where there is an existing agricultural use, and all of the following criteria are met, planning permission is not required for the erection, extension or alteration of a building; the formation, alteration or maintenance of private ways; or any excavation or engineering operations[51]:   9.48

1. the land must form part of a unit occupied for the purposes of agriculture other than fish farming;
2. there must be an existing agricultural use for the purposes of a trade or business;
3. the work must be reasonably necessary for the purposes of agriculture within the unit[52];
4. the agricultural land must have an area of at least 0.4 hectares, comprised in one piece of land, except in the crofting counties where areas of separate parcels of land may be added together;
5. the work must not involve the erection, extension or alteration of a dwellinghouse;
6. any building or structure to be provided must be designed for the purposes of agriculture, thereby avoiding erection of buildings used for keeping livestock, but with the appearance of dwellinghouses;
7. the ground area of any building to be erected, extended or altered, or of any structure (other than a fence) built for the purposes of accommodating livestock, or of any plant or machinery, must not exceed 465 square metres: the ground area is calculated by adding the ground area to be covered by the proposed works to the ground area of any building (other than a dwelling), structure, works, plant or machinery built or provided in the preceding two years within the same unit, any part of which is within 90 metres of the proposed works;
8. the height of the building, structure or works must not exceed 12 metres (three metres if within three kilometres of the perimeter of an aerodrome);

---

[48] s. 277(1).
[49] See the cases cited in Young and Rowan-Robinson, *op. cit.*, p. 155.
[50] *Millington v. Secretary of State for the Environment* [1998] E.G.C.S. 154.
[51] Town and Country Planning (General Permitted Development) (Scotland) Order 1992, art. 3 and Sched. 1, class 18.
[52] *MacPherson v. Secretary of State for Scotland*, 1985 S.L.T. 134.

9. no part of the works must be within 25 metres of the metalled portion of a trunk or classified road; and

10. where the building or structure to be erected or worked upon is or will be used for housing pigs, poultry, rabbits or animals bred for their skin or fur, or for the storage of slurry or sewage sludge, it must be more than 400 metres from the curtilage of any permanent building normally occupied by people or apt for such use, which does not form part of the agricultural unit or another such unit.

If these criteria cannot be met, planning permission will be required. A Certificate of Lawfulness of Proposed Use or Development (CLOPUD) can be obtained from the planning authority in circumstances where it is uncertain whether the criteria have been met (Chapter 4).

The following works also do not require planning permission[53]: the winning and working of any minerals reasonably necessary for agricultural purposes within the agricultural unit, provided the minerals remain within the unit and are used for agricultural purposes; works in connection with the improvement or maintenance of watercourses or land drainage works; and the winning and working of peat by any person for their domestic requirements.

Removal of more than five cubic yards of surface soil from agricultural land in any period of three months is an offence, if planning permission is required but not obtained.[54] This offence also applies to land formerly used for agriculture where that use ceased in consequence of the intention to remove surface soil. It does not extend to the cutting of peat or the removal of such quantities of surface soil as is reasonably necessary in the course of cutting turf.

Prior Notification

9.49   Even if planning permission is not required for works, it may be necessary to give the planning authority prior notification of those works by an application to determine whether the prior approval of the authority is required. This prior notification requirement enables the planning authority to exert some degree of control over the siting, design and external appearance of a building, where planning permission is not required for its erection, alteration or extension.

The prior notification requirement applies to the erection or significant extension or alteration of a building. A building is significantly extended or altered if either the cubic content of the original building is increased by more than 10 per cent or its height is increased. A building can only be significantly altered or extended once without planning permission.

Work cannot proceed until notification is received from the authority that its prior approval is not required, or its approval is received, or 28 days have elapsed since the application was lodged and the authority has

---

[53] PDO, Sched. 1, classes 19, 20 and 21.
[54] Agricultural Land (Removal of Surface Soil) Act 1953, s. 1, as amended.

reached no decision. The work must be carried out in accordance with the approved details or, if no approval is required, in line with the details submitted with the application. In addition, the work must be carried out within five years of the date on which approval was given or if no approval was given, the date of the application.

There is a right of appeal to the Secretary of State against the decision of the planning authority on the application for approval.[55]

Forestry

Similar provisions apply to forestry uses and works. Forestry use   9.50 includes operations necessary to render timber marketable and disposable, even where the operations are carried on some distance from the plantation. Therefore, planning permission was not required for a change of use to use as a timber storage and transfer area.[56] Forestry works do not require planning permission unless: the work involves the provision or alteration of a dwelling; the height of any building or works within three kilometres of an aerodrome would exceed three metres; or any part of the proposed development would be within 25 metres of the metalled portion of a trunk or classified road.[57] There is a similar prior notification requirement for the erection or significant extension or alteration of a building.

Designated Areas

Farming and forestry operations are often affected by some of the   9.51 statutory designations examined above. For example, within NSAs the permitted development rights for the erection for forestry purposes of all buildings or structures over 12 metres high, and for construction of vehicle tracks for agricultural or forestry purposes (except forestry tracks which are part of an approved afforestation scheme), are removed. The result is that an application for planning permission will be required.

Diversification

In the current climate many farmers are considering diversifying from   9.52 farming. Diversification projects will often require planning permission, for example the conversion of farm buildings to non-agricultural use, such as holiday cottages or industrial units, the stabling of horses for riding or breeding, or the erection of houses. Use of the farmhouse for bed and breakfast may require planning permission, depending upon the number of guests and the attitude of the planning authority. As mentioned above, a shop on the farm will not require permission provided it only sells produce from the farm. In general, permission will be required for a caravan site, except for some small-scale activities.[58] Non-agricultural uses of land (but not buildings), for any purpose other

---

[55] TCPSA, s. 47 and Development Procedure Order 1992, art. 23(1) as amended.
[56] *Farleyer Estate v. Secretary of State for Scotland*, 1992 S.L.T. 476.
[57] PDO, class 22.
[58] PDO, classes 16 and 17.

than open-air markets, do not require planning permission, provided the use does not occur for more than 28 days in a calendar year. Moveable structures, such as marquees, may be placed on the land in connection with such use.[59]

Change of Use of Agricultural Land

9.53   Planning authorities are required to notify the Secretary of State where they propose to grant planning permission for a proposed development involving a change of use of 10 (previously two) hectares or more of agricultural land falling within class 1, 2 or 3.1 of the Macaulay land capability classification for agriculture, and either it is contrary to the adopted or approved local plan, or no such plan has been adopted or approved and the Scottish Office Agriculture, Environment and Fisheries Department has advised against granting permission, or have not been consulted.[60] Following notification, the planning authority cannot grant permission until 28 days after the date of receipt by the Secretary of State of the notification. This period enables the Secretary of State to consider calling in the application for his decision or issuing a direction to the planning authority restricting the grant of permission.

DEVELOPMENT IN THE COUNTRYSIDE AND ON GREEN BELT LAND

9.54   The high amenity value of the countryside is acknowledged in the constant pressure for housing development. In order to preserve this amenity, development in the countryside is subject to restrictive policies both at national and local level. National policy states that development in the countryside should be encouraged on suitable sites in existing settlements. The coalescence of settlements and ribbon development should be avoided. Isolated development should be discouraged in the open countryside, except where circumstances are clearly identified in development plans, including where a dispersed pattern of housing might be appropriate in more remote areas, or there are special needs, for example the nature of certain employments requires residence in a particular location.[61] Isolated houses in the countryside are also resisted in local plans. However, there are often exceptions for single house infill within groups of buildings smaller than villages, essential houses for farm workers, replacement houses, restoration of empty or abandoned houses or conversion of redundant agricultural buildings, such as steadings. The siting and design of new housing in the countryside is also a matter of concern[62] and many authorities have published design guides to aid applicants.

---

[59] PDO, class 15.
[60] Town and Country Planning (Notification of Applications) (Scotland) Direction 1997, attached to SDD Circular 4/1997.
[61] NPPG 3, "Land for Housing" (Revised 1996), para. 48 *et seq.* which replaces SDD Circular 24/1985, "Development in the Countryside and Green Belts", para. 3. NPPG 15, "Rural Development".
[62] SDD PAN 36, "Siting and Design of New Housing in the Countryside".

Green Belt is land designated in a development plan to be left open. The purposes of Green Belt land are to check unrestricted sprawl of large built-up areas, to safeguard countryside from further encroachment and preserve it for recreation or institutional purposes. It is also designed to prevent neighbouring towns from merging into one another, to maintain the landscape setting of towns and preserve their identity by establishing a clear definition of their physical boundaries, and to assist in urban regeneration by rendering derelict urban sites more attractive propositions for development.

The Scottish Office guidance states that there should be a general presumption against any intrusion into designated Green Belts (this is the only exception to the presumption in favour of development, see Chapter 5). In particular, approval should not be given, except in very special circumstances, for either the construction of new buildings and the extension or change of use of existing buildings for purposes other than agriculture, horticulture, woodland management and recreation, or establishments and institutions standing in extensive grounds or other uses appropriate to the rural character of the area.[63]

MINERALS

Planning permission is required for mining operations, including the   9.55
removal of material of any description from a mineral-working deposit, deposit of pulverised fuel ash or other furnace ash or clinker, or deposit of iron, steel or other metallic slags, and the extraction of minerals from a disused railway embankment.[64] The extraction of each shovelful constitutes a separate development, and it will therefore be rare for unauthorised mining operations to become legal.[65] There are permitted development rights (Chapter 4) in connection with mineral exploration, development ancillary to mining operations, mining development by the Coal Authority and its licensees, waste tipping at a mine, and removal of material from mineral working deposits.[66]

As a result of the unique problems of mining works, such as the length of the operations, frequent suspension for periods of time and resumption, and the harm caused to the land, the normal planning regime is supplemented by special provisions.[67] Issues such as environmental and visual impact, trade effluent and disposal of mine waste, dust, noise, subsidence, health and safety, site rehabilitation, road infrastructure and the need for the mine, will be relevant to applications for permission for mining operations.[68] It is common for any permission to be combined

---

[63] Circular 24/1985, Annex, para. 4(iv).

[64] TCPSA, s. 26(1) and (5).

[65] *Thomas David (Porthcawl) Ltd v. Penybont RDC* [1972] 1 W.L.R. 1526.

[66] PDO, classes 53–66.

[67] TCPSA, ss. 262; Town and Country Planning (Scotland) (Minerals) Regulations 1998 (S.I. 1998 No. 2193) and Town and Country Planning (Compensation for Restrictions on Mineral Working and Mineral Waste Depositing) (Scotland) Regulations 1998 (S.I. 1998 No. 2914). Circulars 2/1999 and 3/1999.

[68] NPPG 4, "Land for Mineral Working" and PAN 50, "Controlling the Environmental Effects of Surface Mineral Workings".

with a section 75 agreement (Chapter 6), providing for restoration and aftercare of the site, and a bond to cover the cost of these works.

In connection with an application for planning permission for the winning and working of minerals, in addition to the usual notifiable parties, any person with an interest in minerals ordinarily worked for removal by underground or surface working in, on or under the land must be notified of the application as an owner of the proposed development site.[69]

Planning permission may be granted subject to a restoration condition requiring restoration of the site after the winning and working is completed, and an aftercare condition requiring steps to be taken to bring the land to the required standard for either agricultural, forestry or amenity use. Unless a condition expressly specifies a shorter or longer period, the winning and working of minerals or the depositing of mineral waste must cease not later than 60 years after the grant of permission.[70]

Where the winning and working or depositing appears to have permanently ceased, the planning authority may prohibit its resumption.[71] Once the prohibition order comes into force, any planning permission for the development ceases to have effect. If the operations have been temporarily suspended, the planning authority may require steps to be taken for the protection of the environment during the period of suspension, to preserve the amenities of the area, to protect it from damage and to prevent any deterioration in the condition of the land. A suspension order does not prevent recommencement of development provided notice is given to the planning authority. Prohibition and suspension orders do not take effect until confirmed by the Secretary of State and registered in the Land Register or Register of Sasines.

Since January 1, 1997 mineral developments are subject to a review process which requires, in effect, a fresh application for planning permission to be submitted so that the conditions applicable to the development can be updated.[72] This review process is subject to the environmental assessment requirements.[73] Active sites with permissions granted prior to February 22, 1982 have undergone an initial review, and all sites are reviewed 15 years after the initial grant of planning permission and every 15 years from the date of a previous review. At dormant sites, no minerals development can be carried out until a new scheme of conditions has been submitted to, and agreed by, the planning authority. Old mining permissions granted by interim development orders prior to the Town and Country Planning (Scotland) Act 1947, for which application for registration was not made by July 24, 1992, have ceased to have effect.

---

[69] TCPSA, s. 35 and Development Procedure Order 1992, art. 8, as substituted.

[70] s. 41(6) and Sched. 3.

[71] s. 71(8) and Sched. 8.

[72] s. 74 and Scheds 9 and 10, derived from the Environment Act 1995, s. 96 and Scheds 13 and 14. Circular 34/1996, "Review of Mineral Permissions". See Collar, "Mineral Development", 1996 Prop.L.B. 8.

[73] *R. v. North Yorkshire County Council, ex p. Brown*, *The Times*, Feb. 12, 1999 (House of Lords); Circular 25/1998, "Review of Old Mineral Permissions and Environmental Impact Assessment: Notes for Guidance".

CROWN LAND

Crown land is land in which there is an interest belonging to the Queen   9.56
in right of the Crown (adminstered by the Crown Estate Commissioners), or belonging to a government department or Minister, or held
in trust by the Queen for the purposes of a government department or
Minister.[74] Any Crown exemption from planning legislation no longer
applies to health boards.[75]

Crown land and development is largely exempt from planning and
associated controls.[76] For example, development on Crown land (other
than by a person holding a private interest, such as a tenant), or which is
undertaken by the Crown on any other land, does not require planning
permission.[77] However, all Crown bodies have agreed to adhere to a
voluntary arrangement whereby notice of any proposed development is
served on the planning authority and treated as though it were an
application for planning permission. If the Crown body and the planning
authority fail to reach agreement, the proposal is referred to the
Secretary of State to decide whether a planning clearance can be given.[78]

There is provision for application to be made to the planning authority
for permission and other statutory consents in anticipation of the
disposal of Crown land.[79] Planning agreements may be entered into
between the planning authority and the Crown body to secure the use of
Crown land in conformity with the provisions of the development plan,
or to restrict or regulate its development or use, either permanently or
during a specified period.[80] Where a material change in the use of Crown
land is proposed, the planning authority may enter into an agreement
deeming planning permission to be granted for the change of use,
subject to a condition requiring discontinuance of the use after the land
ceases to be used by the Crown.[81] After registration in the Land Register
for Scotland or the Register of Sasines, the agreement will be enforceable against any party acquiring title to the land. A Tree Preservation
Order made by a planning authority over Crown land will not take effect,
without the consent of the Crown body, either until it ceases to be
Crown land or becomes subject to a private interest.[82]

War-time breaches of planning control by the Crown can be subject to
enforcement action by planning authorities for five years after the
disposal of the land by the Crown.[83]

---

[74] s. 242.
[75] NHS and Community Care Act 1990, s. 60.
[76] TCPSA, s. 242 *et seq.*; PLBCASA, s. 74 *et seq.*; but see Scottish Office Environment
Department Consultation Paper, "Removal of Crown Exemption from Planning Law"
(Nov. 1992).
[77] *Lord Advocate v. Dumbarton D.C.*, 1990 S.L.T. 158.
[78] SDD Circular 21/1984, "Crown Land and Crown Development".
[79] s. 248.
[80] s. 246.
[81] s. 250.
[82] s. 249.
[83] s. 251.

Development by Planning Authorities

9.57   To avoid the conflict of interest which would arise if the council as
landowner was required to submit an application for planning permission for proposed development to itself as planning authority, there is a
special procedure for authorising development by a planning authority.[84]
There is also a requirement to notify the Secretary of State where the
planning authority propose to grant planning permission for certain
developments in which they have a financial interest or which are to be
located on land owned by them or in respect of which they may have an
interest (Chapter 5).

Where the authority propose a development, they must undertake the
notification procedures relating to owners, agricultural tenants and
neighbours, and comply with the publicity and consultation requirements, as if it was applying for planning permission (Chapter 5).
Thereafter, a notice must be published in a local newspaper stating its
intention to carry out the development described in the notice, the
address and times at which plans of that development may be inspected,
and that representations may be made in writing to the authority within
21 days of the date of publishing.

If no representations against the development are lodged within 21
days, or such longer period as applies to the notification, publicity or
consultation procedures for planning applications, planning permission is
deemed to have been granted by the Secretary of State. However,
deemed permission cannot be granted for the demolition, alteration or
extension of a listed building or demolition of a building which would
require conservation area consent, or where the Secretary of State has
given a direction restricting the grant of permission for the development
or class of development to which the application relates or a direction as
to how an application is to be determined.

Where representations are received, or deemed permission cannot be
granted, the planning authority sends a notice of intention to develop
(commonly known as an NID) to the Secretary of State, together with
details of the consultation exercise, and copies of representations
received. Thereafter the Secretary of State may require the authority to
submit an application for planning permission to him for the development, which is then treated as a called-in application (Chapter 5). If
after 28 days of receipt of the NID, or any extended period notified to
the authority by the Secretary of State, the Secretary of State has not
required such an application to be made, planning permission is deemed
to be granted. Deemed permission enures for the benefit of the planning
authority and does not transfer with the ownership of the land. In all
other respects, the deemed permission has the same effect as a grant of
planning permission (Chapter 5).

The Scottish Office guidance indicates that NIDs should contain
details of the development, as this procedure cannot be used for outline

---

[84] TCPSA, s. 263; Town and Country Planning (Development by Planning Authorities)
(Scotland) Regulations 1981 (S.I. 1981 No. 829), as amended by 1984 Amendment
Regulations (S.I. 1984 No. 238).

proposals. It states that there is a presumption against an application being required where the proposed development accords with the adopted or approved local plan for the area or has not attracted a significant body of objections. Where the NID is linked to a compulsory purchase order which is to be the subject of a public local inquiry, the NID is likely to be called-in to enable consideration of the planning aspects of the proposal alongside the case for compulsory purchase.[85]

Planning authorities which wish to carry out works requiring listed building or conservation area consent must apply to the Secretary of State.[86]

HAZARDOUS SUBSTANCES

Previously, the development control system only provided the planning authority with the opportunity to control storage of hazardous substances on land if this storage amounted to development (Chapter 4). A new hazardous use could be introduced or an existing operation intensified without any planning permission being required. Since May 1, 1993, hazardous substances consent must be obtained from the planning authority where the aggregate quantity of the substance on, over or under the land exceeds the controlled quantity.[87] The temporary presence of a substance while in transit will be taken into account only if it is unloaded. Deemed consent for the presence of a substance could be claimed as of right until November 1, 1993. 9.58

Hazardous substances consent is obtained by submitting an application in a similar way to an application for planning permission, with owner and neighbour notification and newspaper advertisement. In determining an application, the authority will have regard to any material consideration, including any current or contemplated use of the land to which the application relates, the use and likely use of land in the vicinity, any planning permission granted for land in the vicinity, the provisions of the development plan, and any advice received from the Health and Safety Executive. Consent may be granted subject to conditions specifying the storage or use of the substance and the times between which it may be present.

The control of hazardous substances regime is similar to normal planning controls. There is a right of appeal to the Secretary of State within six months of the date of notice of the decision on the application, or from the expiry of two months (or any extended period agreed in writing with the applicant) from the date of receipt of the application. The planning authority has enforcement powers in situations where consent is required but has not been obtained, or there is a failure to comply with the terms or conditions of the consent.

Hazardous substances consent enures for the benefit of the land and is not personal to the applicant. However, unlike planning permission, the

---

[85] SDD Circular 4/1997, "Notification of Applications", paras 13–18.
[86] PLBCASA, ss. 66 and 73, and Listed Building Regulations (see n. 14), reg. 11.
[87] Planning (Hazardous Substances) (Scotland) Act 1997; Town and Country Planning (Hazardous Substances) (Scotland) Regulations 1993 (S.I. 1993 No. 323).

consent is revoked if there is a change of control of part of the site unless an application for continuation of the consent is made in advance to the planning authority.

The planning authority must consult the Health and Safety Executive before determining an application for planning permission, where a proposed development is within an area notified to the authority by the Executive.[88] Notification takes place because of the presence within the vicinity of toxic, highly reactive, explosive or inflammable substances. This consultation requirement applies where the development involves the provision of residential accommodation, more than 250 square metres of retail floor space, 500 square metres of office space or 750 square metres of floor space to be used for an industrial process, or is otherwise likely to result in a material increase in the number of persons working within or visiting the notified area.

---

[88] DPO, art. 15(f), as amended.

CHAPTER 10

PUBLIC PARTICIPATION

Planning is predominantly about controlling development in the wider 10.01
public interest (a rather sweeping statement of the underlying nature of
planning, but Chapter 1 discusses this matter in more detail). Therefore,
it seems fitting to end this book with an examination of the extent to
which members of the public can participate in the planning system.
Without the interest and input from members of the public, the system
cannot maintain the public confidence which it requires to function
efficiently. Thus it is to be hoped that members of the public will
continue to exercise their rights.

In this context, the terms "members of the public" or "third parties"
are used to denote persons other than the applicant for permission/
developer, the planning authority and bodies which must be consulted as
part of the determination of a planning application. These persons may
be local residents, and might even have been notified as neighbours of
the proposed development, members of a voluntary group such as a
community council or amenity society, or concerned individuals. The
planning system gives all these members of the public various opportunities to make their views known and be taken into account as part of
the decision-making process.

The planning system can be divided into two parts: development
planning and development control (see Chapter 2). The rights of
members of the public in each part are examined below.

DEVELOPMENT PLANS

The development plan is an expression of the views of the planning 10.02
authority with regard to use of the land in its district. The authority has
few powers or opportunities to implement these views itself, and the
provisions of the plan serve more as authoritative guidance to those
wishing to develop land. The plan does not remove the need to obtain
planning permission, even where a development conforms to its provisions, and those provisions form one of the material considerations
taken into account by the authority when determining applications for
planning permission. As explained in Chapters 3 and 5, the introduction
of the plan-led system has resulted in a presumption that planning
permission will be granted for a proposed development which is in
accordance with the provisions of a development plan, unless material
considerations dictate otherwise. It is in this role that the planning
authority can implement its views expressed in the plan, but only to the

extent of granting permission for developments which are in accordance
with the plan and refusing the other applications.

The development plan is actually made up of two separate plans: the
structure plan and the local plan. Both are subject to periodic review,
alteration or replacement by the planning authority, the procedure for
which is discussed in Chapter 3. At each stage the authority is required
to publish notices in local newspapers alerting members of the public to
the opportunity of inspecting proposals or draft plans and lodging
representations. Information displays are often mounted in public buildings such as libraries, and public meetings may be organised. The local
media may carry features on the proposals.

Members of the public should exercise every such opportunity offered
to inspect proposals and lodge written representations making their
views known. As replacement plans have a projected lifespan of at least
10 years, and will form the blueprint for developments during that time,
it is essential that the views of the community are accurately expressed in
the plan which is eventually adopted, not least because it will be difficult
to resist any development which is in accordance with the plan.
Inspection of the proposals will also bring to light any issues which have
escaped the glare of publicity, but are still of importance and worthy of
comment. The opportunity should also be taken to correct any factual
errors. It should be appreciated that the weight given to opposition often
correlates to the number of representations received, and it may be a
mistake to assume that others will object and that your representations
will make no difference.

10.03   Following the initial consultation stage, modified proposals will often
be published. These should be inspected to check whether previous
representations have been incorporated (if not, they can be repeated) or
if representations should be made in relation to fresh proposals. There is
no bar to lodging representations at a later stage which could have been
made in connection with an earlier version of the proposals.

After the consultation stages, the finalised structure plan is submitted
to the Secretary of State for approval, and the public is given an
opportunity to make representations to the Secretary of State. The
provision for an examination in public to be held has fallen into disuse,
and there is no equivalent to the local plan inquiry.

During the replacement or alteration of a local plan, if representations
remain outstanding in relation to the finalised plan, the persons or
bodies maintaining those representations are given the opportunity of
presenting their case at a local plan inquiry. This inquiry is chaired by a
reporter appointed by the planning authority. The reporter is an
independent professional normally employed by the Scottish Office
Inquiry Reporters for determining planning appeals to the Secretary of
State. The inquiry is, therefore, a valuable opportunity to convince a
person independent of the planning authority and the plan preparation
process of the need to modify the proposals. Rather than appear in
person at the inquiry, it is competent to request that the reporter
consider written submissions, which may take the form of the representations previously lodged with the planning authority. While the recommendations made by the reporter are not binding, the authority must
give reasons for rejecting the recommendations. If the authority modifies

the proposals following the report of the inquiry, the public will be given an opportunity to lodge representations in respect of the modified plan.

The legality of the decision of the Secretary of State on the structure plan, or the planning authority on the local plan, may be challenged in the Court of Session by members of the public who are persons "aggrieved", using the statutory review procedure (Chapters 3 and 8).[1] The treatment of third parties in the courts is discussed below.

DEVELOPMENT CONTROL

Development control is the term used to describe the determination 10.04 by the planning authority of applications for planning permission (Chapter 5), and the taking of enforcement action against breaches of planning control (Chapter 7). While it is the former which involves most public participation, members of the public should be prepared to participate in enforcement by reporting activities which are suspected either not to benefit from planning permission or not to conform with the terms and conditions of a grant of permission, rather than relying on detection by under-resourced council planning departments.

The high point of public involvement in the planning system comes with applications for planning permission, where members of the public have the opportunity to lodge representations either with a view towards persuading the authority to refuse permission for the development, or simply expressing views which seem relevant, or in support of the development. The following discussion refers principally to objections, as these are the most common form of representation.

The planning authority is required to take into account representations lodged by certain members of the public, such as notifiable neighbours, or those received following newspaper advertisement or display of site notices. However, even if the application is not advertised, any member of the public can lodge a representation which must be taken into account by the authority to the extent that it raises material planning considerations (Chapter 5).

Part of the reason for the extent of public involvement in the determination of planning applications lies in the publicity requirements (Chapter 5). In submitting the application, the applicant is required to serve notice upon the owners and agricultural tenants of the development site, and neighbouring owners and occupiers (owners, lessees and occupiers of commercial premises). Broadly, only those neighbours within four metres of the site, excluding the width of any road, must be notified. In many circumstances notice of the proposed development must be given by newspaper advertisement, and some authorities have policies of publishing advertisements beyond the statutory requirements. Site notices must be displayed if the proposed development would affect

---

[1] TCPSA, s. 237; *Glasgow for People v. Secretary of State for Scotland*, 1991 S.C.L.R. 775; 1992 S.P.L.P. 35:16; *Scottish House Builders Association v. Secretary of State for Scotland*, 1995 S.C.L.R. 1039; SPEL 52:109. *Lardner v. Renfrewshire Council*, 1997 S.L.T. 1027; SPEL 62:81 shows that challenges by third parties will not always be competent.

the character or appearance of a conservation area or the setting of a listed building. Finally, details of all applications must be entered in a register available for public inspection, allowing concerned members of the public to check regularly on new applications.

10.05   Prior to deciding whether to object, or writing an objection, the plans and other papers lodged with the planning authority in connection with the application should be inspected (the official notices and newspaper advertisements give few details other than the description of the proposed development). It is advisable to check with the authority by telephone that these documents are available for inspection (the application may still be in the initial processing stages), and, if so, at what location and times. Unless the application is for outline permission, or a change of use, the application should include detailed drawings of the buildings or other structures involved. Careful note should be taken of details such as the height of buildings in comparison to others in the vicinity and distance from surrounding properties, the architectural style, any loss of trees, provision for car parking, and vehicular and pedestrian access. The details of the parties notified by the applicant should be checked for any obvious omissions, which should be drawn to the attention of the authority. There should be a duty planning officer present who can explain details of the drawings, and also any policies of the authority which will apply.

In addition to inspecting the drawings accompanying the application, it is important to check with the authority the time limit for lodging objections. The official notices and newspaper advertisements specify time limits, but many authorities do not strictly adhere to these limits. It should also be possible to find out the name of the planning officer dealing with the application, who will normally be prepared to discuss it.

10.06   No procedure is prescribed for lodging objections, but the objection should identify the application concerned, either by reference number, if known, or by repeating the description of the proposed development and specifying the address of the appeal site. It should be in writing, identify the objector and be signed (confidentiality can be requested). Mention should be made of any official notification of the application received by the objector, as this may oblige the planning authority to take the objection into account. Finally, the objections to the proposed development should be listed, together with the reasons for those objections and any supporting information such as plans or photographs.

The grounds of objection will, of course, depend to a large extent on the form of development proposed and the characteristics of the development site and the surrounding area. The planning authority is legally obliged to take into account all material planning considerations and ignore any other issues (even if these issues are raised by parties whose representations must be taken into account). The grounds of objection can, therefore, be compiled from the list of material considerations given in Chapter 5. The level of sophistication of the grounds of objection will depend upon the scale of the development proposed and the views of the objector. While it is not essential that each ground of objection affect the objector directly, some objectors may prefer to limit the objection to the matters most relevant to their personal position. For example, an objection may refer to a traffic problem likely to be caused to residents at one end of a street as a result of the proposed development, notwithstanding that the objector will not suffer any traffic problems.

The planning authority will acknowledge receipt of the objection. Some authorities have a practice of sending copies of objections to the applicant, with the offer of an opportunity of responding to the comments made. When the planning officer comes to consider the recommendation to be made in his report to the authority on the application, the planning considerations raised by any objections will be taken into account. A summary of the considerations (but not usually a copy of the objections) will be included in the report circulated to the councillors who will make the decision.

Objectors may wish to act further than simply lodging an objection. Public opposition to the proposed development can be generated by publicity and meetings. As councillors take account of the number of objections, other members of the public can be encouraged to lodge objections, possibly by the use of style letters which can be photocopied and distributed for signature. Appropriate bodies can be approached with a request for their views. The local councillors, and M.P., can be contacted and made aware of objections. If the local councillor is not a member of the committee which will decide the application, he can be asked to pass views to the councillors on that committee. If the scale or importance of the development justifies it, copies of the objection can be sent to each of the councillors who sit on the committee (the council will provide names and addresses). However, care should be taken not to burden them with too much detail and to avoid too frequent contact, which may result in loss of their co-operation. It is also advisable to delay such communications until a few days before the committee is due to consider the application, so that the views will still be fresh in the minds of the councillors at that meeting.

It is also worth maintaining regular contact with the relevant planning officer, both to check the progress of the application and to discover any problems which are being encountered which may either assist the objection, or with which the objector may be in a position to provide assistance.

Some applications involve the applicant and the planning authority 10.07 entering into a section 75 agreement (Chapter 6). There may be no sinister purpose behind such an agreement, which may be necessary because normal planning powers cannot regulate the development effectively. However, there is concern about the lack of any public participation in the agreement process and the belief that developers "buy" permission by offering planning benefits over and above what is required for the development. (This belief is not borne out by the latest research.) If members of the public are concerned, and not prepared to accept reassurance from the planning department, their only option is to enlist the help of councillors to investigate the terms of any proposed agreement. When it comes to the time for a decision to be made, members of the public are entitled to attend the committee meeting, but it is unusual for them to be allowed to address the committee (although the right of address can always be requested).

Following determination of the application, some but not all authorities notify the decision to all those who lodged representations. If the application has been refused or granted subject to unacceptable conditions, the applicant has six months to lodge an appeal to the Secretary of State (Chapter 8). Any person who lodged a representation in connection with the application will be informed by the planning authority if an appeal is submitted and given the opportunity to lodge further representations (the original representations will be sent to the reporter), or to appear at a public local inquiry which will hear the appeal. Other members of the public will be alerted by newspaper advertisement of the arrangements for the inquiry. Members of the public are entitled to attend the inquiry, and may participate at the discretion of the reporter. Any person aggrieved by the decision of the reporter (or the Secretary of State) may challenge its legality within six weeks in the Court of Session through the statutory review procedure (see below).

If the planning authority grants planning permission for the proposed development, objectors have no right of appeal to the Secretary of State. Their only remedy is to petition the Court of Session for a common-law judicial review of the decision. The limited value of such a remedy is discussed below. Other forms of challenge, such as a complaint to the ombudsman, will not prevent the development from proceeding, and are therefore of limited value.

The lack of an opportunity for members of the public to challenge the merits of a decision to grant planning permission may seem unsatisfactory, but it must be remembered that until the introduction of planning control in 1947 landowners could do as they pleased with their land. For this reason, it has been consistent government policy that there is a presumption in favour of development, and the planning authority must show reasons why development should not proceed (Chapter 5). To allow members of the public a right of appeal against a grant of permission would unduly restrict the rights of landowners, and be contrary to that presumption. Such a right of appeal would also play havoc with developers who often have a tight timescale for a development, and would incur substantial losses if a project was delayed by an appeal lodged by a member of the public. Even if such losses could be claimed against the person following dismissal of the appeal, most members of the public have insufficient assets to make this worthwhile, and the danger of becoming liable for such losses would dissuade members of the public from utilising the right of appeal in the first place. Unfortunately, members of the public must accept that there is no second chance if they fail to persuade the planning authority that permission should be refused, unless there is a legal flaw in the decision which can be challenged in court. The Nolan Committee rejected the introduction of third party appeals (Chapter 2).

MEMBERS OF THE PUBLIC IN COURT

10.08   Following an unsatisfactory planning decision, members of the public often assume that it can be challenged in the courts. Indeed, any person aggrieved by a decision to adopt/approve a development plan, or by the decision of the Secretary of State on appeal, has the right to challenge that decision in the Court of Session through the statutory review procedure, and there is a similar possibility of challenge against a decision of the planning authority on a planning application by the common-law judicial review procedure. These procedures are discussed in detail in Chapter 8.

However, members of the public rarely appreciate the limitations on what can be achieved through the court procedures. The right of challenge only extends to the legality of the decision, and not its planning merits. It is not enough to show that the decision was wrong. A successful challenge requires proof that the authority (or the Secretary of State) incorrectly exercised their powers by taking into account irrelevant matters or by ignoring relevant factors, or that their decision was irrational, or the procedure adopted for making the decision was unfair (Chapter 8). For example, provided the authority has taken all relevant factors into account, the court will not interfere with the weight it chose to place on each factor, unless its decision was irrational. Even if the decision is shown to be illegal, the court has the discretion not to grant any remedy, for example if it decides that the same decision would have been reached in any case. Furthermore, the remedy most likely to be granted is the quashing of the decision. This results in the matter being referred back to the planning authority for a fresh decision to be made. Providing the authority avoids making the same mistake twice, it is likely that it can reach the same decision as before. A successful judicial review may, therefore, be a pyrrhic victory.

Ironically, lodging a comprehensive objection to the application reduces the likelihood of a successful judicial review. The full nature of the objection will alert the planning authority to all the material considerations. It will be difficult to prove that some of the grounds of objection were ignored, as opposed to considered and overruled. Thus the objection will prevent the authority from failing to take into account a relevant consideration and therefore remove one of the grounds for judicial review. This line of reasoning should not dissuade objectors from raising all the grounds of objection, as a successful objection will avoid the need for court action. It is easier for third parties to win (*i.e.* gain refusal of planning permission) in the factual arena of the planning authority, than the legal arena of the Court of Session.

The first edition of this book suggested that if the previous paragraphs paint a bleak scenario, members of the public seeking to challenge a decision should be cheered by the favourable attitude of the Court of Session shown in recent years towards the status (known by lawyers as standing) of third parties to bring such challenges. Reference was made to the two cases which are outlined below. In the intervening period, the approach taken by the court has been less favourable, but as the decision in one of the recent cases shows, members of the public can still bring successful legal challenges (details of the legal requirements of standing are discussed in Chapter 8). The recent successful case involved a group of local residents who successfully challenged the grant of planning permission for a housing development. Reports had been lodged by consultants acting for the applicants and the objectors. These reports contained conflicting views regarding the applicable law. The court held that the Director of Planning should have advised the planning committee on the correct view of the law and approach to be taken. Since his

10.09

report appeared to favour the wrong approach, there was a real risk that the committee were misled as to the correct approach. The report also materially misrepresented the facts in respect of the reduction between the previous and present proposals. Since the report appeared to place importance on the comparison between those proposals, it was likely that the committee took into account irrelevant considerations concerning the extent of the reduction.[2]

Two other recent cases show the less favourable approach by the Court of Session. In the first, a member of the public, whose property was not directly affected by the policies and proposals in a local plan and who took no objection to them during the consultation process, was held not to be a "person aggrieved" and therefore had no right to challenge the local plan.[3] Similarly, a competing developer who sought to challenge the grant of reserved matters for a rival leisure development did not have interest to sue.[4]

The two cases noted in the first edition are still relevant. In the first, a member of the public (L) had complained to the planning authority that he had not been notified of the submission of an application in accordance with the neighbour notification procedures and reserved his right to object to the proposed development once he had received such notification. The authority informed the applicants of the position and, without informing L, subsequently granted permission for an amended application in which the boundaries of the development site had been redrawn to avoid any obligation to notify L as a neighbour. The Court of Session quashed this decision on the grounds that L had been unfairly deprived of his legitimate expectation of being able to lodge an objection. While neither the applicant for permission nor the authority had failed to comply with the statutory procedures, the procedure adopted by the authority was unfair because it prejudiced L's rights as a member of the public.[5]

10.10   The other decision worthy of note possibly goes even further towards protecting third-party rights in the development control process. An application for planning permission was submitted which described the proposed development as a roadside petrol station and service area. This description was repeated in the notices served on neighbours and in the newspaper advertisements. However, the plans submitted with the application showed a separate petrol station for each of two roadside sites and a 40-bedroom lodge, two restaurants and three car parks. A member of the public applied to the Court of Session for the decision to grant permission for the development as shown on the plans to be quashed. The court upheld the application on the grounds that the inadequate description had deprived him of an opportunity to lodge representations which might, at least in his view, have affected the result.[6] The significance of the decision in this case can only be

---

[2] *Campbell v. City of Edinburgh Council*, 1998 G.W.D. 17–877; SPEL 69:99.
[3] *Lardner v. Renfrewshire Council, supra.*
[4] *Bondway Properties Ltd v. City of Edinburgh Council*, 1998 S.C.L.R. 225; SPEL 66:31.
[5] *Lochore v. Moray D.C.*, 1992 S.L.T. 16; 1991 S.P.L.P. 34:78.
[6] *Cumming v. Secretary of State for Scotland*, 1993 S.L.T. 228.

appreciated from a detailed examination of the facts. The member of the public was a businessman who was likely to lose business to the bedroom-lodge part of the development. It seems that the omission of the lodge from the description caused him to assume wrongly that he had no objection to the development, although inspection of the plans would have corrected this mis-assumption. There was some uncertainty whether he could have produced any planning arguments against the development which would have influenced the decision. Perhaps the most telling fact is that he was eventually given full notice of the true extent of the development and given an opportunity to lodge representations before the decision was taken on the application. Despite all of these factors, the Court of Session upheld his right as a member of the public to expect the description contained in an application for planning permission to give full and fair notice of the extent of the development for which permission was sought.

Such a favourable decision cannot be expected at all times, but these two decisions emphasise the importance which the Court of Session now appears to place on third-party rights in planning.

CONCLUSION

Although the Court of Session has on occasion shown a positive attitude towards allowing members of the public to challenge planning decisions, the role of the court is limited to reviewing the decision challenged to ensure that it has been reached within the law. Members of the public have no opportunity to challenge the planning merits of a grant of planning permission or the adoption of a development plan. This emphasises the importance of mounting an effective campaign at the earliest stage. 10.11

APPENDIX 1

STANDARD SCALE OF FINES

[From April 1st, 1996]

Level	Amount
1	£200
2	£500
3	£1,000
4	£2,500
5	£5,000

[Criminal Procedure (Scotland) Act 1995, s.225]

APPENDIX 2

BAD NEIGHBOUR DEVELOPMENT

(1)   the construction of buildings for use as a public convenience;
(2)   The construction of buildings or other operations, or use of land
      (a)   for the disposal of refuse or waste materials, or for the storage or recovery of reusable metal.
      (b)   for the retention, treatment or disposal of sewage, trade waste, or effluent other than
           (i)   the construction of pumphouses in a line of sewers;
          (ii)   the construction of septic tanks and cesspools serving single dwellinghouses, or single caravans, or single buildings in which not more than 10 people will normally reside, work or congregate;
        (iii)   the laying of sewers; or
        (iv)   works ancillary to those described in sub-paragraphs (i) to (ii);
      (c)   as a scrap yard or coal yard; or
      (d)   for the winning or working of minerals;

(3)   the construction of buildings or use of land for the purposes of a slaughterhouse or knacker's yard or for the killing or plucking of poultry:
(4)   the construction of use of buildings for any of the following purposes:
bingo hall
building for indoor games
casino
cinema
dance hall
fun fair
gymnasium (not forming part of a school, college or university)
hot food shop
licensed premises
music hall
skating rink
swimming pool
theatre, or
Turkish or other vapour or foam bath
(5)   the construction of buildings for or the use of buildings or land as
      (a)   a crematorium, or the use of land as a cemetery;

       (b) a zoo or wildlife park, or for the business of boarding or breeding cats or dogs;

(6) the construction of buildings and use of buildings or land for motor car or motor cycle racing;

(7) the construction of a building to a height exceeding 20 metres;

(8) the construction of buildings, operations, and use of buildings or land which will

       (a) affect residential property by reason of fumes, noise, vibration, smoke, artificial lighting or discharge of any solid or liquid substance;

       (b) alter the character of an area of established amenity;

       (c) bring crowds into a generally quiet area;

       (d) cause activity and noise between the hours of 8 p.m. and 8 a.m.; and

       (e) introduce significant change into a homogeneous area.

[Town and Country Planning (General Development Procedure) (Scotland) Order 1992, Schedule 7]

INDEX

Index